The Sower and the Seer

THE SOWER AND THE SEER

Perspectives on the Intellectual History of the American Midwest

EDITED BY

JOSEPH HOGAN, JON K. LAUCK, PAUL MURPHY, ANDREW SEAL, AND GLEAVES WHITNEY

WISCONSIN HISTORICAL SOCIETY PRESS

Published by the Wisconsin Historical Society Press
Publishers since 1855

The Wisconsin Historical Society helps people connect to the past by collecting, preserving, and sharing stories. Founded in 1846, the Society is one of the nation's finest historical institutions.
Join the Wisconsin Historical Society: wisconsinhistory.org/membership

Front cover image: "Crop Rows" by Shane McAdams, photographed by Tom Bamberger

Printed in the United States of America
Cover design and typesetting by Tom Heffron

25 24 23 22 21   1 2 3 4 5

Library of Congress Cataloging-in-Publication Data
Names: Hogan, Joseph, 1992– editor. | Lauck, Jon, 1971– editor. | Murphy,
   Paul V. (Paul Vincent), 1966– editor. | Seal, Andrew, 1984– editor. |
   Whitney, Gleaves, editor.
Title: The sower and the seer : perspectives on the intellectual history of
   the American Midwest / edited by Joseph Hogan, Jon K. Lauck, Paul Murphy,
   Andrew Seal and Gleaves Whitney.
Description: [Madison, Wisconsin] : Wisconsin Historical Society Press,
   [2020] | Includes bibliographical references and index.
Identifiers: LCCN 2020028337 (print) | LCCN 2020028338 (ebook) | ISBN
   9780870209482 (paperback) | ISBN 9780870209499 (ebook)
Subjects: LCSH: Intellectuals—Middle West—History. | Middle
   West—Intellectual life. | Middle West—History. | Middle
   West—Civilization.
Classification: LCC F351 .S69 2020 (print) | LCC F351 (ebook) | DDC
   977—dc23
LC record available at https://lccn.loc.gov/2020028337
LC ebook record available at https://lccn.loc.gov/2020028338

♾ The paper used in this publication meets the minimum requirements of the American National Standard for Information Sciences—Permanence of Paper for Printed Library Materials, ANSI Z39.48-19

To the memory of John E. Miller, Midwestern intellectual

CONTENTS

Sower and Seer

Liberty Hyde Bailey

Full patiently the sower walked on his acres deep and clean
And dropped his handfuls one by one for the harvest full and green,
Full punctually he tilled his lands and groomed his sleek-fed kine
And frugally at sunrise and eve he dressed his yard and vine;
When days were fair he thrust his plow and compelled his clicking drills
And when wilding storms were loosed and raw he sped his barn-snug mills;
And day by day the sun rose and set upon his circling hills.

Full forwardly the seer stood on the rim of circling hills
Where trees were bent on the jagged cliffs and eagles dropped their quills
With shimmering farm-lands far below and spires of roof-flecked vills;
Full eastwardly and westwardly all the sweeping earth lay prone
And upwardly the fleecing clouds in a bondless sunlight shone;
All things beneath and all above were in webs of vision spun
Till every part was as the whole and all the whole was one.

    The sower and the seer each
    Down life's unending way
    Held fast his single speech
    And lived his sep'rate day.

    For one man cast his seed
    And sped the coupled hours,
    He stored his treasured meed
    And plucked his garden flow'rs.

    And one man stood alone
    Where all the world was his,
    All things that men have known
    And all that was and is.

Alack, all ye that sow
And alack, ye that see,
No longer shall ye go
All sep'rate and unfree:

For one shall make far quests,—
The other 'side him fare
And come back from the crests
With star-winds in his hair.[1]

1. Liberty Hyde Bailey, "Sower and Seer," in *Wind and Weather*, (New York: Scribner, 1916), 127–129.

INTRODUCTION

Midwestern "seers," as Liberty Hyde Bailey calls them, are the interest of this collection. They are the writers, thinkers, intellectuals produced by the Midwest. And as Bailey shows, their work cannot be separated from their region. The region is responsible for them, and they for their region, as the sower is responsible for the land, and the land for the sower. The region offers a harvest of knowledge; intellectual and imaginative vision is reaped from it. The region gives its seers perspective, a vantage from which to see "full eastwardly and westwardly." By giving them roots, it sets them free.[1]

And yet, since at least the mid-twentieth century, the dominant assumption about the Midwest, the story often told about it, is that it's a place one leaves—if, that is, one wants to live, to experience, to think, to be free. American literature and criticism has, for years, celebrated a kind of regional brain drain. The "revolt from the village" thesis, first articulated in 1920 by Carl Van Doren in *The Nation*, applauds a certain trend in American writing that opposed the pastoral image of the middle-American small town. Van Doren admired, for instance, Edgar Lee Masters's *Spoon River Anthology* (1915) and Sherwood Anderson's *Winesburg, Ohio* (1919) for their embrace of a "formula of revolt" against provincialism. The idea was, and remains, that the old vision of the wholesome small town ought to be undone; to rebel against it is to rebel against provincialism itself.[2]

F. Scott Fitzgerald's *The Great Gatsby* partly endorses, but in an important sense critiques and improves, this thesis. At the beginning, the Minnesotan Nick Carraway determines to leave the Midwest—"the ragged edge of the universe"—to go to New York, where he has "the high intention" of reading many books: "I was rather literary in college ... and now I was going to bring back all such things into my life and become again that most limited of all specialists, the 'well-rounded man.'" To live on the East Coast, Carraway intuits, is to become capable of gaining membership into a literary elite. But by novel's end, Carraway has returned to the Midwest, having realized that he was "subtly unadaptable to Eastern life," most of all to those people who "smashed up things and creatures and then retreated back into their money or their vast carelessness." One does not get the sense, given Carraway's general disillusionment, that the Midwest presents for him some pastoral ideal, but neither does he romanticize New York.[3]

Despite *Gatsby*'s nuanced portrait of the Midwest and the East Coast, Van Doren's revolt from the village thesis has largely endured. With it has emerged the common assumption that the nation's interior states are excellent seedbeds for the germination of native geniuses—from T. S. Eliot to Jonathan Franzen—but a wasteland for their further growth. This trope has made its way into novels, films, and television. It is as recent as the HBO show *Girls*, whose main character, Hannah Horvath, was raised in East Lansing, Michigan, but moved, after college, to Brooklyn. In her Midwestern parents' hotel room in midtown, Horvath announces that she thinks she might be "the voice of my generation, or at least *a* voice of *a* generation." Indeed, to leave the Midwest for the coasts is to ditch provincialism in favor of something like cosmopolitanism. Or perhaps it is to embrace the default, the thing itself: to think in the Midwest is to think regionally; to think on the East Coast is simply to think. It is to become capable of participating in a nonregional, nonprovincial "great conversation"; it is, regardless of region, to become capable of speaking for one's generation. Or *a* generation.[4]

This collection reveals that assumption to be false. The Midwest has been more than a springboard for the illustrious careers of future expatriates. It has been a hospitable environment for the cultivation of extraordinary communities of intellectuals, for the cross-pollination of a diversity of ideas, and for the harvesting of more than a century of substantial institutional growth. What is more, by attending to the intellectual bounty that remained at "home" in the region, we are better able to make visible and better able to recognize the significance of the multiple traditions and viewpoints that have staked their claim on the Midwest. The region only looks flat and monochromatic when we see it through the expatriate's eyes. From within, the contest of shifting interpretations over the very nature of the Midwest and its history—to some a frontier, to others a colonized space, a breadbasket, a crossroads, a heartland—are readily apparent. The tensions between those interpretations—particularly as they are informed by questions of class, race, gender, indigeneity—are alive and evident in the pages of this collection. What will be clear, by the end, is that the intellectual history of the United States and even of the world would look substantially different without the mental nourishment it has received from the Midwest.

Taken together, these chapters contribute to a recent revival of interest in the region: a revival evidenced by excellent new magazines such as *The New Territory* and the *Middle West Review*, publishing houses such as Belt, and books such as Meghan O'Gieblyn's *Interior States* (2018), Sarah Smarsh's *Heartland* (2018), and Phil Christman's *Midwest Futures* (2020). Among historians, the revival of interest in the Midwest is marked by the founding of the Midwestern History Association in 2014. That association is "dedicated to rebuilding the field of Midwestern history," which its members believe has suffered from "neglect and inattention." [5]

At the same time, this collection joins renewed interest in intellectual history, particularly in the United States, which saw something of a revival at the founding of the Society for US Intellectual History in 2007. That society fosters an interest in the national, whereas the leading organ of intellectual history at the time—*Modern Intellectual History*, itself a relatively new journal, founded in 2004—emphasized the global, especially the transatlantic. Now, this collection merges Midwestern history with US intellectual history.

In the first chapter, "Indigenous Intellectuals and the Colonization of the Midwest: Copway, Warren, Blackbird, and Pokagon," Edward Watts examines how the most lasting conflict between settler and American Indian culture in the formative Midwest during the nineteenth century occurred at the level of ideas. Four Anishnabeg writers—George Copway, William Warren, Andrew Blackbird, and Simon Pokagon—challenged the erasure of settler violence in standard narratives of frontier exploration, tracing these speciously heroic myths to what they argued were debased western intellectual traditions. Their work founded a long-standing culture of intellectual resistance to settler colonialism by Midwestern Native writers and thinkers.

In "'Education for the head, heart, and hands': Populism, Progressive Reform, and Rural School Consolidation," Kerry Alcorn examines how, in the first two decades of the twentieth century, a handful of Midwestern educationists exerted a preponderant influence on the intellectual and policy movement contained within efforts at rural school consolidation. Alcorn uses four case studies of prominent Midwestern reformers to point out a hidden undertone of populism that has eluded previous scholarship on school consolidation. These reformers did not simply seek to make schooling more "progressive," but rather responded sympathetically to the priorities and conditions of rural communities. For them, consolidation's ultimate aim was to preserve life on the farm and, concomitantly, the sacrosanct ethical core of the American ideal—an ideal that, in the first two decades of the twentieth century, was distinctly Midwestern.

In 1868, women in Jacksonville, Illinois, founded a new literary society they called Sorosis, after a women's club founded in New York City just eight months earlier. Rather than taking direction from New York, however, women in Illinois developed leadership from within. As Jenny Barker Devine shows in "'A stamp of femininity': The Sorosis Literary Society, Women's Intellectual Discourse, and Regional Identity in Jacksonville, Illinois, 1865–1900," these women emphasized local connections and negotiated regional identities by cultivating relationships with organizations and individuals outside of their communities while holding fast to Midwestern exceptionalism.

In "Charles G. Finney and the Creation of the Midwestern Evangelical Mind," William Kostlevy contends that—as a noted evangelist, president of Oberlin College, author of a widely circulated revival manual and standard theological textbook, and mentor to literally hundreds of pastors filling Midwestern Congregational pulpits—Charles G. Finney's (1792–1875) impact on the intellectual formation of the Midwest is hard to overestimate. A product of the social and cultural ferment of the so-called Burned-Over District of central and western New York, Finney forged a distinctly Midwestern evangelicalism characterized by a pragmatic suspicion of received tradition, a primitivism associated with a desire to return to first principles, and a perfectionistic ethical activism anticipating a radically altered society.

Marcia Noe, in her chapter, "He Flirted with Euterpe before He Settled Down with Clio: The Education of Frederick Jackson Turner," offers a rhetorical analysis of Turner's 1893 essay "The Significance of the Frontier in American History," demonstrating how the author's intensive reading of literary classics, as well as his responses to them in the commonplace books he kept during his late teens, helped Turner endow his famous essay with eloquence and rhetorical power. Noe demonstrates how this seminal document in American historiography owes much of its cogency and persuasiveness to Turner's skillful use of schemes, tropes, and rhetorical strategies.

In "'Invitation to the Dance': Robert Ingersoll, Dwight Moody, and the Iconoclastic Gilded Age," Justin Clark examines the careers of Robert Ingersoll, an intellectual advocating for freethought, and Dwight L. Moody, an evangelist testifying for Christianity. These two men served as intellectual avatars for the contradictions of the Gilded Age. However, their powerful similarities spoke to a deeper consensus about Midwestern identity during the late nineteenth century. In particular, both men used their public platforms to advance their shared conviction of moral individualism, even while criticizing each other's worldview. As such, their encounters were like a dance, and the public was an eager audience.

The Harvard-educated, Boston-based philosopher Horace Meyer Kallen (1882–1974) is widely recognized as the author of the concept of cultural pluralism, but this idea did not come out of the urban east. According to Michael Steiner in "An Easterner in the Hinterland: Horace Meyer Kallen, the University of Wisconsin, and the Regional Roots of Cultural Pluralism, 1911–1918," it was during his seven years as an instructor at the University of Wisconsin between 1911 and 1918 that Kallen's concept of cultural pluralism reached full expression. Far from being a wasted banishment in a remote hinterland, Kallen's Wisconsin years were essential to his fully developed theory. Kallen's vigorous interactions with a spectrum of Madison colleagues—among them Charles Van Hise, Richard T. Ely, John R. Commons, Edward Alsworth Ross, Max Otto, Julia Grace Wales, and Frederick Jackson Turner (who had just left Wisconsin for Harvard)—helped precipitate his theory and form the heart of this chapter.

Brian M. Ingrassia, in "Modeling 'Civic Effectiveness' in the Midwest: Charles Mulford Robinson's Progressive Era Urban Planning, 1907–1915," takes up the career of Charles Mulford Robinson (1869–1917), who is best known for his writings on the "city beautiful" movement of the early twentieth century. This chapter focuses on the ways that Robinson stressed the creation of parks and playgrounds for midsize cities in Illinois, Indiana, Iowa, and Missouri. He saw Midwestern cities essentially as urban-planning laboratories where he and his students could take ideas from cities the world over and improve them, creating models of civic culture for the entire nation.

The work of agrarian reformer and environmental philosopher Liberty Hyde Bailey Jr. (1858–1954) is the subject of "Agrarian 'Naturism': Liberty Hyde Bailey and the Michigan Frontier." John Linstrom and Daniel Rinn examine the development of Bailey's philosophy from its origins in Michigan soil to its mature formulation as an aesthetic brand of naturalism. A close analysis of Bailey's work on botany and horticulture, as well as his poetry and fiction, reveals a far-reaching environmental cosmology that united nature and culture, art and science, farming and poetry.

In "'The mind and the soil': An Iowa Town That Grows Writers," Cherie Dargan describes how Cedar Falls, Iowa—a town that predates the Civil War by a decade—became an important hub for readers and writers. Five best-selling authors have ties to Cedar Falls: Bess Streeter Aldrich, Ruth Suckow, James Hearst, Robert James Waller, and Nancy Price. The secret of this town's success? A persistent focus by a succession of civic leaders on the fertile blend of literature and the land. Many towns had literary societies, but early Cedar Falls had Peter Melendy, founder of the Cedar Falls Horticultural and Literary Society in 1859. His tagline, "the mind and the soil," bore fruit in the creation of a city with beautiful parks, gardens, and trees complemented by a vibrant literary culture with a modern public library. This chapter explores the city's early history, examines several community organizations that fostered reading and the discussion of ideas, and explains how the community has honored its five best-selling authors.

Allan C. Carlson's chapter, "John C. Rawe and Midwestern Agrarianism," describes the role played by this Jesuit scholar in framing agrarian thought and political action during the 1930s and early 1940s. Born and raised in rural Illinois and educated at Jesuit schools and seminaries in Missouri and Kansas, Rawe (1900–1947) gave a distinctive Midwestern spin to Catholic social teachings that cast the renewal of family-scale agriculture and economically productive homes as solutions to "the social question." According to Rawe, a healthy democracy could be found only "in the country districts and in the rural culture of America."[6]

In "Mari Sandoz: Regional Writer Never at Home," William C. Pratt takes up the work of Sandoz (1896–1966), a historian, novelist, and essayist who was a spokesperson for regional values and concerns in her writings until her death. Sandoz is an example of the complexity of regional identity for intellectuals. Although she lived most of her adult life outside the Nebraska Sandhills where she was born, she renewed her roots by making annual short trips to the area, stating that a writer should not "wander too long from the region with which he is emotionally identified." For her, New York City was an outpost rather than a home, even though she spent the last two decades of her life there.[7]

Kenneth H. Wheeler, in "How the Midwest Encountered Mass Consumer Culture," focuses on the 1920s and 1930s, when a consumer culture eclipsed a producer culture nationally. Midwesterners such as Henry Ford were instrumental in bringing about a consumer culture, yet Ford, we learn, was resistant to the implications of the automobile revolution. Some people, such as Robert S. Lynd, in his studies of Middletown, were shocked and dismayed by Americans' widespread desire for leisure, but others were more sanguine about the changes. All agreed, however, that the idea of the Midwest—so tied to an agrarian and producerist culture—had been altered significantly by the new dominance of a consumer culture.

In "'No Place for Artistes': James Jones's Quest for Authenticity in the Postwar Midwest," Aaron George investigates the life of the renowned war writer and Midwesterner James Jones (1921–1977). Tracing Jones's experiences in World War II, George argues that the ways in which wartime confounded Jones's expectations of heroic sacrifice led him to fashion a notion of manhood predicated on authenticity and camaraderie. Adapting this new ideal as an alternative to what he saw as an emasculating postwar American society, Jones used the rural Midwest as a site to develop a utopic writers' commune that could resist modernity and harken back to an idyllic, authentic American past. An analysis of the commune that resulted—the Handy Writers' Colony—yields fresh insights into the problems of conformity and male authenticity that emerged in the 1950s.

In "Newton Minow, John Bartlow Martin, and the 'Vast Wasteland' Speech," Ray E. Boomhower describes a speech given on May 9, 1961, by Newton Minow, the recently appointed chairman of the Federal Communications Commission. The speech quickly became legendary for its unexpected critique of television's emptiness. "When television is good," Minow claimed, "nothing—not the theater, not the magazines or newspapers—nothing is better. But when television is bad, nothing is worse. I invite each of you to sit down in front of your television set when your station goes on the air and stay there, for a day. . . . I can assure you that what you will observe is a vast wasteland." Minow had able assistance for his speech from his friend and fellow Midwesterner John Bartlow Martin, a Hoosier journalist and respected freelance writer and political speechwriter, and Boomhower shows how this unique partnership produced a speech whose intent and import are still debated in discussions about broadcasting.[8]

In "Cleveland's Anisfield-Wolf Book Awards and Midwestern Racial Liberalism," Andrew Seal examines the history of the Anisfield-Wolf Award, a prize that has been given since 1936 to books that would educate readers on "race relations in the contemporary world." The award, he argues, is a window on the development of a distinctively Midwestern form of mid-twentieth-century racial liberalism. In contrast to the liberalism of elite eastern philanthropic foundations whose attention to "the race problem" was limited in scope to African Americans, mostly in the South, Midwestern racial liberalism encouraged people to think globally and to acknowledge prejudice as a problem affecting many different races and ethnicities. The history of this Midwestern book prize offers a remarkable expression of cosmopolitan, rather than provincial, insights.

In "How the Midwestern GOP Encountered Modernity: Robert Taft, Mobility, and Individualism," William Russell Coil explores how Republican politicians in the Midwest encountered modernity, focusing on the life and career of "Mr. Republican," Robert A. Taft. A US senator from Ohio and three-time failure for the Republican nomination for the presidency (1940, 1948, and 1952), Taft (1938–1953) has frequently been dismissed as a reactionary and an isolationist—someone trying to hold modernization and internationalism at bay. Taft and his followers, however, created their regional identity in conversation with the transnational forces of modernity, selectively embracing, rejecting, negotiating, and adapting as they tried to assert the cultural and political power of the Midwest.

In "The Fusionist Mind of Stephen Tonsor," Gleaves Whitney takes up the life and work of the University of Michigan historian largely remembered for his opposition to the rise of neoconservatives inside the conservative movement and Reagan administration. While Tonsor's fierce wit enlivened contemporary debate, his best work goes far beyond interne-cine struggles in the Republican Party. A Catholic Midwesterner, Tonsor found persuasive the fusionist thinker Frank Meyer, one of the preeminent writers at *National Review* in the 1950s and 1960s. Meyer's fusionism at-tempted to reconcile the libertarian wing of the conservative movement with its traditionalist Catholic wing. Tonsor adopted the fusionist project but ultimately embraced a larger civilizational mission. This chapter of-fers an intimate portrait of Stephen Tonsor and reaches well beyond the politics of Reagan-era conservatism to examine Tonsor's contribution to Catholic humanism and the liberal arts.

David Pichaske and Emily Williamson, in "The Rise and Demise of Rural and Regional Studies at Southwest Minnesota State University, 1977–2010," describe a unique initiative that promised to leverage rural and regional knowledge and pride to create—in the words of President Jon Wefald (1977–1982)—"a school that people in southwestern Minne-sota would want to send their children to." Modeled on urban studies programs, the multidisciplinary Rural and Regional Studies program prospered through the 1980s, receiving many grants, hosting many con-ferences, and spawning many publications. Its true foundation, however, was a general studies requirement that all students, regardless of major, take twelve hours of rural studies courses in history, literature, sociology, physical education, and other subjects. The slow decline of this bold pro-gram in the decades since, however, is a case study in the difficulty of main-taining a commitment to the local and the rural in the twenty-first-century academy.

Sara Kosiba's chapter, "Midwestern Literature and the Literary Canon: When, Where, and How?," attempts to fill in the gaps regarding the his-tory of teaching Midwestern literature at the postsecondary level. Kosi-ba's chapter explores the emergence of Midwestern literature on early twentieth-century American college and university campuses and the prominent scholarly voices, such as those of John T. Flanagan and John T. Frederick, who championed the Midwest in their classrooms. She then contrasts that earlier history with survey data noting the spotty pres-ence of Midwestern literature, particularly as a specific area of study and instruction, on university and college campuses today, and she argues that the region's literature deserves a more prominent place in the contemporary literary canon.

In "The Stars Had Become *My* Stars: Leslie C. Peltier, *Starlight Nights*, and Amateur Astronomy," Robert L. Dorman describes the work of Peltier (1900–1980), a high school dropout from Delphos, Ohio, who became a world-famous comet discoverer. He lived his entire life in the Delphos area and, at age sixty-five, published a memoir that has since been recognized as the definitive portrayal of the amateur astronomy experience. *Starlight Nights: The Adventures of a Star-Gazer* drew from the conventions of books for young boys, nature writing, and Midwestern regionalism to popularize and domesticate the pursuit of science. Writing at the dawn of the Space Age, Peltier exalted the individual amateur at a time when theoretical and technological advances were widening the gulf between amateur and professional scientists. His evocation of the personal experience of observing astronomical objects, coupled with a do-it-yourself ethos depicted in a homely setting, accounts for *Starlight Nights*'s enduring appeal.

John E. Miller admits, in "George McGovern: An Intellectual in Politics," that McGovern (1922–2012) will be remembered for his landslide loss to Richard Nixon in the 1972 presidential campaign, his leading role in opposition to the Vietnam war, and the alleged extremism of his left-wing political views on the floor of the US Senate. But McGovern's major historical legacy, Miller suggests, would better be remembered by the role he played as an intellectual in politics. McGovern would have been perfectly happy to have been a college history professor all his life, as he had intended to be, but circumstances threw him in another direction: he became more a maker of history than an interpreter of it. As such, McGovern was a major figure in Washington, DC, as a two-term congressman and three-term senator, working side by side with other former college professors such as Mike Mansfield, J. William Fulbright, and Eugene McCarthy. In this chapter, Miller examines the Midwesterner George McGovern's intellectual contributions to American political life.

Miller's is the final chapter of a volume that proceeds from the nineteenth century to the end of the twentieth. Each chapter offers a distinct vision of what it means, or has meant, to be a Midwestern "seer." By no means is the volume extensive in this regard. Its aim is to help start a broad examination of the intellectual history of this vast region—an intellectual history not plain but textured, full of multiplicity, diversity, and conflict. Our volume begins with one such conflict, which took place at the level of ideas, between settler and American Indian culture in the formative Midwest.

NOTES

1. Liberty Hyde Bailey, "Sower and Seer," in *Wind and Weather* (New York: Scribner, 1916), 128.

2. See Jon K. Lauck, *From Warm Center to Ragged Edge: The Erosion of Midwestern Literary and Historical Regionalism, 1920–1965* (Iowa City: University of Iowa Press, 2017).

3. F. Scott Fitzgerald, *The Great Gatsby* (New York: Scribner, 2018), 4.

4. *Girls*, season 1, episode 1, "Pilot," directed by Lena Dunham, written by Lena Dunham, aired April 15, 2012, on HBO, www.hulu.com/series/girls.

5. "Midwestern History Association," Midwestern History Association, https://midwesternhistory.com.

6. John C. Rawe, "Agriculture—An Airplane Survey," *Catholic Rural Life Bulletin* 3 (February 1940): 25.

7. Mari Sandoz, "Stay Home, Young Writer!" *The Quill* (June 1937): 9.

8. Newton N. Minow, *How Vast the Wasteland Now?* (New York: Gannett Foundation Media Center, 1991).

CHAPTER 1

INDIGENOUS INTELLECTUALS AND THE COLONIZATION OF THE MIDWEST

Copway, Warren, Blackbird, and Pokagon

Edward Watts

M any current American Indian intellectuals self-identify as members of Midwestern tribes: David and Anton Treuer (Minnesota Ojibwa), Kimberly Blaeser (Wisconsin Ojibwa), Robert Warrior (Kansas Osage), Gordon Henry (Michigan Odawa), Elizabeth Cook-Lynn (South Dakota Sioux), and Gerald Vizenor (Minnesota Ojibwa), to name just a few.[1] These figures work outside the institutional machinations of American academia and the prescribed authority of "western" knowledge long used to validate—intellectually and historically—the de facto genocide of their tribes. Their work, as Cook-Lynn claims, has opened Native studies—specifically work conducted by non-Natives—to completely new lines of inquiry:

> Now that [Native culture] is being examined and criticized by those persons whose intellectual backgrounds are deeply embedded in the oral traditions of the native tribes of North America, new visions are in the offing, mistaken ideas about the native past can be reexamined, and concerns that have not been part of the broad public dialogue can now be addressed.[2]

However, the interventions that Cook-Lynn champions have long been at the center of American Indian intellectual traditions and, more specifically, of Anishnabeg writing. Calling out "mistaken" white conceptions that have led to destructive policies has been the task of Native writers since the late eighteenth century.[3]

Born after the end of the Midwestern Indian Wars (1815), the first generation of literate Anishnabeg negotiated a complex relationship with colonialist "mistakes" that relegated them and their cultures to subhuman or nonhuman status in the eyes of the colonists. These misrepresentations led to and "justified" land seizure and removal.[4] To unveil the ideology beneath the policies, these American Indians challenged white historiography, ethnology, and ideology, revealing the flawed philosophical bases of removal, ethnic cleansing, and other forms of annihilation. The texts produced by members of this generation reflect a necessary double-consciousness: they both assert tribal identity and meet settler standards of cultural legitimacy.[5]

Early Anishnabeg intellectuals transcended mere self-defense by critiquing settler culture's assumption of its supposedly benign and historically inevitable dominion over "its" conquered indigenes. Asserting their claim to govern the indigenes implicitly bolstered settlers' fragile legitimacy and effaced their status as derivative ex-colonials.[6] Midwestern American Indian writers showed how they met a standard of Enlightenment and liberal cultural legitimacy while simultaneously demonstrating how white print culture rarely met that standard itself. The particular circumstances of racial contact in the upper Midwest over the course of the nineteenth century produced a generation of Anishnabeg writers uniquely suited to respond to local manifestations of national transformations in ways not unlike the regionalist response of the region's white writers. Midwestern intellectualism was born in resisting responses to eastern colonialism, nationalism, and empire building.[7]

Intersectional regional connections often go ignored: Toni Morrison, for example, is more commonly considered an African American writer than a Midwestern writer even though most of her work is very specifically situated in that region. Nonwhite Americans are identified more by race than by place. Automatically prioritizing race over region grossly oversimplifies contact and colonial histories: specific circumstances of contact, conquest,

and colonization differed radically from region to region, especially before the Dawes Act and its nationalization of federal Indian policy in 1887.[8]
Effectively, the Dawes Act erased all treaties and racialized all Indigenous
people in the nation, disregarding tribal and local identity. Moreover, even
before 1776, widely varying forms of European colonialism created radically differing forms of Indigenous experience. The history of slaveholding
southerners and the Cherokee in the South shares very little with that of the
freeholding farmers and the Anishnabeg in the upper Midwest. During the
1830s and the 1890s, unilateral race-based policies—first, Andrew Jackson's
1830 Indian Removal Act and then the Dawes Act—nationalized and racialized the previously heterogeneous forms of local interracial relationships
by imposing strictly binary definitions of racial difference.[9]

Yet, as many scholars—settler and Indigenous—have maintained,
the heterogeneity of the frontier Midwest ran counter to the colonialist
narrative, a diversity embodied in the four writers studied here.[10] More
precisely, none of the four described "indigeneity" as an infantilized or
uncorrupted precontact cultural identity despite the consistent identification, in colonial policy and culture, of indigeneity with savagery, noble
or ignoble. All four writers spent time in mission-based boarding schools
and wrote in English, and two married white women. To explain how such
writers could still identify as Indigenous, Patrick Wolfe studies how settler
colonialism transformed the Indigenous to the Native:

> Colonial categories . . . require constant maintenance and refurbish-
> ment, a contestatory process that shifts across time. . . . Rather, in its
> contestedness, the category "Native" takes on transformed historical
> modalities that bear the imprint of anticolonial practice, flexibly regis-
> tering the ever-shifting hegemonic balance between those with a will
> to colonize and those with a will to be free.[11]

In responding to postcontact transformations, the term *Native* grows
beyond implying undiluted indigeneity to denote a more complicated
subjectivity from which meaningful resistance is possible—one reflecting
the complex nature of local and regional conditions. Hence, while some
who recognize indigeneity only in individuals with an undiluted traditional tribal upbringing might question the legitimacy of these authors'

indigenous identities, their accepted status as Natives reflects centuries of transformative defense of tribal lands, culture, and language.

Furthermore, Richard White has famously described the colonial Great Lakes region as a "middle ground" where, until 1815, racial, ethnic, tribal, and religious diversity transcended the usual binaries of Empire.[12] In the process, the white freeholder embodied the righteous American nation, a role few actual settlers could play. Generations of historians of American culture studied how such narratives were deliberately designed to assimilate the divergent frontiersman and other exogenous white populations.[13] However, the region retained middle-ground paradigms well after it was purportedly colonized. Removal and the Dawes Act were not just about American Indians: each was meant to decontaminate the western borders, inoculating white settlers from Native culture, policing the raced nation through ethnic cleansing, and, as that failed, attempting cultural erasure.

As they created their counter-colonialist, alternative histories, the generation of Anishnabeg intellectuals born in the 1820s developed practices of counter-historiography that are still in use by contemporary American Indian intellectuals. This chapter examines how four nineteenth-century Anishnabeg writers responded to the colonization—material, political, and most important, intellectual—of their tribal homelands, from Anglo-American contact (ca. 1820) through Removal (1830–1850) and through the Dawes era (1890–1900). George Copway/Kahgegagahbowh (Minnesota/Ontario Ojibwa), William Warren (Minnesota Ojibwa), Andrew Blackbird (Michigan Odawa), and Simon Pokagon (Michigan Potawatomi) resisted the colonization of what we refer to today as the Midwest by disputing settler culture's colonialist histories of the region and its peoples. In the end, these Anishnabeg writers identify white settlers' writing, as much as their diseases and armies, as implicit in the colonization and corruption of the upper Midwest.

All four worked, traveled broadly, and focused on how their Anishnabeg ancestors had been (mis-)represented in American print culture. However, each also worked and lived among their less fortunate tribesfolk.[14] By merging with and embodying—and then voicing—the diverse and divergent racial, cultural, and tribal presences of the region, their complex identities reproduced the complexities of their subject. These writers envisioned an inevitably multiracial Midwest and how intellectuals might protect it by resisting print-based whitewashing. Copway and Warren wrote mostly in the post-Removal era (1840–1860) and so addressed strategies for resisting the intellectual foundations of overt ethnic cleansing policies at the heart of settler colonialism, while Pokagon and Blackbird responded to later nineteenth-century intellectual assumptions that surrounded the Dawes era. In sum, each resisted colonization at the level of ideas—the true criterion of intellectual utterance.

Copway (ca. 1818–ca. 1869) has a problematic reputation.[15] He was chased out of Canada, accused by his uncle and fellow Ojibwa historian Peter Jones of embezzlement. Copway also embraced Removal, but only if American Indians were given their own state in the Far West under his supervision and named for him, Kahgegaga. Moreover, he was born in Ontario to the Rice Lake Ojibwa but later identified as a Turtle Mountain Ojibwa; and after settling in both Detroit and New York, where he briefly published a newspaper (*Copway's American Indian*), he joined the notorious Know Nothing Party. Worse yet, as a zealous young Methodist missionary, he bragged of desecrating American Indian religious idols by throwing them into the Mississippi River. Despite these actions, Copway's *Traditional History and Characteristics of the Ojibway Nation* (1850) engages issues that would characterize subsequent Anishnabeg challenges to the authority of settler descriptions of both the region and the people of the upper Midwest.

Copway began his book by announcing his goal: "In thus giving a sketch of my nation's history, describing its home, its country, and its peculiarities, and in narrating its traditionary legends, I may awaken in the American heart a deeper feeling for the race of the red men, and induce the pale-face to use greater effort to effect an improvement in their social and political relations."[16] In the age of romantic nationalism, "nations" were viewed as the natural by-product of a community's deep intimacy— in terms of history, demographics, and tradition—with the geographical space it occupied.[17] White settlers, of course, had no access to these authenticating criteria. In his introduction to *The Marble Faun* (1860), Nathaniel Hawthorne complained of the lack of binding foundational narratives in America: "No author, without a trial, can conceive of the difficulty of writing a romance about a country where there is no shadow, no antiquity, no mystery, no picturesque and gloomy wrong, nor anything but a commonplace prosperity, in broad and simple daylight, as is happily the case with my dear native land."[18] Yet, as an Anishnabeg writer, Copway is flush with such narratives.[19]

> There is not a lake or mountain that has not connected with it some story of delight or wonder, and nearly every beast and bird is the subject of the story-teller, being said to have transformed itself at some prior time into some mysterious foundation—of men going to live in the star, and of imaginary beings in the air, whose rushing passage roars in the distant whirlwinds.[20]

Moreover, Copway delineates the influence of the oral tradition on American Indians' community formation and tribal identity: "These legends have an important bearing on the character of the children of our nation. . . . By mingling thus, our social habits are formed and strengthened."[21] One of the main colonialist justifications for the invasion and occupation of areas inhabited by American Indians was that Indigenous populations were nomadic, provisional, and savage. The land in question could then be labeled by settlers as a *terra nullius*, void of genuine human occupation.[22] Thus, by establishing not only the tribe's long-term occupation of the region but also its military and traditional history, Copway showed that the land was in fact inhabited (and had been in perpetuity) based on the very criteria used by the settlers. By this standard, the Ojibwa claim on the land was more authentic than the settlers'.

Much of the remainder of *Traditional History* reprinted already-published accounts of the arrival of whites (as was the custom of the day), especially descriptions of the Ojibwa people's interaction with the Jesuit French in the seventeenth century and the dominance of the fur trade in the eighteenth. Aside from the British trader Alexander Henry—Copway's main source for the aforementioned two accounts—Copway also borrowed from a series of essays that appeared in 1850 in the *St. Paul (Minnesota) Pioneer* written by a young American Indian legislator from the northern part of the state, William Warren. Warren, however, was more concerned with demonstrating how the postcontact merging of people had emerged from the era of French and Ojibwa cohabitation, a multiracialism directly at odds with Removal's intellectual foundation in the emergent and segregationist theories of scientific racism.[23]

Near the end of his brief life, in 1850, Warren traveled to New York with the essays from the *Pioneer* to try to find a publisher to turn them into a book.[24] Aware that the essays had been confined to the generic limitations of white-based print culture, he hoped to produce a follow-up volume that collected Ojibwa folklore and other tribal materials. Unfortunately, with the Civil War looming, American Indian subjects were viewed by publishers as relatively unprofitable, and Warren, rebuffed, trekked home to Minnesota where he succumbed to tuberculosis at age twenty-eight. In 1885, the Minnesota Historical Society reprinted his essays as *History of the Ojibways*. While mostly straightforward history, the book was counter-colonialist in its explicit delineation of the region's long-standing accommodation of multiethnic, multisectarian, and multiracial cooperation, a narrative in which Anglo settlers play only a minor role. This ran counter to the Anglo settler culture's basic assumption of unassailable racial difference. The bad sciences of phrenology and craniology had hardened Anglo ideas about race from the fluid and adaptive paradigm of the eighteenth century into fixed and hierarchical biological categories, theories that later supported the one-drop rule of Jim Crow legislation.

The emergence of such categories marked a profound change in the history of colonial Minnesota. Embodying the problem, Warren was descended not only from Ojibwa leaders but also from the prominent Catholic French mixed-ancestry Cadotte family and Protestant Pilgrim families that came over on the *Mayflower*. In fact, the collected essays in *History of the Ojibways* represented Warren's effort to find his own voice, audience, and identity: he uses *we* and *them* to indicate both Ojibwa and white populations. Warren was educated in private New York schools; however, he never fulfilled the colonialist fantasy of assimilating to white culture as demonstrated in, for example, Lydia Marie Child's *Hobomok* (1823), wherein a biracial man gradually becomes white. Warren's skin remained dark, and he wrote as a Native person.

Warren presented his complex identity in the book's opening materials. In his preface, Warren mouths the standard "vanishing Indian" trope: "The red race is fast disappearing before the onward restless tread of the Anglo-Saxon."[25] Writing for a white culture that, after Removal, had put American Indians out of sight and mind and congratulated itself on its Anglo-Saxon supremacy, Warren advocated for change:

The red man has no powerful friends (such as the enslaved negro can boast) to rightly represent his miserable, sorrowing condition, his many wrongs, his wants and wishes. . . . His condition and character has been so misrepresented that it has failed to secure the sympathy and help which he really deserves.[26]

Warren equated African American slavery and American Indian genocide as paired weapons in the methods of settler colonialism, and he implicated print culture in the propagation of racial violence. Moreover, his use of *Anglo-Saxon* references the settler nation's roots in a borrowed and transplanted Old World foundation, implying the same latent fear exploited by Copway: that the lack of a deep, white continental history delegitimized the settler nation, forcing them to borrow England's, essentially mimicking the colonialism they disavowed. Warren claimed an identity for the Ojibwa that settlers could not for themselves. Thereafter, his *we* might be Anglo, French, or Ojibwa.

As to the historical origins of the settlers' misperception of Ojibwa culture, Warren directly confronted established "experts" on American Indian culture, such as Henry Rowe Schoolcraft and Francis Parkman:

Clashing with the received opinions of more learned writers, whose words are taken as standard authority, [my own opinions] may be totally rejected, in which case the satisfaction will still be left me, that before the great problem had been fully solved, I, a person in language, thoughts, beliefs and blood, partly an Indian, had made known my crude and humble opinion.[27]

Subsequently, Warren further teased his readers by suggesting the Ojibwa might be descended from the Lost Tribes of Israel, a popular argument in antebellum America based in the writings of William Penn, John Eliot, and Roger Williams and later taken up by Nathaniel Hawthorne, James Fenimore Cooper, and the writer William Apess, who was part Pequot by descent.[28] Yet Warren insisted only the "Algics" (his term for speakers of Algonquian languages, including the Ojibwa) might be Lost Jews. By contrast, the Sioux, he suggested, were an Asiatic people who chased the Algics into the New World. However, Warren later undercut the legend:

It requires a most intimate acquaintance with [the Algics] as a people, and individually with their old story tellers, also with their language, beliefs and customs, to procure their real beliefs and to analyze the tales they seldom refuse to tell, and separate the Indian or original from those portions which they have borrowed or imbibed from the whites. Their innate courtesy and politeness often carry them so far that they seldom, if ever, refuse to tell a story when asked by a white man. . . .

These tales, though made up for the occasion by the Indian sage, are taken by his white hearers as their *bona fide* belief, and as such, many have been made public, and accepted by the civilized world.[29]

Assuming the role of the trickster by seizing and inverting the terms of representation through misdirection and mimicry, Warren re-created the tricksterism of Native informants who, by sending the whites off the scent, maintained the privacy and intimacy of elements of Native culture even in the midst of its immersion in settler civilization.

On the other hand, Warren's loyalty to the French—on whom such tricks were not played—suggested a prioritization of character over race. As Warren's own white lineage was both French and Anglo, and because each group treated the Ojibwa differently, for Warren, racial identity was hardly a marker of potential or morality. That the French and the Anglos were both white was beside the point. While the French presence in the region still represented colonialism, Warren argues that the French settlers stressed cohabitation rather than conquest:

The Ojibways received the "heart" of their French brethren, and accepted their proposals of peace, amity, and mutual support and protection. . . . The Ojibways learned to love the French people, for the Frenchmen, possessing a character of great plasticity, easily assimilated themselves to the customs and mode of life of their red brethren. . . . It is an acknowledged fact, that no nation of whites have ever succeeded so well in gaining the love and confidence of the red men, as the Franks.[30]

Warren's juxtaposition of *Franks* against *Anglo-Saxons* is a direct reference to the scientific racism that informed American Indian policy at the time. In making the comparison, he exploited a crucial fissure in the settlers' equation of race and nation: *contra* the binary oppositions that informed Anglo-American settler colonialism, the French embodied the dangerous simultaneity of both whiteness and interracial tolerance. As a legatee of such traditions, Warren insisted that multiracial cohabitation need not evoke racial rivalry, animosity, or violence. For the Anishnabeg historian, cohabitation, not conquest, was the first paradigm of racial interaction.

In the end, Warren posited a vision of the colonial Midwest, much as Richard White did later, as a middle ground wherein a diversity of races, sects, republics, tribes, and villages cohabited in relative peace. While this memory might have been seen through rose-colored glasses, Warren's fundamental intervention in the racist "science" at the core of settler colonialism remained: Removal was founded on false and historically unsupported definitions of racial difference.

Removal's failure is borne out by the presence of Simon Pokagon and Andrew Blackbird in Michigan in the late nineteenth century. Imperial American nationalism, based as it was in racial, economic, and cultural uniformity, shifted from Removal to assimilation, at least among the sympathetic. Advocates of both Removal and assimilation—racist and paternalistic as they were—consistently battled those favoring outright genocide.[31] Faced with settlers boasting "the only good Indian is a dead Indian," whose murderous actions at Sand Creek (1864) and Wounded Knee (1891) demonstrated their intent, many American Indians reluctantly welcomed the notion of "Kill the Indian but not the Man"—the motto of the Haskell (Kansas) Indian Boarding School—and hoped that the Dawes Act would provide the schools, loans, roads, equipment, and teachers it promised to enable Native survival through acculturation.[32]

The Dawes Act reflected a domestic version of the "white man's burden": the self-assigned task of Victorians to use their "natural" superiority over lower races—according to the self-congratulatory social Darwinism at the core of this philosophy—to "civilize" their subjects by making them more Victorian.[33] Mistaking military might for moral authority, they demanded that American Indians convert to Christianity, use the English language, and participate in industrial capitalism. The Native people's lack of progress toward or, worse, resistance to the enforcement of these standards was seen by the Victorians not as just a simple difference in viewpoints but rather as an unregenerated savagery that needed harsh correction in the form of boarding schools, forced acculturation, separation of families, and loss of land. The Dawes Act was enacted in the wake of Helen Hunt Jackson's *A Century of Dishonor* (1881) and the book's unstinting record of the crimes of settler colonialism. To atone for these sins, liberal progressives sought to bear the burden of the crimes, thus the Dawes Act's promises of atonement.

That it failed so completely could not have been foreseen by Blackbird and Pokagon. Writing early in the era of the Dawes Act, both writers supported the economic training of young American Indians to survive in the industrializing white economy. However, within this concession, each insisted on the retention of the cultural and moral authority of Anishnabeg tradition. The full acculturation outlined by the Dawes Act, on the other hand, assumed the moral, as well as the economic and the technological, authority of settler culture. Citing the Act's invasive overextension into the personal and cultural realms of life, both Blackbird and Pokagon challenged the settler culture's claim to moral righteousness that propped up the white man's burden.

Writing after a long career in public service—much of it as a postal worker in L'Arbre Croche near Mackinac—Blackbird was immediately concerned about the moral degradation of the peoples of the region: the Odawa and the Ojibwa (whom he referred to as the Ottawa and the Chippewa, respectively).[34] For centuries, this region had been a crossroads for traders, travelers, miners, missionaries, and many others. In fact, the white press suggested that so much interaction had erased local tribes, a "mistake" Blackbird immediately addresses:

> I have seen a number of writings by different men who attempted to give an account of the Indians who formerly occupied the Straits of Mackinac and Mackinac Island. . . . But I see no very correct account of the Ottawa and Chippewa Indians, according to our knowledge of ourselves, past and present.[35]

In particular, he highlights the many errors in Francis Parkman's account of Pontiac, especially with regard to the British use of bioterrorism in their deliberate spreading of smallpox. Like Copway, Blackbird began by describing a place and a population living in balance prior to contact with settlers. This was not to endorse John Locke's belief in an ahistorical noble savagery ("In the beginning, all the world was America"[36]): when the Seneca from New York chased a smaller tribe into the Straits "five or six hundred years ago,"[37] Blackbird explains, the Ottawas chased them back east. Later, the Mishinimackinawgoes turned down an offer to live with the Anishnabeg and instead became the semi-mythical Windigo, the forest spirits who appear in so much Anishnabeg folklore. Their appearance here also demonstrates how Blackbird transgresses the separation of myth and history upon which colonialist historiography depends to discredit Indigenous trust in oral transmission. Moreover, Blackbird notes that his own family had been captured by an Ottawa war party that had been raiding in the Great Plains and was adopted to offset depopulation from disease, warfare, and starvation. These were not Edenic noble savages living in prehistorical stasis, Blackbird maintains.

Blackbird viewed the destruction of a naturally salutary and self-sustaining Anishnabeg culture as the sin of colonialism, a sin exacerbated by its claimed dominion based in moral and cultural superiority: "But now our living is altogether different, as we are continually suffering under great anxiety and perplexity, and continually being robbed and cheated in various ways."[38] At the center of his account is the story of his brother who was sent to Rome to be ordained as priest. Upon his return, he planned to resist Removal, and so, Blackbird argues, he was assassinated by conspirators acting on the wishes of Andrew Jackson. Blackbird viewed the settlers as hypocritical in their refusal to follow the Christian doctrine they imposed on the American Indians. In turn, the core of Anishnabeg culture was corrupted through its constant exposure to and interaction with morally bankrupt settlers.

Yet Blackbird acknowledged Anglo dominion and sought to use the opportunities offered by the Dawes Act to assure the Ottawas' survival. He drew the line, however, at the cultural transformation essential to the white man's burden. In his penultimate chapter, he suggests:

> Soon as the Indian youths receive an education, they should be
> allowed to have some employment among the whites, in order to
> encourage them in the pursuits of civilization and to exercise their
> ability according to the means and extent of their education, instead

of being a class of persons continually persecuted and cheated and robbed of their little possessions.[39]

While Blackbird seems to be endorsing concession, even to the extent of embracing the individualist ethos of settler culture, in the very next chapter (which was also published separately as an essay), "The Lamentation of the Overflowing Heart of the Red Man of the Forest," he condemns the annihilation of Anishnabeg culture and blames settlers for its destruction:

> When the white man took every foot of my inheritance, he thought
> I should be the slave, Ah never, never! I would sooner plunge the
> dagger into my beating heart, and follow the steps of the footsteps of
> my forefathers, than be slave to the white man.[40]

Blackbird believed American Indian education should enable an individual's economic autonomy but without violating tribal cultural, moral, and linguistic autonomy and sovereignty. The book's final twenty pages outline the structure and working of the Anishnabeg language, recognizing that language preservation is at the core of cultural survival. The burden, then, shifts to the Anishnabeg both to learn white ways *and* to preserve Native identity, just as Cook-Lynn advocates, and for whites to decolonize their binary ontology and explore the potentials of multiethnic cohabitation.

As a young man in an Ohio boarding school, Blackbird roomed with Simon Pokagon, the son of the famous Potowatomi Chief Leopold Pokagon. Much later, the younger Pokagon wrote one of the only nineteenth-century Anishnabeg novels, *Ogimawkwe Mitigwaki (Queen of the Woods)*. Its narrator—also named Simon Pokagon—relates a semi-mythical story of his early marriage to an ethereal Odawa woman whose idyllic life ends when the settlers' "fire-water" corrupts their utopia.[41] Their children die, first by alcoholism and second by abuse from drunken whites. The novel ends with pages of temperance polemic: Pokagon depicts white culture as soaked in alcohol and argues that, rather than improving the Native cultures, the use and distribution of alcohol did only damage and hastened American Indian genocide.[42]

In the 1890s, Pokagon gained a degree of celebrity for his memorable appearance at the World's Columbian Exposition in Chicago in 1893, an event that celebrated the white nation yet took place on Potowatomi land. Pokagon's "Address at the World's Columbian Exposition" reads like Black-bird's penultimate chapter in which he concedes the unfortunate necessity of learning American language, economics, and technologies. A follow-up article in the *Chicago Tribune* described Pokagon as a happy Indian, glad to mimic assimilation's narrative of absorption. However, just as Blackbird's final chapter encouraged American Indians to find a place in but not of the nation, Pokagon's response to the *Tribune* article, "The Red Man's Rebuke," published a few weeks later and printed on birchbark plates, invoked a far more sophisticated rejection of "pale face" culture in both poetry and prose:

> Shall not one line lament our forest race,
> For you struck out from wild creation's face?
> Freedom—the selfsame freedom you adore,
> Bade us defend our violated shore.

> In behalf of my people, the American Indians, I hereby declare to
> you, the pale-face race that has usurped our lands and homes, that we
> have no spirit to celebrate with you the great Columbian Fair being
> held in this Chicago city, the wonder of the World.[43]

Pokagon's vitriol centered on a precontact intimacy with the place un-possessed by settlers: "We trusted in them as infants trust in the arms of their mothers. But again and again our confidence was betrayed, until we were compelled to know that greed for Gold was all the balance wheel they had."[44] "Again and again," Pokagon observed how settlers' actions contra-dicted their words; most directly, he noticed how they imposed a Christian morality on American Indians that they themselves refused to follow. For Pokagon—by far the most literary writer of the four highlighted here—contact, conquest, colonization, and now assimilation demonstrated the deeply sinful nature of settler culture, which possessed a hypocrisy born from greed rather than virtue, idolatry rather than faith. The white man's burden was simply a cover for materialist exploitation.

By identifying and attacking the intellectual cores of settler colonialism, these Anishnabeg writers not only defended their culture as more legiti-mate than the settlers', but also turned the power of intercultural critique back on settler culture. By transcending white claims to heroism, virtue, and sacrifice, Copway, Warren, Blackbird, and Pokagon demonstrated how empire works by controlling the historical master narrative in order to privilege and authenticate white dominion, itself a nervous gesture to minimize America's own late-coming to the company of global empires. In pointing out to white American readers how the settler nation acted more like an empire than a republic, these writers shifted the contest for their own survival from the battlefield to the public sphere. While Midwestern war chiefs such as Pontiac (Illinois Odawa), Tecumseh (Indiana Shawnee), Black Hawk (Illinois Sauk), and Sitting Bull and Crazy Horse (both South Dakota Sioux) overtly opposed settler colonialism, American Indian intellectuals such as Copway, Warren, Blackbird, and Pokagon were opening another, more durable front in the same conflict. While the war chiefs fought for land, the writers fought for ideas, and while the Midwestern land they had occupied was ultimately lost, the battle over the place of Indigenous Americans and their stories in the regional imagination remains unsettled.

NOTES

1. Most of these states are considered Midwestern. See James R. Shortridge, *The Middle West: Its Meaning in American Culture* (Lawrence: University Press of Kansas, 1989).

2. Quoted in Deborah L. Madsen's introduction to *Native Authenticity: Transnational Perspectives on Native American Literary Studies*, ed. Madsen (Albany: SUNY Press, 2010), 9.

3. *Anishnabeg* (in various spellings) identifies the alliance of the Ojibwa (various spellings, including Chippewa), Odawa (various spellings, including Ottawa), and Potowatomi, whose Algonquin-speaking ancestors migrated from the lower to the upper Great Lakes region in approximately the sixteenth and seventeenth centuries. See Richard White, *The Middle Ground: Indians, Empires, and Republics in the Great Lakes Region, 1650–1815* (New York: Cambridge University Press, 1991).

4. Conversations linking representation and policy can be traced to Robert Berkhofer Jr., *The White Man's Indian: Images of the American Indian from Columbus to the Present* (New York: Vintage Books, 1978).

5. "Double Consciousness" was coined by W. E. B. DuBois in *The Souls of Black Folk* (Chicago: A. C. McClurg, 1903). As to its use by "native intellectuals,"

see *Native American Representations: First Encounters, Distorted Images, and Literary Appropriations*, ed. Gretchen M. Bataille (Lincoln: University of Nebraska Press, 2001).

6. See the essays in *The Routledge Handbook of the History of Settler Colonialism*, ed. Edward Cavenagh and Lorenzo Veracini (London: Routledge, 2017). See also Lorenzo Veracini, *Settler Colonialism* (London: Palgrave, 2011) and Walter Hixson, *American Settler Colonialism* (London: Palgrave, 2013).

7. Bethel Saler, *The Settlers' Empire: Colonialism and State Formation in America's Old Northwest* (Philadelphia: University of Pennsylvania Press, 2015), localizes the issue of empire in the upper Midwest.

8. See Reginald Horsman, *Race and Manifest Destiny: The Origins of American Racial Anglo-Saxonism* (Cambridge: Harvard University Press, 1981). See also Thomas King, *The Inconvenient Indian: A Curious Account of Native People in North America* (Minneapolis: University of Minnesota Press, 2013).

9. See the introduction to *The Settler Complex: Recuperating Binarism in Colonial Studies*, ed. Patrick Wolfe (Los Angeles: UCLA American Indian Studies Center, 2016), for a history of binary theory in settler studies.

10. On the French, see Edward Watts, *In This Remote Country: French Colonial Culture in the Anglo-American Imagination, 1780–1860* (Chapel Hill: University of North Carolina Press, 2006).

11. Patrick Wolfe, *Settler Colonialism and the Transformation of Anthropology: The Politics and Poetics of an Ethnographic Event* (London: Cassell, 1999), 9–10.

12. See White, *Middle Ground*. Since its publication thirty years ago, White's book has redirected the study of colonial Midwestern history.

13. On Midwestern multiethnicity, see Edward Watts, *An American Colony: Regionalism and the Roots of Midwestern Culture* (Athens: Ohio University Press, 2002). See Adam Dahl, *Empire of the People: Settler Colonialism and the Foundations of Modern Democratic Thought* (Lawrence: University Press of Kansas, 2018), 23–46, for a greater elaboration of how the Northwest Ordinance was designed to contain regional divergence from eastern dominion.

14. See Kiara M. Vigil, *Indigenous Intellectuals: Sovereignty, Citizenship, and the American Imagination, 1880–1930* (New York: Cambridge University Press, 2015).

15. I use Copway's *The Traditional History and Characteristic Sketches of the Ojibway Nation* (New York: Gilpin, 1850). See George Copway, *Life, Letters and Speeches*, ed. A. Lavonne Brown Ruoff and Donald Smith (Lincoln: University of Nebraska Press, 1997), for biographical information.

16. Copway, *Traditional History*, vi.

17. Anthony D. Smith, *National Identity* (London: Penguin, 1991), has most directly informed my thinking on romantic nationalism.

18. Nathaniel Hawthorne, *The Marble Faun: Or, The Romance of Monte Beni* (Boston: Ticknor and Fields, 1860), vii.

19. Henry James, William Gilmore Simms, and James Fenimore Cooper offered similar complaints about the lack of conventional materials in American history. See Russell Reising, *The Unusable Past: Theory and the Study of American Literature* (Minneapolis: University of Minnesota Press, 1987).

20. Copway, *Traditional History*, 95.

21. Copway, *Traditional History*, 96–97.

22. My ideas about *terra nullius* are based in Robert J. Miller, Jacinta Ruru, Larissa Behrendt, and Tracey Lindberg, *Discovering Indigenous Lands: The Doctrine of Discovery in the English Colonies* (New York: Oxford University Press, 2010).

23. See Robert Bieder, *Science Encounters the Indian, 1820–1880: The Early Years of American Ethnology* (Norman: University of Oklahoma Press, 1986), on the emergence of scientific racism.

24. I use William W. Warren, *History of the Ojibway People* (St. Paul: Minnesota Historical Society Press, 1984), a reprint of the 1885 publication, which was titled *History of the Ojibways*. See also Theresa M. Schenk, *William W. Warren: The Life, Letters, and Times of an Ojibwe Leader* (Lincoln: University of Nebraska Press, 2007).

25. Warren, *History*, 23.

26. Warren, *History*, 23–24.

27. Warren, *History*, 55.

28. See Eran Shalev, *American Zion: The Old Testament as a Political Text from the Revolution to the Civil War* (New Haven: Yale University Press, 2013), 118–50, on lost tribe theory.

29. Warren, *History*, 57–58.

30. Warren, *History*, 132.

31. See Matthew Frye Jacobson, *Barbarian Virtues: The United States Encounters*

Foreign Peoples at Home and Abroad, 1876–1917 (New York: Hill and Wang, 2000), for a discussion of the entanglement of race and nationalism in the Progressive Era.

32. See Katherine Ellinghaus, *Blood Will Tell: Native Americans and Assimilation Policy* (Lincoln: University of Nebraska Press, 2017).

33. Gretchen Murphy, *Shadowing the White Man's Burden: US Imperialism and the Problem of the Color Line* (New York: New York University Press, 2010), discusses nonwhite critiques of American imperialism.

34. I use the undated reprinting of Blackbird's *History of the Ottawa and Chippewa Indians of Michigan: A Grammar of Their Language, and a Personal and Family History of the Author* (Ypsilanti, MI: Ypsilanti Job Printing House, 1887; Petoskey, MI: Little Traverse Regional Historical Society, n.d.). For biographical information, see Theodore J. Karamanski, *Blackbird's Song: Andrew J. Blackbird and the Odawa People* (East Lansing: Michigan State University Press, 2012).

35. Blackbird, *History*, 7.

36. Locke's famous comment can be found in *Locke: Two Treatises of Government*, ed. Peter Laslett (Cambridge, UK: Cambridge University Press, 1988), Treatise II, para. 49.

37. Blackbird, *History*, 23.

38. Blackbird, *History*, 13.

39. Blackbird, *History*, 96.

40. Blackbird, *History*, 102.

41. I use Simon Pokagon, *Ogimawkwe Mitigwaki (The Queen of the Woods)* (East Lansing: Michigan State University Press, 2011). Biographical information of Pokagon is available in the novel's frontmatter by John N. Low (1–30) and Margaret Noori (57–76). "The Red Man's Rebuke" is republished in *American Indian Nonfiction: An Anthology of Writings, 1760s–1930s*, ed. Bernd Peyer (Norman: Oklahoma University Press, 2007), 233–240.

42. On American Indians, alcoholism, and temperance, see Peter C. Mancall, *Deadly Medicine: Indians and Alcohol in Early America* (Ithaca, NY: Cornell University Press, 1997).

43. Pokagon, "Red Man's," 233.

44. Pokagon, "Red Man's," 236.

CHAPTER 2

"Education for the head, heart, and hands"

Populism, Progressive Reform, and Rural School Consolidation

Kerry Alcorn

In the first two decades of the twentieth century, a handful of Midwestern educationists exerted a preponderant influence on the intellectual and policy movement that led to rural school consolidation. A superintendent, O. J. Kern; a college instructor and soon-to-be expert in rural education with the Department of Education in Washington, DC, Harold Foght; and two normal school instructors, Elwood Cubberley and Mabel Carney, both of whom would assume key faculty posts at two of the United States' most prominent faculties of education, wrote monographs on this topic of great concern not only to Midwesterners but to the nation as a whole, including its president.[1] The remarkable homogeneity of all four of their analyses is testament to the intellectual current pervasive among educational experts in this period and the centrality of Midwestern scholars within the field. Indeed, these four scholars had professional connections to Illinois, Indiana, Kansas, Missouri, and Minnesota. A rereading of these key works, published between 1906 and 1914, confirms the prominence of what David Tyack describes as "administrative progressivism," which pitted conservative farmers against educated reformers.[2] What has received less attention, however, but is entirely obvious within the work of these four Midwestern writers, is the *populist* undertone that clearly and consistently positioned country folk against city dwellers. While each of the four authors proposed consolidating the nation's myriad scattered, one-room schools into more modern and efficient district or town schools, often at the expense of some level of local control, their ultimate aim was to use consolidation to preserve life on the farm and, concomitantly, the sacrosanct ethical core of the American ideal—an ideal that, in the first two decades of the twentieth century, was distinctly Midwestern.[3]

I begin this chapter with a brief synopsis of each author's professional connection to the rural Midwest at the time of his or her writing and how that exposure manifested in each author's perspective. I then chronicle their unusually consistent arguments in favor of consolidation, specifically as a means to redress the asymmetric experiences of country students and city students. In conclusion, I synthesize each author's work within a broader populist ideology.

O. J. Kern was the first Midwestern educationist to write at length on the "rural school problem," predating by two years the alarm bell sounded in the final report of Theodore Roosevelt's Country School Commission released in 1908. In 1906, Kern was the county superintendent of Winnebago County, Illinois, a position he held from 1902 through 1915, and was immersed in his own efforts to consolidate the many remote rural schools of his county. Prior to the 1906 publication of his book, *Among Country Schools*, Kern had taken his own sociological tours of other Midwestern states, most notably Ohio and Indiana, to study the merits of consolidation.[4] On these tours, he came to believe that rural school consolidation was essential to improving the experience of country children while simultaneously "spiritualizing" country life. To Kern, the spiritualization of country life included the commandment, or as he described it, single decalogue, "Thou shalt enrich and enlarge the life of the country child."[5]

Similar to Kern, Harold Waldstein Foght viewed "consolidation of schools a panacea" to ensure that rural schools trained students to stay on the farm, not leave it.[6] Foght was the son of Norwegian immigrants who settled in Nebraska when Foght was in his late teens. There he was exposed to the rural school curriculum and its siren call, which could lure one away from the countryside toward the town or city. At the time of *The American Rural School*'s publication in 1910, Foght was a professor of education at Midland College, Kansas, having attended Iowa State College and Augustana College in Rock Island, Illinois. By 1912, he had become professor of rural education and sociology at the State Normal School in Kirkland, Missouri.[7] Foght was the quintessential administrative progressive who, more than the other Midwestern authors mentioned in this chapter, employed statistical and "scientific" methodology to reach the conclusion that administrative reorganization of rural schools was the key to guaranteeing education for children's heads, hearts, and hands.[8]

Much like Foght, Mabel Carney was directly involved in teacher ed-ucation in the Midwest. At the time when her book *Country Life and the Country School* was published in 1912, Carney served as the director of the Country School Department in the State Normal University in Macomb, Illinois. Prior to this, she had been an instructor in the Western Illinois State Normal School. Not surprisingly, she emphasized the key leadership role rural teachers should serve in enhancing the experience of rural stu-dents and in relieving the "undesirable conditions of country life" broadly conceived.[9] Carney's work focused mostly on the country life movement, which emanated from Roosevelt's Country Life Commission. Hers was a book obviously intended for rural teachers—a devotion that ultimately led her to head the Department of Rural Education at Teacher's College, Columbia University, in New York City, beginning in 1917.

Elwood Cubberley, meanwhile, published his *Rural Life and Education* in 1914 while a professor in a fledgling department of education at Stanford University in Palo Alto, California. Cubberley was born and raised in the state of Indiana where he attended Indiana University; spent one year as a schoolteacher; served another year at Ridgeville College in Ridgeville, Indiana; and later became professor and president of Vincennes University in Vincennes, Indiana. While a product of Indiana's system of education, Cubberley spent little time there professionally and is most known for his work in California, which was particularly focused on administration of public schooling. He believed that most commentators on the rural school problem did not see it clearly, and he argued that it must be viewed as a social problem inseparable from the rural life problem.[10] More than his fellow commentators, Cubberley viewed the rural school problem as an issue best understood in its historical and social context. Interestingly, he attributed much of the rural life problem to transient tenant farming, which had a dramatic effect on life in rural America, particularly in the upper Mississippi Valley states.[11] In his mind, nonresident farmers were unwilling to pay the necessary, increased costs for school consolidation and enhanced rural education.

While each of these Midwestern writers emphasized different aspects of the rural school problem on the basis of their unique positions within educational institutions, they were unanimous in their conclusions regarding the centrality of consolidation to resolving the problem. They believed a consolidated rural school would eliminate the "evils" associated with a one-room school and/or small district, where, as Foght argued, "attendance is spasmodic; interest poorly sustained. The work can scarcely be called graded; teachers change with each term, and with every such change the children are 'put back' to do over again work of which no record has been kept."[12] The social advantages gained from a consolidated school, where several teachers and several discrete grades exist within the same, larger, more modern building, were obvious to the four authors. Because more local tax money was devoted to the consolidated school, both students and teachers benefited from an improved building with enhanced tools. Added financial resources, therefore, eliminated the "pernicious" practice of teachers "moving on."[13] As a result, consolidated rural schools retained better teachers because their salaries and working conditions improved dramatically. These effects, the four scholars maintained, would inevitably enrich and enlarge the life of the country child.[14]

Such calls for reform clearly articulated the administrative progressivism described by Tyack. While Tyack makes clear that this reform-minded track first emerged within American urban school systems, in the first two decades of the twentieth century, such reform had clearly migrated to the countryside:

> Articulate professionals mostly agreed on the remedies [for the rural
> school problem]: consolidation of schools and transportation of
> pupils, expert supervision by county superintendents, "taking schools
> out of politics," professionally-trained teachers, and connecting
> the curriculum "with the everyday life of the community." . . . The
> result was to be a standardized, modernized "community" in which
> leadership came from the professionals.[15]

That such reforms would run contrary to the wishes of some rural dwellers is not surprising.

Historians of education have highlighted the struggle between the elite experts in education—such as Kern, Foght, Carney, and Cubberley—on the one hand, and the rural citizens, or "the people," on the other.[16] Superintendent Kern, for example, would have his readers believe that despite initial reservations related to rural school consolidation, the rural farmer would embrace consolidation and never consider returning to the old system once the true value of consolidation was uncovered. Wayne Fuller, however, in *The Old Country School*, suggests that reformers such as Kern oversold the benefits of consolidation to Midwestern country dwellers—so much so that consolidated schools, except in rare circumstances, could not possibly deliver on their promise. As a result, Fuller argues, rural school consolidation in the Midwest inched forward in the first decades of the twentieth century, and in some locations, actively reversed course.[17]

Regardless of the speed at which it was adopted, consolidation persisted as the central intellectual and policy influence among administrative progressives throughout the Midwest and beyond until World War II. From a political cultural standpoint, histories of Midwestern education in this period typically emphasize local farmers' conservative resistance as the foil to the intended progressive reforms of the expert. What has yet to be uncovered, however, is the distinct intellectual overlap between the progressive reformers, such as Foght and Cubberley, and the populist ideology underpinning their reform efforts. While it is true that progressive reforms typically included some form of government intervention into citizens' everyday lives—actions that ultimately weakened the level of local democratic control exercised by those citizens—rural school consolidation was intended to restore to a rural population what it had lost relative to the city dweller. These four Midwestern educationists championed rural school consolidation as a reform that could achieve a central tenet of populist ideology: a guarantee of equality of opportunity for rural citizens relative to those in the city or town.

Each of the four scholars maintained an argument that the ongoing migration from the country into the city eclipsed the "golden age" of country living. The result extinguished equal rights for everyone, much to the advantage of the city dweller. Such premonitory statements preface one of America's earliest and perhaps most noteworthy commentators on this period, Richard Hofstadter, who wrote in 1955:

> The Populist and Progressive movements took place during a rapid and turbulent transition from the conditions of an agrarian society to those of modern urban life. The American tradition of democracy was formed on the farm and in small villages, and its central ideas were founded in rural sentiments and on rural metaphors (we still speak of "grass-roots democracy"). The American was taught throughout the nineteenth and even in the twentieth century that rural life and farming as a vocation was something sacred. Since in the beginning the majority of the people were farmers, democracy, as a rather broad abstraction, became in the same way sacrosanct. A certain complacency and self-righteousness thus entered into rural thinking, and this complacency was rudely shocked by the conquests of industrialization. A good deal of the strain and the sense of anxiety in Populism results from this rapid decline of rural America.[18]

Kern captured the sanctity of rural life, relative to urban America, early in his book when he argued that the movement toward urbanization was regrettable because such a shift tended to increase the nervous strain, or sense of tension, among its inhabitants due to a lack of repose.[19] For him, urban ways and habits now prevailed in the United States, and it was up to country schools to conserve the "divine joy of living in the country."[20] He tended to describe life in towns and cities as artificial and devitalizing, a consistent theme among Midwestern educationists. Kern cites a Mr. Blevett, of St. Louis, Missouri, stating, "However enticing it may be, the life of the great towns is artificial and misshapen by the pressure of the great throngs. In its atmosphere the human forces are devitalized and dwindle into abnormal weakness. This is so true that the great enterprises of the city are sustained only by the infusion of men who have held plow handles or wielded the ax."[21]

Nevertheless, it was the obvious disparity between the experiences of the city student, on the one hand, and the country student, on the other, that most troubled Kern, for the country child simply did not enjoy the same opportunities offered his urban cousin. This Kern quickly outlined in Chapter II, "The Rights of the Country Child": "Our chief concern in this new age should be to secure an equality of educational opportunity for the great mass of country children." [22] Furthermore, Kern made clear that one should never expect the city or town school to teach students about life in the country. He wrote, "Simply to bring the country children into the city and make the country school an annex of the city school will be productive of evil and will intensify city life and degrade country life." [23] For Kern the solution was a simple one: rural residents must spend more money on education and consolidate rural schools to equalize educational opportunity for country children.

Along with Kern, Foght maintained a virulent distaste for city life, declaring the "menace" it posed to the country. In his book's introduction, he describes very clearly what he sees as the negative influence of urbanization and industrialization on the fabric of American society: "City life is terribly devitalizing. In its artificial, hot-house atmosphere the human organism literally starves and early deteriorates." [24] He cites the journal *American Medicine* to confirm that life in the city is "deadly" to the young. Regardless, Foght concludes that the welfare of the city is inextricably linked to the country, since it is from the country youth that the city receives its lifeblood. He believed it was therefore up to the country school to instill in the rural student the sense that country life is complete in itself.[25] Like Kern, Foght concludes, "Consolidation offers opportunities for study under the benign influence of field and grove in the very bosom of mother nature." [26] Indeed, for Foght, rural life in America was the "normal" life.

Foght's populist perspective in *The American Rural School* is ubiquitous. In order to make clear the obvious inequality of opportunity between rural and urban students, Foght and his Midwestern colleagues compared the amount of money spent on urban students relative to rural students. On average, in the first decade of the twentieth century, taxpayers spent $33.01 on a city student but only $13.17 on a rural student.[27] Foght argues, "Let it be kept well in mind that the free school system as established by our forefathers had for its purpose to extend equal opportunities to all members of the commonwealth. . . . In order to reestablish this educational equality it becomes necessary to give the twelve millions boys and girls living in the rural communities just as thorough a preparation in school for their life work as we are now offering city children." [28] Furthermore, like

Kern, Foght maintains that the country child is entitled to a thorough and practical education in his or her own "wholesome country environment" and should not have to move to the city to get it. Regrettably, he wrote, too many boys and girls were "mentally and morally starving" in rural districts. With the advent of the consolidated district school, Foght opines, "shall come a bright dawn for the youth of the farm." [29]

In *Rural Life and Education*, Cubberley was less vehement than his colleagues in his disdain for city life, broadly conceived, but he did repeatedly state the extent to which the city drained the best and brightest from the country, particularly when it came to schooling. He suggests that by 1890 rural boys and girls of "energy and ambition" left for the city at the earliest opportunity, thereby depleting rural communities.[30] Concomitantly, city schools typically syphoned off the best teachers from rural districts. Those teachers who remained in the country—"the city-trained and too often city-sick teacher," as Cubberley described them—had little to offer the rural people or their community.[31]

Much like Foght, Cubberley saw the curriculum and the experience it necessitated in the rural school student—an experience devoted to traditional "city" subjects, like arithmetic and literature, without reference to redirecting or revitalizing rural life [32]—as one key factor in producing disparities between town and country. Furthermore, several realities conspired against the rural school, including its weak financial resources, small number of pupils, "overburdened" programs attempting much that was of no interest to rural students, and teachers and school authorities who lacked ideas for shifting curricular emphasis.[33] Cubberley thought too much time was devoted to subjects such as grammar, mathematics, and geography and far too little to the natural world and life in the open country.[34] As clear as the rural school problem was to Cubberley, so too was its resolution: "If the education of the country boy and girl is as important as the education of the city boy and girl, and if the country boy and girl are ever to secure approximately equal advantages, then country people must see to it that their schools are possessed of as good educational organization and leadership, for their needs, as are the schools of the cities." [35] To put it differently, if the objective was to keep country boys and girls on the farm, and for Cubberley it was, then consolidated schools were the only solution.[36]

Among the four Midwestern writers on the topic of the rural school problem, Mabel Carney was the most measured in her articulation of the antipathy between the countryside and the city. Given her position as the director for rural teacher education in the state of Illinois, it is not surprising that she emphasized the need for appropriate training for those students destined to remain in the countryside. Interestingly, Carney had attended Teacher's College in the heartland of corporate interests, New York City, and was destined to return there, as a faculty member, in 1917.[37] Regardless, she acknowledged that teacher training prepared teachers for work in city schools, not in country schools.[38] Country leaders, she argued, habitually gravitated to cities, which provided advantages to city students. In a similar vein, Carney contended that the best among country students "are turned cityward in search of a more extended training."[39] Though calculated in her criticism of city life, Carney was unequivocal in her statements about the inequality between city and country students.

Toward the end of her book, Carney conveys a decidedly populist stance when she invokes one of its key shibboleths: "*Special privilege* of many kinds is already proving dangerous to our national democracy, and farmers must, and do, for the most part, fully recognize this truth. The facts of the case, however, are that the inherent rights of land owners, for one reason and another, have been over-ridden." She continues by suggesting that the "perpetuation of influences which shall send young people of the farms cityward or hold them countryward" is in the hands of local leaders, particularly educational leaders.[40] For Carney, consolidation was ultimately a righteous cause fought against the unjust treatment of country children, who were not receiving a "square deal."[41]

Given the strong commentary provided by these four scholars on the combative relationship between the city and countryside, the modern-day observer cannot help but read a certain irony into the arguments of Cubberley, Foght, and Carney. Each of these three writers was destined to perform one of the acts they most objected to: that of the accomplished country student moving to the city to serve the needs of the city dweller. When *Rural Life and Education* was published in 1914, Cubberley had already left the rural areas of Indiana where he had worked and moved to the West Coast, having completed his graduate work in education at Teacher's College, Columbia University. In 1915, five years after the publication of *The American*

Rural School, Foght left his position at the State Normal School in Kirkland, Missouri, to join the federal government as an expert on rural education. He went on to complete his PhD at American University in Washington, DC, in 1918. After *Country Life and the Country School* was published in 1912, Carney embarked upon a lengthy career as a faculty member at Teacher's College, Columbia University, beginning in 1917, having spent three prior years as the supervisor of teacher training for the state of Minnesota. In a sense, each reached the pinnacle of his or her career as a progressive expert in education reform, but in doing so, they abandoned their rural, Midwestern homes for metropolises. How do their populist ideologies reconcile with their migrations to more cosmopolitan locales?

It is, I believe, reasonable to conclude that, apart from Kern, who remained county superintendent in Winnebago County, Illinois, following the release of *Among Country Schools*, the publication of sizable monographs on the rural school problem impelled Foght, Cubberley, and Carney to assume their key positions in government and academia. While each book intended to improve the lot of country folk relative to city dwellers, rural residents were not the intended audience for the three authors. Instead, these progressive reformers targeted county and state policymakers, superintendents, and normal school instructors. Essentially, therefore, the ideologies of populism and progressive reform coalesced within these scholars of the rural Midwest. Such harmony occurred frequently during the populist and progressive era of reform.[42] The scholars' promotion into key roles at major institutions further legitimated and expanded the breadth of their influence. Such legitimation was perhaps most obvious in the career of Harold Foght who, although a high-ranking bureaucrat in Washington, DC, devoted much of his career within the federal government to surveying state- and provincial-level school systems across the Midwest and Plains, including the Canadian province of Saskatchewan. Not surprisingly, his policy recommendation remained steadfast throughout his career—rural school consolidation was the critical reform to resolve the inequities between the experiences of rural and city students.

Foght eventually returned to the Midwest and higher education, becoming the president of Wichita State University in Wichita, Kansas, in 1927. In the case of Cubberley and Carney, each researched and wrote widely on a host of topics over the course of extended tenures at two of the foremost faculties of education in the United States (Stanford University and Teacher's College, Columbia University, respectively). Cubberley wrote extensively on school administration, while Carney served as a professor of rural education for nearly three decades. As such, each extended their influence nationally, well beyond what they might have accomplished from within the Midwest. Regardless, apart from Superintendent Kern, who exercised substantial control over rural school consolidation within Winnebago County, Illinois, the scholars were ultimately able to achieve only modest results in the movement toward consolidation up until World War II.[43]

In *The One Best System*, Tyack suggests that around the turn of the twentieth century, university presidents and professors of education across the United States came to favor the study of school administration, thereby creating a consensus among experts in the field.[44] These experts, including Cubberley and later Carney, found a nascent field of study, one they could shape from an early stage. As the preceding narrative suggests, the experts sang in chorus about the merits of consolidation to resolve inefficiencies and improve the experience of students. Among Midwestern experts, however, calls for rural school consolidation maintained a current of populist ideology—an ideology that melded populism and progressivism to ensure that rural students got a "square deal" relative to city dwellers. Notwithstanding such unanimity among experts—apart from Superintendent Kern, who was in the singular position to implement, most readily, rural school consolidation—the remaining Midwestern experts were largely unsuccessful in their attempts at progressive reform, despite their best intentions on behalf of "the people."[45] From an intellectual standpoint, suspicion and mistrust of the city maintained a hold on Midwesterners' mindsets well beyond their departure from the countryside. In a similar fashion, however, mistrust of the expert among rural dwellers persisted in the countryside, even when those experts had sprung from its very bosom.

While Foght and his Midwestern populist brethren articulated arguments that cast the countryside in opposition to the city, such "myths," as historian William L. Bowers describes them, which viewed the city as a parasite preying on rural communities, were only half-truths in the minds of many country dwellers. Bowers argues that while sentimentality and nostalgia prevailed in the minds of many farmers, so too did their belief in the primacy of industrialization and urbanization as a boon to agriculture and country life. Inevitably, the countryside would feed America's growing cities.[46] In addition, the disappearance of readily available productive farmland led to an appreciation in land values, particularly in the Midwest, in the early decades of the twentieth century.[47] Urbanization and industrialization, therefore, held the potential of both enriching and depleting the rural Midwest and those who lived there.

David B. Danbom further argues, and Hofstadter confirms, that because farmers clung to the notion that they were both independent and virtuous and that they formed the foundation for all other vocations, they saw themselves as the political heart of the nation. This sense of independence took many forms. Frequently, farmers exercised autonomy by resisting increases in local taxation. On numerous occasions, rural residents opposed proposed tax increases intended for constructing consolidated rural schools. Not only did rural families resist this system that would force their sons and daughters to spend extra time being conveyed to a distant consolidated school, they also resented the potential drop in their property values should a nearby local school be replaced by a far-flung consolidated school. Danbom argues that this resistance ultimately had political consequences, since independence inevitably gave way to isolation, leading to the decline of populism as a political movement.[48] Regardless, the coupling of progressivism in education reform with populist ideology marks an interesting signpost in the intellectual history of the American Midwest.

NOTES

1. Olly Jasper Kern, *Among Country Schools* (Boston: Ginn & Company, 1906); Harold Waldstein Foght, *The American Rural School: Its Characteristics, Its Future and Its Problems* (New York: Macmillan, 1911); Mabel Carney, *Country Life and the Country School: A Study of the Agencies of Rural Progress and of the Social Relationship of the School to the Country Community* (Chicago: Row, Peterson, 1912); Elwood P. Cubberley, *Rural Life and Education: A Study of the Rural-School Problem as a Phase of the Rural-Life Problem* (Cambridge: Riverside Press, 1914). Theodore Roosevelt fashioned the Commission on Country Life, which reported in 1909.

2. This pitting of the "expert" against the rural dweller is a constant theme within histories of the period. See, for example, Paul Theobald, *Call School: Rural Education in the Midwest to 1918* (Carbondale: Southern Illinois University Press, 1995) and Wayne E. Fuller, *The Old Country School: The Story of Rural Education in the Middle West* (Chicago: University of Chicago Press, 1982), particularly those chapters that focus on consolidation.

3. On the centrality of Midwestern thinking on this theme, see David B. Danbom, *The Resisted Revolution: Urban America and the Industrialization of Agriculture, 1900–1930* (Ames: Iowa State University Press, 1979) and William L. Bowers, *The Country Life Movement in America, 1900–1920* (Port Washington, NY: Kennicat Press, 1974).

4. Daniel T. Rodgers coined the term *sociological tour* in *Atlantic Crossings: Social Politics in a Progressive Age* (Cambridge, MA: Belknap, 2000), 68–69.

5. Kern, *Among Country Schools*, 2.

6. Foght, *The American Rural School*, 22–23.

7. See Kerry Alcorn, *Border Crossings: US Culture and Education in Saskatchewan, 1905–1937* (Montreal: McGill-Queen's University Press, 2013), 94–97, for biographical summary.

8. Foght, *The American Rural School*, 304. Foght's three-pillared emphasis in education—head, heart, hands—includes three of the four terms, represented by a four-leaf clover, that comprise the motto of the 4-H youth organization. The fourth "leaf," which is not part of Foght's slogan, is *health*.

9. Carney, *Country Life and the Country School*, v.

10. Cubberley, *Rural Life and Education*, v.

11. Cubberley, *Rural Life and Education*, particularly Chapter II, "New Rural-Life Conditions," 29–62.

12. Foght, *The American Rural School*, 2.

13. Foght, *The American Rural School*, 115. The term means moving from one rural school to the next, annually, often in search of "greener pastures."

14. Kern, *Among Country Schools*, 177.

15. David B. Tyack, *The One Best System: A History of American Urban Education* (Cambridge, MA: Harvard University Press, 2001), 23.

16. For an excellent discussion of "the people" in populist ideology, see David Laycock, *Populism and Democratic Thought in the Canadian Prairies, 1910–1945* (Toronto: University of Toronto Press, 1990).

17. Fuller argues that Indiana achieved rural school consolidation relatively easily because state legislation had begun the process of forming township districts long before other Midwestern states had made attempts at centralization. Among the key promises made by Kern was that consolidation would reduce the cost to rural residents. This seldom occurred. See Fuller, *The Old Country School*, 229–239.

18. Richard Hofstadter, *The Age of Reform: From Bryan to F.D.R.* (New York: Vintage Books, 1955), 7. See also Jackson Lears, *Rebirth of a Nation: The Making of Modern America, 1877–1920* (New York: Harper, 2009), particularly Chapter 4, "The Country and the City," 133–166, as it relates to the historic divide between country and city. For a more recent account, albeit from a borderlands perspective, and one that focuses on grade schooling, see my *Border Crossings*, particularly Chapter 5, "The 'Populist Moment' in K–12 Education," 92–116.

19. Kern, *Among Country Schools*, 12.

20. Kern, *Among Country Schools*, 13.

21. Kern, *Among Country Schools*, 20.

22. Kern, *Among Country Schools*, 22.

23. Kern, *Among Country Schools*, 245.

24. Foght, *The American Rural School*, 6.

25. Foght, *The American Rural School*, 7.

26. Foght, *The American Rural School*, 23.

27. Foght, *The American Rural School*, 18, 332.

28. Foght, *The American Rural School*, 303.

29. Foght, *The American Rural School*, 134–135, 332.

30. Cubberley, *Rural Life and Education*, 25–26.

31. Cubberley, *Rural Life and Education*, 102.

32. Cubberley, *Rural Life and Education*, 260.

33. Cubberley, *Rural Life and Education*, 166.

34. Cubberley attributed this to untrained teachers, weak supervision, and normal school instruction, which reinforced these weaknesses. Cubberley, *Rural Life and Education*, 256–258.

35. Cubberley, *Rural Life and Education*, 310.

36. Cubberley, *Rural Life and Education*, 278.

37. Richard Glotzer, "Mabel Carney and the Hartford Theological Seminary: Rural Development, 'Negro Education,' and Missionary Training,"

Historical Studies in Education 17, no. 1 (Spring 2005), 55–80, http://historicalstudiesineducation.ca/index.php/edu_hse-rhe/article/view/416/547.

38. Carney, *Country Life and the Country School*, 253.

39. Carney, *Country Life and the Country School*, 140.

40. Carney, *Country Life and the Country School*, 322. [Italics added.]

41. Carney, *Country Life and the Country School*, 248. See page 153 for the "square deal" reference, which was a consistent phrase used by other Midwestern educationists in this period and by populists generally.

42. Lears, *Rebirth of a Nation*, 309.

43. Fuller, *The Old Country School*, 245. Fuller concludes, however, that signs that the one-room schoolhouse was on borrowed time were obvious in the mid-1930s across the Midwest.

44. Tyack, *The One Best System*, 133.

45. Interestingly, in 1916, Foght took his brand of populism to the province of Saskatchewan where, despite providing his expert advice on the benefits of rural school consolidation, he failed to convince its largely rural population to move in such a direction. See Alcorn, *Border Crossings*.

46. Bowers, *The Country Life Movement*, 10–11.

47. Bowers, *The Country Life Movement*, 11.

48. Danbom, *Resisted Revolution*, 35.

CHAPTER 3

"A STAMP OF FEMININITY"

The Sorosis Literary Society, Women's Intellectual Discourse,
and Regional Identity in Jacksonville, Illinois, 1865–1900

Jenny Barker Devine

In the summer of 1868, thirty-three-year-old Josephine Milligan of Delavan, Wisconsin, relocated her family to Jacksonville, Illinois, where her husband had accepted a teaching position at the Illinois School for the Deaf. That same summer, newspaper reporters across the Midwest announced the founding of a new women's club in New York City by writer and feminist Jane Cunningham Croly (who wrote under the pseudonym Jennie June) to "promote agreeable and useful relations among women of literary and artistic tastes." Milligan was inspired by this "mysterious sisterhood" and decided to initiate her own chapter in Jacksonville, a burgeoning city that boosters christened the "Athens of the West." Founded in 1825, Jacksonville boasted a thriving cultural scene fueled by an all-male college, two female seminaries, a female college, the Illinois School for the Deaf, the Illinois School for the Blind, and the Illinois State Asylum for the Insane. Turning intellect into an industry, civic leaders put their faith in these institutions as a vehicle for "civilized" progress.[1]

Within a few months of her arrival, on the cold, rainy evening of November 30, 1868, Milligan opened her home to three female teachers from the Illinois School for the Deaf and the wife of a prominent businessman. Their purpose was to establish their own Sorosis, a literary society dedicated to the "mental, moral, and physical improvement" of its members. Milligan drew inspiration from the women in New York, but the Jacksonville Sorosis did not simply replicate tastes and trends born of eastern cities. Members established intellectual authority within the community through their familiarity with literature, art, and philosophy while building upon an ethos prevalent in central Illinois that situated intellectual achievement within broader frontier mythologies. This chapter focuses specifically on the formative years of the Jacksonville Sorosis, emphasizing the members' interactions with women in New York and Chicago, as well as their collaborations with the Concord School of Philosophy, to illustrate how Midwestern women turned to secular, intellectual organizations to negotiate their shifting perceptions of regional identity.[2]

In forming Sorosis in 1868, members were on the forefront of a nationwide club movement that transformed women's public voices and proved formative in the development of American feminisms. Secular societies founded in the years after the Civil War built on decades of women's involvement with charitable and reform-based organizations but differentiated their various missions by openly emphasizing women's empowerment, education, and individual growth as the basis for larger social reforms. Scholars generally agree that the structure of this club movement, with its emphasis on organization and parliamentary procedure, fostered a consistent middle-class American identity, especially following the founding of the General Federation of Women's Clubs in 1890 and the National Association of Colored Women's Clubs in 1896. The clubs' activities were predicated on new opportunities in women's education, the decline of the church as a central organizing force, and, most important, the consumption of a newly emergent mass media. By the mid-nineteenth century, advances in printing and distribution made books and periodicals affordable for middle-class families. Publishers promoted "classic literature" that promised to elevate readers in a society where many adults were still self-educated. In this context, especially in a period when free public libraries were the exception, literary societies provided for the material needs of members, as well as space and support to share resources and broaden their fields of study.[3]

Literary societies formalized women's long-standing practices of visiting and planning social gatherings among neighbors and relatives predicated on shared work. In striving for "mental, moral, and physical improvement," members of the Jacksonville Sorosis asserted that their meetings were not mere social calls. Rather, they believed engaging with the printed word was a form of work that produced tangible products: educated women, better mothers, and engaged wives. Literary scholar Ann Douglas maintained that "the press offered [club women] the change they were seeking to be unobtrusive and everywhere at the same time." Yet even if mass media acted as a cohesive force, club women were hardly a uniform group. Significant variance in social class, occupation, race, and geography led historian Anne Firor Scott to warn against making broad generalizations regarding the political, intellectual, and social meanings of the club movement. She noted, "Farmers' wives joining village clubs in Kansas were a far cry from the elegant spouses of wealthy businessmen who led the Chicago Woman's Club . . . and both were quite different from the journalists and writers who predominated in New York's Sorosis." [4]

Expressions of regional identity highlight the ways in which geography shaped women's contributions to broader intellectual movements. Scholars of the American West and South have noted the ways in which women's clubs both alleviated and aggravated religious, racial, ethnic, and class divisions, but histories of Midwestern women's clubs have escaped such analysis, perhaps because Midwestern regional identity remains contested and elusive. Historian Wanda Hendricks, in her study of African American women's clubs in Illinois during the Progressive Era, observes that Midwestern regional distinctiveness was characterized by uncertainty and change. Rapid industrialization, urbanization, migration, and immigration exacerbated racial tensions in the Midwest and motivated African American women's clubs to address pressing social and political issues. Historian Sara Egge notes similar pressures in rural areas of the upper Midwest, where women's social and political action relating to suffrage consisted of constant negotiations among diverse ethnic groups. Regional identity, then, was revealed in moments of conflict rather than cohesion, as well as in efforts to negotiate that conflict. Both Hendricks and Egge assert that local studies can help us make sense of "diverse groups of people, living hundreds or even thousands of miles apart, from western Pennsylvania to the plains of the Dakotas," because even amid rapid change and disparate populations, concepts of community and the peculiarity of place remain essential to Midwestern identity. [5]

Like many clubs in the region, Jacksonville's Sorosis was part of Milligan's strategy to create community in the midst of upheaval. Born in Philadelphia in 1835, she grew up as the oldest child in a slave-owning family in Perry County, Tennessee. In the fashion of wealthy southerners, her stepfather, William Ewing, hired private tutors to educate his numerous children. A precocious, intelligent child who harbored fascinations with fossils and wildflowers, Josephine married the family tutor, Harvey Milligan, in 1856. Though he came from a middling family in Massachusetts, the soft-spoken Williams College graduate promised Josephine a bright future in the cosmopolitan city of Philadelphia. There, Harvey worked as a teacher at the Pennsylvania School for the Deaf and, in 1862, earned a doctor of medicine degree from the University of Pennsylvania. In 1865, in the wake of a war that cost Josephine one brother and upended her family's fortunes, the couple moved west, where Harvey served first as superintendent of the Wisconsin School for the Deaf and then as a teacher at the Illinois School for the Deaf. Despite his education and status, one biography described Harvey as hindered by "poor health and a slender purse," which prevented him from practicing medicine and necessitated frequent moves. This certainly created stress for the family. Upon arriving in Jacksonville, Josephine believed she could create a new sense of place by sharing literature and conversation with other women.[6]

How revolutionary was Milligan's idea? In New York City, Jane Cunningham Croly founded Sorosis as an act of defiance after male leaders of the New York Press Club intentionally excluded women from a dinner honoring Charles Dickens. She and several other women sought admission to the dinner not as wives but as established journalists. The incident was so formative in Croly's life that when she wrote a history of Sorosis in 1886, she devoted the first four pages to describing the "churlish" behavior of the Press Club. Though the founding members of Sorosis struggled to define their mission throughout 1868 and 1869, they carefully cultivated a public presence by holding weekly meetings at Delmonico's restaurant and publishing newspaper accounts of the activities. As members of a woman-centered organization with professional aspirations, they publicly antagonized male critics. Addressing the club in April 1868, the first president, Alice Cary, remarked that men's "sneers and sarcasms are, after all, but so many acknowledgements of our power, and should and will stimulate us to braver assertion, to more persistent effort toward thorough and harmonious organization."[7]

Casting aside nearly a century of well-documented women's organizations in the United States, the New York Sorosis closely guarded its self-ascribed status as the first women's club in the nation. In Croly's own telling, Sorosis led the formation of new chapters in a top-down effort by way of members' migrations and personal connections. To this end, she hosted a Woman's Parliament in 1869 and, in 1873, established the Association for the Advancement of Women to shape public discourse around women's issues. The magazine *Godey's Lady's Book* and *The Revolution*, a pro-suffrage newspaper founded by Susan B. Anthony and Elizabeth Cady Stanton, ran stories that hailed the new society for providing a more systematic approach to organizing women and recommended Sorosis as an ideal model for "the formation of such clubs throughout the country." The term *Sorosis* quickly became synonymous with the suffrage movement, used frequently to describe fellowship among women or, among opponents, to identify members of a larger conspiracy to unravel American society.[8]

How Josephine Milligan learned about Sorosis is unclear, though she did not appear to act at the behest of the New York club. Nearly fifty years after the Jacksonville club's founding, member Mary Turner Carriel claimed that they serendipitously came up with the name Sorosis and had no knowledge of the New York club for some years. Most likely, Milligan simply read about Sorosis in the newspaper. Throughout the spring and summer of 1868, newspapers across the country reprinted, from the *New York Herald* and the *New York Tribune*, descriptive stories about the New York women's club. In May 1868, the *Jacksonville Sentinel* published a short squib announcing the formation of Sorosis, and similar stories appeared in newspapers in every Midwestern state and in multiple languages. Within a short time, stories about the founding of local organizations followed. On June 30, the editor of the *Quad-City Times* in Davenport, Iowa, warned the married men of the city that defiant women there planned to establish a chapter of Sorosis. In July, women in Leavenworth, Kansas, established the Leavenworth Club and advised their "lady friends to follow the example of Boston, New York, and Chicago with the organization of Sorosis." The women of Crawfordsville, Indiana, first read about the founding of the New York Sorosis in May, and by September 1868, they had elected officers to their local organization.[9]

Unlike the New York club, the Jacksonville Sorosis was not born of rebellion but rather as a strategy to align middle-class women with the local intellectual community. When Milligan arrived in Jacksonville in 1868, she found herself in a small city with cosmopolitan aspirations. The population nearly doubled between 1860 and 1870, from 5,528 to 9,200, as the city enjoyed significant growth in manufacturing. She understood regionalism well, having grown up in the antebellum South and having begun her adult life in Philadelphia. Like many white migrants, she forged a Midwestern identity that framed imperialism and westward movement as progress. As Egge notes, "Communal institutions, as well as market involvement, were cultural touchstones for Yankees, and they sought to build communities, complete with schools, churches, and local governments, out of the 'barbarism' they saw on the frontier." Of the club's four other founding members, three were single women who had arrived within the previous year to teach at the Illinois School for the Deaf: Belle Woods, Jennie Eggleston, and Anna Osgood. The group's anchor in the community was Maria Gilette McConnel, an 1855 graduate of the Jacksonville Female Academy (JFA) and the wife of a wealthy manufacturer and alderman.[10]

As with many Midwestern cities, Jacksonville's path out of the howling wilderness was paved with volunteerism and the liberal arts. The city teemed with fraternal lodges, benevolent societies, and nonpartisan and nonsectarian voluntary associations for both white and African American citizens. In 1829, several young ministers recently graduated from Yale founded Illinois College (IC) to bring order to the frontier and develop home-grown professionals. Edward Beecher, the first president of IC, and Julian Sturtevant, the college's first professor, collaborated with women both locally and in New England to cultivate female leadership. After establishing the JFA in 1830, Beecher and Sturtevant supported the formation of the Ladies Association for the Education of Females in 1833 to provide financial aid, and they appealed to education leaders Mary Lyon and Zilpah Grant for teachers, ensuring the JFA curriculum would resemble that of leading women's seminaries. The men of IC founded the first literary societies, with Sigma Pi and Phi Alpha in 1843 and 1845, respectively, as independent and unaffiliated with national groups. They hosted debates and oratory contests, offered extensive libraries to members, and created networking opportunities by inviting prominent speakers to campus.[11]

Outside of the college, Jacksonville residents expressed broader interests in bringing intellectual resources to the community. The first men's literary societies, the Club and the Literary Union, were founded in 1861 and 1864, respectively. In 1865, Dr. Hiram K. Jones and his wife, Elizabeth, along with Louise Fuller, Abbie King, and Martha Dwight Wolcott, founded the Plato Club to study Platonism. The Odeon Association formed in 1868 to fundraise and purchase books for a "nucleus" of a town library. Historian Don Doyle found that voluntary associations such as these facilitated upward mobility and served as "bridges over troubled waters" of regional, religious, and political chasms. By providing common spaces and missions to improve local conditions, voluntary associations eased "divisions between community factions."[12]

By 1868, then, Jacksonville's Sorosis was more an inevitability than an exception. Within a month, membership grew to twelve women, including Jones, Wolcott, King, and Belle Paxon Drury of the Plato Club. Members took turns preparing papers, sharing news items, and formulating arguments for debates on controversial questions such as "Do accomplishments enter too largely in the education of women to the exclusion of more solid branches?" and "Is there a stamp of femininity upon the writings of women?" Though their comments are lost to time, members took one another's papers seriously. On December 21, 1868, after Anna Osgood presented a paper titled "Woman Suffrage," the notes recorded members engaged in "criticism and discussion." They pursued studies of author Nathaniel Hawthorne and philosophical questions such as "the natural history of the spirit world." Their thoughts often turned to controversial subjects, and throughout the spring of 1869, topics included temperance, the abolition of the death penalty, equality in education, and "the Influence of woman suffrage on her vocation and wages."[13]

The women of the Jacksonville Sorosis were not subject to the same "sneers and sarcasms" that the women in New York endured. Carriel's history recalls one satirical column that was promptly followed by an editorial by George McConnel, the husband of Maria McConnel, that presented a "royal defense of woman's ability, literary taste, and right to be a writer and a speaker as well as a student." Another paper reported the club's activities as a matter of fact, stating, "We have in this city a society of highly intelligent ladies, called Sorosis organized . . . for the purpose of advocating 'Woman's Rights' and discussing the various items of the day." And in 1891, when recalling their founding, Wolcott stated, "It has always been our good fortune, from the first years of our organization, to meet with the hardiest and most cordial recognition from the several gentlemen's clubs in the City."[14]

The greatest hurdle for the Jacksonville Sorosis was negotiating gendered expectations. For example, when asked to publish their proceedings in 1871, some members objected on the grounds that it would discourage "more timid members . . . and perhaps foster a bad spirit in others." This certainly did not hinder those who wished to publish, as Milligan and Jones became authors in their own right. For most women, though, domestic duties were not negotiable. By the spring of 1869, they decided to hold meetings in the afternoons so that members could be home for evening meal preparation. Pregnancies, births, and childcare, mentioned as carefully coded euphemisms in meeting minutes, were ever-present realities. In October 1871, Milligan noted that she had not finished composing the meeting minutes due to the illness and eventual death of her young son, Charlie. The following week, as the club approached its third anniversary, she simply wrote in the minutes, "Up to the present date, seven children have been born to Sorosis, and one has died." This stark example illustrates a central problem for women's clubs: members' responsibilities at home hampered their desires to collaborate with others outside of their local community.[15]

The early members of the Jacksonville Sorosis were hardly insular, but they had to carefully weigh whether to grow beyond the confines of the city limits and the cost of outside collaborations in terms of maintaining local harmony. Attempted partnerships, first with the Chicago Sorosis and then with the Concord School of Philosophy, demonstrate their commitment to the local club above associations with well-known figures and movements. Early meeting minutes certainly demonstrate an eagerness to cooperate with other clubs. On February 9, 1869, the women addressed a letter of greeting to the Chicago Sorosis on the eve of a suffrage convention featuring national leaders, including Myra Bradwell, Elizabeth Cady Stanton, and Edward Beecher. In their letter, which was read at the convention,

Jacksonville women offered "good will and sympathy in the movement which you have inaugurated in the West." They identified themselves as "earnest co-workers and hearty supporters" and extended best wishes for a successful convention. Yet well wishes did little to quell division and unrest among the women of Chicago. At that moment, as members of Congress deliberated the parameters of the Fifteenth Amendment in Washington, DC, suffragists across the nation were embroiled in their own debate over whether the new amendment designed to enfranchise African Americans should also include women. The debates taking place in the larger suffrage movement so sharply divided the Chicago Sorosis that two factions within that club claimed the name Sorosis and held competing conventions in February 1869. Attendees at both conventions passed resolutions extending olive branches, but the suffrage movement remained divided at the national level for two more decades.[16]

The Jacksonville Sorosis did not record its response to the controversial events in Chicago, but the meeting minutes of March 1, 1869, are telling. Milligan read a letter she received from Chicago, which included warm greetings and suffrage periodicals to circulate among members. Following a general discussion on woman suffrage, "a motion was made and seconded to proceed with the regular exercise." The women of Jacksonville did not abandon the woman suffrage question, but they no longer pursued collaborations with either Chicago faction. The motion to "proceed with the regular exercise" is revealing. In order to keep their club intact, they intentionally evaded the divisions that wrought havoc in Chicago. In 1891, Wolcott recalled that though members differed in age, opinions, and "life theories," they maintained a "tolerant spirit . . . neither embittered by differences nor unduly influencing each other." They welcomed structured debate and diverse opinion, but they prioritized organizational harmony.[17]

This was the moment when the Jacksonville Sorosis members defined their literary society as one devoted to learning broad and diverse topics. The Jacksonville Sorosis was a site of education, not activism. In other words, members could talk about such issues as suffrage or temperance in order to hone their arguments, but they were encouraged to act upon their inclinations through other organizations. Milligan exemplified this approach when, rather than mold Sorosis to fit her interests, she became a member of the Jacksonville Natural History Society, the Household Science Club, the Jacksonville Microscopical Society, the Ladies' Education Society, the Illinois State Historical Society, and the Horticultural Society. In 1905, she reflected on the purely educational purpose of Sorosis in a letter to Jacksonville members when she wrote, "As individuals we are free, as an organization we are bound to the requirements of our constitution; to yield as a body to the numerous demands for civic, political, and philanthropic reform made on women's clubs today would frustrate the object of Sorosis." Recalling the club's early years, Milligan reminded members: "We have not narrowed in our scope. Our themes are yet as wide as the world and high as the heavens. One of our charter members, whose works live after her was heard to say, 'we are for anything that is for the advancement of women.'"[18]

Maintaining a broad agenda could also have its complications when pursuing collaborations. Through their connections to the Plato Club, Sorosis welcomed Amos Bronson Alcott, the transcendentalist philosopher from Concord, Massachusetts, to a private conversation with the club on January 23, 1871. Alcott, who was on a western speaking tour, reiterated the transformative benefits of the club's educational mission. When one Sorosis member asked him why women have "until lately been satisfied with their conditions," he replied, "Women have *always* made a silent protest" (emphasis in original) and noted that their work was critical in elevating the status of women. He told the club's members, "The practical characteristic of the 'Woman's Rights Movement,' is that she makes the same demand upon man which he has always been making upon her. The finest work is never done on platforms. All great movements begin with a few people."[19]

Alcott's visit laid the groundwork for larger projects. Among the key figures in the establishment of his Concord School of Philosophy were numerous Midwesterners, including Jacksonville's Hiram K. Jones and William Torrey Harris, a Hegelian scholar from St. Louis. Between 1879 and 1882, the Jacksonville Sorosis supported Alcott's summer school, a series of lectures on art, literature, and philosophy, in Concord. Elizabeth Jones attended, as her husband was often on the program, and kept a regular correspondence with Jacksonville's *Daily Journal* describing the lectures and the atmosphere. Other members of Sorosis attended as well, but those who could not were "entertained" when Jones shared her notes at club meetings. The women from Illinois made an impression on Bronson's well-known daughter, Louisa May Alcott, who on July 14, 1879, recorded an exchange between Elizabeth Jones and an eastern woman:

> The fresh Westerners will show them all that all the culture in the world is not in Concord. I had a private laugh when Mrs.__ asked one of the newcomers, with her superior air, if she had looked into Plato. And the modest lady from Jacksonville answered, with a twinkle at me, "We have been reading Plato in Greek for the past six years." Mrs.__ subsided after that.[20]

Despite these successful collaborations, after four years the delegation from Jacksonville found annual travel to Massachusetts to be expensive and impractical. In August 1882, Bronson Alcott recorded in his diary that Midwestern members of the Concord School asked that the summer sessions be moved to their region. Alcott refused, writing, "Concord and only Concord is the proper seat of the school." The following year, the Joneses established the *Journal of American Akademe* and established a philosophical school by the same name in Jacksonville. Though Sorosis retained its broad mission, members participated in American Akademe in significant numbers and allowed the activities in one organization to inform the activities of the other.[21]

The question remains: Just how unique was the Jacksonville Sorosis? Not every city was home to one of the nation's leading Platonist philosophers or a concentrated number of educational institutions. The women of Jacksonville understood their club to be one among many literary, voluntary, social, and civic associations in the local community. On the other hand, like many white Midwesterners, they sought cohesion through literature, art, and science and believed their club was part of a larger plan for white Americans to "tame" the howling wilderness. In 1870, when Jacksonville's Sorosis celebrated its second anniversary, Maria McConnel composed an epic poem that characterized the founding members as intrepid travelers making their way through "choking rains," darkness, and ceaseless storms. Drawing upon mythical creation stories, she wrote:

Its natal anthem voiced by mighty gales—
Baptized in furious rain—to seek reform
Sorosis confidently spread its sails.
Resolved all hidden springs of thought to find—
And touch the bottom of creation's plan,
They, with the natural bent of womankind,
Considered first, the "origin of man."

Her poem was so well received, members passed a resolution at the next meeting to copy "said poem for the archives of the society." [22]

In prioritizing the local community, the club members worked to make sense of the upheaval that followed the Civil War and harnessed frontier mythologies that shaped white Midwesterners' belief in regional exceptionalism. In this way, Sorosis was very much typical of the nationwide women's club movement. In 1889, the Jacksonville Sorosis sent a delegate to the meeting where the New York Sorosis established the General Federation of Women's Clubs. It is no surprise that this was the longest collaboration the club ever enjoyed: the federation adopted resolutions and provided suggestions for programming but did not ask local clubs to entirely relinquish their autonomy, take firm positions on controversial issues, or follow a specific philosophy.

Sociologist Elizabeth Long notes that literary societies heightened "the empowerment that literacy often brings in its wake" and granted members the power to "create community, sustain collective memory, generate knowledge, and challenge tradition." In Jacksonville, Sorosis members' weekly discussions barely skirted the public sphere, but they shaped the cultural tenor of the community by allowing middle-class women of means to become intellectual gatekeepers. As they engaged with literature, history, current events, and the arts, these women gained cultural authority over predominantly masculine pursuits in academia, the arts, politics, organized religion, and compensated work. They created cultural and educational institutions, instigated reforms, selected library materials, invited speakers and performers to town, patronized theaters, and influenced educational curricula as teachers, trustees, and alumnae. In 2018, the Jacksonville Sorosis celebrated its 150th anniversary and continues as a traditional literary society. The club's long history illustrates the ways in which Midwestern women fostered community-building through connections to broader intellectual movements without sacrificing the priorities of the local community.[24]

NOTES

The author would like to thank the members of Sorosis who donated their materials to the Khalaf Al Habtoor Archives at Illinois College in 2013, the students who processed those materials, and Samantha Sauer, archivist, who made them accessible. Research for this manuscript was made possible by funds from the New England Regional Fellowship Consortium and the Khalaf Al Habtoor Archives Faculty Research Fellowship. Finally, the author is extremely grateful to Naomi Niemann and Cara Reynolds, who edited final drafts.

1. Helen Hackett, "The Milligan Family," paper prepared for the Household Science Club, Jacksonville, IL, February 19, 1985, Sorosis Collection, Khalaf Al Habtoor Archives, Illinois College, Jacksonville, Illinois (hereafter cited as Sorosis Collection, KAH); Jane Cunningham Croly, *Sorosis: Its Origin and History* (New York: J.J. Little, 1886), 5–8; "The Sorosis Entertain the Press," *New York Times*, April 25, 1869. *Sorosis* is a botanical term for a fruit derived from many flowers, such as a pineapple. The founders of the New York club believed this word represented the fruits of women's collaboration.

2. Meeting Minutes, Book I, November 30, 1868–May 26, 1871, Sorosis Collection, KAH.

3. Karen J. Blair, *The Clubwoman as Feminist: True Womanhood Redefined, 1868–1914* (New York: Holmes & Meier, 1980), 57–60; Anne Ruggles Gere, *Intimate Practices: Literacy and Cultural Work in U.S. Women's Clubs, 1880–1920* (Urbana: University of Illinois Press, 1997), 3; Wanda A. Hendricks, *Gender, Race, and Politics in the Midwest: Black Club Women in Illinois* (Bloomington: Indiana University Press, 1998), xiii; Paula D. Watson, "Founding Mothers: The Contribution of Women's Organizations to Public Library Development in the United States," *Library Quarterly* 64, no. 3 (July 1994), 233–269; Katherine West Scheil, *She Hath Been Reading: Women and Shakespeare Clubs in America* (Ithaca, NY: Cornell University Press, 2012).

4. Nancy Grey Osterud, *Bonds of Community: The Lives of Farm Women in Nineteenth-Century New York* (Ithaca, NY: Cornell University Press,

1991), 231–248; Anne Firor Scott, *Natural Allies: Women's Associations in American History* (Urbana: University of Illinois Press, 1991), 140; Ann Douglas, *The Feminization of American Culture* (New York: Anchor Books, 1988), 9.

5. Hendricks, *Gender, Race, and Politics*, xiv; Sara Egge, *Woman Suffrage and Citizenship in the Midwest, 1870–1920* (Iowa City: University of Iowa Press, 2018), 1–6. Scholars have studied the regional identities of women's clubs in the American West and the South. Historian Suzanne Stauffer, for example, argued that in Progressive Era Utah, clubs provided the means for white, middle-class, Protestant women to create and advance "the established eastern American society and culture in the West, regardless of the racial, socioeconomic, or religious constitution of their communities." Stauffer found that clubs provided space for Protestant and Mormon women to redefine "social and religious boundaries that led to the creation of a new secular culture." Similarly, Mary Jane Smith demonstrated how, during the 1890s, southern white club women expressed regional identities in their intentional and successful efforts to exclude black women's clubs from membership in the General Federation of Women's Clubs, thereby reinforcing a nationwide tendency toward racial segregation in local women's clubs. See Suzanne M. Stauffer, "A Good Social Work: Women's Clubs, Libraries, and the Construction of a Secular Society in Utah, 1890–1920," *Libraries and the Cultural Record* 46, no. 2 (Spring 2011), 137; Mary Jane Smith, "The Fight to Protect Race and Regional Identity within the General Federation of Women's Clubs, 1895–1902," *Georgia Historical Quarterly* 94, no. 4 (Winter 2010), 479–513.

6. Hackett, "The Milligan Family," Sorosis Collection, KAH; "Milligan, (Dr.) Harvey W.," in *Historical Encyclopedia of Illinois and History of Morgan County*, ed. Newton Bateman, Paul Selby, and William F. Short (Chicago: Munsell Publishing Company, 1906), 893; "Harvey William Milligan," *Proceedings of the Seventeenth Meeting of the Convention of American Instructors of the Deaf* (Washington, DC: Government Printing Office, 1906), 186–187.

7. Croly, *Sorosis: Its Origin and History*, 5–8; Jane Cunningham Croly, *The History of the Woman's Club Movement in America* (New York: Henry G. Allen & Co., 1898), 21.

8. Croly, *The History of the Woman's Club Movement*, 26–27; Sorosis Minutes, vol. 1, 1868–1871, in Sorosis Records, Sophia Smith Collection, Smith College, Northampton, MA; Scott, *Natural Allies*, 117–118; *Jacksonville (IL) Sentinel*, May 8, 1868; Mrs. O. Fogey, "Sorosis," *Godey's Lady's Book* (Philadelphia, PA), August 1868; "Sorosis" *The Revolution* (New York, NY), May 28, 1868.

9. Mary Turner Carriel, "Sorosis of Jacksonville, Illinois," *Out West Magazine* 43, no. 3 (March 1916), 133; Phoebe Dummer Bassett, "Of Time and Sorosis," paper presented at the 90th Anniversary exercises, 1958, Sorosis Records, KHA; "Leavenworth Club," *The Leavenworth Times*, July 10, 1868; "Rumored," *Quad-City Times*, June 30, 1868; "Meeting of All the Talents and Graces," *Vincennes Gazette*, May 2, 1868; *Vincennes Gazette*, September 12, 1868. Sorosis was not the only nationally recognized model for organizing. The New England Women's Club, another leader in the women's club movement, was founded in Boston in May 1868.

10. Egge, *Woman Suffrage*, 6; "List of Teachers in the Illinois School," *Thirty-fifth Biennial Report of the Managing Officer of the Illinois School for the Deaf, June 1, 1910* (Springfield: Illinois State Journal Company, State Printer, 1911), 19.

11. Charles M. Eames, *Historic Morgan and Classic Jacksonville* (Jacksonville, IL: Daily Journal Steam Job Printing Office, 1885), 107–108, 120.

12. Betty Carlson Kay and Gary Jack Barwick, *Jacksonville, Illinois: The Traditions Continue* (Charleston, SC: Arcadia Publishing, 1999), 67; Paul Russell Anderson, *Platonism in the Midwest* (Philadelphia: Temple University Press, 1963), 491; Martha Dwight Wolcott, "The Plato Club of Jacksonville, Ill.," *The Bibliotheca Platonica* 1, no. 4 (November–December 1890), 287–301; *Jacksonville (IL) Sentinel*, December 18, 1868; Don Harrison Doyle, *Social Order of a Frontier Community: Jacksonville, Illinois, 1825–1870* (Urbana: University of Illinois Press, 1978), 178–183. The Plato Society inspired others to form similar clubs. In 1866, Sarah Denman of nearby Quincy, Illinois, founded Friends in Council to further discussions of philosophy in that community. See Henry August Pochmann, *New England Transcendentalism and St. Louis Hegelianism: Phases in the History of American Idealism* (New York: Haskell House Publishers, 1970), 72. The citizens of Jacksonville also found alternative approaches to securing intellectual resources for the community. A month after the formation of Sorosis, the *Jacksonville Sentinel* announced the formation of the

Odeon Association, which was open to both female and male members. See *Jacksonville Sentinel*, December 18, 1868.

13. Sorosis meeting minutes, Book I, November 1868–May 1871, Sorosis Collection, KAH.

14. Carriel, "Sorosis," 133; Undated news clipping in Sorosis meeting minutes, Book I, November 1868–May 1871, Sorosis Collection, KAH; Bassett, "Of Time and Sorosis."

15. "Mr. Alcott's Conversation with the Jacksonville Sorosis," in Amos Bronson Alcott, *Notes on Conversations*, ed. Karen English (Madison, NJ: Fairleigh Dickinson University Press, 2007), 212; Sorosis meeting minutes, Book II, September 1871–May 1874, Sorosis Collection, KAH.

16. Sorosis meeting minutes, Book I, November 1868–May 1871, Sorosis Collection, KAH; "Conventions of the Advocates of Female Suffrage," *Chicago Tribune*, February 12, 1869, https://chroniclingamerica.loc.gov/lccn/sn82014064/1869-02-12/ed-1/seq-4.pdf; "Progress of the Female Suffrage Movement in Chicago," *Chicago Tribune*, February 13, 1869, https://chroniclingamerica.loc.gov/lccn/sn82014064/1869-02-13/ed-1/seq-4.pdf.

17. Sorosis meeting minutes, Book I, November 1868–May 1871, Sorosis Collection, KAH; Bassett, "Of Time and Sorosis."

18. Josephine Milligan to Sorosis, February 17, 1905, Sorosis Collection, KAH.

19. Alcott, *Notes on Conversations*, 212–214.

20. Tiffany K. Wayne, *Woman Thinking: Feminism and Transcendentalism in Nineteenth-Century America* (New York: Lexington Books, 2005), 110; Nancy Glazener, *Literature in the Making: A History of US Literary Culture in the Long Nineteenth Century* (Oxford: Oxford University Press, 2016), 123–124; Concord School of Philosophy, scrapbook of Elizabeth Orr Jones, KAH; Sorosis meeting minutes, Book VI, May 1881–May 1884, Sorosis Collection, KAH; Ednah D. Cheney, ed., *Louisa May Alcott: Her Life, Letters, and Journals* (Boston: Roberts Brothers, 1889), 320–321.

21. King J. Dykeman, "Lizzie Orr Jones: 'The Modest Lady from Jacksonville,'" paper presented at the Advancement of American Philosophy, Texas A&M (February 28–March 1, 1980), Sorosis Collection, KAH.

22. Mrs. George M. McConnel, "Anniversary Poem," December 1, 1870, Sorosis Collection, KAH; Sorosis meeting minutes, Book I, November 1868–May 1871, Sorosis Collection, KAH.

23. Watson, "Founding Mothers," 233–269; Elizabeth Long, *Book Clubs: Women and the Uses of Reading in Everyday Life* (Chicago: University of Chicago Press, 2003), 31–32, 35, 39, 46.

CHAPTER 4

CHARLES G. FINNEY AND THE CREATION OF THE MIDWESTERN EVANGELICAL MIND

William Kostlevy

INTRODUCTION

In 1835, Charles Grandison Finney, the country's most famous evangelist, accepted a position as professor of theology at Oberlin College. Over the next three and a half decades, he shaped the coeducational and interracial Ohio school into an important molder of Midwestern cultural and religious identity. The evangelical Christianity nurtured at Oberlin, for good or ill, profoundly shaped the Midwest, and ultimately the world, through such key evangelical institutions, historic and present, as the Woman's Christian Temperance Union, *Christianity Today* magazine, and Wheaton College. All are strategically located in the metropolitan Chicago area. Even today, the urban landscape remains dominated by church spires, with small independent or denominationally based evangelical colleges dotting its outlying areas. The headquarters of the nation's largest Holiness and Pentecostal denominations are in America's "real Bible belt" of the Midwest: Kansas City, Indianapolis, and Springfield, Missouri. Here the legacy of evangelicalism has long been felt in the laws curtailing business activities on Sunday, and especially bans on liquor sales, though such laws have gradually been disappearing. To outsiders, the subtle theological and cultural distinctions that separate what are competing factions of evangelicals often appear trivial, but to insiders, divisions based on ethnic background, doctrine, worship, Christian experience, and even differing views on appropriate dress and diet are matters of spiritual life and death. This chapter provides a brief introduction to the ways Oberlin College theology professor and president Charles G. Finney helped create and shape various strands of Midwestern evangelicalism and, more surprisingly, important nonevangelical movements such as progressivism.[1]

Finney has often been depicted as the crowning figure in an epic narrative, the civilizing and saving not merely of the Midwest but of America itself. In this grand American story of fervid eastern jeremiads, earnest circuit riders, praying mothers and daughters, and heroic itinerants unite to turn the "valley of moral death," as historian Robert Fletcher calls it, into a region of piety, sobriety, and righteousness. For Finney's devotees, this narrative was closely tied to the establishment of Oberlin Collegiate Institute (Oberlin College after 1850), one of the Midwest's most distinctive and important institutions. Many Midwesterners believed the stakes were high. As Henry B. Stanton wrote to Finney in 1835:

> The harvest of the great valley is rotting and perishing for the lack
> of laboring men. . . . The impenitent West is rushing to death,
> unresisted and almost unwarned. The whole valley is over-run with
> antinomianism, Campbelliteism, Universalism and infidelity—while
> Catholicism is fast taking possession of all our strongholds and is
> insidiously worming itself into the confidence of the people, and
> undermining the very foundations of pure religion.[2]

Scholars have often ascribed the evangelical religion that matured in the Midwest during the decades after 1830 with a mythic power and uniformity not sustained by the evidence. Various iterations of evangelical identity were formed during part of what historian Winthrop Hudson called the "Methodist age of American Christianity." Important nonevangelical impulses emerged as early as the second decade of the nineteenth century. The sometimes-Presbyterian Andrew Jackson built a formidable and for a time dominant Midwestern political coalition around southern migrants, Irish and German immigrants, and other critics of moralizing evangelicals. An entire theological tradition dedicated to celebrating antievangelistic practice, the importance of which has probably been overemphasized by scholars who share its prejudices, centered around the tiny central Pennsylvania hamlet of Mercersburg. Similarly, the fact that Peoria, Illinois, was home to America's most famous professional agnostic, Robert Ingersoll, suggests that the epigram "Will it play in Peoria?" speaks volumes about the sectional prejudices and ignorance of coastal Americans. But if Ingersoll never affirmed the evangelical faith of his radical abolitionist father, his aggressive zeal and proselytizing suggests that he was an heir to the evangelical spirit if not the evangelical faith. While acknowledging that antebellum evangelicalism was not ubiquitous, nor did it go uncontested, I argue that it remained a significant cultural force whose historic impact extended beyond the creation of self-acknowledged evangelical institutions. As a precursor to two of the twentieth century's most creative, if moralistic, movements, progressivism and fundamentalism, Finney's impact continues to be felt by many Midwesterners completely oblivious to the existence of the Oberlin divine.[3]

FINNEY: BURNED-OVER DISTRICT ROOTS

Born in Connecticut and raised in central New York, Finney had a promising career in law that was cut short by a dramatic conversion in the fall of 1821. Either refusing the offer of an education or being rejected by Princeton Theological Seminary, Finney began studying for the ministry under the tutelage of a local Presbyterian minister in Adams, New York. As he stepped into the dynamic and democratizing culture of American Christianity, Finney developed a style characterized by dramatic directed appeals, the use of colloquial speech, and a willingness to borrow the highly successful practices of the nation's fastest-growing denomination, Methodism, which proved to be not only innovative but controversial.[4]

Throughout Finney's long ministerial career, he fought against forms of religious determinism that allowed individuals to escape direct responsibility for their own actions. While eventually the determinism of traditional Calvinism would prove to be his greatest nemesis, the earliest serious challenge to his beliefs, and perhaps his earliest temptation, came from the rapidly expanding Universalist movement. As Finney remembered years later, "When I tried to be a Universalist, and . . .

went to their meetings and heard their arguments," he heard the claim that, given his goodness, "God must" forgive all. "I saw at a glance," he continued, "that one might better infer from the goodness of God that He would forgive *none* than that He would forgive all." For if God was a "Being of infinite wisdom and love," Finney reasoned, God's law would be just and would require obedience and, if disregarded, would destroy not only order but justice. Finney did concede one key argument to Universalists. He believed that Universalists who drew on Scripture along with the determinist logic of popular Calvinism had successfully established one key point: Christ's atoning death was for all humans, not merely for the so-called elect. As historian E. Brooks Holifield notes, Finney "criticized Universalists because their doctrine removed a motive for obedience." In effect, for Finney, God had given people blessed with common sense and intelligence a determinative role in deciding their spiritual destinies. Finney's revivals and writings played no small role in the triumph of free will evangelicalism, the opposite of the traditional Calvinist view that the fate of all has been decided by God without regard for human agency.[5]

Much has been made of Finney's most notable evangelistic success, his Rochester, New York, revival of 1830–1831. According to historian Paul Johnson, this revival was used to impose new standards of discipline in the workplace. In the widely read work of Mary Ryan, Finney emerges as a primary catalyst for the formation of the distinctive domestic and family values of the emerging middle class. Both Johnson's and Ryan's interpretations have become fixtures of many standard historical texts amply, if selectively, illustrated by Finney's own writings. Enthusiastic about a surprising number of prominent male converts at the Rochester revival, Finney also celebrated the roles played by young women as the initiators of the revival. Johnson and Ryan, who express little interest in the religious aspects of the revival, fail to account for the power of the revival outside the confines of the marketplace and the middle-class domestic sphere. A more satisfactory interpretation is that of historian Curtis D. Johnson. His telling of the story, like Ryan's, highlights the roles played by evangelical women, but for Curtis Johnson, evangelicalism takes center stage. He argues it is the drama of personal salvation, not class formation or domestic bliss, that motivated the women and men of Rochester. This is verified by Finney, who, while inviting the noted temperance lecturer and later famed abolitionist Theodore Weld to promote the dry cause among the revival's converts, insisted that an interest in reforms like temperance was a matter of secondary importance that flowed naturally from the more important matter of achieving a renewed inner nature. Thus, even temperance, a central concern of both the Rochester revival and evangelical women, was for Finney a penultimate, not the ultimate, concern. Here Finney illustrated one of his most notable characteristics: he was less an innovator than a popularizer. Although he was hardly the first to unite temperance with evangelism, his support of temperance, in retrospect, does seem crucial to the process by which an existing but not normative practice became a common inheritance of evangelicals on both sides of the Atlantic.[6]

In part funded by the famed philanthropists and activists Arthur and Lewis Tappan, Finney served as a pastor in New York City from 1832 to 1837. Skillfully exploiting the emerging print media to spread his message, Finney's supporters founded the widely circulated *New York Evangelist*, edited by the noted journalist and reformer Joshua Leavitt. When Leavitt significantly reduced readership by promoting abolitionism during one of Finney's absences, Finney restored the periodical to financial health by publishing a series of lectures on revivalism later published as *Lectures on Revivals of Religion* (1835). *Lectures on Revivals of Religion* emerged not only as the standard guide for how to conduct a revival but also as a window into the logic of one the most influential nineteenth-century Americans. Consistent with his crusade against Universalism and intent on breaking the back of the logic of a traditional Calvinism that insisted that revivals were the result of supernatural intervention, not human action, Finney insisted that salvation was within reach for all humans and that sin, far from being inevitable, was the product of human choice. In effect, Finney's logic freed women and men not only to respond to God's grace but also to reject sin or selfishness and, in the language of the followers of the great eighteenth-century preacher and scholar Jonathan Edwards, to embrace a "disinterested love" of humanity. In other words, to Finney, salvation was not merely the forgiveness of sin but also a call to personal righteousness and to ethical activism. As historians have long noted, Finney's Burned-Over District in New York, the Western Reserve of Ohio, and the so-called third New England of lower Michigan collectively became the center of a wide range of social reform movements, including the abolition of slavery, temperance, women's rights, health and diet reform, and even a center for sexual experimentation.[7]

FINNEY AND OBERLIN PERFECTIONISM

In 1835, Finney accepted the position of professor of theology at Oberlin College, where he served as the pastor of one of the largest Congregational churches in the United States from 1837 to 1872. He also served as president of the college from 1851 to 1866. As a coeducational and interracial institution, Oberlin was, from its founding, controversial. Despite Finney's lengthy employment there, some have suggested that his commitment to social reform, especially the abolition of slavery, was less than wholehearted. This perspective is based, in part, on Finney's understandable opposition to students abandoning college to become full-time antislavery lecturers. Further, for Finney, the ultimate solution to all problems, whether personal or social, was a change in human motivation. In his logic, the most-needed change was to turn the hearts of sinners from selfishness to disinterested benevolence or love. In effect, evangelism never ceased being the ultimate reform movement for Finney. As his actual record on slavery demonstrates, his abolitionist views went far beyond those held by most in the antebellum North. He was one of the founders and later president of the Ohio Anti-Slavery Society, and over a decade before the concept was popularized by Theodore Parker, Finney insisted that "no human legislation can annul or set aside" God's higher law. In 1846, at the height of the US clamor for war with Mexico, Finney argued that an unjust war in support of a selfish institution, such as slavery, was a sin. "If war has been unjustly waged, if slavery or anything else exists that involves injustice and oppression or sin in any form," Finney asserted, "it cannot be sin to abandon it." For Finney, "no enactment, human or Divine, can legalize selfishness and make it right, under any conceivable circumstances."[8]

Although Finney is rightly recognized as the father of American revivalism, at Oberlin he emerged as a gifted teacher and theologian. Skillfully integrating such popular emphases of the theological heritage of Jonathan Edwards as freedom of the will, disinterested benevolence, the moral government of God, and a modified Wesleyan understanding of Christian perfection, Finney's eclectic theology, though remaining controversial, became a potent shaper of Midwestern evangelical culture. Even Finney's critics, such as Princeton University's Charles Hodge and B. B. Warfield, acknowledged the power of his logic and the importance of his thought. To Warfield, Finney's theology was, in his memorable phrase, "the instinctive thought of the natural man." Hodge, in fact, thought Finney's *Lectures on Systematic Theology* to be "the best refutation that can be given of the popular theology current in many parts of the country." Warfield noted that in Finney's system, the individual, not God, played the decisive role in a person's life, and divine power was limited to moral persuasion. A century after Finney's death, the name of evangelist Billy Graham's periodical *Decision Magazine* continued to remind reformed theological purists that popular evangelicalism, with its emphasis on human agency, remained tied to the logic of one of conventional Calvinism's greatest nemeses. Interestingly, the views of Finney's critics from Princeton would dog him even after death. To this day, many evangelicals find Finney's theology dangerous, and even such nonevangelical critics as historian Richard Hofstadter have found his thought too pragmatic and, ultimately, a typical expression of American anti-intellectualism.[9]

At Oberlin, where most of the student body and even town were acknowledged to be active Christians, Finney made his primary goal not the conversion of sinners but the perfection of believers. As someone who in 1835 had suggested that the long-awaited Christian millennium might, with proper Christian due diligence, arrive in America within three years, Finney quickly shifted his focus from the salvation of the Midwest to its perfection. Fittingly, he rejected traditional Augustinian and classical Protestant understandings of the inevitability of human sinfulness. As Finney saw it, the classic Protestant doctrine of justification by faith alone encouraged ethical indifference. "Finney," the Midwestern historian William Warren Sweet wrote, "made salvation the beginning of religious experience in contrast to the older revivalism which made it the end." In effect, "conversion was not an escape from life, but rather the beginning of new interest in life and in the building of God's Kingdom." As he had looked to the thriving Baptists and Methodists for clues as to how to make evangelicalism successful, Finney now turned to the writings of Methodist luminaries John Wesley and John Fletcher for keys to a fuller Christian life. The resulting doctrine, Oberlin perfectionism, rapidly became as notorious among Finney's critics as the abolition of slavery and the admission of African Americans and women to institutes of higher learning.[10]

Promoted by Finney, Oberlin president Asa Mahan, and such key faculty members as John Morgan and Henry Cowles, the concept of entire sanctification, or Christian perfection, consisted in the consecration of one's entire being to God. As Finney insisted, all acts must be performed in a spirit of entire devotion to God. As might be expected, such an emphasis on duty and law instead of grace, while stimulating moral idealism and social action, led to repeated charges of legalism. Consistent with other aspects of Finney's theology, the theological heritage of Jonathan Edwards and the New England tradition he had inspired underpinned the perfectionist agitation at Oberlin. As Allen Guelzo persuasively argues, "Finney's demand for a holiness that would be visible and public rather than private and sentimental" found natural expression in Oberlin's insistence that Christians refrain from the commission of all known sin, including slavery and intemperance.[11]

Rapidly moving beyond Oberlin's Congregational constituency, Finney's perfectionist theology found a ready audience among other radical evangelicals, including antislavery Methodists, members of United Brethren in Christ, Wesleyan Methodists, Free Methodists, and Free Will Baptists. In England, Finney's thought played no small role in the emergence of the Salvation Army. This perfectionist agitation eventually resulted in the establishment of such core Midwestern evangelical colleges as Wesleyan, Methodist-inspired Wheaton and Adrian Colleges, and Hillsdale College, a closely aligned Free Will Baptist college. Other Midwestern institutions that bore the stamp of Oberlin and promoted its inclusive interracial and coeducational vision were Congregational colleges including Knox in Illinois, Grinnell and Tabor in Iowa, Olivet in Michigan, Carleton in Minnesota, Beloit and Ripon in Wisconsin, Washburn in Kansas, and such non-Congregational Oberlin-inspired schools as Park in Missouri, Wilberforce in Ohio, and Berea in Kentucky. Unlike in the East and South, Oberlin's commitment to coeducation dominated the Midwestern landscape where coeducational colleges, not single-sex schools, became the norm. The journalist, Civil War historian, and Oberlin graduate Bruce Catton would draw much of his inspiration from his experiences growing up in one of the most distinctive Oberlin-influenced Midwestern communities: Benzonia, Michigan. As Catton remembered, Benzonia had two distinct Oberlin-inspired characteristics: discontent with the world as it was and a conviction "that faith without works is of small account." Still dominated by a New England–style Congregational church, Benzonia is located near the aptly named county seat town of Beulah, Michigan. Both Benzonia and Beulah were modeled after Oberlin and founded by one-time Oberlin student and Congregational minister Charles E. Bailey. The name *Beulah* was drawn from the book of Isaiah as read in the light of John Bunyan's *Pilgrim's Progress*. For perfectionist Christians, Beulah described the spiritual perfection possible for Christians in the here and now.[12]

After retiring as president of Oberlin College, Finney, oddly in the minds of many of his supporters, turned his attention to fighting resurgent oath-bound secret societies, especially the Masonic Order. Less controversially, he also began writing his memoirs. Initially serialized in the widely read periodical *Independent*, Finney's writings on Masonry bear all the marks of his mature thought. Placing issues of race and gender at the heart of his critique of Masonic lodges, Finney reminds his readers that Masons excluded women, old men, deformed men, and African Americans from their lodges. "God accepts nothing," Finney argued, "that does not proceed from the supreme love of Him and equal love for fellow-men . . . that is all mankind." While the aging Finney largely withdrew from the organized anti-Masonic campaign, his writings played no small role in the establishment of the National Christian Association, an organization opposed to secret societies headed by Wheaton College president Jonathan Blanchard and largely supported by old abolitionists and radical evangelicals. Fervent supporters of Finney's legacy, these radical evangelicals would keep his writings in print and eventually, during the 1940s, their descendants would play a significant role in the establishment of the National Association of Evangelicals.[13]

Finney's anti-Masonic activity illustrates many of the challenges the older Midwestern evangelicalism faced in the years following the Civil War when the rapid growth of fraternal orders signaled significant cultural shifts, especially among men. Finney's thought found few real echoes in the emerging Romantic-inspired celebration of ritual (new or invented), suspicion of reason, emphasis placed on gradual change as opposed to instantaneous conversions, and historicism focused on organic change over long centuries. In American Christianity, Romantic currents found expression in the anti-conversionist gradualism of Finney's friend and rival Horace Bushnell, the Oxford movement in England, the related growth of high church Anglicanism, and the revitalization of confessionalism among American Lutherans. Trained in Germany and drawing their inspiration from German idealism, younger scholars found little of value in the older Enlightenment-inspired ahistorical rationalism of Finney and other evangelicals rooted in the tradition of Scottish common-sense realism.[14]

Decidedly a product of early nineteenth-century America, Finney remained a primitivist who, in the spirit of his contemporary Alexander Campbell, desired to return to the spirit if not the reality of first-century Christianity. Fittingly, he continued to be deeply suspicious of all historical accretions to the Christian faith, even those inspired by the Protestant Reformation. "None but an omniscient mind," Finney wrote in 1851, "can continue to maintain a precise identity of views and opinions. Finite minds, unless they are asleep or stultified by prejudice, must advance in knowledge. The discovery of new truth will modify all views." In this spirit and much to the horror of his critics at the Princeton Theological Seminary, Finney insisted that it was "ridiculous" for anyone in the nineteenth century "to recognize as a standard of the church" a document so clearly tied to ancient and unprofitable quarrels as the Westminster Confession of Faith. As knowledge in other branches of science changed due to new evidence, Finney maintained that "Christian consistency implied continued investigation and change of views and practice corresponding with increasing knowledge." Finney, consistent with the heritage of Jonathan Edwards, remained a pragmatic ethical activist who emphasized the importance of a disciplined personal life and anticipated a radically altered social order. By uniting the abolition of slavery, temperance, and reforms of dress and even diet with evangelical religion, Finney was a primary shaper of a Midwestern culture that prioritized behavior (both corporate and personal) over a faith that emphasized the forgiveness for sins and the promise of a life of bliss in Heaven after death.[15]

FINNEY'S LEGACY

Finney's preoccupation with obedience was sharply criticized by his most astute critic, B. B. Warfield. Always on the lookout for signs of creeping theological liberalism, Warfield insisted that both Finney's language and his intent closely resembled that of the liberal moralism of German theologian Albrecht Ritschl. To Warfield and his numerous Calvinistic heirs, Finney's theology led not only to a shallow moralism that focused on "prohibitions on all sorts of observable behavior, such as drinking, smoking, dancing, Sabbath-breaking, card playing, and theater attendance" but also, more dangerously, to a superficial moralistic theological liberalism. In other words, if anti-Masonic activity found resonance in such Midwestern institutions as Wheaton College and a cluster of related small denominations, then Oberlin College and much of Finney's Congregational constituency would adopt the seemingly different moralism of the emerging social gospel movement and its slightly more secular expression, progressivism. As historian John Barnard noted, "The ease with which progressive commitment evolved at Oberlin bears witness to the affinity between evangelicalism and progressivism." This point is further illustrated by Oberlin's Henry Churchill King who, like Finney before him, emphasized the ethical as a primary category in theology and saw "benevolence or love as an act of the will." King, an important if now largely forgotten figure in the social gospel movement, was echoing the very words used by Warfield to illustrate his central concern that Oberlin's theology was a mere system of "teleological ethics." If Warfield had been looking for contemporary illustrations, he could have turned to the role played by Oberlin graduate John R. Commons in Wisconsin and national progressivism. A key early social gospel text, Commons's *Institutional Economics* sought morally informed solutions to labor strife. While Commons would abandon evangelicalism, he remained faithful to prohibition, the favorite social cause of his mother, who was also an Oberlin graduate.[16]

Midwest progressivism played a decisive role in the early twentieth-century crusades against liquor and prostitution. Often inextricably tied to debates about gender, these campaigns drew deeply from the Finney legacy. These issues were especially prominent among Holiness bodies. Finney's thought and social engagement found clear expression in the

Salvation Army. With deep roots in the American Midwest, the Army's international war on prostitution and celebration of women's agency united the perfectionism of Methodism and Oberlin. If other Holiness bodies proved less adept at publicity and fundraising, they were no less zealous in fighting the liquor lobby and prostitution and in feeding the hungry. Through Oberlin graduate and evangelist A. M. Hills, Finney's thought also played a key role in the theology of the largest American Holiness denomination, the Church of the Nazarene. In the early twentieth century, the dynamic but theologically unstable Holiness movement divided over the questions surrounding ecstatic experience, especially the practice of speaking in unknown tongues. After World War II, Pentecostalism, a result of this division in the Holiness movement, emerged as the world's fastest-growing Christian tradition, impacting not only Protestantism but Catholicism as well.[17]

In the Midwest, Finney's legacy easily melded with the pietism of Swedish, Finnish, Danish, and especially Norwegian immigrants. Common even among Scandinavian Lutherans, pietist impulses were intensified by immigrants intent on creating their own non-Lutheran sectarian institutions, including such important evangelical colleges as North Park in Chicago; Trinity in Deerfield, Illinois; and Bethel in Minnesota. This immigrant moralism often flowed into political action, as in the case of William T. Evjue, founder of the Madison-based *Capital Times*, whose lifelong struggle against Wisconsin's brewing industry and illicit gaming was matched by his crusades against the Ku Klux Klan, public corruption, and (late in life) the Vietnam War. In Wisconsin, but elsewhere in the Midwest as well, immigrant pietism easily merged with the older Finney-inspired moralism of radical evangelicalism. George McGovern, an ordained Methodist minister, whose father had founded six Wesleyan Methodist churches in South Dakota, would inform a surprised Wheaton College audience that only poverty had kept him from enrolling in Billy Graham's alma mater. The legacy of Finney that found expression in both early and even mid-twentieth-century fundamentalism and progressivism is hard to recognize today among either self-acknowledged evangelicals or progressives. Finney (and most early twentieth-century evangelicals and progressives) would be baffled by the public disregard for Sabbath rest, fiscal dependence on legalized gambling, and relatively unrestricted liquor sales. As for his modern evangelical critics, Finney would dismiss their theology as the logical result of a defeatist determinism that relocates full salvation to a future existence on the other side of death.[18]

NOTES

1. On evangelical diversity, see Molly Worthen, *Apostles of Reason: The Crisis of Authority in American Evangelicalism* (New York: Oxford University Press, 2014). The role of the Midwest in the spread of temperance agitation in the United States is emphasized in Barbara Leslie Epstein, *The Politics of Domesticity: Women, Evangelism and Temperance in Nineteenth-Century America* (Middletown, CT: Wesleyan University Press, 1981), 119–146. Evangelical denominations with headquarters in Indianapolis are the Pentecostal Assemblies of the World, the Free Methodist Church, and the Wesleyan Church; Kansas City is the historic home of the Church of the Nazarene; the Assemblies of God denominational headquarters are in Springfield, Missouri. For an excellent definition of the historic roots of evangelicalism, see Mark A. Noll, *The Rise of Evangelicalism: The Age of Edwards, Whitefield and the Wesleys* (Downers Grove, IL: InterVarsity Press, 2003).

2. Robert Fletcher, *A History of Oberlin College from Its Foundation through the Civil War* (Oberlin, OH: Oberlin College, 1943), 87, 174.

3. On the Methodist Age, see Winthrop S. Hudson, "The Methodist Age in America," *Methodist History* 12, no. 3 (April 1974), 3–15. On the strong antievangelical religious impulses of the antebellum period, see James D. Bratt, "Religious Anti-Revivalism in Antebellum," *Journal of the Early Republic* 24, no. 1 (Spring 2004), 65–106. On Finney as a source of the social gospel tradition, see the classic study of Timothy L. Smith, *Revivalism and Social Reform: American Protestantism on the Eve of the Civil War* (Baltimore: Johns Hopkins University Press, 1980), 235.

4. Nathan O. Hatch, *The Democratization of American Christianity* (New Haven, CT: Yale University Press, 1989). Finney has received unusually negative treatment by scholars. The fairest biography is Charles E. Hambrick-Stowe, *Charles G. Finney and the Spirit of American Evangelicalism* (Grand Rapids, MI: William B. Eerdmans, 1996).

5. Finney discussed his attraction for and rejection of Universalism in "The Rich Man and Lazarus," *Oberlin Evangelist* 9 (November 1853). On his

rejection of the logic of Universalism, see Charles G. Finney, *Sermons on Gospel Themes* (Chicago: Fleming H. Revell, 1876), 236–237, and for a similar point, Charles G. Finney, *Lectures on Systematic Theology Embracing Lectures on Moral Government* (Oberlin, OH: James M. Fitch, 1846), 477. For an astute observation of Finney from a Universalist perspective, see Ann Lee Bressler, *The Universalist Movement in America, 1770–1880* (New York: Oxford University Press, 2001), 38. The Holifield quotation is from E. Brooks Holifield, *Theology in America: Christian Thought from the Age of the Puritans to the Civil War* (New Haven, CT: Yale University Press, 2003), 364.

6. Paul E. Johnson, *A Shopkeeper's Millennium: Society and Revivals in Rochester, New York, 1815–1837* (New York: Hill and Wang, 2004); Mary P. Ryan, *Cradle of the Middle Class: The Family in Oneida County, New York, 1790–1865* (London: Cambridge University Press, 1981); Curtis D. Johnson, *Islands of Holiness: Rural Religion in Upstate New York, 1790–1860* (Ithaca, NY: Cornell University Press, 1989). On the link between conversion and temperance and abolition, see Gilbert H. Barnes, *The Anti-Slavery Impulse, 1830–1844* (New York: American Historical Association, 1933), 162, 275. On Finney as a repackager of standard evangelical practices, see Robert W. Caldwell, III, *Theologies of the American Revivalists: From Whitefield to Finney* (Downers Grove, IL: InterVarsity Press, 2017), 106. These points were first made by Richard Carwardine, "The Second Great Awakening in the Urban Centers: An Examination of Methodism and the 'New Measures,'" *Journal of American History* 59, no. 2 (September 1972), 327–340. See also Richard Carwardine, *Transatlantic Revivalism: Popular Evangelicalism in Britain and America, 1790–1865* (Westport, CT: Greenwood Press, 1978).

7. For the critical edition of *Lectures on Revivals of Religion* with a helpful, if anti-Finney, introduction, see Charles G. Finney, *Lectures on Revivals of Religion*, ed. William G. McLoughlin (Cambridge, MA: Belknap Press of Harvard University, 1960). Also, see Garth M. Rosell, "*Lectures on Revivals of Religion* by Charles G. Finney," *Journal of Presbyterian History* 66 (Winter 1988), 235–240. The term *burned-over district*, greatly popularized by historian Whitney Cross, seems to come from Finney's memoirs. See Charles G. Finney, *The Memoirs of Charles G. Finney: The Completely Restored Text*, ed. Garth M. Rosell and Richard A. G. Dupuis (Grand Rapids, MI: Academie Books, 1989), 78–79. One of the fairest and most fascinating discussions of Finney is in Whitney R. Cross,

The Burned-Over District: The Social and Intellectual History of Enthusiastic Religion in Western New York, 1800–1850 (Ithaca, NY: Cornell University Press, 1950), 3, 151–169. On the role of New England migrants in the creation of the reform culture in antebellum America, see Lois Kimball Mathews, *The Expansion of New England: The Spread of New England Settlement and Institutions to the Mississippi River, 1620–1865* (Boston: Houghton and Mifflin, 1909).

8. For an excellent discussion of Finney's use of the higher law argument, see Charles C. Cole Jr., *The Social Ideas of the Northern Evangelists, 1826–1860* (New York: Columbia University Press, 1954), 209–211. The quotation is from Finney, *Lectures on Systematic Theology*, 444–446. A balanced discussion of Finney's views and actions on reform is found in J. Brent Morris, *Oberlin, Hotbed of Abolitionism: College, Community, and the Fight for Freedom and Equality in Antebellum America* (Chapel Hill: University of North Carolina Press, 2014), 21–23, 91–99.

9. On the relationship of Finney's thought to the heritage of Edwards, see G. Frederick Wright, *Charles Grandison Finney* (Boston: Houghton and Mifflin, 1891), 177–264. Especially helpful is Allen C. Guelzo, "Oberlin Perfectionism and Its Edwardsian Origins, 1835–1870," in *Jonathan Edwards's Writings: Texts, Context, Interpretation*, ed. Stephen J. Stein (Bloomington: Indiana University Press, 1996), 159–174. For Hodge's views on Finney's theology, see Charles Hodge, *Essays and Reviews* (New York: Robert Carter and Brothers, 1856), 245–284. The first quotation from Warfield is from Benjamin Breckinridge Warfield, *Perfectionism*, vol. 2 (New York: Oxford University Press, 1931), 18. See also pages 173–176 for the additional quotation. There is a vast anti-Finney literature in popular evangelicalism. Two examples are Michael S. Horton, *The Christian Faith: A Systematic Theology for Pilgrims on the Way* (Grand Rapids, MI: Zondervan, 2011), 627–628, and Iain H. Murray, *Revival and Revivalism: The Making and Marring of American Evangelicalism, 1750–1858* (Carlisle, PA: Banner of Truth, 1994), 225–298. Finney's greatest academic defenders have been Wesleyans. Especially see Smith, *Revivalism and Social Reform*, 103–113; William Warren Sweet, *Revivalism in America* (New York: Charles Scribner's, 1944); and especially important for my own interpretation, Donald W. Dayton, *Discovering an Evangelical Heritage* (New York: Harper and Row, 1976), 15–24. Hofstadter is very dependent on William

McLoughlin's critique of Finney, and McLoughlin in turn leans heavily on the Princetonians Hodge and Warfield. It should be noted that McLoughlin's interpretation of Finney occurred during the height of Billy Graham's success in the 1950s and 1960s and, in places, seems to interpret Finney in the light of Graham. Hofstadter's somewhat nuanced interpretation of Finney is found in his Pulitzer Prize–winning *Anti-Intellectualism in American Life* (New York: Alfred A. Knopf, 1964), 91–95, 113.

10. Finney, *Lectures on Revivals*, 306. For Finney's view of Augustine, see Finney, *Lectures on Systematic Theology*, 477. On Finney's critique of classic Protestant soteriology, see Wright, *Charles Grandison Finney*, 247. A helpful introduction to Finney and Oberlin perfectionism is Timothy L. Smith, "Holiness and Radicalism in Nineteenth-Century America," in *Sanctification and Liberation: Liberation Theologies in the Light of the Wesleyan Tradition*, ed. Theodore Runyon (Nashville, TN: Abingdon Press, 1981), 116–141, and for its relationship with Methodism, see Donald W. Dayton, *Theological Roots of Pentecostalism* (Grand Rapids, MI: Francis Asbury Press, 1987), 64–70, 100–102. The Sweet quotation is from William Warren Sweet, *The American Churches: An Interpretation* (New York: Abingdon-Cokesbury, 1947), 126–127.

11. Guelzo, "Oberlin Perfectionism," 170.

12. The use of the term *radical* with reference to the groups discussed in this paragraph comes from Victor B. Howard, *Religion and the Radical Republican Movement, 1860–1870* (Lexington: University of Kentucky Press, 1990); these groups are also discussed in the context of Finney in Dayton, *Discovering an Evangelical Heritage*. On the role of Finney in the formation of the Salvation Army, see Norman H. Murdoch, *Origins of the Salvation Army* (Knoxville: University of Tennessee Press, 1994), 5–16. For a list of educational institutions inspired by Oberlin, see Fletcher, *A History of Oberlin College*, vol. 2, 904. On Catton, see Bruce Catton, *Waiting for the Morning Train: An American Boyhood* (Detroit, MI: Wayne State University Press, 1987), 22. For the use of the word *Beulah* in perfectionist religious circles, see Charles Edwin Jones, *Perfectionist Persuasion: The Holiness Movement and American Methodism, 1867–1936* (Metuchen, NJ: Scarecrow Press, 1974), 152–153.

13. C. G. Finney, *The Character, Claims, and Practical Workings of Freemasonry* (Cincinnati, OH: Western Tract and Book Society, 1869), 186–187, 211–212. For a fuller discussion of Finney and Masonry, especially related to

issues of gender, see William Kostlevy, "The Social Vision of the Holiness Movement," in *The Holiness Manifesto*, ed. Kevin W. Mannoia and Don Thorson (Grand Rapids, MI: William B. Eerdmans, 2008), 92–109. Also, see Mark C. Carnes, *Secret Ritual and Manhood in Victorian America* (New Haven, CT: Yale University Press, 1989).

14. On the invention of tradition and its relationship to growing high church sentiments in Anglicanism, see Eric Hobsbawm and Terence Ranger, eds., *The Invention of Tradition* (Cambridge: Cambridge University Press, 1983), 1–15, 131. On the spread of Romanticism among American protestants, see Sydney E. Ahlstrom, *A Religious History of the American People* (New Haven, CT: Yale University Press, 1972), 583–632. On Lutheranism, see Abdel Ross Wentz, *Pioneer in Christian Unity: Samuel Simon Schmucker* (Philadelphia: Fortress Press, 1999), 169–194.

15. Charles G. Finney, *Lectures on Systematic Theology Embracing the Moral Government* (London: William Tegg, 1851), x. This openness to new truth meant that Oberlin, unlike its rival Princeton, was far more willing to embrace new findings in science, including Darwin's theory of evolution, which was defended by Finney's biographer and Oberlin professor G. Frederick Wright. See Ronald L. Numbers, "George Frederick Wright: From Christian Darwinist to Fundamentalist," *Isis* 79, no. 4 (December 1988), 624–645.

16. On the importance of Ritschl in Warfield's thought, see Fred G. Zaspel, *The Theology of B. B. Warfield: A Systematic Summary* (Wheaton, IL: Crossway, 2010). The first quotation is from George M. Marsden, *The Evangelical Mind and the New School Presbyterian Experience: A Case Study of Thought and Theology in Nineteenth-Century America* (New Haven, CT: Yale University Press, 1970), 239–240. Warfield, *Perfectionism*, vol. 2, 195, 200. On the relationship of Oberlin's evangelical tradition to progressivism, see John Barnard, *From Evangelicalism to Progressivism at Oberlin College, 1866–1917* (Columbus: Ohio State University Press, 1969), 126, and Donald M. Love, *Henry Churchill King of Oberlin* (New Haven, CT: Yale University Press, 1956), 170. John R. Commons, *Myself: The Autobiography of John R. Commons* (Madison: University of Wisconsin Press, 1963), 8–22. Also, Robert M. Crunden, *Ministers of Reform: The Progressives' Achievement in American Civilization, 1889–1920* (Urbana: University of Illinois Press, 1984), 6–8.

17. On the wide array of immediate post-Finney evangelical social engagements, see Norris Magnuson, *Salvation in the Slums: Evangelical Social Work, 1865–1920* (Metuchen, NJ: Scarecrow Press, 1977). The Salvation Army engaged in dramatic antiprostitution campaigns in Europe, North America, and most notably Japan. The Army's North American work is discussed in Diane Winston, *Red-Hot and Righteous: The Urban Religion of the Salvation Army* (Cambridge, MA: Harvard University Press, 1990), 156–160. On Finney's role in the development of Pentecostalism, see Dayton, *Theological Roots of Pentecostalism*, 66–72, 100–101, 155–167.

18. In Minnesota, where immigrant pietism easily merged with the older Finney-inspired evangelicalism, see Steven J. Keillor, *Shaping Minnesota's Identity: 150 Years of State History* (Lakeville, MN: Pogo Press, 2008), 195–204.

CHAPTER 5

HE FLIRTED WITH EUTERPE BEFORE HE SETTLED DOWN WITH CLIO

The Education of Frederick Jackson Turner

Marcia Noe

During the summer of 1879, seventeen-year-old Frederick Jackson Turner experienced a serious life crisis. Having contracted spinal meningitis, he was unable to return to the University of Wisconsin for his sophomore year.[1] Instead, he was forced to lead a quiet life at home in Portage, Wisconsin, recuperating from an illness that might have proved a debilitating setback for any other young man.

Ultimately, however, this imposed sabbatical benefited Turner, for he put his downtime to good use, embarking on a program of voracious and intensive reading. The commonplace books that he kept during the early 1880s especially illuminate Turner's intellectual development during his late adolescence. In these notebooks, he made lists of the concerts, plays, and lectures he attended and of the books he read. He compiled quotations from works he admired and recorded his responses as well as his personal observations and notes for further reading and for essays. He translated works of Horace and Heinrich Heine from the original Latin and German, respectively, and he tried his hand at poetry.[2]

These pages reflect his broad intellectual interests: Turner read widely in the disciplines of history, religion, science, philosophy, political philosophy, and literature. While a number of scholars have studied

Turner's rhetorical education and influences, little attention has been paid thus far to his literary education, as documented in his commonplace books, and its impact on his frontier address. This extensive reading, in concert with the stylistic proficiency he developed through his study of rhetoric in high school and college, as well as through his training in Latin and Greek, gave him a literary education that enhanced his growing knowledge of history and elevated his 1893 essay to literary status, endowing it with a rhetorical power that contributed much to its role as a seminal document in American history.[3] The influence of this thorough grounding in literature is evident in "The Significance of the Frontier in American History," for through his carefully chosen tropes and schemes, Turner memorably dramatizes the settling of the frontier. If we weigh the multitude of criticisms against the literary and rhetorical strengths of this landmark essay, it can be argued that its staying power derives as much from Turner's eloquence and rhetorical proficiency as it does from his ideas.

Turner's 1893 essay has survived over one hundred years of academic debate to prevail as one of the classic documents of American civilization.[4] Historians have criticized it as simplistic, inconsistent, and derivative, citing its lack of empirical evidence and comparative methodology and its failure to deal with the class struggle, industrialization, urbanization, and other forces transforming American society.[5] These critiques are succinctly summarized by Doug Kiel: "Historians rightly criticized his vision of the frontier as racist, teleological, unsubtle, outdated, ambiguous, inconsistent, imbued with exaggerated notions of American progress, and, worse yet, conspicuously devoid of empowered women and non-Anglos."[6]

Ray Allen Billington asserts that "Turner was as much an artist as he was a historian. His pen-pictures convinced scholars, not through the process of reason, but in exactly the same way that a fine novel or beautiful painting was 'convincing.'" Henry Nash Smith briefly discusses Turner's rhetorical use of metaphor; Avery Craven, while criticizing Turner's insufficient evidence and misplaced emphases, admits that Turner had "something of the poet in him"; and Benjamin F. Wright Jr., while disputing Turner's notion that American democracy was born on the frontier, describes him as "a poet who wrote in the grand manner" and his essays as "brilliant and moving odes to the glories of the west-ward movement."[7]

The literary elements in Turner's famous essay merit careful consid-eration, for the essay derives much of its cogency from his ability to dra-matize the conflict between the forces of civilization and savagery and to represent the settling of the frontier as a natural event in process rather than a historical abstraction. His skillful use of schemes and tropes add interest, emphasis, and suspense to his discourse, and his ability to stress key ideas through these devices makes them resonate with echoes of classic literary works, giving his essay intellectual weight and persuasiveness and rendering it a powerful and memorable document that would influence generations of Americans.

Turner's critics have leveled charges that he romanticized a bloody, arduous, and imperialistic process and, indeed, his 1881 commonplace book reveals a definite preference for romantic works of literature. Turner read the published essays of Ralph Waldo Emerson and recorded, "I read in Shakespeare nearly every day." A list of books that Turner read in 1880 includes Thomas De Quincey's *Confessions of an English Opium-Eater*; Thomas Carlyle's "Essay on Burns," *The French Revolution*, and *On He-roes, Hero-Worship, and The Heroic in History*; Lord Byron's "Don Juan," "Manfred," and "The Prisoner of Chillon"; James Fenimore Cooper's *The Red Rover*; Washington Irving's *Tales of the Alhambra* and *The Sketch Book*; Nathaniel Hawthorne's *The Scarlet Letter* and *Mosses from an Old Manse*; Johann Wolfgang von Goethe's *Wilhelm Meister's Apprenticeship*; Henry Wadsworth Longfellow's *Outre-Mer* and *Hyperion*; as well as the major plays of Shakespeare and essays of Emerson.[8] Throughout the notebooks appear quotations such as "the cloistered stars that, nunlike, walk through the holy aisles of heaven," from *Hyperion*, and "this journey is written in my mem-ory with a sunbeam" from *Outre-Mer*.[9] On the front inside cover of Turner's 1881 commonplace book is inscribed a quotation from Shakespeare's *The Tempest*: "We are such stuff as dreams are made of" [sic], and to the back in-side cover of his 1883 commonplace book, he affixed a picture of Emerson.[10]

Purple passages such as these captured the imagination of the young Turner and encouraged him to romanticize the process of settling the fron-tier as a triumph of democracy. The Old World drama of many common workingmen prevailing over the wealthy and tyrannical few was similar to the conflict experienced by the persevering pioneers moving westward in struggle against the perils of the wilderness. An excerpt from James Russell Lowell's "A Glance behind the Curtain" that Turner recorded in his commonplace book of 1883 describes this process in stirring language:

> One age moves onward, and the next builds up
> Cities and gorgeous palaces where stood
> The rude log-huts of those who tamed the wild;
> Clearing from out the forests they had felled
> The goodly framework of a fairer state.[11]

In a key passage in his 1893 essay, Turner depicts this process by employing four figures of speech to dramatize his frontier theory: prosopopeia (personification), synecdoche (making a part represent the whole), antithesis (juxtaposing opposites), and the repetition of parallel grammatical constructions. The following passage can serve as a rhetorical microcosm of the essay as a whole, for the devices Turner uses here also appear frequently throughout the essay and can be found in numerous entries in Turner's commonplace books:

> The wilderness masters the colonist. It finds him European in dress,
> industries, tools, modes of travel, and thought. It takes him from the
> railroad car and puts him in the birch canoe. It strips off the garments
> of civilization and arrays him in the hunting shirt and moccasin. It
> puts him in the log cabin of the Cherokee and Iroquois and runs an
> Indian palisade around him. Before long he has gone to planting
> Indian corn and plowing with a sharp stick; he shouts the war cry and
> takes the scalp in orthodox Indian fashion.[12]

This passage personifies the wilderness as a powerful entity that transforms the civilized settler into a primitive man. This process is dramatized, rather than merely explained, through the synecdochal use of "the colonist" to represent all of the pioneers who experienced this transformation and through the use of action verbs in the present tense to create a sense of immediacy. The short, simple opening sentence attracts attention because of its brevity and starkness. Using the device of antithesis, the organizing principle of the passage, Turner places two contending forces in the drama at opposite ends of the sentence, which is balanced on the verb *masters*. The subsequent balanced sentences continually emphasize the contrast seen in the colonist's European clothing and mode of transportation and the parallel aspects of American Indian culture (railroad/birch canoe, garments of civilization/hunting shirt and moccasin). The transformative effect of the frontier is further dramatized through Turner's adroit use of parallel grammatical constructions at the beginning and end of clauses (takes him/puts him, strips off/arrays, planting/plowing, shouts/takes). Through the skillful use of these devices, Turner not only describes but re-creates the process of the wilderness making an American of the colonist.

These four devices, seen repeatedly in entries throughout Turner's commonplace books, also recur in his 1893 essay. Turner employs the first of these, prosopopeia, no fewer than fifteen times throughout his essay. Through this device, he creates a sense of drama and immediacy and gives the frontier the power of a human agent. The clauses "As the frontier had leaped over the Alleghenies, so it now skipped the Great Plains and the Rocky Mountains" and "The stubborn American environment is there with its imperious summons to accept its conditions" represent the frontier as a living, dynamic presence and thus endow it with the democratizing capabilities that he ascribes to it in his essay.[13] This penchant for personification can be traced to passages that appear in his commonplace books. The following excerpt from Longfellow's *Hyperion*, which Turner copied into his 1881 commonplace book, personifies and ennobles nature and suggests the conflict between man and nature that Turner later dramatized in his famous essay.

> O let not the soul that suffers dare to look Nature in the face where she sits majestically aloft in the solitude of the mountains! For her face is stern and hard, and looks not in compassion upon her weak and erring child—it is the countenance of an accusing archangel, who summons us to judgement [sic]- In the valley she wears the countenance of a Virgin Mother looking at us with tearful eyes, and a face of pity and love![14]

Personification appears in many of the original poems and short descriptive prose pieces that appear in Turner's commonplace books, as seen in this paean to autumn:

> "The trees, attired in robes of russet and gold like fair daughters of
> Judea clashed their leafy castenets [sic] in the presence of the Solomon
> of Seasons—languorous, benign old Autumn"; before him ran his torch
> bearers, the astors [sic] and the poppies—Mendota lifted to his lips
> her brimming chalice, and in the west the sunset banners of his pomp
> bring on the outward wall. And yet, through all the glory of the scene
> there crept the breath from Winter's icy realm, that seemed in hollow
> whisper to declare, "Vanity, vanity, saith the preacher, yea, all is vanity
> alone." [15]

Although passages such as this one might strike the modern reader as overwritten, they show that the young Turner was honing his fledgling literary skills, which he later refined and put to more subtle and skillful use in his famous frontier essay.

The second of these devices, synecdoche, is seen in the earlier passage that begins, "The wilderness masters the colonist." Synecdoche is one of the hallmarks of the famous 1893 essay; Turner characteristically writes not of colonists, settlers, trappers, and traders but of *the* colonist, *the* settler, *the* trapper, and *the* trader, using the singular form of the noun to stand for the body of pioneers about whom he writes. When he describes the transformation of the wilderness, he uses this rhetorical device repeatedly: "It begins with the Indian and the hunter; it goes on to tell of the disintegration of savagery; by the entrance of the trader, and pathfinder of civilization."[16] Turner's repeated use of this figure of speech suggests his fascination with the romantic notion of the beleaguered individual who struggles against nearly insurmountable odds, a predilection learned through his youthful acquaintance with the works of Goethe, Byron, and Percy Bysshe Shelley.[17] This romantic bent is also seen in Turner's comment in his commonplace book of 1881 that "Prometheus the representative of suffering and struggling humanity is to be redeemed and perfected by unity with Asia who is the ideal of beauty—the light of life, the spirit of love." A quotation from Shelley's

"Queen Mab" that he copied into the same commonplace book further reveals his idealistic proclivities:

The poor man's God to sweep it
    From the earth
And spare his children the detested
    task
Of piling stone on stone, and poisoning
    The choicest days of life
To soothe a dotard's vanity.[18]

Passages featuring the third device, antithesis, appear throughout Turner's commonplace books, exemplified by this quotation from Emerson's *Representative Men*, which Turner had copied out by hand: "Let a man learn to look for the permanent in the mutable and fleeting . . . let him learn that he is here, not to work, but to be worked upon."[19] Antithesis is used a number of times in Turner's frontier essay to emphasize two main points in his argument: the contrast between European and American and that between East and West. He uses antithesis to emphasize the latter difference when he writes that "the true point of view in the history of this nation is not the Atlantic coast, it is the Great West" and the former when he introduces his famous "the wilderness masters the colonist" passage with this sentence: "Too exclusive attention has been paid by institutional students to the Germanic origins, too little to the American factors."[20]

A fourth rhetorical strategy that appears in the seedbed of Turner's commonplace books, later to take root in the 1893 essay, is the adroit use of syntactic structures. Turner's study of rhetoric in high school and college acquainted him with the Sophists, masters of eloquence who taught that sentence structure and sound patterns could effect persuasion. His omnivorous consumption of poetry as a young man, as recorded in his commonplace books, introduced him to cadences that he would later use skillfully in his essays. A passage from Samuel Taylor Coleridge that Turner paraphrased in his commonplace book of 1881 indicates the source of Turner's inspiration in this regard: "Coleridge remarks very pertinently somewhere, that whenever you find a sentence mystically worded, of true rhythm and melody in the words, there is something deep and good in the meaning, too." A stanza of Turner's own poetry from the same common-place book exemplifies anastrophe, or inverted word order: "Stately down the empyrean paced the moon, / The crescent crowned Queen of Sheba, pale / In the purple sky, with sweet enticement / beaming from her face upon the monarch." [21] Turner employs this device in both the first sentence and the last sentence of his frontier essay and in several other places as well, to effect emphasis: "From the conditions of frontier life came intellectual traits of profound importance"; "With these peoples were also the freed indented servants, or redemptioners, who, at the expiration of their time of service passed to the frontier"; and "The result is that to the frontier the American intellect owes its striking characteristics." [22]

Similar to anastrophe in climactic effect are periodic sentences such as the one that concludes the address: "And now, four centuries from the discovery of America, at the end of a hundred years under the constitution, the frontier has gone, and with its going has closed the first period of American history." [23] Turner uses periodic and balanced sentences frequently, as well as repeated clauses and phrases for rhetorical effect. In the following passage, for example, Turner underscores his stages of history theory by the use of anadiplosis (the repetition of a word or phrase that ends one phrase or clause at the beginning of the next phrase or clause): "The buffalo trail became the Indian trail, and this became the trader's 'trace'; the trails widened into roads, and the roads into turnpikes, and those in turn were transformed into railroads." [24] The repetition of parallel grammatical constructions, so dominant in the "wilderness masters the colonist" passage, is notable throughout the essay, particularly anaphora (the repetition of the same word at the beginning of successive grammatically parallel structures), which occurs in the following passage: "The exploitation of the beasts took hunger and trader to the west, the exploitation of the grasses took the rancher west, and the exploitation of the virgin soil of the river valleys and prairies attracted the farmer." [25]

In addition to the literary devices previously discussed, the young Turner filled his commonplace book of 1881 with passages containing illuminating metaphors, including this one from Emerson's *Representative Men*: "Other men are lenses through which we read our own minds." Turner also employs metaphor, a trope that Aristotle believed to be one of the most persuasive of all literary devices, in his 1893 essay.[26] The controlling metaphor in the essay is one linking water and earth to associate the settling of the frontier with familiar natural processes. "This perennial rebirth, this fluidity of American life, this expansion westward with its new opportunities, its continuous touch with the simplicity of primitive society, furnish the forces dominating American character," wrote Turner near the beginning of his essay, stating his thesis metaphorically.[27]

The essay is replete with water metaphors. Although some of them are dead metaphors, the water imagery is so pervasive that it works effectively as a master trope. Tides and waves are frequently used to describe the movement of settlers across the continent, as seen in the following examples: "Railroads, fostered by land grants, sent an increasing tide of immigrants into the Far West"; "In this advance, the frontier is the outer edge of the wave—the meeting point between savagery and civilization"; "As the eastern lands were taken up migration flowed across them to the west"; "The farmer's advance came in a distinct series of waves"; and "The coast was preponderantly English, but the later tides of continental immigration flowed across to the free lands."[28] Paired with the water imagery are images of fertile earth: "Pennsylvania had been the seed-plot of frontier migration"; "Interstate migration went steadily on—a process of cross-fertilization of ideas and institutions"; "each frontier did furnish a new field of opportunity"; "Thus an intellectual stream from New England sources fertilized the West"; and "At the Atlantic frontier one can study the germs of processes repeated at each successive frontier."[29]

These water and earth metaphors suggest that the process of settling the frontier was as natural to the American nation as the flow of water, the fertilization of land, and the growth of plants from seeds to mature organisms. Turner reinforces this imagery with analogies that also derive from nature: "As successive terminal moraines result from successive glaciations, so each frontier leaves its traces behind it, and when it becomes a settled area the region still partakes of the frontier characteristics," and "What the Mediterranean Sea was to the Greeks . . . the ever retreating frontier has been to the United States directly, and to the nation of Europe more remotely."[30]

The nature imagery that dominates the essay performs an important rhetorical function in suggesting that Turner's account of the succeeding stages of civilization on the frontier describes a natural and inevitable development rather than an academic theory about how the West was settled. Again, we can look to the romantic literature in which Turner engaged as a young man as an influence here, as well as Turner's own poetic efforts recorded in his commonplace books. Into his commonplace book of 1881, he copied Longfellow's translation of a Spanish poem that uses water metaphors in much the same way as Turner does in his essay:

> Our lives are rivers, gliding free
> To that unfathomed, boundless sea
>   The silent wave!
> Thither all earthly pomp and boast
> Roll, to be swallowed up and lost
>   In one dark wave
> Thither the mighty torrents stray,
> Thither the brook pursues its way,
>   And tinkling rill;—
> There all are equal side by side
> The poor man + the son of pride
>   Lie calm and still.[31]

This poem prefigures Turner's frontier thesis essay not only in the pervasiveness of its water imagery but also in its underlying theme of the equality of all men within the human condition.

Turner's commonplace books are of significance to the historian because they reveal his early interest in concepts such as free land, evolution, and other key ideas that he would develop as a mature historian. But to the rhetorician and the literary scholar, they also show Turner's increasing understanding of the persuasive power of literary tropes and schemes. A note of instruction in the commonplace book of 1881 to "read Meditations of a Parish Priest for hint on eloquence" reveals the importance that Turner placed on forms of expression. "A great writer is a man who, having passions, knows his dictionary and grammar," reads a quotation from the French historian Hippolyte Taine that Turner also copied into the same commonplace book—a dictum that Turner would take to heart and practice as a working historian.[32]

The year 2013 marked the 120th anniversary of "The Significance of the Frontier in American History," and the following year saw no fewer than ten scholarly articles that dealt with Turner and/or his landmark essay.[33] Thus, although the new western historians have denigrated the essay for its imperialism and ethnocentrism, its importance must be acknowledged, and that importance is due in great measure to its literary qualities and rhetorical effectiveness.[34] The Midwestern teenager who, faced with a life-threatening illness, confronted it by engaging with "the best that has been thought and known in the world" deserves our attention and admiration.[35] Frederick Jackson Turner flirted with Euterpe before he settled down with Clio and gained much from the infatuation of his early years, for his tryst with the muse of lyric poetry, as documented in his commonplace books, enriched the texture of his signature essay, enhanced its persuasiveness, and helped earn him a place as one of America's foremost historians.

NOTES

1. Ray Allen Billington, "Fred J. Turner: Background and Training," in *The Genesis of the Frontier Thesis: A Study in Historical Creativity*, ed. Ray Allen Billington (San Marino, CA: Henry E. Huntington Library and Gallery, 1971), 15. For a brief discussion of Turner's intellectual activity during his recuperation, including his entries in his commonplace book of 1881, see Ray Allen Billington, *Frederick Jackson Turner: Historian, Scholar, Teacher* (New York: Oxford University Press, 1973), 18–19.

2. Turner's commonplace books are held by the Henry E. Huntington Library and Gallery, San Marino, California (hereafter cited as HEH), and have been touched on by a number of scholars, but no one to date has attempted a focused and well-developed analysis of the relationship between the commonplace books and the 1893 essay. Allan G. Bogue discusses Turner's commonplace books in the first chapter of *Frederick Jackson Turner: Strange Roads Going Down* (Norman: University of Oklahoma Press, 1998), 17–21, and briefly notes the rhetorical effectiveness of "The Significance of the Frontier in American History" in his fourth chapter. John E. Miller, *Small-Town Dreams: Stories of Midwestern Boys Who Shaped America* (Lawrence: University Press of Kansas, 2014), 26–46, opens with a biographical sketch of Turner in which his oratorical skills

are lauded and his wide reading, as recorded in his commonplace books, is also briefly discussed. Henry Nash Smith mentions two entries in Turner's commonplace books in the last chapter of *Virgin Land: The American West as Symbol and Myth* (New York: Vintage Books, 1957), 294–295. Merrill Lewis, in his "Language, Literature, Rhetoric, and the Shaping of the Historical Imagination of Frederick Jackson Turner," *Pacific Historical Review* 45, no. 3 (August 1976): 399–424, draws from Turner's commonplace books to argue that Turner built a bridge between literature and history that informed his way of thinking about and doing history. Ronald H. Carpenter, who has published extensively on Turner's rhetorical training and influences, also mentions the commonplace books in *The Eloquence of Frederick Jackson Turner* (San Marino, CA: HEH, 1983), 11, 14, 17, 18, 21–22, 95.

3. Turner's classical and rhetorical training is well documented. Ray Allen Billington states that Turner added "a special preparatory 'Greek Course' to his heavy senior schedule in high school, mastering Xenophone's *Anabasis*, beginning Homer's *Iliad*, and suffering stiff doses of Greek grammar to meet the university's requirements for its 'Ancient Classical Course'" (Billington, *Frederick Jackson Turner*, 18). Allan G. Bogue reports that at his high school commencement, Turner earned the prize for the best oration (Bogue, *Frederick Jackson Turner*, 17) and notes that before he taught history at the University of Wisconsin, Turner taught classes in oratory and rhetoric (38), a phase of Turner's life that is chronicled in detail in Goodwin F. Berquist Jr., "The Rhetorical Heritage of Frederick Jackson Turner," *Transactions of the Wisconsin Academy of Sciences, Arts and Letters* 59 (1971): 23–32. Berquist notes the influence of the young Robert M. La Follette's prize-winning oration, "Iago," on Turner, as does Ronald H. Carpenter in "The Stylistic Identification of Frederick Jackson Turner with Robert M. La Follette: A Psychologically Oriented Analysis of Language Behavior," *Wisconsin Academy of Sciences, Arts and Letters* 63 (1975): 102–115, and also in "On Eloquent Style and Rhetorical Impact" in *The Eloquence of Frederick Jackson Turner*, 14–19. Merle E. Curti, in "Frederick Jackson Turner," *Wisconsin Witness to Frederick Jackson Turner: A Collection of Essays on the Historian and the Thesis*, ed. O. Lawrence Burnette Jr., (Madison: State Historical Society of Wisconsin, 1961), 178, remarks on the "thorough classical training" that Turner received

during his studies at the University of Wisconsin. "The sensitiveness to literary style thus cultivated was another foundation for Turner's later career," Curti argues. "His fluid and balanced sentences, his liking for the apt epithet, owed something to his classical studies." Curti also notes in the same essay that during his time at the university, Turner gave "two orations, one . . . in his junior year, and one at commencement in 1884 [in which] Turner expounded his faith in democracy and in a democratic culture" (179); both orations won prizes. Turner's rhetorical education was also informed by Adams Sherman Hill, *Principles of Rhetoric* (New York: Harper and Brothers,1878), a textbook widely used by undergraduates of Turner's generation, called "an exceptionally influential textbook during the nineteenth and twentieth centuries" for its emphasis on style in written discourse by James A. Berlin in his *Writing Instruction in Nineteenth-Century American Colleges* (Carbondale and Edwardsville: Southern Illinois University Press, 1984), 67. Carpenter's *The Eloquence of Frederick Jackson Turner* reprints Turner's prize-winning orations and several of his key eulogies and addresses, including "The Significance of the Frontier in American History" and "American Colonization." In a long introductory essay, "On Eloquent Style and Rhetorical Impact," Carpenter discusses Turner's rhetorical influences and argues that the latter speech is a stylistic precursor of the frontier essay through an analysis of the specific rhetorical devices used in both addresses (3–111).

4. The paper that J. A. Burkhart says "had perhaps more profound influence than any other essay or volume ever written in American historiography" went nearly unremarked upon among the two hundred historians gathered on July 12, 1893, at the summer meeting of the American Historical Association, held concurrently with the World's Columbian Exposition in Chicago ("The Turner Thesis: A Historian's Controversy," in Burnette, *Wisconsin Witness*, 160). However, within the next few years it began to gain notice and, as Merle E. Curti reports, soon earned Turner a national reputation ("Frederick Jackson Turner," 199). An anti-Turner backlash developed, beginning in 1926 and continuing through the Great Depression, when emphasis shifted to the economic issues that dominated the day. Curti observes that "from that decade to the present [the 1960s] it has been subjected to increasing criticism" (194). Under the influence of the new western historians of the 1980s and 1990s, "The Significance of the Frontier

in American History" was viewed negatively as a document that endorsed colonialism and imperialism. However, despite (or perhaps because of) the numerous criticisms leveled against it, continuing interest in the Turner thesis can be well documented. Since the turn of the twenty-first century, more than twenty scholarly essays have been published in academic journals. The first issue of the *Middle West Review* featured two essays and one interview that engaged substantially with the Turner thesis. See Doug Kiel, "Untaming the Wild Frontier: In Search of New Midwestern Histories," *Middle West Review* 1, no.1 (Fall 2014): 10–38; John E. Miller, "Frederick Jackson Turner and the Dream of Regional History," *Middle West Review* 1, no.1 (Fall 2014): 1–8; and Jon K. Lauck, "The Last Prairie Historian: An Interview with Professor Allan G. Bogue, Historian of the American West," *Middle West Review* 1, no. 1 (Fall 2014): 91–105. See also Cole Harris, "The Spaces of Early Canada," *The Canadian Historical Review* 91, no. 4 (December 2010): 725–759; Alex Wagner Lough, "Henry George, Frederick Jackson Turner, and the 'Closing' of the American Frontier," *California History* 89, no. 2 (2012): 4–54; Albert L. Hurtado, "Bolton and Turner: The Borderlands and American Exceptionalism," *Western Historical Quarterly* 44, no. 1 (Spring 2013): 5–20; Max J. Skidmore, "Restless Americans: The Significance of Movement in American History (With a Nod to F. J. Turner)," *Journal of American Culture* 34, no. 2 (June 2011): 161–174; Hillary A. Jones, "'Them as Feel the Need to Be Free': Reworking the Frontier Myth," *Southern Communication Journal* 76, no. 3 (July–August 2011): 230–247; Richard R. John, "Turner, Beard, Chandler: Progressive Historians," *Business History Review* 82, no. 2 (Summer 2008): 227–240; Brian Diemert, "Uncontainable Metaphor: George F. Kennan's 'X' Article and Cold War Discourse," *Canadian Review of American Studies* 35, no. 1 (2005): 21–55; Guy Reynolds, "The Winning of the West: Washington Irving's 'A Tour on the Prairies,'" *Yearbook of English Studies* 34 (2004): 88–99; Allan G. Bogue, "'Not by Bread Alone': The Emergence of the Wisconsin Idea and the Departure of Frederick Jackson Turner," *Wisconsin Magazine of History* 86, no. 1 (Autumn 2002): 10–23; Richard W. Etulain, "Western Biographies in Transition," *Western Historical Quarterly* 42, no. 3 (Autumn 2011): 349–354; Jon K. Lauck, "The Old Roots of the New West: Howard Lamar and the Intellectual Origins of 'Dakota Territory,'" *Western Historical Quarterly* 39, no. 3 (Autumn 2008): 261–281; Thomas Bender, "Commentary: Widening the Lens and Rethinking Asian American History," *Pacific Historical Review* 76, no. 4 (November 2007): 605–610; David M. Wrobel, "A Place for Regions in the Modern US Survey?," *Journal of American History* 94, no. 4 (March 2008): 1203–1210; Mark Fiege, "The Nature of the West and the World," *Western Historical Quarterly* 42, no. 3 (Autumn 2011): 305–312; María E. Montoya, "From Homogeneity to Complexity: Understanding the Urban West," *Western Historical Quarterly* 42, no. 3 (Autumn 2011): 344–348; Kevin J. Fernlund, "To Think Like a Star: The American West, Modern Cosmology, and Big History," *Montana: The Magazine of Western History* 59, no. 2 (Summer 2009): 23–44, 93–95; Albert L. Hurtado, "Romancing the West in the Twentieth Century: The Politics of History in a Contested Region," *Western Historical Quarterly* 32, no. 4 (Winter 2001): 417–435; and Patricia Kelly Hall and Steven Ruggles, " 'Restless in the Midst of Their Prosperity': New Evidence on the Internal Migration of Americans, 1850–2000," *Journal of American History* 91, no. 3 (December 2004): 829–846. Over fifty years after the publication of Burkhart's essay, John Mack Faragher echoed Burkhart's assessment, stating that Turner's essay is the "single most influential piece of writing in the history of American history" in his *Rereading Frederick Jackson Turner: "The Significance of the Frontier in American History" and Other Essays* (New York: Henry Holt, 1994), 1.

5. Representative of the new western historians of the 1980s and 1990s is Patricia Nelson Limerick, who, in her introduction to *The Legacy of Conquest: The Unbroken Past of the American West* (New York: W. W. Norton, 1987), 21, describes the Turner thesis as a biased, exclusionary, and inaccurate model of the western frontier. Quoting Howard Lamar's assertion that it is a "useless guide for the present and future," Limerick enumerates the negative effects of the Turner thesis on both the scholarship and pedagogy of American historians. In his afterword to *Rereading Frederick Jackson Turner*, John Mack Faragher offers a fairly comprehensive summary of criticism from this period and directs the reader to Gerald D. Nash, *Creating the West: Historical Interpretations, 1890–1990* (Albuquerque: University of New Mexico Press, 1991), for an even fuller discussion of these arguments.

6. Doug Kiel, "Untaming the Wild Frontier," 16.

7. See Billington, *Frederick Jackson Turner*, 426; Smith, *Virgin Land*, 297–298; Avery Craven, "Frederick Jackson Turner, Historian," in *Wisconsin*

Witness, 110, 115–116; and Benjamin F. Wright Jr., "Political Institutions and the Frontier," in *The Turner Thesis: Concerning the Role of the Frontier in American History*, ed. George Rogers Taylor (Lexington, MA: D.C. Heath, 1972), 4, 41.

8. Frederick Jackson Turner, "1881 Commonplace Book," *Commonplace Book 1881–1887*, TU Vol. 3, n. pag., HEH.

9. Turner, "1881 Commonplace Book."

10. Turner, "1881 Commonplace Book" and "1883 Commonplace Book," *Commonplace Book 1881–1887*, TU Vol. 3, n. pag., HEH.

11. Turner, "1883 Commonplace Book." Although the words "Cricket Hill" are penned beside these lines that Turner copied into his commonplace book, they are actually excerpted from a long poem by James Russell Lowell, "A Glance behind the Curtain," in *The Early Poems of James Russell Lowell* (New York: Thomas Y. Crowell Publishing Company, 1892), 169.

12. Turner, "The Significance of the Frontier in American History," in *Rereading Frederick Jackson Turner: "The Significance of the Frontier in American History" and Other Essays*, ed. John Mack Faragher (New York: H. Holt, 1994), 33.

13. Turner, "The Significance of the Frontier."

14. Turner, "1881 Commonplace Book." This quote has been transcribed exactly as it appears in Turner's book.

15. Turner, "1881 Commonplace Book."

16. Faragher, *Rereading Frederick Jackson Turner*, 33.

17. Billington, *Frederick Jackson Turner*, 18–19.

18. Turner, "1881 Commonplace Book."

19. Turner, "1881 Commonplace Book."

20. Faragher, *Rereading Frederick Jackson Turner*, 32.

21. Turner, "1881 Commonplace Book."

22. Faragher, *Rereading Frederick Jackson Turner*, 47, 59.

23. Faragher, *Rereading Frederick Jackson Turner*, 60.

24. Faragher, *Rereading Frederick Jackson Turner*, 40.

25. Faragher, *Rereading Frederick Jackson Turner*, 44.

26. Turner, "1881 Commonplace Book." See Lane Cooper, *Aristotle on the Art of Poetry*, rev. ed. (Ithaca: Cornell University Press, 1947), 74, and Aristotle's *On Rhetoric: A Theory of Civic Discourse*, trans. George A. Kennedy (New York: Oxford University Press, 1991), 22.

27. Faragher, *Rereading Frederick Jackson Turner*, 32.

28. Faragher, *Rereading Frederick Jackson Turner*, 36, 32, 44, 47.

29. Faragher, *Rereading Frederick Jackson Turner*, 51, 53, 59, 58, 37.

30. Faragher, *Rereading Frederick Jackson Turner*, 34, 59–60.

31. Turner, "1881 Commonplace Book."

32. Turner, "1881 Commonplace Book."

33. See Kiel, Miller, and Lauck, as well as Thomas Devaney, "The Contested Legacy of a Romantic Historian," *Reviews in American History* 42, no. 2 (June 2014): 303–308; Michael C. Steiner, "Utopias West: Or the Trouble with Perfection," *American Studies* 53, no. 1 (2014): 183–193; John Munro, "Interwoven Colonial Histories: Indigenous Agency and Academic Historiography in North America," *Canadian Review of American Studies* 44, no. 3 (Winter 2014): 402–425; Scott Andrews, "The Significance of the Frontier in Comanche Poetry," *Western American Literature* 49, no. 1 (Spring 2014): 9–28; Christina Henderson, "A Fairy Tale of American Progress: Frances Hodgson Burnett's Two Little Pilgrims at the World's Fair," *Children's Literature* 42 (2014): 108–135; Jared van Duinen, "The Borderlands of the British World," *Journal of Colonialism and Colonial History* 15, no. 1 (Spring 2014); and David Willbern, "Dialogic Frontiers: History and Psychology in *Lonesome Dove* and *Blood Meridian*," *Arizona Quarterly: A Journal of American Literature, Culture, and Theory* 70, no.1 (Spring 2014): 81–108.

34. See George Wilson Pierson, "American Historians and the Frontier Hypothesis in 1941 (I)," in *Wisconsin Witness*, 129.

35. Matthew Arnold, *Culture and Anarchy*, ed. and intro. J. Dover Wilson (Cambridge: Cambridge University Press, 1960), 70.

CHAPTER 6

"Invitation to the Dance"

Robert Ingersoll, Dwight Moody, and the Iconoclastic Gilded Age

Justin Clark

Introduction

In his 1927 essay, "Invitation to the Dance," journalist H. L. Mencken lamented the poor condition of American freethought during his life. "What this grand, gaudy, unapproachable country needs and lacks is an Ingersoll," Mencken quipped. He may have been on to something. An iconoclast in his own right, Mencken was reflecting on the age of Robert Green Ingersoll, when religion faced fiercer public criticism. He believed that Ingersoll, America's respected popularizer of freethought and secularism during the late nineteenth century, needed an heir apparent. He also understood Ingersoll's intellectual foils and their influence on America. "Moreover, a high tide of evangelistic passion was running," wrote Mencken, "it was the day of Dwight L. Moody, of the Salvation Army, of prayer-meetings in the White House, of eager chapel building on every suburban dump."[1] Moody, evangelical minister and founder of the Chicago Evangelization Society, was Ingersoll's ecclesiastical parallel. Both were Illinoisans and exceptional orators, and both possessed a moralistic passion that guided their intellectual lives.

Mencken's musings illuminated a tension at the heart of nineteenth-century American life; it was an age of reason, industrialization, and liberalism contrasted by an ever-growing evangelicalism. Ingersoll, the agnostic advocating for freethought, and Moody, the evangelist testifying for Christianity, served as intellectual avatars for this contradictory age. Yet, their powerful similarities spoke to a deeper consensus about Midwestern identity during the late nineteenth century. Both men used their public platforms to advance a shared conviction of rational individualism while simultaneously, and graciously, criticizing each other's worldview. As such, their encounters were like a dance and the public was an eager audience.

Two Illinoisans

Born August 11, 1833, Ingersoll grew up with a tender father who valued education. "My father [the minister John Ingersoll] was one of the most affectionate of men," Ingersoll wrote in 1887, who believed "that his children should think and investigate for themselves." [2] In this atmosphere, young Ingersoll read the Bible, Robert Burns, William Shakespeare, Voltaire, and Thomas Paine, whose own religious criticism, particularly *The Age of Reason*, impacted Ingersoll's critiques of Christianity. [3] After many years and many homes, in 1858, Ingersoll finally settled with his brother Clark in Peoria, Illinois, where they began a law practice. [4] Ingersoll's Illinois years proved to be significant; while honing his practice of law, he refined his religious skepticism. For much of the 1850s and 1860s, Ingersoll (echoing Paine) subscribed to a liberal deism that saw god as an "infinite being who created and preserves the universe." [5]

Two consequential events during Ingersoll's Peoria years pushed him toward agnosticism: his Civil War service and his marriage to Eva Parker. Ingersoll mustered into the 11th Regiment of the Illinois Volunteer Cavalry in 1861, later fighting in the battle of Shiloh. He was appointed chief of cavalry on December 2, 1862, but only sixteen days later, Nathan Bedford Forrest's troops captured and held him as a prisoner of war for four days. Ingersoll left the Illinois Volunteer Cavalry in 1863, but the carnage of battle never left him; it shaped his views on war's religious underpinnings. "The religion of Jesus Christ, as preached by his church," he wrote in 1884, "causes war, bloodshed, hatred, and all uncharitableness." [6] The other prominent influence on Ingersoll's freethought was his wife, Eva Parker, whom he married on February 13, 1862. Parker descended from a long line of freethinkers; her grandmother was a known skeptic who, like Ingersoll, read Voltaire and Paine.[7] Ingersoll dedicated his lecture "The Gods" to Eva, whom he called a "woman without superstition."[8]

Still, it took Ingersoll years of continued study to finally abandon any religious inclinations. With the publication of his 1869 lecture "Humboldt," Ingersoll openly announced his agnosticism. He passionately defended reason and science against superstition, declaring, "Superstition has always been the relentless enemy of science; faith has been a hater of demonstration; hypocrisy has been sincere only in its dread of truth, and all religions are inconsistent with mental freedom."[9] By the time he published his seminal 1872 lecture, "The Gods," in which he rejected Biblical wisdom and argued that gods were manmade, Ingersoll established himself as an infidel preachers would excoriate from the pulpit.[10]

Moody also solidified his career in Illinois, but through the churches of Chicago. Born February 5, 1837, Moody came from even humbler roots than Ingersoll. After his father's early death, young Moody and his mother worked to make ends meet. With only a slight education in Unitarianism, Moody did not fully accept Christianity until his move to Boston at the age of seventeen. Under the tutelage of his Sunday School teacher Edward Kimball, Moody accepted Christ as his lord and savior in 1855.

A year later, he left for Chicago. Initially, he worked as a shoe salesman, but after a few years volunteering in some of Chicago's most distressed areas, he decided that evangelizing for Christ was the correct path for him. He opened a church in 1863 and became heavily involved in the creation of the Chicago branches of the Young Men's Christian Association (YMCA).[11] According to historian August Fry, "Moody changed the YMCA from a group of frightened business men, praying for their tottering fortunes, to a society for the evangelization of the city [of Chicago]." Moody also honed his theology during his Chicago years, adopting a personal form of Christianity that celebrated "a belief that God is involved in the cares of men, a profound conviction that God has taken an interest in each individual."[12] Moody's Christianity, much like Ingersoll's freethought, centered on individualism, an interest they both developed during their time in Illinois.

Moody's oratorical career exploded during the 1860s and 1870s, with revivals even in Great Britain; more than 2.5 million people attended his sermons in Greater London in 1875. Equipped with an organizational zeal gained from his YMCA work and a new evangelizing partner, songwriter Ira Sankey, Moody returned to Chicago as a national figure in 1876. He built a new church, christened the "Moody Tabernacle" by newspapers, and reignited his evangelizing. He created a network of nearly one hundred churches that disseminated his religious materials and advertised his sermons. By the time his Chicago campaign ended in January 1877, Moody had reached approximately one million people, with nearly a third seeing him "in the revival's final month." [13] Moody became a formidable figure in American Protestantism during the mid- to late nineteenth century. His sermons co-opted the revivalism of the Second Great Awakening while infusing it with a newly articulated "social gospel." [14] His mantle as "America's evangelist" would remain unchallenged for decades.

While they lived in many places during their early lives, Ingersoll's and Moody's pivotal years in Illinois shaped their respective intellectual and cultural values. Both came from modest beginnings and little formal education to become two of the nineteenth century's most popular and influential public intellectuals. As such, it was inevitable that the two men would connect, either in person or in the press. The latter became true. Moody and Ingersoll likely never met, but their similar styles permeated their public debates in pamphlets and the press.

SHARED INDIVIDUALISM, DIFFERING PHILOSOPHIES

A major component of Moody's evangelism and Ingersoll's agnosticism was a commitment to rational individualism. In particular, Moody's came from two key aspects: a religious principle and a social/political principle. With the broader religious principle that influenced Moody, a belief in "religious activism, combined with the demand for personal conversions, created within evangelicalism a heavy stress upon individualism." [15] Moody believed that the best way to convert others to Christianity was by encouraging them to assert their own lives within their faith. The social/political principle stemmed from what historian Daniel J. Elazar called an "individualistic political culture," which "holds politics to be just another means by which individuals may improve themselves socially and economically. In this sense politics is a 'business' like any other that competes for talent and offers rewards to those who take it up as a career." [16] Economic historian William N. Parker agreed, writing that Midwestern culture emerged from a "blending of opposites," namely "a family-centered individualism and a community-centered corporate spirit." [17] Moody applied an individualistic, commerce-oriented political attitude to his evangelism, stressing the connection between Christianity and self-reliance.

Ingersoll's individualism shared with Moody's the social/political dimension celebrated by those from the Midwest but replaced Moody's religious dimension with a philosophical one. In particular, Ingersoll's individualism stemmed from the classical liberalism of the eighteenth and nineteenth centuries, which championed human reason, self-determination, religious toleration, and economic freedom.[18] In particular, Ingersoll expressed an affinity for the philosopher Herbert Spencer.[19] Of Spencer, Ingersoll wrote, "He sees that right and wrong do not depend upon the arbitrary will of even an infinite being, but upon the nature of things; that they are relations, not entities, and that they cannot exist, so far as we know, apart from human experience." [20] Spencer's naturalistic ethics deeply impacted Ingersoll's individualism. Yet, again, Moody's and Ingersoll's commitment to individualism emanated from their respective religious and nonreligious beliefs—Moody's evangelism and Ingersoll's agnosticism.

Moody's sermon *Heaven* (1880) and Ingersoll's lecture *Hell* (1882) serve as prime examples of their shared rational individualism but discordant philosophies.[21] Moody opens *Heaven* by addressing skeptics like Ingersoll and their view of the afterlife. "A great many persons," declared Moody, "imagine that anything said about heaven is only a matter of speculation. They talk about heaven like the air." To Moody, the inspired word of Scripture countered Ingersoll's skepticism. "What the Bible says about heaven, is just as true as what it says about everything else," Moody exclaimed. "It is inspired. What we are taught about heaven could not have come to us in any other way but by inspiration." [22] While Moody believed that the Bible was written "with more than human skill," he believed it to be compatible with human reason. As Moody further noted:

> If the Bible had anything in it that was opposed to reason, or to our sense of right, then, perhaps, we might think that it was like all the books in the world that are written merely by Men. . . . There is nothing at all in the Bible that does not conform to common sense.[23]

This argument was known as "supernatural rationalism," the view that the Bible aligns with human reason and God's revelation in nature.[24] Ingersoll, in his parallel lecture *Hell*, fiercely countered this argument, claiming, "Whenever a man appeals to a miracle he tells what is not true. Truth relies upon reason, and the undeviating course of all the laws of nature."[25] While Moody argued for a supernatural universe, Ingersoll showed the errors of reasoning within Moody's arguments. In other words, they both acted within a point-counterpoint structure, which highlighted Ingersoll's role as a critic of religion.

Moody saw heaven as the "place of victory and triumph" where believers who labored for their own salvation and rectitude resided after their death.[26] Accordingly, he believed skeptics and infidels could not vanquish believers' commitment to God. "All the infidels in the world could not convince me that I have not a different spirit than I had before I became a Christian," he declared. "'That that is born of the flesh is flesh, and that that is born of the spirit is spirit,' and a man can soon tell whether he is born of the spirit by the change in his life."[27] Moody intentionally delineated the difference between the natural and supernatural; as Ingersoll did to believers, Moody often spoke or wrote to nonbelievers in the hope that they would convert to Christianity. In the closing of his sermon, he reaffirmed this goal, stating, "Your turn and mine will come by-and-by, if we are but faithful; let us see that we do not lose the crown. Let us awake and put on the whole armor of God."[28] Moody's *Heaven* provided far more than just his take on the afterlife. It also demonstrated his belief in the supernatural preceding the natural, as well as the individual commitment one makes to God in the face of earthly problems.

Naturally, Robert Ingersoll's *Hell* presented a counterexample to a faith he saw riddled with barbarism and superstition.[29] His opening conjured a vastly different picture of the afterlife and of Christianity. "The idea of a hell," Ingersoll noted, "was born of revenge and brutality on the one side, and cowardice on the other. In my judgment the American people are too brave, too charitable, too generous, too magnanimous, to believe in the infamous dogma of an eternal hell."[30] In Ingersoll's mind, believing in the eternal torture and torment of hell ran counter to everything that he, in his modern existence and with his ethics, desired. Moody's "heaven" might be as wonderful as it appeared, but to Ingersoll, that never justified the sheer inhumanity of the doctrine of hell.

Rebuking Moody's delineation between natural and supernatural, Ingersoll outlined his view of the origins of religion. He believed that "every religion in this world is the work of man" and that "every idea in the world that man has came to him by nature."[31] Thus, he reasoned, religion was a human invention, born out of an inability to understand the natural world. What helped humanity grow beyond the superstitions of the past was increased understanding of the natural world brought forth by science and ethics. In his words, "Science has done it; education and the growing heart of man has done it."[32] In contrast to Moody's belief that evangelical progress would occur in heaven, Ingersoll believed that human progress would occur if his fellow citizens abandoned doctrines such as hell.

In later passages of his lecture, Ingersoll addresses the doctrine of divine justice, specifically the threat of eternal punishments as a means of inciting ethical change. As he wrote, "It is in the very nature of things that torments inflicted have no tendency to bring a wicked man to repentance. Then why torment him if it will not do him good? . . . Punishment inflicted for gratifying the appetite makes man not afraid but debases him."[33] Ingersoll's rational individualism influenced his belief in the rehabilitation of offenders in this life, not the supposed afterlife. Instead of anticipating the future justice of God, the position Moody defended, Ingersoll placed his confidence in the natural world and human justice.[34] Ingersoll saw earthly justice, flawed though it may be, as preferable to the malevolent threat of eternal damnation.

In his closing, Ingersoll declared that he was "willing to give up heaven to get rid of hell. I had rather there should be no heaven than that any solitary soul should be condemned to suffer for ever and ever." He also restated that the "doctrine of hell is infamous beyond all power to express. I wish there were words mean enough to express my feelings of loathing on this subject." He echoed reformers of the nineteenth century, many of whom were Protestants, when he called for a time "when every penitentiary will become a reformatory; and that if criminals go to them with hatred in their bosoms, they will leave them without feelings of revenge." Ingersoll's steadfast devotion to the real world expressly repudiated the divine pronouncements of justice by preachers like Moody. To improve the world, Ingersoll maintained, we must acknowledge it is all we have and adhere to "the great harmonies of science, which are rescuing from the prisons of superstition the torn and bleeding heart of man." [35]

With *Heaven* and *Hell*, Moody and Ingersoll grounded their moral arguments in rational terms, making the case for spiritual and humane justice, respectively. They also established their own forms of ethics, with Moody's dedicated to the higher purpose of God and Ingersoll's to the higher purpose of mankind. Their differences also highlighted their similarities. While Ingersoll denounced the Bible and Moody celebrated it, they had equally mastered the text, quoting from it copiously in each lecture and tying their arguments to Biblical explanations or obfuscations. As such, *Heaven* and *Hell* demonstrated Moody and Ingersoll's relationship as foils in the public debate between evangelicalism and freethought during the era.

A more direct exchange between them occurred after Moody published his 1896 sermon, *Sowing and Reaping*.[36] In it, he made the case that individual initiative and personal responsibility were ways to become closer to God. "Our whole life is thus bounded and governed by laws ordained and established by God," Moody declared, "and that a man reaps what he sows is a law that can be easily observed and verified, whether we regard sowing to the flesh or sowing to the Spirit." [37] Moody, framing divine law as "sowing and reaping," gave believers in his version of Christianity a sense of *agency*—reasserting the role of the individual. Ingersoll, with his own commitment to individualism, would have appreciated Moody's pronouncement about agency but would have balked at the idea that such agency came from God.

Continuing on this theme, Moody added, "Just as we cannot reap a good harvest unless we have sown good seed, so we cannot reap eternal life unless we have sown to the spirit." In other words, our ability to reap the fortunes of God relied on our making "the most of the opportunities God has given us. It depends a good deal on ourselves what our future shall be." An individual's material and ethical success translated into spiritual success. However, Moody continued, "be not deceived" and commit the error of worshipping riches, for "he who sets his heart upon money is sowing to the flesh, and shall of the flesh reap corruption."[38] Moody believed in a Christianized ethic of self-reliance whereby material success fostered ethical and spiritual responsibilities. Thus, Moody's individualism also contained a component of duty, in which one's personal choices must reaffirm one's commitment to God.

Even though *Sowing and Reaping* became a successful lecture for Moody, Ingersoll wasted no time in criticizing it. In an undated article, Ingersoll laid out his objections.[39] "The trouble with this sermon," wrote Ingersoll, "is that he [Moody] contradicts it." He elaborated:

> There is no forgiveness in nature. But Mr. Moody tells us that a man may sow thistles and gather figs, that having acted like a fiend for seventy years, he can, between his last dose of medicine and his last breath, repent; that he can be washed clean by the blood of the lamb, and that myriads of angels will carry his soul to heaven—in other words, that this man will not reap what he sowed, but what Christ sowed, that this man's thistles will be changed to figs. . . .
>
> This doctrine, to my mind, is not only absurd, but dishonest and corrupting.[40]

To Ingersoll, no amount of "sowing" a person did in this life equaled the forgiveness of sins through Christ. According to Moody, a person could be terrible, what he called "sowing seeds of the flesh," and be forgiven in a flash, negating whatever that person had previously done. Ingersoll's criticism of *Sowing and Reaping* insisted that secular individualism was not only more logical but also more ethically applicable than Moody's individualism.

Ingersoll ends the article expressing his dedication to his own ethics and with a bromide to Moody. "Theology is a curse," wrote Ingersoll, "Science is a blessing. We do not need preachers, but teachers; not priests, but thinkers; not churches, but schools; not steeples, but observatories. We want knowledge. Let us hope that Mr. Moody will read some really useful books."[41] Ingersoll placed his own individualism within the confines of reason and reality, as he saw it. There was no need for calls to do right in anticipation of some eternal reward. Humans should be good to each other now, when it counted, because it did not matter to God's supposed plan. While they both held individualism and rationality as key values, Ingersoll placed his ethics within a secular framework, whereas Moody championed a Christian one.

1897–1898: THE CRUCIAL YEARS

Moody and Ingersoll spent 1897 and 1898 practically following each other on the lecture circuit, both in the hopes of good news coverage and to have public intellectual battles. One interesting encounter was recorded by the *St. Louis Post-Dispatch*. In April 1897, Moody and Ingersoll both passed through St. Louis and ended up at the same hotel.[42] In an interview with the *Post-Dispatch*, Moody challenged Ingersoll to find faults in his lecture *Sowing and Reaping*, putting Ingersoll on the defensive. "You go to Ingersoll when he gets here and show him my sermon on 'Sowing and Reaping,'" Moody said. "If he denies anything in it you let me know. Send me a marked copy of the paper, will you? I'd just like to see what he'd say about it." It is unclear whether Moody actually received something from the St. Louis reporters, but his taunting arguably inspired Ingersoll's later comments on *Sowing and Reaping*.[43] They also gave orations in St. Louis within days of each other; Moody delivered *Sowing and Reaping* on April 8 and 9, and Ingersoll delivered *Truth* on April 12.[44] They also answered questions for a joint interview in the *New York Journal*. Moody responded that he prayed for Ingersoll's conversion because "he is a better man than Saul of Tarsus. . . . I understand that he is a moral man, an exemplary husband and father."[45] Ingersoll replied in kind, saying Moody "is a good man, but his ideas are too old."[46] Even at their most contentious, their disagreements were intellectual, not personal.

By 1898, Ingersoll's and Moody's parallel speaking dates moved to Indiana. This is when Moody appeared too close, to the displeasure of Ingersoll. On April 30, 1898, Ingersoll wrote to his daughters from Fort Wayne, days after he delivered a lecture on Abraham Lincoln to an enthusiastic crowd in Indianapolis. However, the lecture had been met with some criticism. "Many tried to heal me in that town," wrote Ingersoll. "The Christians sent and got Mr. Moody to come and hold two tree meetings [likely sermons] on the same day."[47] Moody did, in fact, hold two prayer meetings in Indianapolis shortly after Ingersoll reportedly gave his lecture, but the *Indianapolis News* failed to mention Ingersoll.[48] Regardless, the claim Ingersoll made of hostile crowds in Indiana holds weight, seeing as he was harassed by ministers in Terre Haute when he delivered his lecture "Why I Am an Agnostic" there in May 1898.[49] As with their intellectual sparring in the press, Ingersoll and Moody continued to serve points and counterpoints back and forth on their lecture circuit, with Moody responding to Ingersoll and vice versa. Sadly, this lively intellectual back-and-forth ended less than a year later.

Conclusion: A Complicated Relationship

On July 21, 1899, Robert Ingersoll died of heart failure at his home in New York; tributes from friends and foes filled the newspapers. A few days later, the press asked Moody about the orator's death, and while he reaffirmed his belief that Ingersoll was an "exemplary man in his home life," he nonetheless regarded Ingersoll's view of Christianity as "twisted" by its "dark side."[50] Paralleling Ingersoll again, Moody died just months later, also of heart failure, on December 22, 1899. Ira Sankey, his former songwriting partner, commented that Moody was "one of the most remarkable men of the century, distinguished especially for his devotion to the cause of Christ and the preaching of the Gospel to the world."[51] It was truly the end of an era.

Ingersoll and Moody represented two sides of America's intellectual identity: one steeped in faith and another enriched by freethought. While they never faced off in person, Ingersoll and Moody shaped each other's arguments and oratory for the American public, at least in relation to their views of one another. However, to simply call them orators would be a disservice to them both. Ingersoll was a public intellectual who synthesized philosophy, theology, and science into evidences and arguments the average American could understand. Moody was a talented evangelist who dedicated his life to broadening the appeal of Christianity to the masses, particularly those living in a new capitalist age.

More important, they each cultivated a compelling, moralistic view of rational individualism. Moody's rational individuals concerned themselves with living exceptionally through their faith in Christ. Ingersoll, by contrast, believed that this earthly life was the only guaranteed life and that we should live as reasonable, ethical individuals in order to build a better society. Their individualism, cultivated in part by their years in the Midwest, inexorably tied them together. As the *Fond du Lac Reporter* wrote, "Moody says Bob Ingersoll is a good man, but misguided. Ingersoll says Moody is misguided, but is a good man. According to their estimates of each other, there does not seem to be much difference between the two gentlemen."[52] The *Reporter* and Mencken were right: Robert Ingersoll and Dwight Moody were complementary partners in an intellectual dance that reshaped American thought during the late nineteenth century.

NOTES

1. H. L. Mencken, *Prejudices: Fourth, Fifth, and Sixth Series*, ed. Marion Elizabeth Rodgers (New York: Library of America, 2010), 525, 527.
2. Robert Ingersoll to S. C. Windsor, November 9, 1887, in Robert Ingersoll, *The Letters of Robert G. Ingersoll*, ed. Eva Ingersoll Wakefield (Westport, CT: Greenwood Press, 1951), 293.
3. Robert Ingersoll to Isaac H. Julian, Esq., July 18, 1892, in Ingersoll, *The Letters of Robert G. Ingersoll*, 335.
4. Orvin P. Larson, *American Infidel: Robert G. Ingersoll* (New York: Citadel Press, 1962; Madison: Freedom from Religion Foundation, 1993), 39.
5. Robert Ingersoll to General Charles H. T. Collis, February 15, 1893, in Ingersoll, *The Letters of Robert G. Ingersoll*, 342; Larson, *American Infidel*, 75–77.
6. Robert Ingersoll, "Orthodoxy," in *The Works of Robert G. Ingersoll*, ed. C. P. Farrell, vol. 2, *Lectures* (New York: Ingersoll League, 1929), 380.
7. Larson, *American Infidel*, 51–52.
8. Robert Ingersoll, "The Gods," in *The Works of Robert G. Ingersoll*, ed. C. P. Farrell, vol. 1, *Lectures* (New York: Ingersoll League, 1929), iii.
9. Robert Ingersoll, "Humboldt," in *The Works of Robert G. Ingersoll*, ed. C. P. Farrell, vol. 1, *Lectures* (New York: Ingersoll League, 1929), 99, 104.
10. Ingersoll, "The Gods," 7–90.
11. James F. Findlay Jr., *Dwight L. Moody: American Evangelist, 1837–1899* (Chicago: University of Chicago Press, 1969), 26–53; J. C. Pollock, *Moody: A Biographical Portrait of the Pacesetter in Modern Mass Evangelism* (New York: Macmillan Company, 1963), 17; August J. Fry, *D. L. Moody:*

The Chicago Years, 1856–1871 (Amsterdam: Free University Press, 1984), 15; Edwin Gaustad and Leigh Schmidt, *The Religious History of America: The Heart of the American Story from Colonial Times to Today* (San Francisco: Harper San Francisco, 2002), 222.

12. Fry, *D. L. Moody*, 12, 33, 71.

13. Bruce J. Evensen, *God's Man for the Gilded Age: D. L. Moody and the Rise of Modern Mass Evangelism* (Oxford: Oxford University Press, 2003), 43, 136–144, 156.

14. Findlay Jr., *Dwight L. Moody*, 3.

15. D. L. Moody, *Heaven: Where It Is, Its Inhabitants, and How to Get There* (Chicago: F. H. Revell, 1880), 43; Findlay Jr., *Dwight L. Moody*, 82.

16. Daniel J. Elazar, *American Federalism: A View from the States* (New York: Thomas Y. Crowell, 1966), 86–87.

17. William N. Parker, "From Northwest to Midwest: Social Bases of a Regional History," in *Essays in Nineteenth Century Economic History: The Old Northwest*, ed. David C. Klingaman and Richard K. Vedder (Athens: Ohio University Press, 1975), 13.

18. On classical liberalism, see George H. Smith, *The System of Liberty: Themes in the History of Classical Liberalism* (Cambridge, MA: Cambridge University Press, 2013).

19. For Spencer's concept of individualism, see Mark Francis, *Herbert Spencer and the Invention of Modern Life* (Ithaca, NY: Cornell University Press, 2007), 310–311.

20. Robert Ingersoll, "Preface to Prof. Van Buren Denslow's *Modern Thinkers*," in *The Works of Robert G. Ingersoll*, ed. C. P. Farrell, vol. 12, *Tributes and Miscellany* (New York: Ingersoll League, 1929), 10–11.

21. Robert Ingersoll, *Hell: Warm Words on the Cheerful and Comforting Doctrine of Eternal Damnation* (London: Watts & Co., 1882); Moody, *Heaven*.

22. Moody, *Heaven*, 7.

23. Moody, *Heaven*, 7.

24. Conrad Wright, *The Beginnings of Unitarianism in America* (Boston: Starr King Press, 1955), 135.

25. Ingersoll, *Hell*, 4.

26. Moody, *Heaven*, 65.

27. Moody, *Heaven*, 67–68.

28. Moody, *Heaven*, 107.

29. Ingersoll, *Hell*, 4.

30. Ingersoll, *Hell*, 3.

31. Ingersoll, *Hell*, 3.

32. Ingersoll, *Hell*, 4.

33. Ingersoll, *Hell*, 12.

34. Ingersoll, *Hell*, 13.

35. Ingersoll, *Hell*, 14; Jennifer Graber, *The Furnace of Affliction: Prisons and Religion in Antebellum America* (Chapel Hill: University of North Carolina Press, 2011).

36. The title and overall concept came from a passage in Galatians: "Be not deceived; God is not mocked: for whatsoever a man soweth, that shall he also reap." (Galatians 7:7–8, as quoted in Dwight Moody, *Sowing and Reaping* [Chicago: Fleming H. Revell Company, 1896], 9, Project Gutenberg).

37. Moody, *Sowing and Reaping*, 14–15.

38. Moody, *Sowing and Reaping*, 19–20, 24, 40.

39. Robert Ingersoll, "Sowing and Reaping," in *The Works of Robert G. Ingersoll*, ed. C. P. Farrell, vol. 11, *Miscellany* (Dresden, NY: Dresden Publishing Company, 1902), 887–895, Project Gutenberg. This likely appeared originally as "Ingersoll on Moody," *Chicago World*, April 7, 1897, reel 32, slides 58–59, Robert Ingersoll Papers, Library of Congress.

40. Ingersoll, "Sowing and Reaping," 889–890.

41. Ingersoll, "Sowing and Reaping," 895.

42. "Evangelists and Infidel," *St. Louis Post-Dispatch*, April 8, 1897, 3, reel 32, slide 82, Robert Ingersoll Papers, Library of Congress.

43. "Ingersoll Not in His Class," *St. Louis Post-Dispatch*, April 9, 1897, reel 32, slide 82, Robert Ingersoll Papers, Library of Congress.

44. "Moody's Words Brought Tears," *St. Louis Post-Dispatch*, April 8, 1897, 12, Newspaper Microfilm Collection, Library of Congress; "Dwight Moody's Closing Talk," *St. Louis Post-Dispatch*, April 9, 1897, 7, Newspaper Microfilm Collection, Library of Congress; "Col. Ingersoll on 'Truth,'" *St. Louis Globe Democrat*, April 12, 1897, 2, Newspaper Microfilm Collection, Library of Congress.

45. "Ingersoll, Moody, and Miss Couzens—Hear Them," *New York Journal*, April 12, 1897, reel 32, slide 100, Robert Ingersoll Papers, Library of Congress.

46. "Ingersoll, Moody, and Miss Couzens."

47. Robert Ingersoll to "Girls," Fort Wayne, Indiana, April 30, 1898, box 1, folder 5, Gordon Stein Collection of Robert Ingersoll, Southern Illinois University Special Collections. It is unclear what Ingersoll meant by "tree meeting." Perhaps it was an outside gathering, which Moody had done scores of times in the past (Evensen, *God's Man for the Gilded Age*, 62–65).

48. "The Moody Meetings," *Indianapolis News*, April 13, 1898, 9, Hoosier State Chronicles.

49. "Colonel Robert G. Ingersoll," *Saturday Evening Mail* (Terre Haute, IN), April 30, 1898, 5, Hoosier State Chronicles; "Short and Spicy," *Hoosier State* (Newport, IN), May 18, 1898, 1, Newspaper Archive.

50. "Col. Ingersoll Dies Smiling," *Chicago Daily Tribune*, July 22, 1899, 1, Newspaper Microfilm Collection, Library of Congress; "Moody's View of Ingersoll," *Chicago Tribune*, July 24, 1899, 2, Newspaper Microfilm Collection, Library of Congress.

51. "Dwight L. Moody, Preacher to 7,000,000, Dies in the Hope He Offered to Others," *New York World*, December 23, 1899, 15, Newspapers.com.

52. *Fond du Lac Reporter*, April 1897, reel 32, slide 90, Robert Ingersoll Papers, Library of Congress.

CHAPTER 7

An Easterner in the Hinterland

Horace Meyer Kallen, the University of Wisconsin, and the Regional Roots of Cultural Pluralism, 1911–1918

Michael C. Steiner

Jewish American philosopher Horace Meyer Kallen (1882–1974) is widely recognized as the creator of the concept of cultural pluralism. He lived a long and remarkably productive life, one that included teaching at the New School for Social Research in New York City for fifty-four years, publishing thirty-nine books and more than three hundred articles on a vast range of topics, receiving a string of academic accolades and honorary degrees, and corresponding with many of the most significant figures of the twentieth century, including T. S. Eliot and Albert Einstein. Of these many achievements, cultural pluralism is his lasting legacy, the continually relevant idea that remains connected to his name.

Kallen's role in the birth of cultural pluralism has been thoroughly debated and dissected, but missing from this literature is careful consideration of how the concept was shaped by where Kallen lived. The idea reached its full expression in the Midwest during Kallen's seven eventful years there between 1911 and 1918. Elements of cultural pluralism had been slowly evolving in Kallen's consciousness since his education at Harvard from 1900 until 1906, but only after moving to Madison five years later to teach at the University of Wisconsin did those intellectual seeds take root and flower in full form.

The few critics who have mentioned Kallen's Midwestern years consider them to be a largely fruitless exile in an inhospitable hinterland.

Images of a disgruntled expatriate, a stranger in a strange land, counting the days until he can return to a more congenial place, dominate Kallen scholarship. Many otherwise deeply thoughtful scholars interpret Kallen's Wisconsin years as a disappointing interlude that came too late to shape his theory. Milton Konvitz argues, for example, that all of the "essential ingredients of what later came to be known as cultural pluralism" were in place before Kallen arrived at Wisconsin in 1911 and that he spent the next seven years longing "to be in Boston or New York where he could attend meetings . . . and influence men and action." Sara Schmidt simply states, "Kallen never really adjusted to Wisconsin," and concludes, "Perhaps alone at Madison, he felt the need to assert his Jewish selfhood more strongly." Matthew Kaufman's recent assessment that "Although he had been at the University of Wisconsin since 1911, he had been unhappy there almost from the beginning" sums up the standard interpretation of Kallen's heartland years.[1]

Kallen's Midwest experience was far more consequential than we have been led to believe. His highly eventful years of teaching in and traveling throughout the region precipitated a concept that continues to reverberate. How the Midwest molded this idea is a complex story with many strands and contributing actors. This chapter focuses on one dimension of that narrative: how Kallen's experiences and interactions at the University of Wisconsin in Madison, especially during his first four years there, from 1911 to 1915, shaped a concept that has influenced discussions of diversity ever since.

Twenty-nine-year-old Horace Kallen arrived in Madison in mid-September 1911 to start a tenure-track teaching position in the philosophy and rhetoric departments. The deeply rooted New Englander had a complex reaction to his radically new environment. Growing up in Boston as the son of an impoverished rabbi; studying at Harvard where he had worked closely with intellectual luminaries William James, George Santayana, and Josiah Royce; teaching briefly at Princeton; and traveling to Oxford and Paris on a postdoctoral fellowship right before accepting the position at Madison, Kallen was a devoted and ethnically sensitive easterner. He had never ventured west of the Hudson and was wary about what he would meet in Wisconsin, and his first impressions of the region were understandably mixed, filled with apprehension and cautious enthusiasm about this dramatically different place.

Kallen's new university had been established in 1848, the year of Wisconsin's statehood. It became a land grant university under the Morrill Act in 1866, launched doctoral programs in the 1890s, and by 1900 had emerged, according to historian David S. Brown, as "the Middle West's most dynamic educational center."[2] The university's reputation continued to grow over the next decade, and when Kallen arrived in 1911, his Harvard mentors cheered him on, praising the upstart Midwestern campus. "The clouds have broken for you," exalted Kallen's Harvard undergraduate advisor, Barrett Wendell. "Here you have . . . a real chance to make yourself a future at what I have come to believe the best of all our Western universities; and this means in my heart of hearts of America."[3]

With over 3,400 students and 188 faculty members by 1910, the University of Wisconsin was one of the nation's largest and most respected universities when Kallen arrived. The city of Madison, with 25,000 people, presented a sharp contrast to the dense polyglot metropolis of 650,000 inhabitants Kallen had just left in Boston. His new campus, despite its bucolic, small-city setting on the south shore of Lake Mendota, was justifiably proud of its emerging cosmopolitanism and connections across the state's ethnically diverse countryside. University alumnus and recently elected US Senator Robert M. La Follette was at the height of his career as a driving force for progressive reform. Paralleling these efforts, the Madison campus had launched a vigorous program of university outreach in 1904 known as the Wisconsin Idea. As articulated by university president, Charles Van Hise, who in 1905 declared, "I shall never be content until the beneficent influence of the University reaches every family of the state," this progressive effort attracted national attention as a model of statewide cultural experimentation.[4]

Kallen had tangled emotions and mixed impressions as he began a new life at this rising Midwestern university. He arrived in Chicago in early September 1911, lingering there for several days before taking the train 150 miles north to Madison. His first impressions of Chicago and Madison and of the university and its faculty were vividly expressed in two personal sources: in a private journal Kallen kept during his first two months in the region and in letters to family and friends back in Boston. His letters are often filled with the day-to-day concerns and anxieties of a new faculty member, while his journal tells a more impressionistic and often buoyant story.

From his hotel room in Chicago on September 15, 1911, Kallen noted in his journal, "I have a Jewish impression and that is that Chicago has no Jews. The most notable thing is the dominance of business. . . . Everything is scattered pell mell & smoke & railroads are pervasive."[5] Kallen's sense of Chicago as a great powerhouse remained; his impression that "Chicago has no Jews," on the other hand, quickly changed as he became acquainted with the city's German Jewish elite within a year, exchanging ideas and socializing with renowned Judge Julian Mack, Reformed Rabbi Emil Hirsch, philanthropist Julius Rosenwald, writer Ben Hecht, and others on frequent trips to the city.[6]

Arriving in Madison after his exposure to Chicago, Kallen noted in his journal, "The hopefulness and pride of place which marked Chicago are unmistakable here," and he then wrote a sweeping, sensitive portrait, in many ways a paean to Wisconsin and the Midwest. Of his new surroundings Kallen commented, "There is a pagan Hellenistic quality in the civic sense. The abyss of corruption . . . & the hardship of pioneer life are *just* behind. The call of the wild is still audible & sometimes insistent. . . . The beast is conquered, but not assimilated." Creatively mixing classical Greek history with a sense of the American frontier, Kallen observed, "The civic pride of Wisconsin is much like the pride of the Hellenes—like Aristotle—that they are not cannibals. And La Follette, indeed, occupies a place in their minds not unlike that of Theseus in the minds of Athenians. He has led them from savagery to some kind of civilization."[7]

Commenting on the "hard-headed" and "earthbound . . . Northern European peasants" who had settled this new land, Kallen voiced the Turnerian hope that "the last 20 years seem to have given the children of these people a new tone—the necessary inward spirit which . . . gives rise to hopefulness, to illusion." He concluded, "I realize here for the first time in my life, what is meant when it is said that this country is a 'new country,'" and he would soon learn that this fresh landscape brimmed with ethnic and intellectual complexity.[8]

Kallen's complex feelings about his new environment and university were expressed again in a highly detailed ten-page journal entry on October 11, 1911. After attending a late Monday afternoon gathering of the University Literary Club and listening to academic papers presented by four new colleagues, Kallen wrote a striking account of his extremely mixed reactions. Impressed with thoughtful presentations by historians Carl Russell Fish and Frederic Logan Paxson, and heartened by Jewish American psychologist Joseph Jastrow's talk on Zionism, Kallen was appalled by the last talk of the evening, the extemporaneous comments given by a distinguished colleague described by Kallen as "a man above middle height, thinnish, gawky, dressed in a swallow tail, with large hands & monotonous voice."[9]

Discussing racial distinctions, the final speaker argued, in Kallen's recollection, that "the negroes in their own country have contributed nothing to civilization. The white, the yellow, & the brown races have. Not so the negroes. Wherever they are left to themselves they are barbarous. In Brazil, in Haiti, in America. In truth the leaders of negroes are negroes who are ½ or ¼ white." As Kallen recalled, the colleague then declared, "Wherever the negroes are left to themselves, there is filth, disease, lechery," and concluded, "Negroes are a conquered people." Expressing disgust with this racist rant, Kallen noted in his journal: "The man's delivery was extraordinary . . . a curious staccato" filled with "a strangely disagreeable ineptitude and insufficiency." When Kallen asked his new friend, Jastrow, who sat nearby, "Who was this person?" Jastrow whispered: "Why that's president Van Hise, haven't you ever met him?"[10] This was a ragged start for the young philosopher, who found himself in a surprisingly stimulating yet deeply disturbing academic environment that would both inspire and provoke him over the next seven years.

As his astute observations reveal, Kallen was at the peak of his powers and deeply sensitive to racial and ethnic slights and injustices. His dismay over Van Hise's blatant racism was countered by his delight in discovering Jastrow and other Zionists and progressive thinkers on campus. Tall and physically robust, Kallen was keenly sensitive to countering the popular stereotype of Jewish men as being physically weak and mentally devious, and ethnic uplift and Zionism became increasingly important driving forces in his new environment.[11]

Kallen's letters to family and friends in Boston are far less exuberant than his journal entries. Responding to his early complaints about being isolated and overworked, Kallen's former Harvard colleague Ralph Barton Perry wrote on November 1, 1911, "I am sorry to hear that things are not more to your liking at Madison" and urged him to seek out other displaced easterners on the faculty. Ten days later, Alice James, the widow of Kallen's mentor, William James, wrote to the young, seemingly stranded philosopher, urging him to be more open to his new place and wisely emphasizing, "After all one must take people and places for what they are—not for what they are not."[12]

His sense of displacement seemed to pass through several phases, waxing and waning as Kallen grew more accustomed to his new university and region. In March 1913, philosopher Hugo Munsterberg encouraged his former student, stressing that "Wisconsin must be full of interest and intellectual stimulation. A certain time of new adjustment is of course needed, but I feel sure you will be very happy there." As late as December 1916, Kallen reported to his sister Miriam that "nothing happens at this end. I find I simply cannot write and teach too; the distractions are too much for concentrated work."[13] Yet despite these complaints, it became clear through his early journal entries and increasing connections with a variety of new colleagues and campus visitors that Kallen soon followed Alice James's advice to accept new people and places "for what they are— not for what they are not," and he began to realize that Madison, Chicago, and the Midwest in general were, in Munsterberg's words, "full of interest and intellectual stimulation."

At the same time that he expressed frustration with his surroundings, Kallen gingerly embraced his new university, state, and region, expanding his frame of reference and learning to value the state and region's political culture and ethnic diversity. The Midwest, and Wisconsin in particular, was fertile ground for pluralist thought. German, Scandinavian, and Polish immigrants and their children constituted more than 50 percent of Wisconsin's population during Kallen's years there, making it the state with the second-highest proportion of foreign-born residents (next to Minnesota) in the years leading up to World War I. Wisconsin also had a rich mosaic of other European groups, including 28,500 German and Eastern European Jews living primarily in its urban centers, and the state's residents of "native white heritage" were a distinct minority, constituting less than one-third of the state's population in 1910.[14]

Wisconsin was especially ripe for pluralist thought during the decade before the war, and after moving beyond his initial sense of dislocation, Kallen became deeply impressed with the state's vital ethnic matrix. By

1912, he was journeying across the state and region to give talks promoting Zionist organizations at college campuses, small towns, and cities. A tireless Zionist circuit rider, Kallen visited Chicago, Cleveland, St. Louis, Minneapolis, St. Paul, Cincinnati, Kansas City, and smaller Midwestern towns within his first three years at Madison, promoting the cause across the region and eventually the nation. His discovery during these travels of a mosaic of interacting immigrant communities across a wide regional landscape informed his pluralist vision. The rising region became the geographical template for cultural pluralism, and it was with the publication of "Democracy Versus the Melting Pot" as a two-part article in two issues of *The Nation* in February 1915 that Kallen's theory reached its full form indelibly shaped by the Midwest.[15]

In addition to Kallen's experiences in the regional hinterland, his emerging relationships with colleagues at Madison, especially during his first four years there, profoundly shaped his theory. Despite complaints and professed isolation, he soon became involved in a lively campus culture. During his first months at Madison, he met Milwaukee's socialist mayor Emil Seidel as well as future Pulitzer Prize–winning playwright Zona Gale from Portage, who both spoke at the university.[16] By November 1912, the vigorous young instructor was participating in university theatrical productions, writing and acting in several plays and historical pageants sponsored by the Wisconsin Players, and performing across the state.[17]

During his frequent trips to Chicago, Kallen often visited the office of the literary journal *The Dial* on South Dearborn Street. He soon became a frequent contributor and a close friend of the magazine's young editor, George Bernard Donlin. Kallen also spent time with playwright Maurice Browne, who had emigrated from England in 1912 to launch the influential Chicago Little Theatre with his American wife, actor Ellen Van Volkenburg. Kallen was a frequent member of Browne and Van Volkenburg's Sunday afternoon discussion group in the Fine Arts Building where he interacted with many of Chicago's literary figures, including Theodore Dreiser, Vachel Lindsay, Harriet Monroe, and Carl Sandburg. Writing in 1914 to Henrietta Szold, the founder of the major women's Zionist organization Hadassah, Kallen described his Chicago meetings and how Browne and Van Volkenburg had "enthusiastically agreed to organize a company of Jewish players who will present nationalistic plays all over the country, in the same way the Irish Players are presenting Irish plays." He added that he had agreed to write three plays of his own, "one of which must be a comedy."[18]

These Herculean outreach efforts bore fruit in surprising ways. Literary historian Howard Mumford Jones, for example, recounted acting as a Wisconsin undergraduate in the years right before World War I in a play that was written, directed, and co-acted by Kallen. In this play depicting the trials of Job and produced by the Wisconsin Players, Jones recalled, "Horace Kallen was Job, and I played the role of Bildad the Shuhite . . . looking as mournful as I could while Kallen recited despairing cadences."[19]

The gregarious young instructor interacted with students in other ways. Undergraduate philosopher and future historian Marvin Lowenthal warmly recalled Kallen's many lunch and dinner conversations with groups of students in Lathrop Hall and his riveting Zionist beliefs. Political activist Ammon Hennacy, who would become a leading Catholic Worker advocate, had positive memories from his time as a Wisconsin undergraduate of "a seminar of an unofficial sort at the home of radical Horace M. Kallen," and the young instructor also held a series of off-campus gatherings to discuss philosophical radicalism and encourage ethnic pride among Jewish students.[20]

Kallen promoted the university's extension and outreach efforts. In a direct link to the Wisconsin Idea, Kallen invited Mary Antin, a fellow Boston-based Jewish intellectual and author of the best-selling assimilationist autobiography *The Promised Land* (1912), to teach a summer extension course at Madison. "I still thrill over the idea of the university going to the people," she wrote him. "I haven't got over that phase of my appreciation of things American, and never shall, I fear."[21]

The versatile young philosopher made lasting intellectual friendships with a cross section of his Wisconsin colleagues. He came to know famed psychologist Joseph Jastrow, who, along with his wife, Rachel Szold, and her sister, Henrietta, worked with the philosopher to promote Zionism and the Hadassah movement in the Midwest and elsewhere. He crossed paths with a young Polish-born and Wisconsin-trained economist and labor historian, Selig Perlman, whose *A Theory of the Labor Movement* (1928) remains a classic analysis of American labor history.[22]

Kallen was also undoubtedly aware of the work of two prominent university antiwar advocates: English instructor Julia Grace Wales and campus peace activist Louis Lochner. At the outbreak of war in Europe, Canadian-born Wales began working with Jane Addams, and Wales's vision of a "Neutral Conference for Continuous Mediation," commonly known as the Wisconsin Plan, became a centerpiece of Addams's ill-fated antiwar efforts at the Women's Peace Conference at The Hague in April 1915.[23] Lochner, who became a Pulitzer Prize–winning journalist in 1939 for his coverage of the rise of Nazism, began his long career as a writer and crusading pacifist as a student activist at Madison. Founder of the campus International Club in 1907 and editor of the *Wisconsin Alumni Magazine* from 1909 until 1916, Lochner was deeply involved, along with Wales and Addams, in peace efforts leading up to and during World War I, serving as director of the Emergency Peace Foundation in Chicago in 1915 and delegate to The Hague several times between 1909 and 1915 in an antiwar capacity.[24]

While Kallen was acquainted with Wales and Lochner through their antiwar efforts, he began lifelong, deeply influential friendships with two Madison faculty members with firm pacifist beliefs. Vivian Trow Thayer was a philosophy graduate student and progressive educator who eventually became head of the Ethical Culture Society in Manhattan. Max Otto was a German-born philosopher who shared Kallen's bitter disillusionment at the height of the campus loyalty crusade of 1917 and 1918. Kallen and Otto met one another as boarders at the Thayer house during Kallen's first year at Madison, and the three young philosophers formed lasting friendships. Kallen's connection with Thayer continued during their later New York years, but his friendship with Otto was especially profound, lasting throughout their long careers as influential public philosophers, Otto at Wisconsin from 1908 until 1968 and Kallen at the New School for Social Research in New York from 1919 until 1974.[25]

Kallen had more distant but highly significant relationships with three prominent social scientists on the faculty. Progressive economists Richard T. Ely and John R. Commons came to Madison in 1892 and 1904, respectively, and firebrand sociologist Edward Alsworth Ross arrived in 1906, a few years after being fired at Stanford University for making anti-Chinese statements. As moderate Christian socialists, both Ely and Commons had been victims of witch hunts early in their careers:

Commons was dismissed from Syracuse University in 1899 for being a radical, and Ely was summoned before a Wisconsin faculty committee in 1894 on charges of promoting socialist doctrines. Ely's exoneration, with his former Johns Hopkins student Frederick Jackson Turner leading the defense, was a milestone in academic freedom, giving birth to the university's ringing declaration later that year of the need to "ever encourage that continual and fearless sifting and winnowing by which alone the truth can be found."[26]

Although Turner left Wisconsin for Harvard in 1910, the year before Kallen arrived at the Madison campus, the young philosopher was clearly influenced by Turner's as well as Josiah Royce's pioneering theories of the section and the province as seedbeds of cultural diversity and bulwarks against tidal waves of mass emotion. As early as 1901, Royce, who was one of Kallen's Harvard mentors, had promoted a "wise provincialism" to serve as a breakwater for minority groups against the "mob spirit" of the nation-state; by 1909, Turner used his native Wisconsin as a model for advocating a healthy "sectionalism" (a label he used instead of "regionalism") for its ability to "check the deadening uniformity of national consolidation."[27]

While Kallen was inspired by Turner's and Royce's theories, his relationship with Ely and Commons was deeply conflicted, especially with the approach of war. Although he benefited from Ely's early free-speech stand and admired Commons's pro-union vision of labor history, both economists held repressive beliefs that Kallen rejected. Each supported severe immigration quotas and the eugenics movement. Both men voiced occasional anti-Semitism and would strongly endorse the brutal 1917 campus loyalty crusade and champion efforts to censure and remove La Follette from the US Senate—all causes and ideologies Kallen scorned.[28]

Ely's and Commons's positions were mild compared with Ross's virulent xenophobia and outspoken anti-Semitism. He became, in many ways, Kallen's intellectual nemesis and academic provocateur. A lightning rod of controversy throughout his long and prolific career, Iowa-born Ross, who has been described as "the founding father of modern American sociology," championed ideologies across the political spectrum.[29] As a free speech advocate, moderate feminist, and committed socialist, Ross came close to being fired for promoting anarchist Emma Goldman's campus visit in 1910, stood for women's suffrage, and admired the Bolshevik Revolution after traveling across Russia in 1917.[30]

Yet, as a staunch Nordic supremacist, vigorous eugenicist, and champion of severe immigration restriction, Ross embodied many of the most reactionary aspects of American progressivism. He coined the popular concepts of race suicide and social control in 1901, and in 1914 he published an influential exclusionary treatise, *The Old World in the New*, one of a series of increasingly shrill xenophobic tracts that included David Starr Jordan's *The Blood of the Nation: A Study of the Decay of Nations Through the Survival of the Unfit* (1910), Madison Grant's *The Passing of the Great Race* (1916), and Lothrop Stoddard's *The Rising Tide of Color Against the White World-Supremacy* (1920). While Kallen scathingly dismissed Grant's dangerous message with a swift one-sentence analysis—"Moral: Restrict immigration and compel blonds to breed"—his rejoinder to Ross's quasi-scientific tract was more complex and deeply consequential.[31]

The Old World in the New stoked nativist fears by railing against a flood-tide of inferior races on the American shore. Distressed by the death of the frontier and its dwindling ranks of Anglo-Saxon settlers, Ross intoned that "we now confront the melancholy spectacle of this pioneer breed being swamped and submerged by an overwhelming tide of late comers from the old-world hive." He warned that "the blood now being injected into the veins of our people is 'sub-common,' and the Caliban type shows up with a frequency that is startling." This dark vision of prolific "sub-common" hordes swamping a frontierless nation outraged Kallen, and sharing a campus with one of the nation's foremost xenophobes had a galvanizing effect on his thought.[32]

Ross's Nordic racism and exclusionism were antithetical to Kallen's commitment to Zionism and to the revitalizing influence of open immigration. As an influential public intellectual and exclusionary firebrand on the same campus as Kallen, Ross was impossible to ignore. His ruthless critique of Jewish immigrants in particular, asserting that "lower class Jews of Eastern Europe reach here moral cripples, their souls warped and dwarfed by iron circumstances" and that they soon develop "a monstrous and repulsive love of gain," affronted Kallen personally and intellectually. Ross's contention, for example, that "Hebrews are the polar opposite of our pioneer breed. . . . They are undersized and weak-muscled . . . shun bodily activity and are excessively sensitive to pain," demanded a response, and within a few months Kallen published his withering rebuke, "Democracy versus the Melting Pot" (1915), that marked the full expression of his seminal concept.[33]

Complicating Kallen's retort was Ross's position as both an ardent exclusionist and a cautious assimilationist, viewpoints Kallen found almost equally distasteful. Ross's scurrilous images of Jewish immigrants were countered, ironically enough, by his notion that if Jews arrived in controlled numbers, they would happily discard their old culture and eagerly assimilate to the new. In words that offended Kallen's pluralist convictions, Ross speculated, "America is probably the strongest solvent Jewish separatism has ever encountered," and he concluded that "immigrant Jews are being assimilated outwardly." "The long coat, side curls, beards and fringes, the 'Wandering Jew' figure, the furtive manner, the stoop, the hunted look," he asserted, "disappear as if by magic after a brief taste of American life."[34]

"Democracy versus the Melting Pot" responded to Ross on several levels. While Ross's overriding anti-Semitic exclusionism was blatantly disturbing to Kallen, he was also alarmed by Ross's counter-contention that, if held to a tight quota, the select Jews who immigrated would quickly cast off their corrupt culture. This toxic combination of the desire for most Jews to be excluded and for a few to be completely assimilated was antithetical to Kallen's ethnic pride, belief in open immigration, and faith in national rejuvenation through cultural diversity. Ross's offensive stereotype of Jews as furtive, "stooped shouldered," and "undersized and weak-muscled" also personally affronted Kallen with his robust, athletic presence and personality.[35]

Ross's positions jolted his younger colleague into action, and the sociologist's ideas are mentioned more than a dozen times throughout Kallen's landmark essay. On the opening page, Ross is introduced as a "nervous professor, in embattled defense," whose shrill xenophobia and fear of race suicide make him one of "the enemies of democracy, the antithesis of the fundamentals of the North American Republic." Described at another point as a "trained economist" blinded by "race prejudice, primitive, spontaneous and unconscious," Ross was Kallen's intellectual antithesis and campus irritant demanding an immediate response.[36]

Kallen's theory was motivated not only by colleagues in Madison but also by a Jewish playwright in London. If Ross's racist exclusionism gave the final push to Kallen's theory, English-born Israel Zangwill and his popular parable of assimilation, *The Melting-Pot*, gave Kallen's essay its title and an added impetus. Kallen had been at Oxford when Zangwill's play, personally dedicated to Theodore Roosevelt, premiered to great acclaim in Washington, DC, in October 1908, and Kallen's reaction to it had been simmering ever since. Although Zangwill was far from the first to use the melting pot metaphor to describe immigrants happily discarding their home cultures and blending into a radically new and better amalgam, and Zangwill's personal position on Jewish identity was more complicated than complete assimilation, his play fired the public imagination and popularized the image. President Roosevelt's exclamation at the end of its opening night—"That's a great play, Mr. Zangwill! A great play!"—underscored how this parable of peaceful accommodation helped ease anxieties for some about massive immigration. Roosevelt's repeated use of Zangwill's imagery, declaring, for example, only a few weeks before his death in early 1919, "We have room for but one language here. . . . We intend to see that crucible turn our people out as Americans, and not as dwellers in a polyglot boarding house," echoed the nationalistic appeal of the play.[37]

In Zangwill's melodrama, David, a young Jewish composer and recent Russian immigrant in New York, falls in love with Vera, a young woman from a Russian Orthodox family who is involved in settlement work. David is in the midst of composing a sweeping "American symphony" celebrating the merging of all old cultures into an entirely new one. Early in the play, David, eager to erase dark Old World memories, declares to Vera: "America is God's Crucible, the great Melting-Pot where all the races of Europe are melting and reforming." Prefiguring the play's conclusion, Zangwill's hero proclaims, using metaphors that would affront Kallen, "These are the fires of God! A fig for your feuds and vendettas! . . . Into the crucible with you all! God is making the American. . . . He will be the fusion of all races, perhaps the coming superman. Ah, what a glorious finale for my symphony!"[38]

As the plot develops, David learns that Vera's military officer father was responsible for the deaths of David's mother and sister in a Russian pogrom. Confronted with this awful truth, Vera's father asks for and receives David's forgiveness and then blesses the couple's interethnic union. Zangwill's drama ends with the young lovers embracing and gazing out over a glorious New York sunset as they envision a future free of ethnic conflict and hatred. Beckoning to a horizon that is "one glory of burning flame," David declares, "It is the fires of God around His Crucible." Then, speaking in forceful words, appalling to Kallen but heartening to eager assimilationists, David asserts:

> There she lies, the great Melting Pot—listen! Can't you hear the roaring and the bubbling? There gapes her mouth . . . the harbor where a thousand mammoth feeders come from the ends of the world to pour their human freight. Ah, what a stirring and a seething! Celt and Latin, Slav and Teuton, Greek and Syrian,—black and yellow—

And speaking softly, Vera suggests: "Jew and Gentile—" before David continues:

> Yes, East and West, the North and the South, the palm and the pine, the pole and the equator, the crescent and the cross—how the great Alchemist melts and fuses them with his purging flame! Here shall they all unite to build the Republic of Man and the Kingdom of God![39]

This fiery consolidation of every ethnic, racial, regional, and religious difference into a uniform American who would be "a fusion of all races, perhaps the coming superman" cheered audiences fearful of diversity. But Zangwill's image of cultural alchemy creating a monolithic superior race and of a symphony celebrating the erasing of cultures alarmed Kallen and others who saw multiplicity as the nation's greatest strength and safeguard against militant uniformity.

Zangwill's play is mentioned only twice in Kallen's groundbreaking essay, yet it provided him with a dramatic title and vivid metaphors for the perils of assimilation. As rabbinical scholar Jonathan Sacks argues, Zangwill was writing "as a Jew who no longer wanted to be a Jew. His real hope was for a world in which the entire lexicon of racial and religious differences would be thrown away."[40] This desire to discard race and religion was echoed by Kallen's friend Mary Antin, who celebrated her thorough

Americanization in her autobiography, *The Promised Land*, published three years after Zangwill's play. After emigrating at thirteen with her family from Russia to Boston in 1894, Antin fully embraced her new culture and rejoiced being relieved of a weighty past. "I have thoroughly assimilated my past," she declared. "I have done its bidding—I want now to be of today. It is painful to be consciously of two worlds. The Wandering Jew in me seeks forgetfulness." America, she concluded, "invites me to a glad new home. . . . My spirit is not tied to the monumental past. . . . The past was only my cradle, and now it cannot hold me, because I am grown too big."[41]

Zangwill's and Antin's apparent eagerness to discard their respective pasts was antithetical to Kallen's ethnic pride and faith in cultural diversity. Ironically, Kallen maintained a warm friendship with Antin, and Zangwill's positions on Jewish identity shifted dramatically over the last fifteen years of his life to the point that by 1923 he was eager to meet Kallen to share common ideas.[42] But eleven years earlier, Kallen's first gut-level critique of melting pot assimilation and of Zangwill's play was revealed in a March 1912 letter from his British friend, political theorist Alfred Zimmern. "I am grateful to you for showing me how absurd the melting pot idea is," Zimmern wrote to Kallen. "It is a varnish pot. A little mercantile polish and chewing gum and a belt and a free and easy manner and a square chin . . . and lo! an American. But these are only transient things."[43] Whether or not Zangwill's wildly popular play endorsed such radical transformation, it redoubled Kallen's faith in cultural distinctiveness and diversity.[44]

Zangwill's all-absorbing melting pot also served as a negative counterpoint to the equally grim alternative of Ross's xenophobic exclusionism. Cultural pluralism, born in the Midwest, was Kallen's response to these distressing extremes. Extolling the invigorating impact of non-Anglo immigrants and the flowering of their distinctive cultures across the region and nation, Kallen was sharply critical of both slate-cleaning assimilation and racist nativism. His benchmark theory grew from this intellectual tug-of-war between cultural obliteration and segregation; it provided a dynamic alternative to the erasure of immigrant cultures advocated by melting-pot enthusiasts and the blanket rejection of them advanced by Anglo-Saxon exclusionists. Cultural pluralism, as it emerged in 1915, offered a fertile middle ground between two deeply troubling ideologies.

Published in early 1915, Kallen's far-reaching vision of diversity was deeply shaped by his ever-widening interaction with colleagues at the University of Wisconsin, and his theory would continue to be influenced by visiting intellectuals and events leading up to the nation's 1917 entry into war. On the eve of war, in early January 1917, for example, Kallen brought together fiery New York writers Max Eastman and Randolph Bourne for an informal gathering in his apartment near campus. The two cultural radicals lived in Greenwich Village, but they first met in Madison. Eastman, who had just been barred from lecturing on Madison's campus, was among several of Kallen's friends, including pacifist and future Nobel Peace Prize winner Norman Angell, who would be denied campus speaking privileges due to deepening wartime oppression in the coming months.[45]

Although Eastman was forbidden from public lecturing in early January 1917, his private interactions with Bourne, Otto, Kallen, and other campus radicals left a deep and positive impression on all of them. Soon after this Madison gathering, Bourne noted to an East Coast friend that "my little group of friends there exceeded in charming soundness anything I even remotely apprehended at Columbia or indeed anywhere in New York," and concluded, "I renounce Boston for Madison as my city of refuge."[46] Writing to Kallen a few days after his visit, Bourne affirmed, "I am glad I stayed in Madison. It was delightful to sit around and talk with you. . . . Seriously, I am starved in New York, like an ass between a thousand bundles of hay." After thanking his friend for arranging the meeting with Eastman, Bourne concluded, "Really the Middle West is the place for me. It was a great misfortune to be born in New Jersey and go to arrogant Columbia."[47]

January 1917 marked a turning point in Kallen's growing appreciation of his adopted university and region. The rabid xenophobia and blind wartime repression that soon swept across the Madison campus, the Midwest, and the nation within a month of Bourne's and Eastman's visits and continued during Kallen's last two years at the university were deeply disillusioning. After resigning from the university in December 1918 and returning to the East Coast to become a founding faculty member of the New School in Manhattan in 1919, Kallen would look back on this final period in the Midwest at Madison as "a black interlude, a crisis whose acid test very few people, academic or lay, survived in courage or integrity."[48]

Despite the dark conclusion to Kallen's heartland years, they also marked the zenith of his remarkably productive career. For most of his time there, the region and the university helped inspire and complete his path-breaking theory. Far from being a time of wasted exile in the remote hinterland, Kallen's Midwestern years were essential in positive and negative ways to his fully developed vision of cultural pluralism. In addition to forcing this uprooted easterner to expand his spatial consciousness beyond the Hudson River, Kallen's midlife immersion in a sprawling and diverse region added much-needed geographical breadth to his theory, allowing him to declare in his most fully conceived vision of cultural pluralism that "historic sectional differences between North and South, East and West . . . have added diversity to diversity." "In the spaces of the continent," he stressed, "democracy could not but prevail, and the lives of cultural groups retain their integrity even as the lives of individual spirits."[49]

Wisconsin itself initially offered far more inclusive political ideals and experiments than Kallen had experienced back East. Despite his professed discomfort in Madison, he found much to admire there in the years before the repression of war. In an obscure but revealing autobiographical passage written sixteen years after he left Wisconsin, the philosopher warmly recounted the state's civic virtues. Admitting that "I stayed, not easily, not quietly, seven years," he stressed that "for the most of these years, as I journeyed here and there in the State, lecturing, looking, I found something like a renovation of my young, young dream of the American way of life." He relished Wisconsin's "quality of civic integrity," and it was during this period before the "black interlude" of war that "those thoughts to which I gave expression in *Culture and Democracy in America* came to their maturity."[50]

Largely ignored by Kallen scholars, this autobiographical passage reveals the deep regional roots of cultural pluralism and how the Midwest as a diverse region and home of a vibrant university gave birth to a theory a hundred years ago that grips the nation today. Kallen's vision of a nation embracing multiplicity and inclusion rather than division and distrust persists as an elusive yet compelling ideal in the twenty-first century.

NOTES

Portions of this chapter have been adapted from material in my book *Horace M. Kallen in the Heartland: The Midwestern Roots of American Pluralism* (Lawrence: University Press of Kansas, 2020). Among the many people who have helped me shape this chapter, I would especially like to thank Jon Lauck, James Leary, Paul Murphy, and Andrew Seal for encouraging my interest in cultural pluralism in the Midwest. I also express deep appreciation to Mark Cowett, Dana Herman, and Mark Raider for introducing me to Jewish American intellectual history in the region.

1. Milton R. Konvitz, "Horace M. Kallen," in *The 'Other' New York Jewish Intellectuals*, ed. Carole S. Kessner (New York: New York University Press, 1994), 154; Milton R. Konvitz, "Horace M. Kallen: In Praise of Hyphenation and Orchestration," in *The Legacy of Horace M. Kallen*, ed. Milton R. Konvitz (Rutherford, NJ: Farleigh Dickinson Press, 1987), 18; Sarah Schmidt, *Horace M. Kallen: Prophet of American Zionism* (Brooklyn, NY: Carlson Publishing, 1995), 28–29; Matthew J. Kaufman, *Horace Kallen Confronts America: Jewish Identity, Science, and Secularism* (Syracuse, NY: Syracuse University Press, 2019), 123. Also see John Higham, *Send These to Me: Jews and Other Immigrants in Urban America* (New York: Atheneum Press, 1975), 206, for another insightful discussion that slights the significance of Kallen's Midwestern years.

2. David S. Brown, *Beyond the Frontier: The Midwestern Voice in American Historical Writing* (Chicago: University of Chicago Press, 2009), 16.

3. Barrett Wendell to Horace M. Kallen, August 14, 1911, box 31, folder 7, MSS 1, Horace M. Kallen Papers, American Jewish Archives, Hebrew Union College, Cincinnati, Ohio (hereafter cited as Kallen Papers). I wish to thank the thoughtful, endlessly encouraging staff at the American Jewish Archives, especially archivists Joe Weber, Steve Collins, and Juliana Witt and director of research and publications, Dana Herman.

4. See Charles McCarthy, *The Wisconsin Idea* (New York: Macmillan, 1912), for the first full expression of this progressive concept. Also see Lincoln Steffens, "Sending a State to College: What the University of Wisconsin Is Doing for Its People," *American Magazine* 67 (November 1908–April 1909): 349–364; and Vernon Carstensen, "The Origin and Development of the Wisconsin Idea," *Wisconsin Magazine of History* 39, no. 3 (Spring 1956): 181–188, for early and retrospective accounts of this educational

experiment. Student and faculty numbers at Madison in 1910 are found at https://registrar.wisc.edu/enrollments_1888_to_present.htm.

5. Horace Kallen, journal entry, September 15, 1911, box 89, Kallen Papers.

6. Walter Roth, *Avengers and Defenders: Glimpses of Chicago's Jewish Past* (Chicago: Chicago Review Press, 2008), 157.

7. Kallen, journal entry, September 30, 1911, box 89, Kallen Papers.

8. Kallen, journal entry, September 30, 1911, box 89, Kallen Papers.

9. Kallen, journal entry, October 11, 1911, box 89, Kallen Papers.

10. Kallen, journal entry, October 11, 1911, box 89, Kallen Papers.

11. See Sarah Imhoff, *Masculinity and the Making of American Judaism* (Bloomington: Indiana University, Press, 2017), for a penetrating analysis of this pernicious and persistent antimasculine stereotype and brief mention (pp. 52–53) of Kallen's sense of himself as providing a vigorous counterimage.

12. Ralph Barton Perry to Horace Kallen, November 1, 1911, box 24, folder 28, Kallen Papers; Alice James to Horace Kallen, November 12, 1011, box 14, folder 3, Kallen Papers.

13. Hugo Munsterberg to Horace Kallen, March 11, 1913, box 23, folder 3, Kallen Papers; Horace Kallen to Miriam Kallen, December 13, 1916, box 94, folder 1, Kallen Papers.

14. US Bureau of the Census, *Thirteenth Census of the United States Taken in the Year 1910*, vol. 3, *Population* (Washington, DC, Government Printing Office, 1913), 135, table 15. In this census, Minnesota, Wisconsin, and North Dakota stood out as having the highest percentage of residents with "Foreign or Mixed Parentage" of any states at 45.3 percent, 44.8 percent, and 43.5 percent respectively. See Sheila Terman Cohen, *Jews in Wisconsin* (Madison: State Historical Society of Wisconsin, 2016), for statistics and an overview of Jewish culture in the state. Also see Richard L. Pifer with Marjorie Hannon Pifer, "An Evolving Population," in *The Great War Comes to Wisconsin: Sacrifice, Patriotism, and Free Speech in a Time of Crisis* (Madison: Wisconsin Historical Society Press, 2017), 22–26, for an effective overview of the state's ethnic diversity in the years leading up to the war.

15. Although Kallen did not put the phrase *cultural pluralism* into print until the publication of his compendium of previously published essays, *Culture and Democracy in the United States* (1923), his theory appeared in full form eight years earlier as a two-part article, "Democracy versus

the Melting Pot," *The Nation* 100 (February 18–25, 1915): 190–194, 217–220. On Kallen's missionary work across the Midwest and elsewhere during his Wisconsin years, see Sarah Schmidt, "A Conversation with Horace M. Kallen: The Zionist Chapter of His Life," *Reconstructionist* 41 (November 1975): 28–33. Voluminous correspondence regarding Kallen's ever-widening regional organizing is found in several folders marked "Provisional Committee for Zionist Affairs" in box 4, folder 11; box 12, folder 17; and box 19, folder 9, Kallen Papers.

16. Kallen, journal entry, October 27, 1911, box 89, no folder, Kallen Papers.

17. Horace Kallen to Miriam Kallen, November 8, 1912, and Horace Kallen to Miriam Kallen, n.d., box 94, folder 1, Kallen Papers. In the undated letter, Horace writes that he has been working on a pageant, "a very big one— on the history of Madison and of Wisconsin." "Otherwise," he concludes, "I have been very lazy."

18. Horace Kallen to Henrietta Szold, October 28, 1914, box 29, folder 1, Kallen Papers. The extensive Kallen–Donlin correspondence between 1916 and 1920 is contained in box 7, folder 18, Kallen Papers. Regarding Browne's and Van Volkenburg's roles as founders in 1912 of the Little Theatre Movement in the United States in Chicago, see Charles Lock, "Maurice Browne and the Chicago Little Theatre," *Modern Drama* 31, no. 1 (Spring 1988): 106–116. See Maurice Browne, *Too Late to Lament: An Autobiography* (Bloomington: Indiana University Press, 1956), 134, for a vivid description of Kallen debating Theodore Dreiser at a Chicago Little Theatre gathering.

19. Howard Mumford Jones, *Howard Mumford Jones: An Autobiography* (Madison: University of Wisconsin Press, 1979), 52. This play was published with extensive commentary in Horace Meyer Kallen, *The Book of Job as a Greek Tragedy* (New York: Moffat, Yard, 1918).

20. Marvin Lowenthal, cited in Susanne Klingenstein, " 'Not the Recovery of a Grave, but of a Cradle': The Zionist Life of Marvin Lowenthal," in *The "Other" New York Jewish Intellectuals*, ed. Carole S. Kessner (New York: New York University Press, 1994), 212. Ammon Hennacy, *The Book of Ammon* (Eugene, OR: Wipf and Stock, 1994), 7. Describing a living room gathering of Jewish students, Kallen reported to his sister, "They are all inhibited Jews—Russian extraction who had been hurt by being Jews." Horace Kallen to Miriam Kallen, n.d., box 94, folder 1, Kallen Papers.

21. Mary Antin to Horace Kallen, November 29, 1916, box 2, folder 4, Kallen Papers.

22. Perlman, a Jewish immigrant and life-long socialist, was deeply influenced by a course he took at Madison in 1909 on the American West taught by progressive historian Frederick Jackson Turner, who inspired the young economist to compare Russian and American frontiers and their impacts on labor movements in each society. Selig Perlman, 1950 interview, cited in Brown, *Beyond the Frontier*, 48.

23. See Mary Jean Woodard Bean, *Julia Grace Wales: Canada's Hidden Heroine and the Quest for Peace, 1914–1918* (Ottawa: Borealis Press, 2005).

24. Louis P. Lochner, *Always the Unexpected: A Book of Reminiscences* (New York: Macmillan, 1956). Especially useful are chapters three through six (pp. 18–78). Also see Meg Jones, "Our Man in Berlin," *On Wisconsin Magazine* (Summer 2017).

25. The extensive Kallen–Otto correspondence between 1918 and 1961 is located in box 24, folder 12, Kallen Papers. In letters of condolence written on Kallen's death in February 1974, V. T. Thayer and Florence Thayer warmly recount their friendship with Kallen and the year that "Horace and Max Otto lived with us" (box 94, folder 1, Kallen Papers).

26. See Theodore Herfurth, *Sifting and Winnowing: A Chapter in the History of Academic Freedom at the University of Wisconsin* (Madison: University of Wisconsin Press, 1949). Also see Brown, *Beyond the Frontier*, 16–24, for a brief overview of Ely, Commons, and Ross and their impact at Madison.

27. Josiah Royce, "Provincialism," in *Race Questions, Provincialism, and Other American Problems* (New York: Macmillan Company, 1908), 57–104. Royce's extended discussion of "wise provincialism" as a breakwater against the "mob spirit" is found on pages 80–102. An earlier version of this essay was published in 1902, as a thirty-page pamphlet: "Provincialism: An Address to the Phi Beta Kappa Society of the State University of Iowa." Frederick Jackson Turner, "The Ohio Valley in American History," (1909), in Turner, *The Frontier in American History* (New York: Henry Holt and Company, 1921), 158. On the relationship among Turner, Royce, and Kallen and their related theories, sectionalism, provincialism, and cultural pluralism, see Michael C. Steiner, "The Birth of the Midwest and the Rise of Regional Theory," in *Finding a New Midwestern History*, ed. Jon C. Lauck, Gleaves Whitney, and Joseph Hogan (Lincoln: University of Nebraska Press, 2018),

15–16. For more detailed discussion of Turner's regional thought and its roots in Wisconsin and the Upper Midwest, see Michael C. Steiner, "The Significance of Turner's Sectional Thesis," *Western Historical Quarterly* 10, no. 4 (October 1979): 437–466.

28. See Thomas C. Leonard, *Illiberal Reformers: Race, Eugenics, and American Economics in the Progressive Era* (Princeton, NJ: Princeton University Press, 2017); and Luca Fiorito and Cosma Orsi, "Anti-Semitism and Progressive Era Social Science: The Case of John R. Commons," *Journal of the History of Economic Thought* 38, no. 1 (March 2016): 55–80. Ely, Commons, and Ross's fears of race suicide and advocacy of eugenics are examined throughout Leonard's book. For a detailed account of the campaign by Ely, Commons, and others to stifle free speech during World War I, see Murray N. Rothbard, "World War I as Fulfillment: Power and the Intellectuals," in *The Costs of War: America's Pyrrhic Victories*, ed. John V. Denson (New Brunswick, NJ: Transaction Publishers, 1999), 277–284.

29. Isabel Heinemann, "Preserving the Family and the Nation: Eugenic Masculinity Concepts, Expert Intervention, and the American Family in the United States, 1900–1960," in *Masculinities and the Nation in the Modern World*, ed. Pablo Dominguez Andersen and Simon Wendt (New York: Palgrave Macmillan, 2015), 75.

30. Ross's role in Goldman's controversial 1910 campus visit is discussed in Merle Curti and Vernon Carstensen, *The University of Wisconsin: A History, 1848–1925*, vol. 2 (Madison: University of Wisconsin Press, 1949), 63–68, and in Sean H. McMahon, *Social Control & Public Intellect: The Legacy of Edward A. Ross* (New Brunswick, NJ: Transaction Publishers, 1999), 93–95. Ross's views on women's suffrage and birth control are analyzed in McMahon, 107–135. For his glowing personal account of the Bolshevik Revolution after traveling across Russia for five months in 1917 and 1918, see Ross, *Russia in Upheaval* (London: T. Fisher Unwin, 1919). Dismissing criticisms of the Revolution, Ross asks, "Ought we not rather discern in the many similarities between the Russian people and the American people the natural foundation for the firmest friendship? . . . Why should not the two peoples feel the pull and sympathy and become like brothers?" (129, 130).

31. Ross introduced the notion of race suicide in "The Causes of Racial Superiority," *Annals of the American Academy of Political and Social Sciences*

18 (July 1901): 67–89. His theory of social control was outlined in *Social Control: A Survey of the Foundations of Order* (New York: Macmillan, 1901). For Kallen's succinct rejection of Grant's thesis, see his review essay in *The Dial* 62 (May 17, 1917), 433.

32. Edward Alsworth Ross, *The Old World in the New: The Significance of Past and Present Immigration to the American People* (New York: Century Company, 1914), 282, 285.

33. Ross, *The Old World in the New*, 154–155, 289. Horace M. Kallen, "Democracy versus the Melting Pot," *The Nation* 100 (February 18–25, 1915), 90–194 and 217–220. This two-part article was republished as chapter 2 of Kallen's *Culture and Democracy in the United States* in 1924. Ross's chapter 7, "The Eastern European Hebrews," 143–167, is a largely negative analysis that ultimately depicts Jews as being more easily absorbed into American culture than most non-northern European immigrants.

34. Ross, *The Old World in the New*, 166–167.

35. See Imhoff, *Masculinity and the Making of American Judaism*.

36. Kallen, "Democracy versus the Melting Pot" (1915), in *Culture and Democracy in the United States* (New York: Boni and Liveright, 1924; New Brunswick, NJ: Transaction Publishers, 1998), 61, 83.

37. See Guy Szuberla, "Zangwill's *The Melting Pot* Plays Chicago," *MELUS* 20, no. 3 (Autumn 1995), 3, for reference to Roosevelt's often-quoted 1908 praise of Zangwill's play; "Abolish Hyphen, Roosevelt's Last Words to Public," *Chicago Daily Tribune*, January 7, 1919, 4.

38. Israel Zangwill, *The Melting-Pot* (1909; New York: American Jewish Book Company, 1921), 50–51.

39. Zangwill, *The Melting-Pot*, 265–267.

40. Jonathan Sacks, *The Home We Build Together: Recreating Society* (New York: Continuum Press, 2007), 26. Sacks also emphasizes that Zangwill was an early Zionist who rejected the movement in 1905 just as Kallen was embracing it.

41. Mary Antin, *The Promised Land* (Boston: Houghton Mifflin, 1912), xxii, 364.

42. Zangwill visited the United States in late 1923, and he and Kallen exchanged warm letters, hoping to arrange a meeting. Although they missed the opportunity to meet, Zangwill praised *Culture and Democracy in the United States*, writing to Kallen's publisher: "His theme, the future

of America, is literally the most important in the world, for there all races are met to create a really New World, or to fall back into the old chaos. . . . No intelligent American, honestly perplexed by his country's problems, should overlook this contribution to solution." Israel Zangwill to Messrs. Boni & Liveright, telegram, n.d., YIVO Institute for Jewish Research, New York City, Horace Kallen Papers, RG-317, folder 889. I am grateful to YIVO archivist Gunnar Berg for helping me locate this among the eight items of the Zangwill–Kallen correspondence between early October and late December 1923.

43. Alfred Zimmern to Horace Kallen, March 21, 1912, box 32, folder 20, Kallen Papers.

44. See David Weinfeld, "*The Maccabean* and the Melting Pot: Contributionist Zionism and American Diversity Discourse, 1903–1915," *American Jewish Archives Journal* 70, nos. 1 & 2 (2018), 1–37, for an insightful discussion of underlying similarities between Kallen's and Zangwill's visions of cultural diversity.

45. Kallen complained about "the denial of the halls of the university" for Angell's talk in a letter to Alfred Zimmern, on April 16, 1918, box 32, folder 20, Kallen Papers. On campus wartime repression at Madison, see Erika Janik, "The Great War at Home," *On Wisconsin Magazine* 118, no. 1 (Spring 2017), 22–29; George T. Blakey, *Historians on the Homefront: American Propagandists for the Great War* (Lexington: University Press of Kentucky, 1970), 77–81; and Pifer, *The Great War*, 206–210.

46. Randolph Bourne to Alyse Gregory, Sunday (January 1917), in *The Letters of Randolph Bourne: A Comprehensive Edition*, ed. Eric J. Sandeen (Troy, NY: Whitson Publishing Company, 1981), 293, 394.

47. Randolph Bourne to Horace Kallen, "Milwaukee, Sunday," n.d., box 4, folder 7, Kallen Papers.

48. Horace Kallen, *Individualism: An American Way of Life* (New York: Liveright, 1933), 12.

49. Kallen, "Democracy versus the Melting Pot" and "Culture and the Ku Klux Klan," in *Culture and Democracy in the United States*, 89, 35.

50. Kallen, *Individualism*, 11–12.

CHAPTER 8

MODELING "CIVIC EFFECTIVENESS" IN THE MIDWEST

Charles Mulford Robinson's Progressive Era Urban Planning,
1907–1915

Brian M. Ingrassia

"Cities are not made to be looked at, but to be lived in," asserted Charles Mulford Robinson (1869–1917) in his influential book *Modern Civic Art; or, The City Made Beautiful*. This book, which first appeared in 1903 and was republished in three subsequent editions through 1918,[1] was a thorough articulation of the early-1900s City Beautiful movement, the Progressive Era push to redesign urban space for aesthetic appeal and public coherence.[2] In his final years, Robinson devised plans for several Midwestern cities and taught at the University of Illinois, where he helped pioneer the nascent discipline of urban planning. Robinson wanted cities to be beautiful, but it is clear from his reports for Midwestern urban centers that he also saw them as orderly and efficient places—as pragmatic spaces for early-1900s Americans.

Historians tend to focus on Robinson's major publications and his plans for big cities, including Denver (1906) and Los Angeles (1909).[3] Yet he also submitted reports advising a number of smaller cities in Illinois, Indiana, Iowa, and Missouri between 1907 and 1914,[4] and his University of Illinois students collaborated on a plan for the twin cities of Champaign and Urbana in 1915. Scholar Emily Talen calls Robinson a "tactical urbanist who advocated small scale, incremental improvements" and "saw the potential of the City Beautiful to effectuate broader change."[5] He was a visionary who frequently focused on details.[6] Although not a landscape architect like George Kessler or Jens Jensen, Robinson was clearly someone who shaped "the raw, new cities and vast rural spaces of the nation's heartland."[7] Historian Jon Peterson calls Robinson a "lucid and prolific writer"[8] who was "master scrivener of the beautification movement." Since Robinson's drafting skills were limited, Peterson explains, "Clients did not *look at* a Robinson plan; they read it."[9] One scholar has deemed Robinson, who had no formal training in urban planning, an "amateur" and "dilettante."[10] Yet such training was scarce in late-1800s America, and Robinson may best be seen not as a dabbler but as a pioneer who increased "public interest in the possibilities of more beautiful and more efficient urban environments."[11] Robinson represented the specialized expert of America's Progressive Era, a reformer who hoped to solve the problems of urban-industrial society. He worked to craft urban spaces—one city at a time, if necessary—to increase beauty, efficiency, and profitability. By improving heartland cities, he believed, the nation's entire urban archipelago could rise to a more productive and pleasing level. This chapter focuses especially on Robinson's ideas about playgrounds and parks, which he viewed as inspiring yet orderly spaces where democratic citizens, efficient workers, and public life were formed.

Robinson was born in 1869 and raised in Rochester, New York; he graduated from the University of Rochester in 1891. After college, he worked as a journalist, editing Rochester's *Post Express* for a decade. His early writings touched on issues of urban character and growth. Starting in 1899, he wrote pieces for *Atlantic Monthly* and *Harper's Magazine*, which gained him recognition. Buffalo, New York, commissioned his first city plan in 1902.[12] He was perhaps best known, though, for his influential books. *The Improvement of Towns and Cities* (1901) was "the first book on city planning written by an American,"[13] the virtual "birth certificate" of the City Beautiful movement.[14] Robinson invoked broad knowledge of cities, including Paris, Vienna, Boston, and San Francisco, in his influential second book, *Modern Civic Art*. As historian Daniel T. Rodgers has shown, Robinson was one of many social scientists and planners inspired by turn-of-the-century European cities to reform America's urban life. This expertise prompted Detroit's board of commerce to commission Robinson's plan for Michigan's metropolis. The result was too grandiose, though, and Detroit rejected it after consulting with Frederick Law Olmsted Jr. Subsequently, Robinson crafted more modest plans.[15] His ideas changed over time, too. Around 1910, Robinson shifted from the City Beautiful to an orientation scholars call the "City Practical" (or City Efficient or City Scientific). This change was due, at least in part, to Robinson's 1910 sojourn as a special student at Harvard University, where he studied with James Sturgis Pray, a landscape architect who had worked with Olmsted's firm. At Harvard, Robinson drafted *The Width and Arrangement of Streets* (1911), republished as *City Planning: With Special Reference to the Planning of Streets and Lots* (1916). The University of Illinois appointed him chair in civic design in 1913. In this position, the first such chair at an American university, Robinson shaped the incipient field of urban planning, traveling to Urbana several times each year to offer instruction. Robinson's career, though, was cut short when he died of pneumonia in 1917 at age forty-eight.[16]

In *Modern Civic Art*, Robinson discussed many aspects of public space, from civic centers to parks to street layouts and statues, fountains, and lighting. He wrote that cities on an ocean, river, or lake could reclaim the waterfront from commerce for use as parks or administrative centers. For all cities, but especially landlocked ones, he thought railroad stations were important entrance portals requiring attractive landscaping. First impressions were important to Robinson: an area's economic well-being might depend on how well it impressed potential residents with aesthetically pleasing spaces.[17] In his 1908 plan for Cedar Rapids, a city of 33,000 on the Cedar River, Robinson wrote that urban beauty attracted a "desirable sort of people," thus augmenting business, growing residential neighborhoods, and "increasing assessable values."[18] In his 1910 report for Hannibal, Missouri, a city of 18,000 perched on bluffs overlooking the Mississippi River, Robinson argued that although a city had to be attractive for its citizens' "pleasure," aesthetics also lured tourists, "new residents," and businesses, thus improving the town's "reputation in the world."[19]

Robinson hoped to elevate the character of public spaces above their basic economic functions via the civic center, a central and aesthetically pleasing grouping of municipal buildings. His physiological metaphors portrayed the civic center as a city's "heart," or one of the "nerve centres" from which urban energy flowed. He thought public buildings should be grouped at the center of the progressive body politic, increasing civic pride and facilitating "co-operation." [20] The civic center's location depended on local geography. Some cities might locate it on the waterfront, while others might choose an elevated point. Robinson implicitly invoked John Winthrop's 1630 "city upon a hill" by suggesting that municipal buildings placed on an elevated spot "would visibly dominate the town." People could "look up" to government, and this location would protect "public buildings from the intrusive elbowing of private structures that might dwarf them, that might screen them from view, or might shut out their light." [21] Like other progressives, Robinson wanted public life to be protected from corruption.[22] In his 1908 Cedar Rapids report, he proposed the city purchase an island in the Cedar River for a civic center. With "domes and towers . . . rising above the trees," Mays Island would be an exceptional example of "civic beauty," with water protecting it from downtown fires and commercial development. Cedar Rapids had a natural advantage, Robinson argued, which cities like Boston sought; it just had to act. If the town built an island civic center, other cities would "have something to learn of civic effectiveness from the Middle West." [23]

Even before *Modern Civic Art*, Robinson developed an urban model intended to be seen by people throughout the Midwest and the world. This was the circular, ten-acre Model City, intended, but never built, for St. Louis's 1904 Louisiana Purchase Exhibition. Possibly drawing from Englishman Ebenezer Howard's 1898 garden city idea, Robinson planned an "exemplary" town-site that, as imagined in 1902, would have made his ideas visible to world's fair visitors. The Model City would be surrounded by a ring road (perhaps inspired by Vienna's *Ringstrasse*) partially landscaped into a "beautiful park road." At the town center, a rail terminal with a plaza was "an unmistakable entrance." Everything would be "orderly, cleanly, and dignified" in the Model City. Yet it could include "an amusement and exhibition section" and "recreation district" with "outdoor restaurants, a band stand . . . and other amusement features." [24]

Recreational spaces were an important part of Robinson's plans, and he dedicated a significant portion of *Modern Civic Art* to parks and parkways.[25] In his 1907 report for the Mississippi River city of Dubuque, Iowa, then home to 38,000 residents, he declared the need for "ornamental" and neighborhood parks, playgrounds, "recreative fields," and larger municipal parks. He argued Dubuque also needed parkways tying together this "park system." Ornamental parks would be "irregular little spaces," river bluffs or disjointed intersections crafted for pleasing aesthetics. A neighborhood park would function as "a public room out of doors, where children can play, where mothers can sit to sew and talk, where neighbors can meet in the evenings." Playgrounds would augment public schools by "keeping the children off the streets" and "affording elementary instruction in industrial handicraft." Meanwhile, recreational fields would serve industrial laborers. Fields for sports like baseball and cricket would provide space for "healthy and enjoyable exercise in the open air." Robinson said Dubuque's major industries could purchase land near the Chicago Great Western Railway's facilities "or some similar tract" and donate it "as a playfield for operatives." Robinson admitted that parks, playgrounds, and parkways would cost money. But he contended they were "municipal necessities," as important as streets, sewers, lighting, and police.[26]

Robinson thus contributed to the burgeoning playground movement, in which reformers such as Chicago settlement-house pioneer Jane Addams built play spaces in Progressive Era cities. Around 1908, Robinson told a New York audience how playgrounds were "little oases of country," with ornamental elements like trees, flowers, and small bodies of water. These features delighted children and helped them explore aspects of nature they otherwise might not encounter.[27] Historian Dominick Cavallo portrays Robinson (perhaps unfairly) as an idealist who saw the playground merely as a beautiful place, a "sylvan sanctuary" from urban life that "might attract fairies" and would do little to help "slum children."[28] Yet it is clear that Robinson, especially in his post-1910 reports, was more practical than this characterization lets on. Robinson wrote that playgrounds provided "social service" for young people. His report for St. Joseph, Missouri, a Missouri River meatpacking city with 77,000 residents in 1910, noted that the city needed more play spaces. Sounding like progressive educator John Dewey, Robinson argued that playgrounds helped children develop social skills and democratic civic mindedness. St. Joseph's children merely had "vacant lots," where "only the gang spirit" could "exercise a primitive kind of control" over interactions. If the city could not enlarge its small schoolyards, Robinson argued, it needed parks with playgrounds.[29]

He made similar prescriptions elsewhere. He contended that Swinney Park in Fort Wayne, Indiana, a metropolis of 65,000, needed a fully "equipped and directed playground."[30]

Robinson did not fail to note that playgrounds required supervision. Without oversight, he wrote, even the best-equipped space was "only a battlefield where might is right and where at last only the strong survive, to make themselves a nuisance to the neighbors."[31] An unsupervised playground was "like a school without a teacher," instilling "lawlessness, the destruction of property, [and] the survival of the fittest physically." Only "the most unfit morally" could thrive there.[32] Robinson clearly invoked Darwinian natural selection in such passages. Yet he used the term to articulate what historians call "reform Darwinism" rather than the social Darwinism of Herbert Spencer. Instead of arguing that society should emulate naturalistic competition to eliminate the weak, reformers used the rhetoric of natural selection to promote progressive causes.[33] In Robinson's case, he hoped supervised child's play would develop both efficient and democratically minded citizens.

Robinson's plans also demonstrated progressive ideals about the health-giving nature of recreation. Historian Colin Fisher writes that urban reformers such as Jacob Riis and Graham Taylor proposed small parks in working-class neighborhoods where workers might get "recreation that would restore them from long hours of mechanized labor and render them more efficient and productive when they returned to the factory floor." While reformers may have intended such spaces for social control, workers appear to have utilized parks for their own purposes, including indulging the impulse to escape seemingly "artificial" cities and enjoy green spaces. Scholar Robin Bachin writes that Chicago's reformers sought an "urban aesthetic" that "combined moralism with scientific management, art with efficiency, and open space with the promotion of democracy and citizenship."[34] Robinson extended the idea of recreational parks—which could bolster both industrial efficiency and workers' quality of life—to smaller Midwestern cities.

When he recommended that Dubuque's factories furnish a recreational field, Robinson ventured into welfare capitalism, an early-1900s idea originally conceived as "welfare work." Historian Andrea Tone writes that companies such as National Cash Register of Dayton, Ohio, formed sports leagues or built recreational spaces in order to maintain productivity and limit workers' political radicalism or labor organization.[35] Robinson used this then-innovative impulse to argue for urban leisure spaces. In 1910, he theorized that for adult men and women working long hours in a laborious "grind," parks provided education via entertainment. "When one is entertained," he wrote, "labor ceases and care is forgotten, the old tired muscles relax, [and] nerves are at rest." Thus "public recreation facilities" were "a free and popular antidote to task-driving conditions." And education was a "by-product" of recreation: sports like golf and tennis gave "pleasure and health" and "encourage[d] muscular proficiency and mental alertness." Parks, which served as "outdoor school[s]," opening the senses and instilling civilization, were a municipal "investment" paying "daily dividends on the common stock of human experience."[36]

In his St. Joseph report, Robinson argued that a "field for baseball and other sports" located "near the great packing houses" on the city's west side would give laborers places to play so they could be "better citizens" and "more efficient workers."[37] Robinson quoted Addams when observing that factory work created great "nervous strain."[38] A city like Fort Wayne needed baseball diamonds and gymnastic apparatus to provide "healthful outdoor exercise" for "mechanics, clerks," and other workers, which would in turn aid the city's economy, society, and health—and even attract more industry.[39] Waterloo, Iowa, a city of 27,000 upriver from Cedar Rapids, needed a "reservation" in its industrial section where workers could "indulge in healthful sports."[40] Hannibal, meanwhile, needed a field with running track, baseball diamond, or even an ice skating rink. This field might host interfactory contests so male and female laborers could "exercise other muscles than the single set of which modern piece work makes demand." They might be "more contented" as well as "efficient" at work.[41] In his 1911 report for Freeport, Illinois, a city of 18,000 near the Wisconsin border, Robinson argued that attractive parks should give "opportunities for healthy exercise in the open air where employees may be invigorated." Parks on the city's edge could include spaces for recreation and "athletic sports." They should also provide "tranquil views" of nearby hills that were "soothing to weary city nerves."[42]

In attempting to calm nerves, Robinson was addressing a turn-of-the-century Euro-American concern that the nervous exhaustion caused by modern life was destroying minds and bodies. Historian David Schuster writes that innovations in communications and industry seemingly "created a fast-paced, modern society that sickened citizens." Physicians frequently diagnosed *neurasthenia*, a disease with numerous symptoms including depression, insomnia, and impotence. Some psychiatrists even grew concerned about supposed "male hysteria."[43] How could society prevent this mental deterioration? Many believed strenuous sports were one way to bolster modern nerves,[44] and parks seemed to be good places for such activities. Robinson urged Freeport to acquire a one-hundred-acre tract called Globe Park on the city's southwest edge, which could "serve the entire city" with its "picnic groves" and "romantic walks and water stretches."[45]

Robinson's writings vacillated between animistic and mechanistic views—between seeing public spaces as providing spiritual inspiration and seeing them as providing active benefits. In his St. Joseph report, he proposed transforming King Hill into a pleasant, accessible park with "outlooks and benches" to be enjoyed by many. Instead of a billboard advertising soap at the hill's pinnacle, a "memorial tablet" could make it "a monument to the vanished races which here lighted their signal fires." (While American Indians may have been pushed off Missouri lands by 1910, they had by no means disappeared from the American landscape.) Echoing mid-1800s transcendentalists like New Englander Henry David Thoreau, Robinson said this hill, which might once have been a *deus loci* (god of place), could now inspire "hope and courage" in nearby residents while also providing "an active social and hygienic service" to the city.[46]

Robinson thought playgrounds and parks had to be accessible in order to promote social order and development. If possible, they should be located on thoroughfares serviced by streetcars.[47] But as automobiles became more common after 1908—when Henry Ford introduced the Model T and more cities began paving their streets—Robinson considered cars' increased usage for enjoying scenery in places like Council Bluffs, Iowa, a city of about 30,000 residents across the Missouri River from Omaha, Nebraska.[48] Boulevards and parkways could connect more urban dwellers to parks.[49] For Hannibal, Robinson proposed a road emulating Kansas City's Cliff Drive to "tie together all the large parks into a system, and make a loop drive around the city as amazing in its practicalness as in its variety and attractiveness."[50] A projected parkway in Fort Wayne would be "a connecting link, tying together the river drives, and making one beautiful and extensive system of the whole."[51] Yet, he maintained, it was best if playgrounds were not located directly on a busy parkway, since educational spaces worked best "when not too much in public view."[52] This dictum echoed early-1800s physical-culture proponents who argued that gymnasia should not be places of spectacle.[53] Since Robinson died in 1917, before the automotive boom of the 1920s, it is not clear how his later plans might have accommodated increased usage of private vehicles.

Robinson's last report for a Midwestern city was for Alton, Illinois, a Mississippi River town of 18,000 near St. Louis. Not surprisingly, he echoed ideas from other post-1910 reports, which fell more on the side of the City Practical. He proposed riverfront improvements but did not advocate a grand union station; he discussed municipal buildings yet stressed a proper street grid rather than a magnificent civic center. Still, Robinson continued to see parks as an integral part of cities. He contended that Alton's "park system" should not consist of little, detached "oases in the desert of streets"; it should rather be "a pervasive pattern woven into the fabric of the town" that "stamp[ed] it all with beauty and charm." Industrial workers, he wrote, needed "places where strained eyes can be rested by long views, where the stifling air of the shops can be exchanged for fresh winds." Robinson stressed practicality alongside beauty. He criticized Alton, he explained, only because it held so much potential: "It is because Alton has so plainly the making of a beautiful, livable, efficient city . . . that it is worth while to point out every untoward thing that stands in the way of its progress."[54]

Robinson conveyed such ideas to his pupils at the University of Illinois. In 1915, his students collaborated on a report for the twin railroad and college towns of Champaign and Urbana, then with a combined population of 23,000. In one chapter, the student-authors stated that parks were both beautiful and useful, increasing adjoining property values and thus augmenting tax revenues. Since east-central Illinois possesses no significant hills or bodies of water, Champaign and Urbana had to make do with "the characteristic flatness of the prairies." But even parks on flat land could provide refuge. For instance, White Park near downtown Champaign (today's West Side Park) provided "social service" because of its "proximity to the shopping district." Weary "shoppers and store employees" could "find a change of scene" there "and obtain rest for strained nerves in its restful beauty."[55] The authors also commented favorably on other parks, including Urbana's Carle, Crystal Lake, and Leal Parks. With some improvements, they wrote, the parks of Champaign and Urbana could be "models" for other small "modern cities."[56] The students also noted that enhanced playgrounds could improve the cities' "moral and physical tone."[57] The report's introduction, likely penned by Robinson, observed that when children could only play on streets, they could not really "develop into the type of men and women" a city demanded.[58]

Were Robinson's ideas put into practice? In some cases, yes. Cedar Rapids purchased Mays Island and built public buildings there; for nearly a century, the river-bound civic center stood in the midst of the regional metropolis until floodwaters devastated it in 2008. In 1912, Freeport voters overwhelmingly approved the acquisition of Globe Park, today called Krape Park. In other cases, certainly, Robinson's plans went un-realized. But it is beyond this chapter's scope to survey the results of Robinson's reports. Rather, it is the intent of this chapter to view his work and thought as part of what historian Kathryn Oberdeck (writing about Kohler, Wisconsin) calls the "unbuilt environment": a cache of ideas for city life that had an impact on residents' hopes and dreams—and sometimes resentments—beyond their early-1900s genesis.[59] Robinson's writings illustrate that the Progressive Era Midwest was both an excep-tional and unexceptional place: a region where people borrowed ideas from around the world to improve their cities and, potentially, provide an example for everyone else.

Charles Mulford Robinson was a City Beautiful pioneer, but he did not only try to make cities prettier. He sought to make residents efficient workers and effective citizens by developing public spaces, including those for recreation. A typical self-trained expert of America's early-1900s Progressive Era, Robinson utilized the Midwest's midsized cities as his (and his students') urban-planning workshop between 1907 and 1915. This region grew as people moved from the East, the rural countryside, and other nations to work in factories springing up in cities along rivers and railroads. The early-1900s Midwest, poised near the center of American culture,[60] was a beacon. As Robinson told Cedar Rapids in 1908, with properly developed spaces, Midwesterners could model civic culture for an entire nation.

NOTES

1. Charles Mulford Robinson, *Modern Civic Art; or, The City Made Beautiful*, 4th ed. (New York: Putnam, 1918; New York: Arno Press, 1970), 29.
2. William H. Wilson, *The City Beautiful Movement* (Baltimore: Johns Hopkins University Press, 1989), 38.
3. Wilson analyzes Denver in *City Beautiful Movement*, 235–238. Los Angeles is discussed in Jeremiah B. C. Axelrod, *Inventing Autopia: Dreams and Visions of the Modern Metropolis in Jazz Age Los Angeles* (Berkeley: University of California Press, 2009), 22–24; Mansel G. Blackford, *The Lost Dream: Businessmen and City Planning on the Pacific Coast, 1890–1920* (Columbus: Ohio State University Press, 1993), 85–91; and Kevin Starr, *Material Dreams: Southern California through the 1920s* (New York: Oxford University Press, 1990), 105.
4. For a list of plans, see Jon A. Peterson, *The Birth of City Planning in the United States, 1840–1917* (Baltimore: Johns Hopkins University Press, 2003), 176, 296. Peterson does not mention Robinson's reports for Hannibal, St. Joseph, Freeport, or Council Bluffs. The first three, apparently unpublished, are held at the University of Pennsylvania and are analyzed subsequently.
5. Emily Talen, "Charles Mulford Robinson: A Tribute" (n.d.), 1, www.urban.illinois.edu/images/site-content/DURP100essay-1Talen.pdf.
6. Jon A. Peterson, "The City Beautiful Movement: Forgotten Origins and Lost Meanings," *Journal of Urban History* 2, no. 4 (August 1976), 420–421; and *Birth of City Planning*, 190.
7. William H. Tishler, "Introduction: Shaping America's Heartland," in *Midwestern Landscape Architecture*, ed. William H. Tishler (Urbana: University of Illinois Press, 2000), 2.
8. Peterson, "City Beautiful Movement," 426.
9. Peterson, *Birth of City Planning*, 190.
10. Axelrod, *Inventing Autopia*, 27.
11. Sherry Piland, "Charles Mulford Robinson: Theory and Practice in Early Twentieth-Century Urban Planning" (PhD diss., Florida State University, 1997), 10.
12. Piland, "Charles Mulford Robinson," 13–16, 21; Park Dixon Goist, *From Main Street to State Street: Town, City, and Community in America* (Port Washington, NY: Kennicat Press, 1977), 121–123; Peterson, *Birth of City*

Planning, 120. Many natives of New England and upstate New York shaped the turn-of-the-century Midwest; James Gilbert, *Perfect Cities: Chicago's Utopias of 1893* (Chicago: University of Chicago Press, 1991), 37–39.

13. Goist, *Main Street to State Street*, 122.

14. Peterson, *Birth of City Planning*, 120.

15. Peterson, *Birth of City Planning*, 190–191; Daniel T. Rodgers, *Atlantic Crossings: Social Politics in a Progressive Age* (Cambridge, MA: Harvard University Press, 1998), 169.

16. Piland, "Charles Mulford Robinson," 8, 24–25, 27, 94–97, 262–268.

17. Robinson, *Modern Civic Art*, 42–50, 62–65. M. Christine Boyer discusses Robinson's focus on water and rail approaches in *Dreaming the Rational City: The Myth of American City Planning* (Cambridge, MA: MIT Press, 1983), 51–52.

18. Charles Mulford Robinson, *Report of Charles Mulford Robinson with Regard to Civic Affairs in the City of Cedar Rapids, Iowa with Recommendations for City Improvement and Beautification* (Cedar Rapids, IA: Torch Press, 1908), [28]. Brackets here and elsewhere in the notes indicate page numbers I have assigned to a text without page numbers.

19. Charles Mulford Robinson, "The Improvement of Hannibal, Mo." (1910), 6, 17, typescript copy, MS 1010, Charles Mulford Robinson Papers, Kislak Center for Special Collections, Rare Books, and Manuscripts, University of Pennsylvania, Philadelphia, Pennsylvania (hereafter cited as Robinson Papers).

20. Robinson, *Modern Civic Art*, 81–86.

21. Robinson, *Modern Civic Art*, 90–91.

22. For an overview of Progressive Era reformers, see Michael McGerr, *A Fierce Discontent: The Rise and Fall of the Progressive Movement in America, 1870–1920* (New York: Oxford University Press, 2003), xiv–xv; Shelton Stromquist, *Reinventing "The People": The Progressive Movement, the Class Problem, and the Origins of Modern Liberalism* (Urbana: University of Illinois Press, 2006), esp. 3–4.

23. Robinson, *Report [on] Cedar Rapids*, [33]. Mays Island, along with its civic buildings, was devastated by floodwaters in 2008, a century after Robinson's report.

24. Charles Mulford Robinson, "The Plan of the Model City," *The Criterion* 3 (March 1902): 34–48. For an overview of the St. Louis Model City,

see Peterson, *Birth of City Planning*, 147–149. On the "garden city," see
Ebenezer Howard, *Garden Cities of To-Morrow*, edited with preface
by F. J. Osborn and introduction by Lewis Mumford (London: Swan
Sonnenschein, 1898; Cambridge, MA: MIT Press, 1965). On Vienna's
Ringstrasse, see Carl E. Schorske, *Fin-de-Siècle Vienna: Politics and Culture*
(New York: Knopf, 1979), 24–115. Piland contends that Robinson was
familiar with the "garden city" concept ("Charles Mulford Robinson," 194).

25. Robinson, *Modern Civic Art*, 307–354.

26. Charles Mulford Robinson, *Report on the Improvement of the City of Dubuque,
Iowa* (Dubuque, IA: Joint Committee Representing Dubuque Commercial
Club, Civic Division of Dubuque Woman's Club, and Trades and Labor
Congress, 1907), 6, 10–12, 23. Boyer briefly discusses Robinson's idea of
parks as worker leisure spaces in *Dreaming the Rational City*, 36.

27. Charles Mulford Robinson, *Landscape Gardening for Playgrounds*,
reprinted from *Proceedings of the Second Annual Playground Congress for
the Playground Association of America* (New York: Russell Sage Foundation,
1909), 4.

28. Dominick Cavallo, *Muscles and Morals: Organized Playgrounds and Urban
Reform, 1880–1920* (Philadelphia: University of Pennsylvania Press, 1981),
17, 25–26. All quotations are Cavallo's.

29. Charles Mulford Robinson, "The St. Joseph of the Future" (1910), 20–21,
Robinson Papers.

30. Charles Mulford Robinson, *Report of Charles Mulford Robinson for Fort
Wayne Civic Improvement Association* (Fort Wayne, IN: Fort Wayne Printing
Company, 1910), 76.

31. Robinson, "Improvement of Hannibal," 46. Robinson noted that in
Los Angeles, young playground volunteers told "stories" and provided
"instruction in gymnastics" or "gardening"; Charles Mulford Robinson,
"Park System for Freeport, Ill." (1911), 14, Robinson Papers.

32. Robinson, "Park System for Freeport," 12.

33. See Robert C. Bannister, *Social Darwinism: Science and Myth in Anglo-
American Social Thought*, rev. ed. (1979; Philadelphia: Temple University
Press, 1989).

34. Colin Fisher, *Urban Green: Nature, Recreation, and the Working Class in
Industrial Chicago* (Chapel Hill: University of North Carolina Press, 2015),
18, 22, 26 (quotation), 115; Robin F. Bachin, *Building the South Side: Urban*

Space and Civic Culture in Chicago, 1890–1919 (Chicago: University of Chicago Press, 2004), 128.

35. Andrea Tone, *The Business of Benevolence: Industrial Paternalism in Progressive America* (Ithaca, NY: Cornell University Press, 1997), 93–97. On "cheap amusements" and the ways workers used them, see Kathy Peiss, *Cheap Amusements: Working Women and Leisure in Turn-of-the-Century New York* (Philadelphia: Temple University Press, 1986); Nan Enstad, *Ladies of Labor, Girls of Adventure: Working Women, Popular Culture, and Labor Politics at the Turn of the Twentieth Century* (New York: Columbia University Press, 1999). Robinson was aware of National Cash Register's desire to locate plants in cities with parks; Boyer, *Dreaming the Rational City*, 36.

36. Charles Mulford Robinson, "Educational Value of Public Recreation Facilities," *Annals of the American Academy of Political and Social Science* 35, no. 2 (March 1910): 350–355.

37. Robinson, "St. Joseph of the Future," 20–21. Robinson suggested something similar in his 1911 plan for Binghamton, New York; Goist, *Main Street to State Street*, 126–127. St. Joseph received a Swift meatpacking plant in 1896; William Cronon, *Nature's Metropolis: Chicago and the Great West* (New York: Norton, 1991), 257.

38. Robinson, "St. Joseph of the Future," 10–13.

39. Robinson, *Report for Fort Wayne*, 68, 81–82.

40. Charles Mulford Robinson, *The Wellbeing of Waterloo: A Report to the Civic Society of Waterloo, Iowa* (Waterloo, IA: Matt Parrott & Sons Co., 1910), [33].

41. Robinson, "Improvement of Hannibal," 9–10.

42. Robinson, "Park System for Freeport," 2–3.

43. David G. Schuster, *Neurasthenic Nation: America's Search for Health, Happiness, and Comfort, 1869–1920* (New Brunswick, NJ: Rutgers University Press, 2011), 1; Mark S. Micale, *Hysterical Men: The Hidden History of Male Nervous Illness* (Cambridge, MA: Harvard University Press, 2008).

44. Gail Bederman, *Manliness and Civilization: A Cultural History of Gender and Race in the United States, 1880–1917* (Chicago: University of Chicago Press, 1995), 88–101; Brian M. Ingrassia, *The Rise of Gridiron University: Higher Education's Uneasy Alliance with Big-Time Football* (Lawrence: University Press of Kansas, 2012), 71–92.

45. Robinson, "Park System for Freeport," 5–6.
46. Robinson, "St. Joseph of the Future," 8–9. On the animistic and mechanistic, see Carolyn Merchant, *The Death of Nature: Women, Ecology, and the Scientific Revolution* (New York: Harper, 1989), 100, 192–193. Piland notes the transcendentalist influence ("Charles Mulford Robinson," 105). I am indebted to graduate assistant Jared Haines for some insights in this paragraph.
47. Robinson, "Improvement of Hannibal," 58.
48. Charles Mulford Robinson, *Report on a Park System for Council Bluffs, Iowa, Made to the Board of Park Commissioners* (Council Bluffs, IA: Monarch Printing Co., 1913), 9–12, 21.
49. Robinson, *Report [on] Cedar Rapids*, [3–5].
50. Robinson, "Improvement of Hannibal," 66.
51. Robinson, *Report for Fort Wayne*, 105.
52. Robinson, "Park System for Freeport," 20.
53. Ingrassia, *Rise of Gridiron University*, 17–19.
54. Charles Mulford Robinson, *The Advancement of Alton, Illinois: A General City Plan Study for The Board of Trade* (Alton: Melling & Gaskins, 1914), 17, 26, 41–42 (last quotation).
55. H. S. Mueller and H. T. Reeves, "The Parks," in Charles Mulford Robinson et al., *Notes for a Study in City Planning in Champaign-Urbana by the 1913 and 1914 Classes in Civic Design at the University of Illinois* (Chicago: R.R. Donnelly & Sons Co., 1915), 34–35, 37. The idea that parks increased property values was common then; see Blackford, *The Lost Dream*, 64, 74–75.
56. Mueller and Reeves, "Parks," 44.
57. C. B. Andrews, Jean K. Ripley, W. L. Ramsey, and W. M. Welty, "Playgrounds," in Robinson et al., *Notes for a Study in City Planning*, 51.
58. Robinson et al., *Notes for a Study in City Planning*, 1.
59. Kathryn J. Oberdeck, "Archives of the Unbuilt Environment: Documents and Discourses of Imagined Space in Twentieth-Century Kohler, Wisconsin," *Archive Stories: Facts, Fictions, and the Writing of History*, ed. Antoinette Burton (Durham, NC: Duke University Press, 2005), 251–273.
60. Jon K. Lauck, *From Warm Center to Ragged Edge: The Erosion of Midwestern Literary and Historical Regionalism, 1920–1965* (Iowa City: University of Iowa Press, 2017).

CHAPTER 9

AGRARIAN "NATURISM"

Liberty Hyde Bailey and the Michigan Frontier

John Linstrom and Daniel Rinn

INTRODUCTION

It was haying time on a small Midwestern farm in the latter half of the nineteenth century. Liberty Hyde Bailey Jr. watched as his father, scythe in hand, joined other farmers in mowing an open meadow. It was a recurring, seasonal event in which farmers cut and dried grasses for later use as animal fodder. A young boy, Bailey did not participate in the mowing itself—he was not big enough to swing a scythe to much effect. He aided the effort in different capacities, sometimes providing food and water to the men working or, at other times, simply taking a hand rake to the ground to consolidate the fallen grasses into neat piles. More often than not, perhaps, he simply watched. While the grasses ran high, the meadow had contained mysteries. Rabbits, birds, and other natural wonders seemed to be contained within. Yet the meadow was "forbidden territory" to young Bailey, off limits until it was time to process the hay. His curiosity hard to contain, he skirted every inch of the meadow's perimeter, climbed atop fence rails, scaled a large stump for an aerial view, and relied on any means possible to glean an insight into "the grassy wilderness." Haying time, then, was a very special event. He and his childhood friends knew "there must be strange things in the depths of the grass. The mowing would disclose it all; and eagerly we would watch the mowers." With interest, he watched and waited for "a new landscape" to emerge as the grasses fell.[1]

Haying time was fixed at an important intersection in Bailey's understanding of the world. Such labor required the help of neighbors, which in turn provided an opportunity for sharing stories and forming personal relationships. It required, too, sweat, exhaustion, investing one's sense of self in the land. Maybe most important, harvesting the meadow's grasses was an aesthetic experience. He found a certain beauty in the way a landscape seemed to change, and coevolve, as humans interacted with the natural world. For Bailey, the meadow was a *natural* landscape year-round—as such, it sometimes included tall grasses and hidden wildlife, and at other times it included farmers and threshers. No matter the time of year, one could witness evolutionary processes continuously at work. As Bailey would later describe in many lectures, books, and poems, humanity and nature were deeply interwoven. If scientists failed to recognize this entanglement, then they failed to understand and express the quality of the landscape. Indeed, this responsibility would ultimately fall on the shoulders of horticulturists—the farmers and gardeners who understood nature's beauty as well as its botany. Aesthetic experience and expression were the tenets of a far-reaching environmental cosmology that, for Bailey, united nature and culture, art and science, farming and poetry. And despite its nearly impossible breadth, this was a naturalism rooted in Michigan's soil.[2]

AMATEUR NATURALIST

Liberty Hyde Bailey Jr. was born in a newly built, five-room frame house, on a two-year-old farm with an orchard not yet bearing fruit in the woods of southwest Michigan, just over a mile from the shore of Lake Michigan, in 1858. His father, the senior Liberty Hyde Bailey, had moved west from Vermont in 1842, working for a family friend in the Vermont Land Company as a land locator and buyer in the spring, summer, and fall and working in lumber mills in the winter. He evidently undertook this labor in order to eventually purchase his own land and establish a farm similar to what he had known in Vermont. Building a life in Michigan was a gradual process for the elder Bailey, one that involved acquiring land, starting a family, selling an initial farm in order to move closer to the Lake Michigan shoreline in 1856, and welcoming his third and last child, Liberty Jr., to the family in 1858.

The junior Bailey would recount his memories of growing up as a child in the swamps, forests, and sand dunes of Michigan, as well as his memories of farm labor and the work ethic imposed by his father, in essays and books throughout his life. He would recall spending hours at the side of a brook that ran through the farm, studying the insects and other animals that lived in the interesting habitat, and riding his horse Ed through the woods. He also recounted the rainy work days spent pulling nails from old boards, the dreaded chore of cleaning out the bottom of the cistern, the creative fun of grafting as many varieties of apple and pear as he could to a single experimental tree at the back of the house, and the sultry days when he walked the rows of corn with his father hoeing weeds.[3] He also recalled spending considerable time with the "three hundred [Potawatomi] Indians wigwamed on that land" purchased by his father, with whom he trapped passenger pigeons, among other activities, and who would freely come in and out of his family's house when he was young. "I knew the Indians," he said at his ninetieth birthday party, "and I picked up something of their outlooks."[4] Indeed, it was during his childhood years that Bailey would begin defining his own naturalistic "outlook."

Bailey's numerous childhood excursions into the garden, fields, and forests near the South Haven farm had suggested the plasticity of the boundaries that humans laid upon the landscape. Nature, he believed, contained mystery that invited curiosity, even awe and wonder, as he explored cultivated and wild landscapes alike. He was a devotee of a brand of naturalism that recognized no hard boundaries between natural and unnatural, wilderness and civilization. He would bring more nuance and shape to these ideas in his years as a student and, much later, professor at Cornell University.

Bailey's formal education began in Michigan. "It was called a high school, because one room was over the other," he later recalled of the two-story building.[5] His studies continued at the State Agricultural College (now Michigan State University)—he graduated with his bachelor's degree in 1882 at age twenty-four, with a major in botany. Through the recommendation of his professor and noted botanist William J. Beal, he secured a research position in the Harvard herbarium of Asa Gray. Gray was a towering figure, the foremost American botanist of his day and adamant defender of scientific evolution alongside theism, whom Charles Darwin held in high esteem.[6] His brand of naturalism would have a lasting impact on Bailey, though the two men did not always see eye to eye.

When, in 1884, Bailey accepted an offer to chair the nation's first Department of Horticulture and Landscape Gardening at his alma mater in Michigan, Gray reportedly expressed his disappointment in the decision. He had thought that this new protégé of his desired to become a *botanist*, to which Bailey responded that he believed a *horticulturist* ought to *be* a botanist, eliciting Gray's retort, "Yes, but he needs to be a horticulturist, too."[7] Horticulture, in other words, was no science to the gatekeepers of academic botany. Gray was not alone in these beliefs. Michigan was something of a national leader in the effort, during the nineteenth century, to centralize education and provide professional training for teachers. As numerous educational institutions—ranging from the small, single-room schoolhouse for children and young adults to academic centers such as the University of Michigan—began to proliferate around the state, policymakers began debating the question of "practical" training in agriculture. Against calls from Michigan farmers to create agricultural schools, administrators such as Henry Tappan, who championed an elite brand of academic learning at the University of Michigan, emphasized scholarship in literature and the sciences over practical training.[8] But Bailey had grown up with his feet and hands in the soil—he found it difficult to conceive of science as fixed within the confines of a cold, sterile method aimed primarily at "objectivity" or distanced from everyday experience. Over his years as an academic, his thought would coalesce around one consistent drive: looking back to his experiences of nature at home, he sought to blunt the harder edges of a scientific naturalism that ignored culture.

NATURALISM: A DIVIDED LANDSCAPE

Bailey had Gray's comments in mind when he entered a lecture hall at 7:30 p.m. on December 1, 1885, to give a talk. A tall, thin twenty-seven-year-old man at this point, his striking blue eyes took stock of the audience at the Massachusetts Board of Agriculture's annual meeting. He stepped forward to the lectern and began: "Horticulture, the art, is old. It had its origin, with twin agriculture, in the fertile valleys of Asia while yet the world was new. Man early learned to till the soil. He was a farmer." Tilling the soil was an art, as he would make clear, and cultivating plants functioned as an aesthetic experience. "Surely ours is a goodly heritage," he continued. He would go on to quote Shakespeare, Goethe, and—repeatedly—Darwin, whom he called "the grandest horticulturist of any generation" and who had written, after all, that "one new variety raised by man will be a more important and interesting subject for study, than one more species added to the infinitude of already recorded species." [9]

"The fence that stands between theory and practice is relative," Bailey stated. "It exists and it does not exist." And, later: "Then do not discourage the pursuit of science, however much you may have been taught to regard it as opposed to practice. Science is practice." These quotations from the lecture, which he titled "The Garden Fence," summarize much of Bailey's thinking: science is that which unites theory with practice and book-learning with fieldwork, rendering the divisions relative. Bailey knew from the outset, however, that treating horticulture as a "science" would not be uncomplicated. Farmers and scientists both had been taught to maintain the "garden fence" separating them, for reasons Bailey maintained some ambivalence about (the fence "exists and it does not exist," after all). But the notion that botanists belonged on the theoretical side, along with the plants of the forest and field, and farmers and plant breeders belonged on the practical side, in the garden, struck him as a division just as arbitrary as the divisions he had known between farm fields growing up—and he had crossed those boundaries easily enough. Moreover, if "science must climb the garden fence," Bailey believed, it was not because farmers were not already practicing science but because the experiments of the everyday farmer were not being recorded or transmitted sufficiently enough to be useful. [10]

While Bailey acknowledged in "The Garden Fence" that "those antagonistic notions which have been a feud between the farmer and the botanist" [11] exist on either side of the imagined garden fence, he nevertheless saved his heaviest rhetorical critique for the *scientists* who avoided crossing the fence into the garden:

The botanist claims the plant when it is a part of wild nature, but loses his interest when it becomes immediately useful to man. Is this

a legitimate division of labor? Is the scientist scientific? Does a horse
cease to be a horse when it is put into the harness?[12]

No, Bailey argued. In refusing to climb the fence, the "scientist" here has
ceased to be "scientific" and the "division of labor" no longer "legitimate."
Just as the horse is as much a horse when domesticated as when wild, so
with the cultivated apple and the wild apple. But how does a scientist
become scientific, and when does this division of labor become legitimate?
The crisis, for Bailey, originates with a misinterpretation of the more-than-
human world.

THE "NATURIST" AND SCIENTIFIC EXPRESSION

As a young man, Bailey had been a serious student of philosophy and
aesthetics, both in his reading and his early journalistic work, and if he
understood horticulture as continuous with botany, he also understood
philosophy and the arts as continuous with science. While this theme
emerges in his writing as early as "The Garden Fence," it first comes
into notable prominence in Bailey's unpublished 1888 travel narrative,
Onamanni: An Outing. Bailey had enjoyed reading travel narratives by
popular authors like Samuel Baker as a boy growing up on the South Haven
farm. He was barred from reading fiction, as well as even such improbable
biblical texts as the Book of Jonah,[13] by his Puritan-influenced Vermonter
father, although he read fiction widely as an adult.[14] So, when he had
the opportunity to join the Minnesota Geological Survey as botanist in
the Boundary Waters of northern Minnesota, a region then considered
"wilderness" and not heavily botanized, Bailey evidently saw an opportunity
to write the kind of book he had enjoyed reading so much as a child.

In *Onamanni*, Bailey again directly confronts the limits of disciplinary
science practiced in isolation, lamenting that "science oftener stifles inspiration than awakens it" and even "may lead away from nature." The
problem he identifies is one of analysis: "Ultimate analysis is a process
of detachment. The plant becomes a mere collection of cells. Nature in
its wholeness is a stranger." He goes on to specify that the problem has
to do with the collection of facts becoming ends in and of themselves.
As in "The Garden Fence," in which the unscientific scientist begins with

taxonomy rather than with the physical plant, Bailey argues in *Onamanni* that a glorification of "facts" can lead the scientist away from the kind of science Bailey practiced as a child in Michigan. To come closer to "nature in its wholeness" and avoid "detachment" from that wholeness, he believed the scientist needed to be grounded in the environment both intellectually and physically. But this grounding required the intervention of a very different mode of inquiry.[15]

"The scientist," Bailey wrote, "should at times escape his study. He should see nature externally. He of all others should see beauty. He should know the choicest scenery, the handsomest, most fragrant flowers. He should be capable of ecstasy, enthusiasm." If in "The Garden Fence" Bailey had concerned himself with the manner in which the scientist ought to be scientific, in *Onamanni* he takes issue with the scientist who has not learned to be *poetic*. The unpoetic scientist's "confin[ed] mental vision" leads to the sad state in which "few scientists see great expression in nature." His feeling that the scientist should "at times escape his study," "see nature externally," "see beauty," and "be capable of ecstasy, enthusiasm," indicates the scale of the problem, in Bailey's eyes, when scientists fail to experience the world poetically and hence misinterpret the radical interconnection of "nature in its wholeness" that is actually at work in the world.[16]

In Bailey's view, the atomization that might render a full plant "a mere collection of cells" required an illusory division between the observer and the thing observed, a distance that would "confin[e] mental vision" and render the scientist incapable of "ecstasy, enthusiasm." He states, "Few scientists see great expression in nature," and defines *expression* as "the utterance of some thought, feeling, the representation of an idea." The expression he takes for his example is that of "a giant oak, gnarled, leaning from a cliff." In his transcription of the tree's expression into written language, Bailey resorts to listing qualities represented by the individual oak, but he makes the point of stressing at the beginning of the sentence that "its expression is individual." The oak may express only *itself* in this formulation, but, at least in that sense, it does *express*. And the scientist—at least the "scientific" one, who ought also to be poetic—has a responsibility to that expression. The true naturalist needs somehow to bear witness to such expression as it arises in the more-than-human world rather than silencing such expression and replacing the living tree with the simple form of the *species* oak, with its then seemingly predictable arrangement of cells—which, of course, from tree to tree, are not predictable to any significant degree at all. To the poetic scientist, the source of the specific oak's individual expression remains a mystery—related to "what we don't know about horticulture." Bailey clearly does affirm an active, communicative relationality between the human and the more-than-human.[17]

In *The Outlook to Nature* (1905), Bailey continued exploring the contours of a non-reductive view of the natural world. Consisting of four lectures, the book emphasizes perception (outlook) as a means for shaping personal philosophy and conduct. In its ideal form, such an outlook would closely resemble that of the farmer. Suggesting the enduring importance of his childhood in Michigan, Bailey argues in the lecture titled "The Realm of the Commonplace,"

> What is now much needed in the public temper is such a change of
> attitude as will make us see and appreciate the commonplace and
> the spontaneous, and to have the desire to maintain and express our
> youthful and native enthusiasms. And it is my special part to try, so
> far as is possible, to open the eyes and the heart to nature and the
> common-day environment.

The farmer, Bailey argues, has access to something that others lack: the experience of direct and self-directed labor on the land, which for Bailey seemed to lend itself, as a lifestyle, to the appreciation of the "realm of the commonplace" more than the lifestyles of most urban dwellers. By necessity, he writes, "the farmer is a naturalist. In proportion as he is a good naturalist he is a good farmer." Not only for the sake of individual rural livelihoods but for the sake of a flourishing landscape, body politic, and democracy, rural life had to be protected from the economic and social pressures building against it at the turn of the century. A key tool for fighting the stereotypes that both drove rural people away from their farms and reinforced the belittling rhetoric of urban dwellers against "rubes" and "hayseeds," Bailey thought, would be a new rural literature— to make accessible the advantages of rural life to the broader public on the one hand, and to celebrate a culture that an increasingly industrialized capitalist society sought to marginalize on the other.[18]

While the relative isolation that a farmer experienced, compared to a city person, need not indicate "intellectual poverty," a certain literature would increasingly be needed to combat the idea of such poverty—the sort that, by 1905, Bailey had been writing and publishing in an increasingly wide array of rural periodicals across the country:

> The farmer needs literature,—literature that is bright, true and relevant. Most of the books that he reads—as also most of those that his children study—are made for townspeople. Where is the fiction that portrays the farmer without overdrawing or caricaturing him? Where are the candid and interesting farm sketches? The farm poems? The writing that will do for the farm what has been done to interest persons in nature? A good technical agricultural literature is now developing, and this is certain to be followed by a new range of literary writing.

In many ways, Bailey here sets out the importance of much of the writing he would do over the following decades.[19] If, as Bailey declares elsewhere in *The Outlook to Nature*, he would "stand, then, for the open country, for its affairs, for the trees that grow there, for the heaven above, for its men, for its women, for its institutions . . . [and] for them I mean to labor as long as I have strength and life," his most public and sustained means for such labor would be just as much *literary* as scientific labor. The pride in one's "calling" that Bailey hoped to inspire in more farmers would develop primarily through the farmer's realization "that he constitutes the most important nature-factor in our civilization."[20]

The chapter titled "Evolution: The Quest of Truth" begins to theorize the ways in which Darwinian evolution reshapes the human imagination in terms of literature, theology, and philosophy. Bailey returns to the same interest he expressed in "The Garden Fence" with the idea that "we are rapidly emancipating ourselves from the dogma of 'species,'" citing Hugo de Vries, who had just two years earlier published the second volume of his landmark *The Mutation Theory*, which put forward the concept of random mutation, by which evolution would take place much more quickly than in Darwinian gradualism. Bailey notes that "the very essence of [De Vries's] contention is that the differences between organisms must be measured by their qualities, not by their names," meaning their species names. The analytical categories of naturalism, now more than ever, needed to account for *experiential quality*, rather than "objective" description. Taxonomy necessitated aesthetic expression. It was on this point that Bailey signaled his entrance into an ongoing literary controversy concerning "sham naturalists." [21]

The "Burroughs-Long controversy," as he addresses it in the final chapter of the book, presented a particularly interesting problem for Bailey's literary/aesthetic project, as it seemed to pit a kind of scientific naturalist (a position the naturalist and writer John Burroughs defended) against the perspective of a more personable, yet attentive, amateur nature writer (a more generous version of Burroughs's characterization of Rev. William J. Long). Bailey then relates this focus on the individual rather than on the species to a shift in imaginative focus to "individual animals as personalities rather than to species and groups," or a shift from the old book-learning to a nature-study way of knowing the natural world. He continues:

> The Burroughs-Long controversy, aside from its incidents and its disputes as to matters of fact, brings up the deeper question as to how far particular animals have strong individual traits that are not common to the species as a whole. . . . The boy knows what the squirrel does day by day,—where it lives, when it goes and comes, what it eats, what it says. He knows the fields and the woods and the fishing-hole, without knowing that he knows them. If we could have the intimate unconscious boy kind of knowledge put into books, it would almost make a new natural history.

This unsettling of authority from the taxonomist to the author with "the intimate unconscious boy kind of knowledge"—specifically, the kind of knowledge *rural* children possessed—would lead to nothing less than "a new type of monographs, written directly from the field, without reference to the museums or to the kind of information that we have read about." [22]

While both Burroughs and Long would have agreed (vehemently) that natural history, or nature-study texts, must be "written directly from the field," this "new type of monographs" proposed by Bailey would still fly in the face, somewhat, of the tradition Burroughs defends in his essay

"Real and Sham Natural History"—a tradition that begins in the field but then involves the painstaking work of cross-referencing the body of extant text in search of other members of the species in question described as exhibiting similar behavior. Yet Bailey does not dismiss Burroughs so much as he dismisses the premise around which Burroughs and Long seem to have lost themselves—the controversy's "incidents and its disputes as to matters of fact," which do not interest him nearly as much as the "deeper question" as to the level of difference among individuals of a species. Moreover, these new monographs, Bailey continues, "will contain the least possible contamination of the author and the greatest possible content of crow or frog." [23]

Bailey does not resolve the tension between authorial relinquishment and the inherent anthropocentrism of the author's utterance here, which is partly why he is able to bypass the quagmire of the Burroughs-Long debate and move to the crucial significance of a natural history based around *individual* animals rather than abstract collections of species traits. He aligns "contamination of the author" not with misleading artistic flourishes (Burroughs's central complaint) but with the practice of *imposing book research onto depictions of living individuals*, thereby turning part of Burroughs's argument on its head. Close and prolonged attention to the individual—the kind of attention he attributes to farm children—would actually allow the "crow or frog" to live more fully in the text than it would through an author's painstaking attention to scientific precedent. Bailey does not suggest a new atomization, however—he asserts several pages later that "the fragmentary phenomena which we are able to observe are parts in some great system" but also that the only way for "the philosopher" to "construct a retrospect and to make a prophecy" is through the study of "fragmentary knowledge," recognizing the vast limits of human understanding. Considering the individuality of every living organism on the planet, the kind of authoritative debate over the possible habits of crows that Burroughs engages in his attack of Long begins to seem silly. Bailey wants the writer of his "new kind of monographs" to be attentive to the facts of the world, but precisely so that she does not fall into the privileging of supposed scientific facts over the realities of individuals. [24]

Rather than throw out science, Bailey again seeks to reorient it and in turn to reorient the outlook of an increasingly scientific society away from the myth of finality of fact and toward the indeterminacy of an uncountable number of unaccountably varied organisms all bound together in a system much too vast for human comprehension. Bailey believes the best one can do is apprehend what is around one and be led by those apprehensions to a deeper awe of the whole. Only then, if one is so fortunate, may one come into some greater, but self-consciously incomplete, understanding. Bailey's scientific scientist would seek to lean into and deepen that awe rather than search for its final explanation. "Science gives us prevision," he writes, but only if followed with the curiosity of the farm child with time and space to roam. Therefore, the best scientists, as well as the best naturalists, would not necessarily be found in the concentrated centers of academia—fittingly, Bailey dedicates *The Outlook to Nature* "to my father, whose more than four-score years have been lived on the farm—naturalist without knowing it." [25]

The controversy between Burroughs and Long is usually considered to have been ended finally by then-president Theodore Roosevelt's essay in defense of Burroughs titled "Nature Fakers," which ultimately gave the debate the name by which it is remembered to this day. [26] The "deeper question" that the debate raised for Bailey, however, continued to inform his emerging "earth-philosophy" and his convictions about the right way to approach the more-than-human world. [27] Tiring of the contentious connotations of the very term *naturalist*, which stemmed in part, no doubt, from the nature-faker scandal, in 1915 Bailey wrote, "I would like to use some other word for the man or woman who is both the nature-student and the nature-lover. I suggest that we adopt the old word 'naturist,' which now has no particular application and, therefore, no history to live down." [28]

THE ECOPOETICS OF NATURISM

In the 1908 collection, *Poems*, Bailey opens with a concrete description that seems to fit his theory, avoiding moralizing and abstractions in favor of a relatively "short, sharp, quick, direct word-picture," [29] although it leads him to abstraction by the end of the stanza:

I lie on my back on the shingle shore
Subdued by the wind and the pebbly roar;

I see the white clouds in their domes of air
And the specks of birds that are floating there;
And the earth is small and the sky is large—
I forget the sense of my time and charge;
I am lost in the awe of the Great Program—
Only this I know: I know that I Am.[30]

After the fourth line, the particulars of the shoreline where the poet lies begin to give way to a simultaneously expanding and contracting sense of scale—"the earth is small and the sky is large." As the speaker loses a sense of "time and charge" in the reverie of scale that the sensory experience gives rise to (the feeling of the "shingle shore," the sounds of wind and waves, the sight of the clouds and "specks of birds"), he begins to imagine a "Great Program," which Bailey describes in characteristically vague and undogmatic terms but which indicates a system connecting him to a long line of naturists like Darwin and Alexander von Humboldt who extrapolated larger patterns from commonplace particulars. While Bailey departs from the project of "direct word-pictures" at this point in the poem, he has demonstrated the idea that direct encounters with the "realm of the commonplace" allow one to observe the parts of greater wholes and the interconnectedness of Earth's elements, in this case the individual poet connecting to the small earth, the large sky, the specks of birds above, and the shingle shore below.

The penultimate poem in the collection, "Brotherhood," takes up more directly the theme of the interrelatedness of life, which Bailey would explicate seven years later in "The Brotherhood Relation" chapter of *The Holy Earth*. In the poem, he anticipates his argument that human kinship extends to the whole biotic community and that the teachings of Darwin necessitate a reconsideration of human morals to encompass the more-than-human world. Rather than rely on Darwinian evolutionary science here, though, Bailey appeals to the experiences of the open fields, listing an astonishing variety of more-than-human entities:

Weather and wind and waning moon,
Plain and hilltop under the sky,
Ev'ning, morning and blazing noon,

Brother of all the world am I.
The pine-tree, linden and the maize,
The insect, squirrel and the kine,
All-natively they live their days—
As they live theirs, so I live mine.
I know not where, I know not what:—
Believing none and doubting none
What'er befalls it counteth not,—
Nature and Time and I are one.[31]

The whole poem employs the form of the list, and while the poem goes on to include four stanzas that are more imagistic than this first, Bailey here establishes the breadth of his kinship as "brother of all the world."

Bailey had experienced poetry and the literary arts throughout his childhood in rural Michigan—his neighbor and mentor, the peach farmer A. S. Dyckman, regularly published sprawling, mini-epic poems in the local *South-Haven Sentinel* memorializing local events and individuals under the flamboyant pseudonym Veritas, and he galvanized members of the community to raise the town's first theater, a barnlike structure where a young Bailey attended his first performance of Shakespeare.[32] Dyckman was also among the first successful orchardists in the region, along with Bailey's father. Years later, Bailey's work at Cornell continually reaffirmed his belief in poetry's role in rural society. He held weekly meetings of students at his home, where each week he made a habit of sharing poems by some of his favorite poets, who ranged from Shakespeare to Rupert Brooke. One of these students, he recalled, "had to support himself and help members of his family." One day the student approached Bailey with some embarrassment and asked to borrow a copy of one of the poems in order to memorize it, "for he could not afford to buy."[33]

The new nature poetry, as Bailey described his poetic vision, would help to inspire the "outlook to nature" that his whole book of that title seeks to direct its readers toward.[34] This poetry would encourage readers to pursue moral or ethical answers through firsthand encounters and relationships with the world that the poem depicts, rather than seeking some sort of truth contained in the poem itself and potentially abstracted from the world. After reading, in other words, the reader would be redirected by the poem back toward the natural world. In a poem like "The Farmer" (which is also included in *Poems*), rather than valorize farm labor, Bailey describes and formally represents the repetitiveness of farm labor without allowing that aspect of the labor to be either subsumed by or opposed to natural beauty. In Bailey's evocation, beauty exists in productive tension with work. Rather than dismiss the hard-working farmer as incapable of literary appreciation and expression, Bailey indicates that, in fact, the contribution of the farmer would be vitally central to the new nature poetry.

THE ECOLOGICAL COSMOLOGY OF CULTIVATED LANDSCAPES

In one of his most fully realized literary agrarian texts, *The Harvest of the Year to the Tiller of the Soil* (1927), Bailey reflected on the incidents of his childhood on the farm through memoir. For Bailey, one of the largest flaws underlying the industrial "prophecy" that "in the future we are to have corporation farms of 5000 acres and more," which sounds all too real to those familiar with the history of farming in the century since, was that "the public little recognizes the farmer's place in nature," and public policy had grown around the urban ignorance of that ecological place held uniquely by the farmer. In the midst of agriculture's demotion in public discussions to "mere commercial valuations," Bailey believed that "we are now direfully in need of a spiritual awakening." [35]

In other words, Bailey believed the project of worldview transition needed to reach into the core of a rural cosmology to awaken farmers as well as everyone else to humans' sense of kinship with, rather than dominance over, the more-than-human world. But as he approached his seventieth year and watched as many of the rural reforms he had fought for seemed to be drifting in more industrial directions, Bailey feared he might be wrong. If, in fact, he had slid into an irresponsibly romantic notion of the agrarian farmer's spiritual awareness of human frailty and the interrelatedness of all life (even extending beyond the biotic) and the value and beauty of that interrelationality, then the cosmological core of his political praxis would be inherently false. Out of fear that he might have lost touch with the grinding labor of farming and had romanticized it, he sent a simple circular to his farmer correspondents across the United States and Canada, informing them of his inquiry: "Now that the discouragements of agriculture are so much stressed, I am asking farmers in various parts of the country whether they really experience joy in farming and to indicate to me, if they will, what is the main satisfaction they find in the farmer's life." He received letters from 129 farmers, "sometimes more than one letter," and from all over the continent.[36] He concluded his book with excerpts from these responses, letting the voices of the working farmers have the last word.

The collective voice that emerges in those excerpts reflects something of the cosmological mode of kinship that Bailey had explored throughout his life. "I grew up here on this farm," one writes. "Like Walt Whitman's child, I went forth every day and the things I saw became part of me." The idea that the land contained generations in it, and that individuals had fitted themselves to the land or had been shaped by the land into relationship with it, recurs multiple times in Bailey's excerpting. Some respondents indicated their involvement in larger political and social organizing:

> The raising of better cattle and crops than the average brings a
> sense of satisfaction difficult to duplicate. Further than this a close
> contact with cooperative buying and selling organizations which
> show enough progress to furnish the courage necessary to insure the
> continuance of this work is satisfying.

Confirming Bailey's reading of his childhood meadow as a social (as well as a "natural") space, another writer, self-identified as "a farm wife," describes joy "in working in the soil, the wind and rain in our faces . . . the wild flowers and the birds . . .; we enjoy the community contacts and the local and State fairs and the folks down at our State College." Another, specifically addressing labor, describes "freedom of action that once enjoyed could not suffer to be abridged. The spirit of creating, always hoping, always expecting, never on the dead level of monotony." Bailey, evidently, was not the only naturist in North America—perhaps every farm had its own.[37] But naturism would be found not only on the farm.

Over a decade later, in 1938, an eighty-year-old Bailey published *The Garden of Pinks*, a book that explored the environmental cosmology of the garden. Writing about the varieties of Dianthus in his Cornell herbarium (which he named a "Hortorium," emphasizing horticulture's root *hortus*, for garden), he offered personal reflections on gardening as he explored scientific method and the process of taxonomy. At the same time, however, the book reveals that Bailey, even in his old age, was still grounded in the landscape of his childhood:

> From earliest boyhood the pinks have been my companions. Mounds
> and rings of grass pinks were in the front yard, left there by my
> mother, so different in their delicacy from the weeds and brush
> and deep smells of the forest from which the farm was cut that they
> seemed like tokens from another and remoter earth.[38]

The flowers were "left there" by Bailey's mother after her death; in the only book-length biography that Bailey partially oversaw, Andrew Denny Rodgers III emphasizes the importance of that garden, observing that "for years [Bailey] watched it, tended it, and kept the same plants growing in it. Indeed, when he became professor of horticulture at Cornell University, he took with him roots of some of the plants from this garden."[39] That first garden of pinks represented a touchstone in Bailey's autobiographical imagination. After his mother died from diphtheria when he was four years old, his father took him into the garden in front of the small frame house and taught him to tend the small plot of pinks his mother had left there, and he would seek to plant and tend a garden every year of his life afterward.

In *The Garden of Pinks*, Bailey remembered the variety of pinks from his mother's garden first by his family's name for them, "grass pinks," a name he "liked," but which he ultimately thought "is not a good name, seeing that all pinks are grass-like," as well as John Gerard's 1597 name "Plumarius, or feathered pinke," which Bailey ironically dismissed as "a name for tomes and those who persist in writing them." He ultimately concluded, "To me the plant is Cottage pink, and so I call it in this my book."[40]

He also harked back to his introduction, as a four year old, to that 1862 garden of pinks in his first-ever radio address on February 17, 1930, which was broadcast by the National Broadcasting Company chain as the inaugural address in the National Garden Bureau's "National Chain Broadcast of Garden Talks." On the radio, Bailey stated, "Every year for sixty or more recurring seasons I have had a garden, under my own hand."[41] His motivation for gardening stemmed less from an interest in developing "special gardening skill or material for floral display, or [to]

make a good-looking space," and more from a desire to "ever increase
. . . my range of acquaintanceship."[42] So, in the drama of Bailey's own
autobiography, pinks represented a sustained connection to the land
through the growing of and "acquaintanceship" with cultivated plants—a
connection that bridged art, science, and "practice," insisting, in fact,
on the continuity rather than the exclusivity of these categories. Bailey
was a taxonomist, but his was the taxonomy of a broadly conceived environmental outlook. Indeed, across Bailey's oeuvre, the praxis of the
horticulturist provides a corrective to the atomizing abstractions of the
unscientific scientist.[43]

CONCLUSION

Liberty Hyde Bailey Jr. continuously drew on examples for his books from
his own childhood experience of gardens, farms, and greenhouses. Even
in The Pruning-Manual, a book largely characterized by the matter-of-fact
tone of authority one might expect from a distinguished professor writing
on a specialty, we find passages such as this one:

> Of all the operations connected with horticulture, pruning, shaping,
> and training bring the person into closest contact and sympathy
> with the plant. One directs and cares for the plant tenderly and
> thoughtfully, working out his ideas as he would in the training and
> guiding of a child. . . . If a person cannot love a plant after he has
> pruned it, then he has either done a poor job or is devoid of emotion.[44]

Apple pruning had been a major part of Bailey's work as a child on the farm
in South Haven where he joined his father in testing experimental pruning
methods.[45] The reference to the benefits of pruning, then, should not come
as a surprise. Bailey clearly believed a central feature of naturism was an
ability to envision one's *home* in the natural world.

He believed the "brotherhood relation" of kinship with all life, seemingly with all of nature, emerged out of the poetic sensibility that one
cultivated through experience in the outdoors—just as the farmer would
"gather the wind with the grain," as Bailey wrote in his poem "The Farmer,"
she would also gather a poetic understanding of the place of contingency

that she occupied in the universe.[46] Everyone lived in such a state of radical contingency, but awareness of that state required an awakened vision to the "realm of the commonplace." As a result, Bailey consistently maintained that his philosophy and work should necessarily and organically emerge in cultivated landscapes, standing not only, as he wrote in *The Outlook to Nature*, for "the open country" but also for "its affairs, for the trees that grow there, for the heaven above, for its men, for its women, for its institutions," and for them—all of them—he succeeded in his goal to "labor as long as I have strength and life."

NOTES

1. Liberty Hyde Bailey, *The Harvest of the Year to the Tiller of the Soil* (New York: Macmillan, 1927), 25–26.
2. This chapter is adapted from a longer chapter in John Linstrom's dissertation on land and labor in the literary cosmologies of American writers during the Progressive Era. For further discussion of Bailey's cosmological engagement with land and environment, and on the central role of such engagement to Bailey's lifework and impact on environmental literature, see Linstrom's "Editor's Introduction" to the centennial edition of Bailey's *The Holy Earth* (Berkeley: Counterpoint, 2015), as well as The Liberty Hyde Bailey Library, a forthcoming series of books by and about Bailey that Linstrom will edit under the Comstock imprint of Cornell University Press.
3. These stories appear in a number of Bailey's works, including *The Nature-Study Idea* (1903) and his ninetieth birthday speech in *Words Said about a Birthday*, as well as in the biographies by Rodgers and Dorf, but the most sustained childhood reminiscences occur in Part II of Bailey's *The Harvest*.
4. *Words Said about a Birthday: Addresses in Recognition of the Ninetieth Anniversary of the Natal Day of Liberty Hyde Bailey*, 1948, Liberty Hyde Bailey Papers, #21-2-3342, Division of Rare & Manuscript Collections, Cornell University Library, Ithaca, NY.
5. *Liberty Hyde Bailey*, handsewn pamphlet of local South Haven newspaper clippings, Liberty Hyde Bailey Museum, unnumbered.
6. Harlan P. Banks, "Liberty Hyde Bailey: 1858–1954," *Biographical Memoirs of the National Academy of Sciences* 64 (1994): 1–32.
7. This tension between Bailey and Gray has been noted in Andrew Denny Rodgers III, *Liberty Hyde Bailey: A Story of American Plant Sciences* (New

York: Hafner, 1965), 86; Philip Dorf, *Liberty Hyde Bailey: An Informal Biography* (Ithaca, NY: Cornell University Press, 1956), 48; and Banks, "Liberty Hyde Bailey," 7.

8. References to the debates surrounding education in Michigan during the nineteenth century are drawn from Willis Frederick Dunbar and George S. May, *Michigan: A History of the Wolverine State*, rev. ed. (Grand Rapids, MI: W. B. Eerdmans, 1980), 329–347.

9. Liberty Hyde Bailey, "The Garden Fence," in *The Liberty Hyde Bailey Gardener's Companion: Essential Writings*, ed. John A. Stempien and John Linstrom (Ithaca, NY: Comstock-Cornell University Press, 2019), 227, 228, 234.

10. Bailey, "Garden Fence," 232, 259, 252.

11. Bailey, "Garden Fence," 245.

12. Bailey, "Garden Fence," 257.

13. Liberty Hyde Bailey, "Some Reminiscences of the Development of the American Country Life Movement," *The Rural Church Institute Mimeograph Series* 33 (1943), 7.

14. Dorf, *Liberty Hyde Bailey*, 47.

15. Liberty Hyde Bailey, *Onamanni: A Gardener's Vacation*, 1886–1899, Liberty Hyde Bailey Papers, #21-2-3342, box 18, folders 15–18, Division of Rare and Manuscript Collections, Cornell University Library, Ithaca, NY.

16. Bailey, *Onamanni*.

17. Bailey, *Onamanni*.

18. Liberty Hyde Bailey, *The Outlook to Nature* (New York: Macmillan, 1905), 4, 68.

19. Such fiction would appear briefly in *Universal Service* (1918) and in book-length form in *The Seven Stars* (1927); such "sketches" would form the second half of *The Harvest* and are scattered throughout his oeuvre; and such poems he had already begun to publish, more and more widely in journals, and would collect first in the chapbook *Poems* (1908, printed by the Roycrofters) and then in the full-length collection *Wind and Weather* (1916).

20. Bailey, *The Outlook to Nature*, 127, 81–82, 112.

21. Bailey, *The Outlook to Nature*, 267.

22. Bailey, *The Outlook to Nature*, 267–269.

23. Bailey, *The Outlook to Nature*, 270.

24. Bailey, *The Outlook to Nature*, 172, 176.

25. Bailey, *The Outlook to Nature*, 274, v.

26. Ralph H. Lutts, *The Nature Fakers: Wildlife, Science & Sentiment* (Golden, CO: Fulcrum, 1990), 129–138.

27. Baily coins the term *earth-philosophy* in Liberty Hyde Bailey, *Universal Service* (New York: Macmillan, 1918), 16.

28. Liberty Hyde Bailey, *York State Rural Problems II* (Albany, NY: Lyon, 1915), 40.

29. Bailey outlined his desire for this type of writing in *The Outlook to Nature*, 22–33.

30. Liberty Hyde Bailey, *Poems* (Ithaca, NY: Cornell Countryman, 1908), 7.

31. Bailey, *Poems*, 19.

32. See Dorf, *Liberty Hyde Bailey*, and Margaret Beattie Bogue, "Liberty Hyde Bailey, Jr. and the Bailey Family Farm," *Agricultural History* 63, no. 1 (1989): 26–48.

33. Bailey, *The Outlook to Nature*, 34–35.

34. Bailey, *The Outlook to Nature*, 29–30.

35. Bailey, *The Harvest*, 102, 110.

36. Bailey, *The Harvest*, 196.

37. Bailey, *The Harvest*, 200, 204.

38. Liberty Hyde Bailey, *The Garden of Pinks, with Decorations* (New York: Macmillan, 1938), 1.

39. Rodgers, *Liberty Hyde Bailey*, 8. See also Dorf, *Liberty Hyde Bailey*, 7.

40. Bailey, *The Garden of Pinks*, 1.

41. Liberty Hyde Bailey, "Gardening and Its Future" (1930), in Stempien and Linstrom, *The Liberty Hyde Bailey Gardener's Companion*, 39.

42. Bailey, "Gardening and Its Future," 40.

43. As Daniel Rinn writes of the philosophy espoused in "The Garden Fence," "The intellectual edifice on which scientific naturalism rested began to crumble in the hands of gardeners" (122). Rinn, "Liberty Hyde Bailey: Pragmatic Naturalism in the Garden," *Environment and History* 24, no. 1 (2018): 121–138.

44. Liberty Hyde Bailey, *The Pruning-Manual: Being the Eighteenth Edition, Revised and Reset, of The Pruning-Book, which was First Published in 1898* (New York: Macmillan, 1946), 108.

45. Bogue, "Liberty Hyde Bailey," 40.

46. Bailey, *Poems*, 21.

CHAPTER 10

"THE MIND AND THE SOIL"

An Iowa Town That Grows Writers

Cherie Dargan

INTRODUCTION

Cedar Falls, Iowa, was established on the banks of the Red Cedar River in 1850,[1] eleven years before the start of the Civil War. A railroad town by 1861, it became a college town in 1876 with the founding of the Iowa State Normal School, Iowa's sole college at the time for training teachers.[2] During and after the Civil War, Cedar Falls, like other Midwestern towns, became a hub of intellectual activity with the advent of a newspaper, a lending library, several reading societies, and a handful of discussion groups. Unlike other Midwestern towns, this community of approximately 41,000[3] fostered five nationally known best-selling writers[4] and a number of other writers, while establishing several cultural groups that flourish to this day. The secret of this town's success? A persistent focus by a succession of civic leaders on the fertile blend of literature and the land. Many towns had literary societies, but early Cedar Falls had Peter Melendy, founder of the Cedar Falls Horticultural and Literary Society in 1859.[5] His tagline, "the mind and the soil," bore fruit in the creation of a city with beautiful parks, gardens, and trees complemented by a vibrant literary culture.

Cedar Falls became home to such nationally known, best-selling writers as Bess Streeter Aldrich, Ruth Suckow, James Hearst, Robert James Waller, and Nancy Price, among others.[6] Other local authors wrote memoirs, short stories, novels, blogs, and histories of the area. The university enriched the community with lectures, music, dramatic performances, and art exhibits. Its faculty became part of the community, joining numerous groups, such as the Cedar Falls Supper Club and the Final Thursday Reading Group.

How did Cedar Falls develop a culture that valued literacy, encouraged so many writers to tell their stories, and produced so many readers eager to read those stories? Furthermore, how did Cedar Falls become a place where people gathered to present and discuss ideas?

An analysis of its early history points to three reasons and at least three early leaders who shared a vision for a community that valued "the mind and the soil." First, the town valued literacy from the very beginning. Early leaders like Melendy organized the Cedar Falls Horticultural and Literary Society and gathered five hundred books for the first lending library in 1859 and 1860.[7] Second, the town valued its history: both Melendy and Roger Leavitt served as early historians, and a number of the city's writers have produced histories of the early settlers or personal memoirs of their lives in town. Finally, the college brought educated people to the community to serve as its faculty, giving townsfolk opportunities to interact with them in clubs like the Cedar Falls Parlor Reading Circle. Melendy was part of the effort to establish the normal school: teacher Moses Bartlett and President James C. Gilchrist became part of the Parlor Reading Circle early on in 1876.[8]

Without these men and women, Cedar Falls would not be the community we know today as "an Iowa Town that Grows Writers."[9]

Peter Melendy and the Horticultural and Literary Society

Let's begin by looking at how Cedar Falls established the value of literacy in its community when it formed its first school in 1847 with six students and Mrs. Jackson Taylor serving as the teacher—there were only forty people living in the village at the time. This was two years after William Sturgis and his brother-in-law, Erasmus Adams, established the town, which was then called Sturgis Falls. The men were drawn to the area for the timber, the land for farming, and the Red Cedar River (later called the Cedar River) for transportation, power for lumber and grist mills, and drinking water.[10] In 1847, brothers John Milton Overman and Dempsey Overman, along with their friend John T. Barrick, arrived in Sturgis Falls; they bought out the Sturgis family and renamed the town Cedar Falls in 1849 in honor of the Cedar River. Within its first decade, the town established a post office (1849), a schoolhouse (1853), a newspaper (the *Banner*, in 1853), and a county court (1853).[11]

As settlers moved west, they sought better lives for their children, wanting them to be able to read and write, use math, and discuss the issues of the day. The settlers who came to Cedar Falls moved west for the fertile land but also wanted intellectual opportunities for their children. The community grew rapidly, reaching around sixteen hundred by 1860 and crowding the school, where the first log cabin had been replaced by a frame schoolhouse.[12]

One of the obstacles early schools faced was a lack of books, as pointed out by a teacher's guide from Nebraska. Students had to furnish books, slates, and chalk. Often, they brought "a Bible, an Almanac, or old textbooks brought on the westward trip."[13]

Melendy moved to Cedar Falls in 1857, after farming in Ohio for several years. In that state, he had subscribed to a number of farm journals, attended fairs, asked questions, and learned all that he could before moving west. Melendy believed that farmers needed to learn about soil conservation, and they needed "agricultural enlightenment." In other words, they needed to learn all they could about the profession of farming.[14] Melendy and his wife, Martha, enrolled twelve-year-old Charles and eight-year-old Luetta in school in Cedar Falls and became involved as patrons, coming to hear the children's recitations on Fridays. Melendy "pronounced the words in Webster's old Blue Back Speller and spelled the children down," according to his biographer Luella Wright. Later, Melendy and his wife worked to get the funding to build a new, bigger building.[15]

The town's first newspaper, the *Banner*, established in 1853, was the only newsroom west of Dubuque and north of Cedar Rapids. When the *Banner*'s editors moved their paper to Waterloo in 1858, Henry ("H. A.") and George Perkins arrived in the spring of 1860, bringing their printing press with them. They were already proficient editors, printers, publishers, and reporters at the ages of twenty-four and twenty, respectively.[16]

Melendy became friends with the Perkins brothers and agreed to write a "Field and Garden" column for the *Cedar Falls Gazette*. In one column, he wrote, "The mind and the soil is our platform and we would make a thorough business of each, could we have our way."[17] That issue of the *Gazette* also included a history of the Cedar Falls Horticultural and Literary Society's first year, with its twin goals of beautifying the city and developing an appreciation of learning and literature.[18] Furthermore, the editors promised that Melendy's columns would "promote scientific horticulture."[19]

The phrase "the mind and the soil" led to the formation of the Cedar Valley Horticultural and Literary Society in 1859, which developed a small lending library for its members and encouraged residents to beautify the city with garden plots, fruit trees, ornamental shrubs, and flowers.[20] Melendy called Cedar Falls "the Garden City" and set a good example: his own garden was the "show garden" of Cedar Falls.[21] In addition, as Luella Wright put it in her 1947 biography, "he desired to see his fellow townsmen become lovers of books and of reading. . . . [In] Peter Melendy's scheme of social values two things seemed paramount—opportunities for mental stimulation and closer solidarity of town and country."[22]

The Horticultural and Literary Society addressed both objectives. Members collected one hundred books in their first year, after going door to door to collect books from neighbors on two different occasions.[23] The group purchased a Bible and a dictionary and subscribed to farm journals, including the *Ohio Farmer*, the *Prairie Farmer*, and the *New England Farmer*, as well as *Scientific American* and the *Horticulturist* and the *Annals of Congress*.[24] They purchased an additional one hundred books each year, until they had a total of five hundred books in their lending library. To put that accomplishment into context, consider that in the mid-nineteenth century most families had few books: perhaps a family Bible and *The Old Farmer's Almanac*, maybe a hymnbook, an old *McGuffey's Reader*, a book of poetry, *Pilgrim's Progress*, or *Paradise Lost*.[25] Gathering five hundred books was quite an accomplishment at the time.

In 1861, the group purchased 105 books at a little less than a dollar per book, and then another 77 in 1862. The *Gazette* listed all of the books, including many American and British classics, such as Elizabeth Gaskell's *The Life of Charlotte Brontë*, Richard Henry Dana Jr.'s *Two Years Before the Mast*, David Livingstone's *Explorations in Africa*, James Russell Lowell's

Biglow Papers, Herman Melville's *Moby-Dick* and *Typee*, and Alfred Lord Tennyson's *The Princess*.[26]

The society also offered prizes for the best vegetable garden, the best arranged dooryard, and best combined fruit and vegetable garden, and this led villagers "to develop a sense of civic pride." [27] In 1859, the group hosted a series of forums at which agricultural, social, and political questions could be discussed, and then it became a lyceum providing an early form of adult education. Topics included soil conservation, fruit grafting, increasing the potato crop, the culture of bees, the construction of hot beds, the care of sick hogs, the mechanics of the new threshing machines, and the advantages of various kinds of plows.[28]

As the Civil War drew closer, the society began to feature political debates, and Melendy enlisted local ministers to help serve as moderators. He reported that because of these debates, the "minister . . . preached more thoughtful sermons[,] . . . George D. Perkins wrote better editorials and Zimri Streeter and J. B. Powers gained ability to speak forcefully before caucuses and conventions." [29]

In 1865, the society donated its books to the new library association and disbanded. When the city voted to support a free library in 1878, the library association turned over 1,301 books, and Cedar Falls became the third city in the state to have a tax-supported library.[30] During Melendy's tenure as mayor, 1895–1901, the city planned the construction of the Dayton-Carnegie Public Library.[31] Throughout its history, Cedar Falls has upheld Melendy's dual commitment to "the mind and the soil" with its many beautiful parks, public art, and modern library.

Valuing History: The Work of Local Historians

From the very start, Cedar Falls placed value in the collection of its stories and the preservation of its history. Several men stand out as local historians. Later in his life, Melendy wrote *Historical Record of Cedar Falls*, a book about the first fifty years of Cedar Falls.[32] The second local historian was banker Roger Leavitt: born in 1860 in nearby Waterloo and educated at Beloit College, he spent sixty-one years living and working in Cedar Falls.

Leavitt was the unofficial historian of Cedar Falls, keeping numerous scrapbooks, which he used to write *When Cedar Falls Was Young* (1928) and *Main Street* (1948).[33] When he was seventy, Leavitt met with Bess Streeter Aldrich when she was visiting town in 1930 and urged her to write a book about her family's arrival in Cedar Falls. Leavitt sent her eighteen pounds of documents, including correspondence and clippings, which resulted in her novel *Song of Years* (1938). She credited Leavitt's materials with giving her the information needed to bring the story and characters to life.[34]

After Leavitt, Cedar Falls residents continued to write a remarkable number of histories of the area. Professor Tom Connors compiled a list of twenty-four books about Black Hawk County and Cedar Falls, and another eight about the history of the University of Northern Iowa, in 2014. The list includes biographies of William Sturgis and Peter Melendy and is available on the Cedar Falls Authors Festival website.[35]

Many citizens wrote memoirs of their own lives or biographies of others living in Cedar Falls. Connors lists sixteen books and shorter works that fit into this category, including James Hearst's autobiography describing his diving accident and long recovery in *My Shadow Below Me* (1981), as well as Carol Miles Petersen's biography of Bess Streeter Aldrich, *The Dreams Are All Real* (1995).[36]

THE PARLOR READING CIRCLE AND THE NORMAL SCHOOL

Cedar Falls became home to the Iowa State Normal School in 1876. Several of those first teachers and administrators became involved in the community when faculty members Wright, Bartlett and Gilchrist joined the Cedar Falls Parlor Reading Circle, which had been established the previous year.[37] Parlor reading circles were a fad around the state; however, few cities documented their efforts as well as Cedar Falls did. In an age before radio or television, people relied on the recitation of poetry, vocal and instrumental performances, lectures, and book discussions for entertainment.

The lovely Victorian home in present-day Cedar Falls that houses the Cedar Falls Historical Society was once the home of Walter and Cornelia Bryant, who hosted musical performances, as well as many of the Cedar Falls Parlor Reading Circle meetings, in their parlor in the 1880s.[38] The group met every other week in various members' homes to discuss assigned readings and topics.

Another one of the first faculty members at the Iowa State Normal School, David Sands Wright, described his friend Moses Bartlett's contribution to the reading circle:

> [Bartlett] became immediately its lion. For many years he served as president of the Circle. . . . The Cedar Falls Circle is still a flourishing organization. It has survived the storms of fifty-six Iowa winters. . . . Perhaps the impact of Professor Bartlett's personality is a partial explanation of the secret of its longevity.[39]

Wright provided details about one evening in 1877:

> The program was opened by Miss Nellie Cameron with a piano solo from "Il Trovatore." Her rendition was followed by a reading . . . "very happily rendered from Dickens in which Tattleby, his wife and babes were characterized by Mrs. Ella (Mrs. Elias) Overman." Then "in a plain and intelligible manner" Mrs. B. Thorpe read a selection from Washington Irving. The piece de resistance of the evening, however, "was a paper on Language, prepared and read by Prof. M. W. Bartlett of the Normal School to which the Society listened attentively."[40]

Bartlett explained that the society's members "desired more rational and profitable entertainment than is found in the average society gathering." Membership was limited to thirty and was open to men and women. According to Bartlett, "Few towns . . . are more interested in social and intellectual culture than [Cedar Falls]."[41]

Roger Leavitt joined the group in 1888, and in 1926, he presented a paper about the history of the Cedar Falls Parlor Reading Circle.[42] After Walter Bryant died, Leavitt was instrumental in leading the group. The unofficial historian became a key member of the reading circle, made up of community members and faculty of the normal school. In an article for the 1934 issue of the *Iowa Journal of History and Politics*, Professor Luella Wright suggests that the reading circle owed a great deal to the Horticultural and Literary Society as well as to its successor, the Library Association, which prepared the way for future groups where town and gown could interact.[43]

THE CEDAR FALLS SUPPER CLUB

More than sixty years after the Cedar Falls Parlor Reading Circle began meeting, the Cedar Falls Supper Club grew out of a conversation in 1940 between a group of men who wanted to form a group to connect the college and community. Once founded, the group was alternately called the No Name Club, Town and Gown, and the Cedar Falls Supper Club.[44] Cedar Falls native Ferner Nuhn was one of the supper club's five founders, along with poet James Hearst, professor Harry Willard "Bill" Reninger, professor Martin Grant, and businessman Paul Diamond. They recruited seven other local men, kept rules to a minimum, and encouraged lively conversation and debate at gatherings.[45] Each monthly meeting included one member's presentation followed by a discussion of the topic. Even today, the member in charge of each meeting reminds all visitors that they are expected to participate.[46]

The Cedar Falls Supper Club had its first meeting in February 1941 with twelve members. Looking back after forty years, the poet James Hearst explained, "We were hungry for serious discussions of what life was like for the other fellow. . . . We were interested in controversy, in the opposition of faiths, beliefs, and . . . in a man's reasons for being."[47] The titles of some early speeches reveal the intellectual nature of the group: "Humanity's Destiny," "Authoritarianism/Conformity," "Surrealism in Politics," "Conscientious Objectors," "Failure of Education," "Our Unfinished Civil War," and "McCarthy: Substance & Shadow."[48]

The Cedar Falls Supper Club evolved from a men-only club that invited visitors (often spouses) one month a year to a more diverse club with women members in 1986. One of the first women to join was Dorothy Grant—the wife of founder Martin Grant—who wrote an informal history of the club in 1992. Another woman, Judith Harrington (who became a member in March 1988), is still active in the club today, serving as its secretary.[49] More than one hundred people have been members of the supper club since its founding, and current member Michael Dargan keeps a blog where he archives the speeches.[50]

Many of the club's members throughout the years have been writers or mentors to writers. For example, Professor Reninger taught Mona Van Duyn, who was later appointed United States Poet Laureate and won a

Pulitzer Prize for her poetry.[51] Reninger published articles and coauthored literature textbooks, and "he is also remembered for bringing James Hearst, one of Iowa's finest poets, to the college faculty."[52] Nuhn wrote short stories, essays, articles, and one book; he was married to novelist Ruth Suckow. Hearst wrote poetry, as well as an autobiography, and taught at the Iowa State Teachers College. His connection to his family's farm outside Cedar Falls permeates his work. Hearst is the literary and historical "grandchild" of Melendy's vision.

To say that the Iowa State Normal School and its faculty helped shape the town is an understatement: the town and the college grew up together, as is evident from the school's evolving name and mission. The normal school became the Iowa State Teachers College in 1909, the State College of Iowa in 1961, and the University of Northern Iowa (UNI) in 1967.[53] In 2012, the students in Thomas Connors's Iowa history class at UNI developed a website, *Historical Cedar Falls*, "to provide stories about the people and events that built this city."[54] The students write:

> From the beginning, [Cedar Falls] has placed a focus on literature.
> . . . The city and the University of Northern Iowa have created an
> atmosphere that supports authors and offers an idyllic setting for
> literature. . . . The presence of the University has brought authors to
> Cedar Falls, both in its faculty, and as visiting authors, and helped
> create a literary community.[55]

THE CEDAR FALLS AUTHORS FESTIVAL

As noted previously, Cedar Falls has the distinction of having five nationally known, best-selling authors with ties to the city: Bess Streeter Aldrich, Ruth Suckow, James Hearst, Nancy Price, and Robert James Waller. Three attended the college (Aldrich, Price, and Waller), all five taught there (Suckow as a guest lecturer), and three were born in Cedar Falls (Aldrich, Price, and Hearst), reflecting again the important role of the college in bringing writers to the community.[56] They give literary and poetic expression to Melendy's pairing of the soil and the mind. In the fall of 2016, a group of retired professors and community leaders created the Cedar Falls Authors Festival to celebrate these authors and their contribution to the literary and intellectual history of Cedar Falls.[57] The year-long festival, beginning in May 2017 and continuing through June 2018, featured more than sixty events, highlighting the five best-known authors and recognizing many other local authors.[58] The festival is the most recent contribution by the residents of Cedar Falls to Melendy's vision of a city that values both its rich farmland and its literary and intellectual legacy.

Aldrich, Suckow, Hearst, Price, and Waller shared an appreciation for Iowa's farms and fields, the cycle of planting and harvesting, and Iowans' connection to the soil. James Hearst grew up on a farm and wrote about the hard work of farming and the people who tend the soil. Novelist Ruth Suckow was known for her realistic, gorgeous descriptions of country fields, which bring to mind Grant Wood's rich agricultural paintings of the Midwest. Suckow was a city-dweller, having lived in a number of towns around the state, but she often visited relatives on their farms. Suckow's husband, Ferner Nuhn, wrote about her love of Iowa: "Always she returned to Iowa, rejoicing in the superb farm land, tree-shaded towns, and unpretentious friendly people."[59] Bess Streeter Aldrich vividly described the physical environments that surrounded her novels' characters, including their fields, homes, and small towns. In 1933, she wrote the essay "Why I Live in a Small Town," which included a photograph of her yard filled with trees, bushes, and plants that would have made Melendy proud.[60] Robert James Waller set several of his novels in little Iowa towns like Cedar Falls and filled them with lyrical sentences like this one, from *The Bridges of Madison County*: "There are songs that come free from the blue-eyed grass, from the dust of a thousand country roads."[61] Nancy Price spent her early life in cities but set her novel *Sleeping with the Enemy* in Cedar Falls. References to local stores, streets, and other establishments are sprinkled throughout the novel.

These five authors also write about relationships between friends, family, and community. Aldrich is the pioneer storyteller, describing the struggles of early settlers in Iowa battling sickness, bad weather, and loneliness. Suckow tells the stories of several families over multiple generations and their struggles with farming, raising families, and understanding the next generation. Aldrich and Suckow capture the minutia of daily life and allow their readers to imagine living in a bygone era. Hearst describes the relationship of the farmer to the soil, his neighbors, and his community.

The Hearst Center for the Arts

Before the creation of the authors festival in 2016, residents of Cedar Falls found another way both to remember and contribute to the literary and intellectual output of their city. Suckow's husband, Nuhn, established the Cedar Falls Art League in the early 1940s.[62] Several decades later, Nuhn donated some paintings created by his artist sister, Marjorie, to the city of Cedar Falls. After Hearst left his home to the city, requesting that it be used for a community arts center, Marjorie Nuhn's paintings became part of the collection of the Hearst Center for the Arts, which opened in 1989 and has provided space for a number of programs in the community.[63]

The Hearst Center for the Arts offers its Final Thursday Reading series, hosted by University of Northern Iowa associate professor Jim O'Loughlin, who also happens to be a long-time member of the Cedar Falls Supper Club. This series, held on the last Thursday of each month, begins with an open mic for local writers to share five minutes of poetry, fiction, or creative nonfiction. Then the attention shifts to a featured reading by a published author, who reads from his or her work.[64] In addition, O'Loughlin maintains the James Hearst Digital Archive.[65]

The Hearst Center features a sculpture garden (including one sculpture that was dedicated to Ruth Suckow and Ferner Nuhn during the Cedar Falls Authors Festival), beautiful grounds, and art exhibits, and it also hosts lectures. Melendy would be proud to see his legacy thus passed down to the current generation.

Conclusion

From the city's early days, the residents of Cedar Falls have enjoyed access to a public library, good schools, a college/university, and community groups like the Horticultural and Literary Society, the Cedar Falls Parlor Circle, and the Cedar Falls Supper Club that promote reading, speaking, and critical thinking to promote better understanding of opposing views. Programs at the Hearst Center for the Arts and the public library encourage writers to share their work. In addition, the city has nurtured five best-selling, nationally known authors: Bess Streeter Aldrich, Ruth Suckow, James Hearst, Nancy Price, and Robert James Waller.

With its rich pioneer history, university influence, and the vision of early leaders like Peter Melendy, Roger Leavitt, and Moses Bartlett, among others, the community of Cedar Falls continues to foster creativity and intellectual development. Melendy dubbed Cedar Falls "the Garden City" in 1893. In doing so, he seemed to underestimate the lasting power and importance of his dual commitment to the soil and mind. Cedar Falls has indeed been the Garden City, but it has just as much been, and remains, "an Iowa town that grows Writers." [66]

NOTES

1. "History," Cedar Falls, Iowa, www.cedarfalls.com/336/History.
2. "History and Traditions," University of Northern Iowa, https://uni.edu/resources/history-traditions.
3. "Quick Facts for Cedar Falls," United States Census Bureau, www.census.gov/quickfacts/fact/table/cedarfallscityiowa/PST045217.
4. "Our Five Authors," Cedar Falls Authors Festival, www.cfauthorsfestival.org/.
5. Luella M. Wright, "The Mind and the Soil," *The Palimpsest* 17, no. 11 (1936): 373–394.
6. "Our Five Authors," Cedar Falls Authors Festival.
7. Luella M. Wright, "The Cedar Falls Parlor Reading Circle," *Iowa Journal of History and Politics* 34, no. 4 (October 1936): 339.
8. Wright, "The Cedar Falls Parlor Reading Circle."
9. Barbara Lounsberry, "Authors Festival Final Report to the City Council," personal communication, August 23, 2018.
10. "Cedar Falls History Timeline," Cedar Falls Historical Society, www.cfhistory.org/copy-of-dig-deeper-cf-history.
11. "Cedar Falls History Timeline," Cedar Falls Historical Society.
12. Peter Melendy, *Historical Record of Cedar Falls* (1893), *Iowa Book Gallery*, 22, https://scholarworks.uni.edu/iowabooks/22/.
13. "Fort Worth Log Cabin Village Pioneer School: Teachers Guide," Log Cabin Village, 1995, https://topslide.net/view-doc.html?utm_source=pioneer-school-log-cabin-village.
14. Luella Wright, *Peter Melendy: The Mind and the Soil* (State Historical Society of Iowa, 1943), 69–70.
15. Wright, *Peter Melendy*, 69–70.

16. John C. Hartman, *History of Black Hawk County, Iowa, and Its People*, vol. 1 (Chicago: S. J. Clarke, 1915).

17. Wright, "The Mind and the Soil."

18. Wright, "The Mind and the Soil."

19. Wright, "The Mind and the Soil."

20. Wright, *Peter Melendy*, 121.

21. Wright, "The Mind and the Soil."

22. Wright, *Peter Melendy*.

23. Wright, *Peter Melendy*, 133–135.

24. Wright, *Peter Melendy*, 135.

25. Iowa History Project: Stories of Iowa for Boys and Girls, Chapter XXVIII, Going to School in Pioneer Days, http://iagenweb.org/history/soi/soi28.htm.

26. Wright, "The Mind and the Soil."

27. Wright, *Peter Melendy*, 124.

28. Wright, *Peter Melendy*, 130.

29. Wright, *Peter Melendy*, 131.

30. Wright, *Peter Melendy*, 138.

31. Wright, *Peter Melendy*, 298.

32. Melendy, *Historical Record of Cedar Falls*.

33. "Literature," Historical Cedar Falls, 2012, https://sites.google.com/site/historicalcedarfalls/home/categories/literature.

34. Carol M. Petersen, *Bess Streeter Aldrich: The Dreams Are All Real* (Lincoln: University of Nebraska, 1995), 157–160.

35. Thomas Connors, "Resources for Cedar Falls Local History," Cedar Falls Authors Festival, 2014, www.cfauthorsfestival.org/home/list-of-resources-on-cf-history.

36. Connors, "Resources for Cedar Falls."

37. Wright, "The Cedar Falls Parlor Reading Circle."

38. "Dig Deeper—Victorian Home," Cedar Falls Historical Society, www.cfhistory.org/newpage1.

39. D. S. Wright, "Moses Willard Bartlett," *The Palimpsest* 13, no. 1 (1932): 25–35. https://ir.uiowa.edu/palimpsest/vol13/iss1/5.

40. Wright, "Moses Willard Bartlett."

41. "Literature," Historical Cedar Falls.

42. Wright, "The Cedar Falls Parlor Reading Circle."

43. Wright, "The Cedar Falls Parlor Reading Circle."

44. Dorothy Grant, "The Supper Club of Cedar Falls," Martin L. Grant and Dorothy S. Grant Papers, Archives Record Series 15/02/21, box 1, University Archives, Rod Library, University of Northern Iowa.

45. Grant, "The Supper Club of Cedar Falls."

46. Grant, "The Supper Club of Cedar Falls."

47. Grant, "The Supper Club of Cedar Falls."

48. Grant, "The Supper Club of Cedar Falls."

49. Grant, "The Supper Club of Cedar Falls."

50. Cedar Falls Supper Club Blog, http://cedarfallssupperclub.blogspot.com/.

51. "H. Willard Reninger" [biographical sketch], University of Northern Iowa, https://scua.library.uni.edu/university-archives/biographies/h-willard-reninger.

52. "H. Willard Reninger," University of Northern Iowa.

53. "Brief History of UNI, 1876–1995 (with addendum, 1995–2017)," University of Northern Iowa, https://scua.library.uni.edu/university-archives/articles/brief-history-uni-1876-1995-addendum-1995-2017.

54. "Literature," Historical Cedar Falls.

55. "Literature," Historical Cedar Falls.

56. "Our Five Authors," Cedar Falls Authors Festival.

57. "Our Five Authors," Cedar Falls Authors Festival.

58. "Our Five Authors," Cedar Falls Authors Festival.

59. "Ferner Nuhn: Founder of the RSMA," Ruth Suckow Memorial Association, www.ruthsuckow.org/home/ferner-nuhn.

60. Bess Streeter Aldrich, "Why I Live in a Small Town," reprinted from *Ladies' Home Journal*, 1933, Bess Streeter Aldrich Foundation Web Site, www.bessstreeteraldrich.org/small_town.html.

61. Robert James Waller, *Bridges of Madison County* (New York: Warner Books, 1992).

62. "Ferner Nuhn," Ruth Suckow Memorial Association.

63. "About," Hearst Center for the Arts, www.thehearst.org/about/.

64. Jim O'Loughlin, personal communication, May 20, 2018.

65. "The James Hearst Digital Archive," University of Northern Iowa, https://hearstarchive.uni.edu.

66. Lounsberry, "Authors Festival."

CHAPTER 11

JOHN C. RAWE AND
MIDWESTERN AGRARIANISM

Allan C. Carlson

The 1930s witnessed the last serious, idea-centered campaign to preserve an agrarian order on the American landscape. With thirty-one million persons still residing on farms, and with the urban-industrial order created by liberal capitalism in seeming permanent crisis, agrarians sought to restore a healthy, family-scale farming system. They looked to land redistribution, rural development, and subsistence homesteading as vehicles for invigorating the agrarian republic. The best-known voices in this effort were the Twelve Southerners centered around Vanderbilt University, the coauthors of *I'll Take My Stand: The South and the Agrarian Tradition*, published in 1930. Equally important at the time, though, were the Roman Catholic agrarians, geographically centered in the Midwest. Inspired by recent papal social encyclicals, and appreciating the standard, 160-acre family farm still dominant in their region, they worked to renew and replicate this model nationwide.[1] The boldest, most radical figure in this campaign was John C. Rawe.

Rawe was born December 19, 1900, near Carrollton, Illinois. He was the eldest of eight children born to his German immigrant parents. He grew up and worked on the family farm, learning the realities of American agriculture during a relatively prosperous period. Graduating from the Carrollton public high school in 1918, he entered St. Louis University, a school of the Society of Jesus. In four years, he earned both a bachelor's and a master's degree in law. He also resolved to enter the Jesuit order.[2]

It was a time when the Society of Jesus was in full flower, growing in size and influence. During the 1930s, the number of Americans in the order surpassed that of Spain, so becoming the largest single national group. Jesuit training was rigorous, involving fifteen years: two as a novitiate, two in classical studies, three studying philosophy, three as a teacher in one of the order's high schools or colleges, four studying theology, and a final tertianship year. The Jesuit spirit of the period was invigorating, combining spiritual, philosophical, and military disciplines. As historian Peter McDonough writes, "The model was one of a muscular Christianity and imperturbable masculinity." Tales of past Jesuit martyrdom combined with youthful enthusiasm to make the years of training both tolerable and exciting. As one novice of the era wrote, these were young men "grounded in the spirit of St. Ignatius—men of generous heart and powerful physical constitution equipped, themselves, to vanquish Satan and to snatch from the jaws of Hell souls who were made for Heaven and Happiness." Not coincidentally, Jesuit seminaries, such as the ones Rawe attended in Florissant, Missouri, and St. Mary's, Kansas, were set in rural locales. These religious refuges, far removed from the corruptions of urban-industrial life, were well-suited to nourish agrarian sentiments.[3]

The social encyclicals of recent popes also fed this agrarianism. Leo XIII's 1891 *Rerum Novarum* (*The New Age*), for example, held that all wealth ultimately derived from the land: "The earth, even though apportioned among private owners, ceases not thereby to minister to the needs of all, in as much as there is not one who does not sustain life from what the land produces." This encyclical further affirmed the concept of "labor property," grounded in the "law of nature." As Leo wrote, "Now, when man thus turns that activity of his mind and the strength of his body toward procuring the fruits of nature, *by such acts he makes his own that portion of nature's field which he cultivates*" (emphasis added). Turning toward solutions to the great inequalities created by the industrial order, Leo also favored agrarian approaches. "The law should favor ownership," he explained, "and its policy should be to induce as many as possible of the people to be owners." This would resolve the era's "social question," for "if people can be encouraged to look forward to obtaining a share in the land," then "the gulf between vast wealth and sheer poverty will be bridged over."[4]

In 1931, Pope Pius XI issued *Quadragesimo Anno* (*Forty Years After*), with the sweeping subtitle *On Reconstruction of the Social Order*. In part, it was a celebration and reaffirmation of *Rerum Novarum*, which had "laid down for all mankind the surest rules to solve aright . . . 'the social question.'" It also, he said, had given rise to "a true Catholic social science." The new document became much more specific in policy terms. Pius condemned both communism and democratic socialism as "fundamentally contrary to Christian truth." More startling, in certain respects, were his celebration of the fall of "the idols of Liberalism," his assertion that economic life "cannot be left to a free competition of forces," and his condemnation of "individualistic economic teaching." Pius reaffirmed his predecessor's agrarian postulates yet added a call for new mechanisms to secure "harmonious cooperation of the Industries and Professions." He urged the creation of "guilds or associations" that would combine all workers, owners, and firms within each distinctive economic sphere. These associations, or syndicates, would then govern wages, work rules, prices, and profit-sharing for the presumed good of all involved. Pius also praised those Catholic clerics and members of the laity who now engaged in "Catholic Action," activities that pressed for "the reconstruction and perfection of social order."

Quadragesimo Anno held a special importance for Jesuits. Having resolved to commemorate Leo's work, Pius had charged Wlodimir Ledóchowski, the Polish-born superior general of the Society of Jesus, to craft the encyclical. A staunch anti-modernist, Ledóchowski saw liberalism and secularism as on the verge of exhaustion, a theme that would drive the subsequent encyclical. In turn, he recruited another Jesuit, theologian and sociologist Oswald von Nell-Breuning of Germany, to draft the actual document. As the latter later reported, Ledóchowski "accepted my material and as a rule agreed to my proposals." Pius did as well.[5] This special role played by Jesuits was known within the order, generating a kind of "ownership" of *Quadragesimo Anno* that carried into the work of John C. Rawe.

From 1932 to 1936, Rawe studied theology at St. Mary's College, a small Jesuit seminary in Kansas. There he joined a "zealous seminar of rural life advocates," turning him into a lifelong advocate for agrarian restoration.[6] This seminar contributed to the drafting of "An Integrated Program of Social

Order," first published in 1935 by the Queen's Work forum in St. Louis. The pamphlet was notable for its radical language and specific policy platform. Labeling the Catholic Church as "the first and only Supernational," it called on Christian "comrades" everywhere to repudiate war, class conflict, all forms of exploitation, and "unbridled economic competition." The family was "a natural society," the pamphlet proclaimed, the primary unit of civil life, with a "right to soil and fireside." It was the duty of the state "to facilitate and further all that tends to stabilize a family economy." Taxation should be used to break up excessive concentrations of land and wealth. Farmers must be assured of "proper land distribution and land finance, making possible widespread ownership of productive soil." They should also be guaranteed control over their "economic salvation through marketing, purchasing, and credit organizations," backed by government "sanctions" when necessary. Land speculation and industrialized farming should be banned.[7] Other products of the St. Mary's seminar included published papers on the "American Catholic Village," "Catholicizing the 4-H Clubs," and "Private Property: Who Owns the Farms?"[8]

Ordained in 1935, Rawe became active in the National Catholic Rural Life Conference, founded a dozen years earlier by Fr. Edwin O'Hara, originally from Minnesota. In a lengthy essay for *American Review*, Rawe praised the farming communes of the Catholic Worker movement in the northeastern states associated with Dorothy Day and Peter Maurin. And he welcomed the "practical projects" of the Rural Life Bureau of the National Catholic Welfare Conference. He gave special praise to the "cultured Southerners" who had produced *I'll Take My Stand*, which he called a "trenchant" guide "to a saner, far happier, more correct way of living." He acknowledged the welcome contributions of the English distributists Hilaire Belloc and G. K. Chesterton in seeking to restore systems of small holdings.[9]

More directly, Rawe was one of three Jesuits who in June 1936 attended a meeting in Nashville, Tennessee, to promote "closer ties between the Americans and the English Distributists." Southerners present included Donald Davidson, Cleanthe Brooks, John Crowe Ransom, and Allen Tate.[10] Also in attendance was historian Herbert Agar who, together with Tate, had compiled and edited a second agrarian manifesto, *Who Owns America?: A New Declaration of Independence*. John C. Rawe wrote the informal "Catholic Essay" for the compilation, focused on the flawed legal status of business corporations. Agar would also prove to be the driving force behind the creation of a new monthly journal, *Free America*, launched in January 1937. It claimed to be equally opposed to communism, fascism, and finance capitalism; *Free America* favored a decentralist, agrarian social order focused on independent living. Rawe would be an occasional contributor. In 1939, the National Catholic Rural Life Conference resolved to publish *A Manifesto on Rural Life*. The nominal creators were Aloisius Muench (the bishop of Fargo, North Dakota) and Vincent J. Ryan (soon to be named the bishop of Bismarck). The "ghost" author was Rawe.[11] The following year, he coauthored with Luigi Ligutti the "Summa" of Catholic agrarianism: *Rural Roads to Security: America's Third Struggle for Freedom*. It was the most explicit and thorough presentation of interwar Catholic agrarian philosophy.[12] The more ideologically charged sections of this volume were clearly the product of Rawe.

In this work, Rawe focused on eight basic themes; each had a distinctive Midwestern spin. To begin with, he was an unabashed American. Among early twentieth-century Jesuits in the United States, the reputation of the medieval era was high; the thirteenth had been the greatest of centuries.[13] When turning to examples of a well-ordered agrarian life, Jesuit writers also referred almost exclusively to European examples, such as the Jobbist movement in Belgium or Action Populaire in France. Rawe, in contrast, stayed firmly in American history and precedents. He wrote, "There is a wise, democratic, Jeffersonian political economy in family owned subsistence farming."[14] Rawe praised nineteenth-century American innovations such as the Homestead Act of 1862, which strongly encouraged settlement on the land by agricultural families, as opposed to earlier forms of land distribution that favored speculation. He affirmed in particular the 160-acre model that took root in the Midwest, one specifically designed for "the support of the family."[15] Social disorders in the 1930s, he said, derived from an American "failure to practice democracy in the ownership and control of productive goods," a "turn to homes without function," and "land robbery," or the stripping of life from the soil.[16] To repair the damage, he summoned "the great wisdom" of the American founders "who made provision for a widely diffused freehold ownership" of land as the basis of their republic.[17] As McDonough nicely summarizes, Rawe avoided old European sentiments: "the times he yearned to restore were Jeffersonian."[18]

Second, Rawe openly called for a "Green Revolution," one "far removed from the red rags of communist tyranny and the wriggling swastikas of frenzied dictatorships." This revolution would be "Green" for it would take place on rich land owned by "patient, productive, profitable, democratic, free" farm families, seeking a "constitutional restoration of private property and personal rights." While always peaceful, constitutional, and just, this revolution would represent "a determined reaction against complete industrialization."[19] In *Rural Roads*, Rawe and Ligutti relabeled this Green Revolution as America's "third struggle for liberty." The first, they argued, had come in 1776 in reaction to British oppression that "threatened the human rights and happiness" of Americans. However, "liberty for all, Black and White," required a second war, this time in the 1860s. American liberties then fell prey to an alien "liberalistic system which Europe had fostered" that delivered "mammoth-scale industry, commercialized farms, human lives ground by marvelous machines, efficiency substituted for liberty, money codes displacing justice, with God and his spirit forgotten." The third American campaign for liberty must now commence, Rawe and Ligutti urged, demanding a new foundation of "family unit operation and fee-simple, family-basis ownership of land based on religious principles."[20]

In pursuing this restoration of an agrarian order, Rawe was stridently anti-urban. He argued that "the roots of democracy" were to be found "in the country districts and in the rural culture of America." In contrast, cities were "mere concentrated, collectivized aggregations of helpless dependent individuals, a dying population."[21] He described cities on the American East Coast as comprising "congested housing, the families living in brick caves and canyons of steel and stone." Rawe despaired over "the gigantic size of the belching factories," the millions of men, women, and children wholly dependent on "low-wage incomes from subdivided, dehumanized, unskilled, monotonous" factory jobs, and the absence of children among deliberately sterile or "one-child" couples.[22] He saw the industrial system as actually destroying the cities it had created, consuming adult lives, discouraging the birth of children, and leaving behind ugly and barren landscapes.[23]

Rawe also built a strong legal and historical case against the American corporate order. Initially trained in law at St. Louis University, he focused his ire on federal court decisions that had transformed commercial corporations into "artificial persons" bearing rights found in the US Constitution. He blasted, in particular, the twisting of the Fourteenth Amendment from an instrument to guarantee "the liberation of the black man" into an "opportunity for the economic enslavement of both the white man *and* the black man" (emphasis added). In Rawe's view, court decisions striking down state laws seeking to restrain or dissolve corporate monopolies made joint stock corporations "a radically new danger in the history of mankind." Family and state, he held, were "natural societies," while the Church was a "supernatural" one. In contrast, corporations were artificial and utilitarian, entitled to no more legal claims than those provided within specific state-granted charters. With the "dictatorial power and unrestrained greed" of commercial corporations now enjoying legal protection, Rawe argued that the only alternative was for the federal government to proceed against them as "internal enemies."[24]

As a key step in this "new cause of liberty," Rawe endorsed a proposed constitutional amendment that would end the effective treatment of corporations as citizens. In its opening sentence, the proposal reads: "No right, privilege, or immunity granted or secured to the individual citizen in this Constitution shall be construed either directly or indirectly to apply to any joint stock corporation engaged in commerce." Driving home the point, this passage continues: "No joint stock corporation engaged in commerce is a citizen according to the terms used in this Constitution." In harmony with *Quadragesimo Anno*'s call for industrywide guilds, Rawe urged the creation of industrial code corporations that would "protect the natural rights of all those, whether capitalist or laborer, who are occupied in a definite industry." This measure, he believed, would restore to the nation's commercial life an "organic form." Seeking to avoid European terminology, he directly compared the American style of this scheme to existing municipalities, labeling the new versions "industrocipalities" and "industropolises." He also praised the business codes of the National Industrial Recovery Act advanced by "the New Dealers" as important precedents for a Christian social order.[25]

As another positive remedy, Rawe held that the US Constitution "implied the right and imposed the duty on government" to secure "distributism in private property" for real citizens.[26] This required well-dispersed private ownership of farms, with families restored as "the basic economic unit."[27] Drawing on his own experience growing up on an Illinois farm, Rawe looked to units of forty to two hundred acres and wrote: "Rich acres and productive plants are safe only in the hands of a small owner . . . a family man, who can respect and cooperate with the laws of nature, make provision for crop rotation, prevent erosion, and give paternal care to the plants and animals that feed and shelter him and his dear ones."[28] Refugees from the city, he imagined, would find a home on three to five acres to be an admirable site for part-time farming, allowing for a high degree of self-sufficiency in food. In these ways, the American spirit would be reborn through a rich natural culture. "The agrarian wants a balanced life for all," Rawe explained, "lived out in a definite social tradition, a life in which religion, the arts, good manners, conversation, hospitality, sympathy [and] family life" can thrive, within "an equitable economy founded on the right relation of man to nature."[29]

Regarding families, Rawe emphasized their need to be refunctionalized. He saw the urban-industrial family as having been weakened as task after task was turned over to the commercial order or to the state, resulting in fewer marriages, a plummeting birth rate, and divorce. Rawe was insistent: "We must have a rising birth rate. We must have a new vitality in Christian home life and home culture."[30] The "only way" to accomplish this, he argued, "is to provide for some family-centered production . . . where the child can soon become an economic asset instead of remaining an economic liability." To secure this end, Rawe insisted that every housing development be a "productive home" program, houses with small acreages attached.[31] New multilane highways could link urban centers to such semi-rural, function-rich homes. Government-backed thirty-year mortgages should require that new houses include workrooms and kitchens suitable for food preservation. Recent technological innovations—the rural electrical grid, the small electric motor, the portable internal combustion engine—made such decentralization both desirable and efficient. In these places, families would find themselves again surrounded by "independence, security, economic-liberty, and work-liberty."[32] For Rawe, "the natural family unit" was and must be a productive unit, in food and related handcrafts.[33]

Cooperatives were another mechanism through which Rawe sought to bring the arguments of the papal encyclicals to fruition. Families in homesteads, he wrote, would "strive to play a leading part in the building of an agricultural occupation group" in line with those needed in the industrial sector. This unit would work to form "cooperative economic enterprises" in health, recreation, education, and culture.[34] More concretely, he praised the Rochdale consumer cooperative model and credit unions spreading rapidly in rural America. These "democracies of consumers," controlled by their members on the "one man, one vote" principle, allowed members to escape corporate retailers and the large banks. They retained capital locally and gave preference to the sale of local products.[35]

Finally, Rawe somewhat awkwardly embraced biodynamic agriculture. This was the brainchild of the German polymath Rudolf Steiner. As explained in his 1924 volume *Spirit and Foundations for the Renewal of Agriculture*, Steiner believed a "farm is healthy only as much as it becomes an organism in itself," where the farmer stands "in living interaction" with larger ecological and spiritual realities. Biodynamics differed from organic farming in its appeal to "cosmic and terrestrial forces" and "life energy," reflecting Steiner's personal grounding in spiritualism and theosophy. Mechanisms to capture positive spiritual forces included special "preparations" to be applied to soil or growing plants and the "Cosmic Pipe," which would draw healthy "etheric forces" into the soil through a crystal.[36] Rawe tactfully avoided these references to non-Christian spiritualism and magic. However, he praised the close attention that biodynamic farmers brought to their work. For example, he celebrated the earthworm as a welcome visitor to a biodynamic farm, for this creature "is a connoisseur of the better soils." In one of his few references to Europe, Rawe favorably reported on the extended visit by Chauncey Stillman, a wealthy Catholic convert and the publisher of *Free America*, to hundreds of biodynamic farms in Switzerland and the Rhine Valley. Some villages, Rawe noted, were more than 80 percent biodynamic, successful islands portending a new agrarian age.[37]

During the academic terms of 1938 and 1939, Rawe served on the faculties of St. Louis and Creighton (Omaha) Universities, teaching philosophy, rural sociology, and economics. He was then dispatched to New York City, where he became a founding member of the Institute of Social Order (ISO). This new organization, long in the planning, was "to encourage unification and coordination of all the Jesuit forces . . . behind the movement to create

a Christian Social Order" in the United States. This national center for
Catholic Social Action would be modeled on Action Populaire in France,
which served as a "think tank" on ways to implement the spirit and ideals
of *Rerum Novarum* and *Quadragesimo Anno*. Rawe became the ISO "expert"
on rural life.[38]

Unfortunately, he served the project for only six months. His experience
there actually revealed the shortcomings of Midwestern Catholic
agrarianism within an overwhelmingly urban church. For example, in
an ambitious attempt to unify Catholic "Social Thought" on one page, he
cited the problem of extreme concentrations in property ownership, urban
living, money and finance, and so on, and results such as "proletarianism,"
"family shrinkage," "social disorders," and the change of humans into
"obedient economic slaves." Rawe's "remedies"—all agrarian in practice—
included "some self sufficiency in homes," "biodynamic farming," and
"decentralization of urban inhabitants in part-time farming communities."
However, his supervisor, it appears, inserted the word "some" before
"urban inhabitants" in the last phrase, greatly reducing its sweep.[39] More
tellingly, Rawe contributed passages to an ISO teaching curriculum,
which included his usual denunciations of urban life: "Show some of the
artificiality of city living, the crowded apartments, the artificial recreation,
the absence of real family life," he wrote. "Show the effect of apartment
living and city life on the family, the falling birth rate, the ever-growing
selfishness even of Catholic families, standardization of everything from
food to thought." However, inserted then in parentheses was a curious
rejoinder: "This does not mean an attack on all city life. It is an attack on
'urbanism,' a false philosophy that more and more concentration, more
and bigger cities are infallible signs of progress and civilization."[40] Rawe's
radical ruralism simply seemed out of place in a Manhattan-based center,
and he soon returned to Omaha.

Rawe's last years bear a kind of awful symbolism, as stillborn projects
and poor health paralleled the disruptions of American rural life brought on
by America's entry into World War II. Back in Nebraska, a fine opportunity
seemed to emerge when a university trustee donated the use of a 220-acre
farm to create the Creighton University Rural Life Institute, with Rawe
as its director. The institute would provide a twelve-month course for up
to a dozen young men seeking to become farmers. University publicity

featured the institute's biodynamic system of soil renewal, "stewardship farming," and scientific farm practices. The actual course outline was closer to Rawe's heart, focused on "The Rural Family and the Way-of-Life on the Land," "The Family: Social and Economic Unit on the Farm," "Production on the Farm for the Family," as well as the more practical subjects.[41] Alas, the attack on Pearl Harbor occurred just as the institute was being launched. In less than a year, all eight of the initial students had been drafted into the military. Meanwhile, soaring food prices led the original owner to reclaim the farm for commercial production.[42]

In 1943, Rawe's father provincial assigned him to serve as the director of farm and rural life at the Jesuits' Indian Mission in St. Stephens, Wyoming. His task was to guide the American Indian boys in the operation of the mission's eight-hundred-acre farm. Rawe soon managed to produce a surplus of crops and animals for sale. However, the brutal cold took its toll on his health. Rawe contracted severe blood poisoning and nearly died.[43] After a difficult recovery, entreaties by John LaFarge, the influential editor of the Jesuit magazine *America*, led to Rawe's assignment in mid-1945 to manage rural life training for African Americans at the Cardinal Gibbons Institute, in the village of Ridge, St. Mary's County, Maryland. Rawe had already drafted part of a new agrarian book, and his father superior assured him that his new duties would be light, allowing him ample time to finish the volume and write for *America*, as well. As matters turned out, the assignment was a failure. In January 1946, Rawe reported that he had no farm equipment and no help. Only eight students enrolled in the program, and he was "teaching farming to boys who don't want it." Their parents "recreate in the bars" nearby, Rawe said, while he was left to do most of the physical work. He added: "I have not done any writing for the second book or for articles since I have been here." In August 1947, his health collapsed and he was hospitalized with anemia, a bad heart, and failing kidneys. Rawe died on September 7 at age forty-six. His unfinished manuscript passed through several hands and eventually disappeared at St. Mary's College.[44]

How should John C. Rawe's career be assessed? In the obvious aspects, he failed. The reconstructed social order of which he dreamed—factories decommissioned and cities emptied, replaced by productive homesteads and family-scale, 160-acre biodynamic farms; commercial corporations stripped of unintended constitutional protections; families broadly refunctionalized; cooperatives waxing in strength and economic influence—did not emerge. Post-1945 America went in other directions, undergoing a vast industrial boom as intact American factories churned out products for a shattered world; producing more densely packed suburban developments that rested on companionship and informed consumerism, rather than production for use; experiencing an accelerating consolidation of agriculture, as power machinery largely banished true horsepower; and seeing the zealous corporate protection of inherited constitutional rights.

And yet, there are better ways to understand Rawe's legacy. McDonough correctly notes that "Rawe wanted to restore a true Americanism," unlike other Catholic writers from the era who praised "a foreign model exhumed from an era" before Columbus. McDonough adds: "Rawe's forte was the making of homely poetry out of a way of life."[45] Christopher Hamlin and John T. McGreevy find in Rawe's "Midwestern Catholicism" a distinct understanding of nature. Where others saw beauty and value in wild and scenic places, Rawe focused on "organic processes and temporal cycles." For him, nature was not sacred; however, "work in nature *was* sacramental" (emphasis added). This aesthetic "grounded in the agricultural Midwest" focused on "sky and soil, watching small parts of nature change through the seasons."[46]

Most notably, in all of his arguments, Rawe anticipated the better known, more recent, and more complete message of the Kentuckian Wendell Berry. Every major theme in Berry's numerous works of fiction, poetry, and agrarian polemics is anticipated in Rawe, albeit with Midwestern and Catholic sensitivities: the importance of attachment to a specific geographic place, the power of a web of memory, the necessity of a "beloved community," resistance to the dominion of science and machines, opposition to the commercial corporate order, the powerful importance of marriage and the procreation of children, the necessity of being a generalist in the skills of life, the power and beauty of the productive home economy, and communion with God the Creator.[47]

Rawe's real legacy may lie in a future rediscovery of his work by young, twenty-first-century Roman Catholics in America, looking for a postmodern agrarian model fully compatible with their faith.

NOTES

1. Allan Carlson, "'Flee to the Fields': Midwestern Catholicism and the Last Agrarian Crusade," in *The Midwestern Moment: The Forgotten World of Early Twentieth-Century Midwestern Regionalism, 1880–1940*, ed. Jon Lauck (Hastings, NE: Hastings College Press, 2017), 185–206.

2. Personal file card from personnel file and obituary, "Fr. John C. Rawe S.J. Dies in Baltimore," n.d., box 5.011, folder MIS 8.1, Missouri Province, Jesuit Archives and Research Center, St. Louis, Missouri (hereafter cited as Jesuit Archives–St. Louis.)

3. Peter McDonough, *Men Astutely Trained: A History of the Jesuits in the American Century* (New York: The Free Press, 1992), 144–159. The quotation comes from novice Frank Wilson.

4. Pope Leo XIII, *Rerum Novarum* [May 1891], 3–5, 12, 14, http://w2.vatican. va/content/leo-xiii/en/encyclicals/documents/hf_l-xiii_enc_15051891_ rerum-novarum.html.

5. McDonough, *Men Astutely Trained*, 66–68.

6. "Obituary: Reverend John C. Rawe, S.J.," *The Province Newsletter* (Missouri Province), October 16, 1948, 106.

7. A Committee on Social Order of the Jesuit Provinces of the United States and Canada, *An Integrated Program of Social Order* (St. Louis, MO: The Queen's Work, 1943 [1935]), 8–9, 13, 17–18.

8. *Study Project No. 1: Private Property, Prepared by The Land Owners and Operators Committee of St. Mary's College* (St. Louis: The Queen's Work, 1936), cover and index.

9. John C. Rawe, "Agrarianism: The Basis for a Better Life," *American Review* 6 (December 1935): 180–181.

10. Minutes of the Convention of the Committee for the Alliance of Agrarian and Distributist Groups, Nashville, Tennessee, June 4–5 ,1936, Vanderbilt University Archives; from McDonough, *Men Astutely Trained*, 518, n66.

11. "Obituary: Reverend John C. Rawe," 106. The volume was published as *Manifesto on Rural Life* (St. Paul, MN: National Catholic Rural Life Conference, 1939).

12. Christopher Hamlin and John T. McGreevy, "The Greening of America, Catholic Style, 1930–1950," *Environmental History* 11, no. 3 (July 2006): 467.

13. McDonough, *Men Astutely Trained*, 52–55.

14. John C. Rawe, "Life, Liberty and the Pursuit of Happiness in Agriculture," address to the October 1936 session of the National Catholic Rural Life Conference, Fargo, North Dakota, 12, in series 8/1, box 2, National Catholic Rural Life Archives, Marquette University, Milwaukee, Wisconsin.

15. John C. Rawe, "Agriculture and the Property State," in *Who Owns America? A New Declaration of Independence*, ed. Herbert Agar and Allen Tate (Wilmington, DE: ISI Books, 1999 [1936]), 57, 60.

16. John C. Rawe, "Agriculture—An Airplane Survey," *Catholic Rural Life Bulletin* 3, no. 1 (February 1940): 25.

17. Rawe, "Agrarianism," 187.

18. McDonough, *Men Astutely Trained*, 89.

19. Rawe, "Life, Liberty, and the Pursuit of Happiness," 18.

20. Luigi Ligutti and John C. Rawe, *Rural Roads to Security: America's Third Struggle for Freedom* (Milwaukee, WI: Bruce Publishing, 1940), 3, 9–10.

21. John C. Rawe, "Rural Life Conference Plans a Sound Democracy," *America* 64, no. 4 (November 2, 1943), 94.

22. Rawe, "Agriculture—An Airplane Survey," 1–2.

23. John C. Rawe, "The Home on the Land," *Catholic Rural Life Bulletin* 2 (February 1939), 24–25.

24. John C. Rawe, "Corporations and Human Liberty: A Study in Exploitation. I. Real and Artificial Persons," *American Review* 4 (January 1935): 255–271.

25. John C. Rawe, "Corporations and Human Liberty: A Study in Exploitation. II. Regaining the Rights of the Individual," *American Review* 4 (February 1935): 472–489.

26. Rawe, "Corporations and Human Liberty. I.," 273.

27. Rawe, "Life, Liberty, and the Pursuit of Happiness," 3.

28. John C. Rawe, "Homesteading Solves the Problem of Farm Decline," *America* 60 (December 3, 1938): 200; Ligutti and Rawe, *Rural Roads*, 104.

29. Rawe, "Agrarianism," 182.

30. Rawe, "The Home on the Land," 25.

31. Ligutti and Rawe, *Rural Roads*, 108.

32. Rawe, "Rural Life Conference," 95.

33. Rawe, "Homesteading," 201.

34. Rawe, "Homesteading," 201.

35. John C. Rawe, "A Fair Deal to All through the Cooperatives," *America* 64 (February 15, 1941): 514–515.

36. Rudolf Steiner, *Spiritual Foundations for the Renewal of Agriculture*, ed. M. Gardner (Junction City, OR: Biodynamic Farming and Gardening Association of the USA, 1993 [1926]); Steve Diver, *Biodynamic Farming and Compost Preparation* (Fayetteville, AR: Appropriate Technology Transfer for Rural Areas, 1999), 2–4.

37. John C. Rawe, "Biological Technology on the Land," *Catholic Rural Life Bulletin* 2 (August 1939), 21–22; Rawe, "Agriculture—An Airplane Survey," 25.

38. "Prospectus for the American Social Action Institute [1939?]"; John P. Delaney to "Reverend Father Rector," March 4, 1940; and John LaFarge, "Memorandum on The Present Status of the Institute for Social Order in New York City," May 7, 1940—all three items located in box 3.0058, New York Province, Jesuit Archives–St. Louis.

39. [John C. Rawe], "To organize and correlate problems in the Social Order for the purpose of unification of Social Thought," box 5.0111, personnel file, folder MIS 5.1, Jesuit Archives–St. Louis.

40. "Institute of Social Order. Service Bulletin: Catholic Social Teaching through the Regular Curriculum," September 1940, box 3.0051, New York Province, Jesuit Archives–St. Louis.

41. "Creighton Sponsors Rural Life Institute," *The Creighton Alumnus* 16 (February 1942): 6; and *Forward on the Land*, promotional brochure of the Creighton University Rural Life Institute, Elkhorn, Nebraska, box 5.011, manuscript, folder MIS 8.1, Missouri Province, Jesuit Archives–St. Louis.

42. "Death of Fr. Rawe Great Loss to American Rural Cause," obituary published by the National Catholic Rural Life Conference, September 26, 1947, box 5.0111, manuscript, MIS 8.1, Missouri Province, Jesuit Archives–St. Louis.

43. E. O. Mullaney to Joseph Zuercher, November 7, 1944; attached hospital scrawls of John C. Rawe, "am left alone"; and Joseph P. Zuercher to John C. Rawe, November 11, 1944—all three items located in box 5.0111, personnel file, folder MIS 5.1, Missouri Province, Jesuit Archives–St. Louis.

44. Joseph Zuercher to John C. Rawe, May 24, 1945; John C. Rawe to Joseph Zuercher, January 28, 1946; Office of the Provincial, Maryland Province, to Joseph Zuercher, August 19, 1947; and Joseph Zuercher to Sister

Ignatius Loyola [Rawe's biological sister], November 6, 1947—all four items located in box 5.0111, personnel file, folder MIS 5.1, Missouri Province, Jesuit Archives–St. Louis.

45. McDonough, *Men Astutely Trained*, 94.

46. Hamlin and McGreevy, "The Greening of America, Catholic Style," 484.

47. On these themes in Berry's work, see Allan Carlson, "Wendell Berry and the Agrarian Recovery of the Human Person," in *Figures in the Carpet: Finding the Human Person in the American Past*, ed. Wilfred M. McClay (Grand Rapids, MI: William B. Eerdmans, 2007), 290–317.

CHAPTER 12

Mari Sandoz

Regional Writer Never at Home

William C. Pratt

Historian, novelist, and essayist Mari Sandoz (1896–1966) established herself as a spokesperson for regional values and concerns in her writings from the 1930s until her death in the mid-1960s.[1] This chapter is based upon her correspondence, local newspaper accounts, nonfiction publications that address the issue of regionalism, and two of her novels: *Slogum House* (1937) and *Capital City* (1939). Sandoz saw herself as a product of the trans-Missouri West, especially the Sandhills of western Nebraska, but she lived most of her adult life in cities—first Lincoln, Nebraska, then Denver, Colorado, and finally Greenwich Village, where she spent the last twenty-four years of her life. While residing in urban areas, she often traveled across the Midwest and West for research and personal reasons, maintaining ties particularly in Nebraska, to which she returned throughout her life after 1940. She had endured a hardscrabble upbringing on the frontier, and only through sheer determination and talent was she able to finally succeed as a writer with the publication of *Old Jules* (1935), which made her reputation.

Among the major influences on Sandoz were the rationale for the passage of the 1862 Homestead Act and the frontier thesis. Such influences were reshaped or shaded by her early life experiences, first her tough upbringing in the Nebraska Sandhills and then her struggles to establish herself as a writer in Lincoln during the 1920s and Depression years. What we find in her correspondence and writing is a lament over the ultimate failure of the Homestead legislation and the closing of the frontier as outlined by Frederick Jackson Turner in his 1893 essay "The Significance of the Frontier in American History."[2] One very big difference between Sandoz and the proponents of the first Homestead Act and Turner is her view toward American Indians, and it is her treatment of the first Americans for which Sandoz is much remembered and honored. That topic, however, has been treated in depth by others and is outside my concerns in this chapter. Here, I want to examine particular intellectual influences that helped shape Sandoz's thinking, her views on regionalism, and finally her experience over the last three decades of her life when she achieved prominence as a writer.

Sandoz attended the University of Nebraska intermittently between 1923 and 1932 and saw that experience as extremely important to her intellectual development. She never graduated from high school, though she taught in rural schools for several years before moving to Lincoln. During her college years, she studied under John D. Hicks, who served on the Nebraska faculty from 1928 to 1932, during which time he had researched and published his classic work on Populism, *The Populist Revolt* (1931). Sandoz had enrolled in Hicks's History of the Frontier since 1829 course in the spring of 1932. At the time, Hicks clearly was influenced by Turner and saw the frontier experience as the major influence on American historical development.[3]

In Sandoz's 1939 novel, *Capital City*, one of the main characters wants to study with Hicks, but since he has already moved to the University of Wisconsin, she decides to attend the state university where she lives. In another passage, which shows the provincialism of the town's citizens, some of them warn students against taking Hicks as a professor apparently because of his progressive views.[4] In Sandoz's correspondence, she praised Hicks for not moving to Harvard, as Turner had done, and for staying in the West by moving to Berkeley: "I took my Frontier history under John Hicks who refused to follow the humbling path of Turner, from Wisconsin to Harvard, and went to California instead."[5]

To Sandoz, and she wrote these words near the end of her life, "The Homestead Act was the hope of the poor man."[6] While not inclined to discuss the ins and outs of the Turner thesis, Sandoz seemed to be a strong proponent of the safety value hypothesis and referred to it often. In both *Slogum House* and *Capital City*, she makes references to the disappearance of free land and the dire consequences that followed. Of course, the idea of the significance of free land and the opportunities that it would provide for would-be settlers predated Turner.[7]

In fact, Hamlin Garland's *Main-Travelled Roads* may well have been more influential to Sandoz than Turner's thesis. In 1937, she wrote, "For me, the most important themes of Nebraska will always be those of the farmer and his dispossession. Hamlin Garland's 'Under the Lion's Paw' grew out of the nineties. . . . Doesn't anyone here see that the story of a man who broke out the first sod on his government claim, thirty, forty years ago, clung to it until 1929, and lost it is a [worthy] theme [for a contemporary writer]?"[8] Gulla Slogum, the archvillain of *Slogum House*, orchestrates a plot more dastardly than that of Garland's "Under the Lion's Paw," when she forces a sheriff's sale of a farm on which she holds the mortgage. Lincoln Loder had settled there in the 1880s and made numerous improvements on the land with "a fine ten-acre grove on the old timber claim [and a] windbreak for the house and the yard." Following the sale, which leaves Loder with "a deficit of three dollars an acre," he shoots his elderly wife and commits suicide, a grimmer conclusion than Garland had envisioned as a possibility in his story.[9]

The increase in farm tenancy was a serious concern for Sandoz, and she portrayed its perils in both *Slogum House* and *Capital City*. Land monopoly troubled earlier proponents of the Homestead Act idea, who saw free land as an opportunity for poor farmers and city dwellers to escape bad economic circumstances. But such legislation had been stymied in Congress until the Panic of 1857, when industrialists and some others who had earlier opposed the measure, according to Sandoz, had a change of heart. Now they wanted "to get the restless unemployed out of the east," as well as develop a new territory for investment.[10]

Whether or not Hicks was as influential on Sandoz's thinking as she suggested, he was a historian with whom she wished to be identified.[11] *The Populist Revolt* became the standard account on the topic for a generation.[12] But perhaps more influential for Sandoz than Hicks's history of this third-party movement was a 1928 essay that Hicks published in the *Prairie Schooner*, "Our Pioneer Heritage." Only thirteen pages long, it built on

Turner's 1893 essay and argued that "a frontier—has been, we doubt not, the most important single factor in the making of the United States." In the same paragraph, Hicks asserted: "The frontier acted as automatically as a safety-valve to relieve the pressure of developing industrial conditions in the East." While life on the frontier was hard, Hicks argued, especially for wives, who "for the most part [were] unwilling pioneers," overall the pioneer experience was a positive one, and now those days were over.[13] In some respects, Hicks had updated the Turner thesis, but then Turner himself had elaborated upon it over the years as well. There is no question that Sandoz was familiar with Hicks's essay before she enrolled in his course in 1932, as she herself had a piece published in the same issue of the *Prairie Schooner*. In fact, it appeared in the magazine immediately following "Our Pioneer Heritage."[14]

Sandoz probably acquired more hands-on experience as a historian from her work at the Nebraska State Historical Society under the supervision of Addison E. Sheldon, the society's director, than she did from her one semester in Hicks's course. She did quite a bit of research at that institution and worked there between 1931 and 1935, serving as associate editor of *Nebraska History* and as a supervisor for a Works Progress Administration project.[15] Among her tasks at the society, she assisted Sheldon in the completion of his *Land Systems and Land Policies in Nebraska*, a book based on his 1918 Columbia PhD dissertation.[16] Whatever her formal training in historical research methods, Sandoz had a great deal of hands-on experience with primary sources and newspapers, not to mention extensive experience with oral histories, both using those collected by others and conducting her own in preparation of her biography of her father, Jules Sandoz.[17]

Hicks's 1932 course may have helped Mari Sandoz frame her previous experience or perhaps even validate it as real history. But her view of the Sandhills frontier experience was roughly compatible with the Turner thesis in that she believed free land provided real opportunity for poor people, native born or immigrant, and also that the frontier's closure resulted in hardship and a loss of opportunity for many of the people who had relocated there. Sandoz's 1937 novel, *Slogum House*, however, showed the dark side of frontier life and how settlers were often exploited by the greed of predatory forces, some of which emerged out of the frontier experience. Sandoz believed opportunity was reduced or even extinguished with the closing of the frontier, but some of the problems that settlers confronted came from their neighbors. What one reviewer wrote of *Old Jules* could easily be applied to *Slogum House*, that it "depict[s] pioneering at its worst."[18]

Regionalism was in the air in the 1930s, and Sandoz emerged as a strong proponent of this approach.[19] Schooled as a critic of the East at an early age, she became an articulate spokesperson for regionalism after moving to Lincoln. Perhaps her most developed expression on this subject was in a talk to a local audience that was subsequently published in *The Quill* under the title "Stay Home, Young Writer!" A number of articles on the state of American letters had recently been published, and Sandoz sought to encourage Nebraska writers to stick with local topics. She might well have borrowed Booker T. Washington's command, "Cast down your bucket where you are," as she suggested one topic after another for local writers: "As I look over the state I see a dozen fine locales for important novels, and you will see many more." After listing possible topics in Havelock, Nebraska City, the North Platte Valley, Omaha, and Lincoln, as well as wondering why a good novel on the Winnebagoes had not yet been written, she offered a rationale for writers to set their work in this region, followed by an explanation of why that was not happening. Central to her argument that writers should not write about far-off locales is the emotional attachment one has to home:

> I believe that it is not good for the writer to wander too long from the
> region with which he is emotionally identified, no matter what the
> locale of his writing of the moment may be. Expatriation seems to
> devitalize the artist, particularly the one who deals with the people.

Yet, she warned, while a writer needs to be close to the sources of his inspiration, his neighbors and townsmen often discourage him and drive him out. Sandoz could name only one well-received Nebraska writer, Bess Streeter Aldrich, who still remained in the state. (Though born and raised in Iowa, Aldrich achieved her prominence as a writer in Nebraska.)[20]

Interestingly, this argument, which Sandoz made in 1937, soon applied to her, as she left the state in 1940 and never again lived in Nebraska. The *Omaha*

World-Herald published the headline, "Miss Sandoz Quits Lincoln, Sees Culture Dying There." [21] First she moved to Denver, and then to Greenwich Village, where she maintained a residence until she died in 1966. [22] Over time, her view of Lincoln mellowed, as her association with the University of Nebraska Press and then Nebraska Educational Television, along with her book signings, required frequent returns to the city. Throughout her life, Sandoz maintained a dogged affection for the state and a pronounced verbal aversion to the East, which was reinforced by her persistent disagreements with eastern publishers. At one point late in her career, she wrote a private letter to the *Lincoln Journal and Star* denying a report that she had expressed her dislike of eastern Nebraska at a book signing in Denver. She claimed that she had been misunderstood and announced: "It's the east and New York that I hate." [23] Later, in the last year of her life, she told an Omaha reporter, "I have a great deal of work to do—the book about General Custer and the Battle of Little Bighorn and a book about this city, 'I hate New York.'" [24] As Sandoz was prone to occasional exaggeration, perhaps this comment was an example of frontier hyperbole—the file folder in her papers that includes this phrase contains just two pages, complaining about medical care she had received in New York.

While living in Lincoln prior to her 1940 departure, Sandoz had been very critical of the town, revealing some of her bitterness toward it in *Capital City*. But by the 1950s, she had a change of heart. At that time, she was often invited back to speak and appear at book signings, and she had very positive things to say about her earlier experiences there. In 1959, the Miller & Paine department store decided to run an "I remember Lincoln" feature in six installments in the Lincoln papers as part of a commemoration of the city's centennial. Sandoz was invited to write one of these autobiographical pieces, which appeared in May of that year. [25] Titled "I Remember Lincoln— As Our Greenwich Village," the piece celebrated her years in Lincoln, making it sound like it had been a very cosmopolitan place:

> There was a place near the campus and later at the bus depot where we could drift in and talk all evening with others interested in the arts for the price of the coffee—talk about the *Dial*, about D. H. Lawrence, James Joyce, Dos Passos, Sherwood Anderson and *The Torrents of Spring*, or about *Spoon River Anthology*, *Main Street* and

Babbitt. . . . But much of our talk was about the writing around us: poems by Loren Eiseley and Mabel Langdon, stories . . . of Dorothy Thomas, Lasalle Gilman and Lowry C. Wimberly. Later we included the work of Rudolph Umland and Weldon Kees.[26]

It sounded like a remarkable change of heart from the person who left Lincoln in 1940 declaring that its culture was dying and that all the artistic people had left.

There was more than a hint of truth in Sandoz's 1959 Miller & Paine essay. In the late 1920s and 1930s, she had been part of a group of young writers associated with the *Prairie Schooner* and later with the Works Progress Administration Writers' Project. Though not involved herself with the Writers' Project, a number of her friends were, including Umland and Kees. In a memoir account published years later, Umland writes of a lively cultural life in Lincoln during that era and Sandoz's involvement in it.[27] Also during those years, Sandoz had justified her remaining in Lincoln, writing, "With Toscanini ready at the turn of a knob and with books almost as available here as anywhere, only plays and art galleries can drag me on periodical trips out of the middle west. But I always come back. There's a vigor here, and a broadness of horizon. Besides, I believe that the creative worker must not wander too far from the earth of his emotional identity."[28] By the late 1930s, however, this type of comment would seem out of character for her, and she left Lincoln for good in 1940.

After close to three years in Denver, Sandoz moved to New York, where she maintained a rigorous work schedule. Often, she took extended research trips, visiting and revisiting archives and sites, especially in the West, and observing the environments about which she wrote. Between 1947 and 1956, she taught in the summer writers' program at the University of Wisconsin and turned down an offer to work in the Iowa Writers' Workshop.[29] With the death of Willa Cather in 1947, Sandoz became Nebraska's best-known author. She was now in demand as a speaker and that often presented her with opportunities to return to Nebraska. By the 1950s, Sandoz was being regularly honored in her native state, and any traces of resentment over her novels *Slogum House* and *Capital City* had dissipated. In 1950, the University of Nebraska awarded her an honorary degree, and four years later, the Nebraska governor declared Mari Sandoz Day.[30]

Beginning in the 1950s, she established a close working relationship with the University of Nebraska Press, and ultimately the Press published and reprinted a number of her books. She seemed to take particular interest in the development of Bison Books, the Press's first trade imprint, which would publish paperbacks on Western history.[31] She also continued to support the *Prairie Schooner*, contributing stories and essays and sponsoring an annual prize.[32] In the early 1960s, both Omaha's Joslyn Art Museum and the University of Nebraska invited Sandoz to work in their facilities, but she declined to move.[33] She was already overcommitted with book projects under contract and preferred to stay in Greenwich Village, where she had many of her files.

But Sandoz never saw New York as her home; rather it was nothing more than "a sort of outpost" for her.[34] In 1963, she even published an essay in the *Prairie Schooner* titled "Outpost in New York."[35] Almost thirty years earlier, the *Yale Review* had published a review of *Old Jules* under the heading, "A Nebraska Outpost."[36] The titles and venues of these pieces reflect two different perspectives on the work of this Nebraska writer, not to mention the nature of historic regionalism in American culture. From the perspective of an easterner, even a sympathetic one (as was Stanley T. Williams from the *Yale Review*), western Nebraska was a distant, strange place. But to Sandoz, despite living in New York for two decades, her life in the East seemed a temporary expedient, necessary but not home.[37]

Sandoz wrote twelve of her sixteen books while residing in her Greenwich Village outpost, and she died there of cancer in 1966. Her last book, *The Battle of the Little Bighorn*, was released later that year.[38] She was buried in the Nebraska Sandhills on a hill owned by the Sandoz family. After years of self-imposed exile, Mari Sandoz returned home for good.

NOTES

1. Helen Winter Stauffer, *Mari Sandoz: Story Catcher of the Plains* (Lincoln: University of Nebraska Press, 1982). For shorter, more recent studies, see Betsy Downey, "'She Does Not Write Like a Historian': Mari Sandoz and the Old and New Western History," *Great Plains Quarterly* 16, no. 1 (Winter 1996): 9–28; John R. Wunder, "Mari Sandoz: Historian of the Great Plains," in *Their Own Frontier: Women Intellectuals Re-Visioning the American West*, ed. Shirley A. Leckie and Nancy J. Parezo (Lincoln: University of Nebraska

Press, 2008), 97–135; Robert L. Dorman, "Blowout Grass: Mari Sandoz, Historical Pessimism, and Great Plains Regionalism," in *Regionalists on the Left: Radical Voices from the American West*, ed. Michael C. Steiner (Norman: University of Oklahoma Press, 2013), 93–109.

2. *Rereading Frederick Jackson Turner: "The Significance of the Frontier in American History" and Other Essays*, ed. John Mack Faragher (New Haven, CT: Yale University Press, 1998).

3. John D. Hicks, *The Populist Revolt: A History of the Farmers' Alliance and the People's Party* (Lincoln: University of Nebraska Press, 1961). For his experience at the University of Nebraska, see "My Nine Years at the University of Nebraska," *Nebraska History* 46, no. 1 (March 1965): 1–27.

4. Mari Sandoz, *Capital City* (Lincoln: University of Nebraska Press, 1982), 271, 284.

5. Mari Sandoz to M. S. Wyeth Jr., September 6, 1961, in *Letters of Mari Sandoz*, ed. Helen Winter Stauffer (Lincoln: University of Nebraska Press, 1992), 375.

6. Mari Sandoz, "The Homestead in Perspective," in *Sandhill Sundays and Other Recollections* (Lincoln: University of Nebraska Press, 1970), 3. This essay was published originally in *Land Use Policy and Problems in the United States*, ed. Howard W. Ottoson (Lincoln: University of Nebraska Press, 1963).

7. For antecedents of the frontier thesis, see Roy Marvin Robbins, "Horace Greeley: Land Reform and Unemployment, 1837–1862," *Agricultural History* 7, no. 1 (January 1933): 18–41; Henry Nash Smith, *Virgin Land: The American West as Symbol and Myth* (Cambridge, MA: Harvard University Press, 1970); Lee Benson, "The Historical Background of Turner's Frontier Essay," *Agricultural History* 25, no. 2 (April 1951): 59–82.

8. Mari Sandoz, "Stay Home, Young Writer!" *The Quill* (June 1937): 9. In a 1931 letter, Sandoz wrote that native-born settlers in the Sandhills "came to escape the high rentals and the sharp practices exposed in Garland's 'Under the Lion's Paw.'" Mari Sandoz to Mr. M—, May 28, 1931, in *Gordon Journal Letters of Mari Sandoz*, ed. Caroline Sandoz Pifer (Crawford, NE: Cottonwood Press, 1991), 26. For "Under the Lion's Paw," see Hamlin Garland, *Main-Travelled Roads* (Lincoln: University of Nebraska Press, 1995), 130–144. This story originally was published in *Harper's Weekly*, September 7, 1889. See Barbara Martinec, "Hamlin Garland's Revisions

of Main-Travelled Roads," *American Literary Realism, 1870–1910* 5, no. 2 (Spring 1972): 167. Stephen Vincent Benet also made a connection between Sandoz and Garland in his *New York Herald Tribune* review of *Old Jules*, saying that it was "the best and most honest picture of its kind [a pioneer account] since Hamlin Garland's 'Son of the Middle Border.'" Quoted in George Grimes, "Among the New Books," *Sunday Omaha World-Herald*, November 10, 1935.

9. Mari Sandoz, *Slogum House* (Lincoln: University of Nebraska Press, 1981), 301–302. A Nebraska journalist characterized Gulla Slogum as "perhaps the most malevolent figure in all American literature." Eva Mahoney, "An Interview with the Author," *Sunday Omaha World-Herald*, November 26, 1939.

10. Mari Sandoz to Walter Johnson, December 21, 1939, Mari Sandoz Papers, Archives & Special Collections, University of Nebraska–Lincoln Libraries, Lincoln, Nebraska.

11. Downey, "'She Does Not Write Like a Historian,'" 10.

12. *The Populist Revolt* has proved to have a long shelf life, especially on the movement in the Midwest. See Martin Ridge, "Populism Redux: John D, Hicks and The Populist Revolt," in *American Retrospectives: Historians on Historians*, ed. Stanley I. Kutler (Baltimore: Johns Hopkins Press, 1995), 19–31; Robert C. McMath Jr., "Politics Matters: John D. Hicks and the History of Populism," *Agricultural History* 82, no. 1 (Winter 2008): 2–6. For more recent broad treatments on this topic, see Lawrence Goodwyn, *Democratic Promise: The Populist Moment in America* (New York: Oxford University Press, 1976); Gene Clanton, *Populism: The Humane Preference in America, 1890–1900* (Boston: Twayne Publishers, 1991); and Robert C. McMath Jr., *American Populism: A Social History, 1877–1898* (New York: Hill & Wang, 1993).

13. J. D. Hicks, "Our Pioneer Heritage," *Prairie Schooner* 2, no. 1 (Winter 1928): 17, 19. Hicks later would revise his emphasis on the significance of the frontier. See John D. Hicks, "Our Pioneer Heritage: A Reconsideration," *Prairie Schooner* 30, no. 4 (Winter 1956): 359–361. See also John D. Hicks, "The 'Ecology' of Middle-Western Historians," *Wisconsin Magazine of History* 24, no. 4 (June 1941): 377–384.

14. Marie Macumber, "Old Potato Face," *Prairie Schooner* 2, no. 1 (Winter 1928): 29–35. Marie Macumber was Sandoz's legal name when she first enrolled at

the University of Nebraska. On the advice of an agent, she started going by
the name Mari Sandoz in 1929. Stauffer, *Mari Sandoz*, 71–72.

15. Sandoz had a part-time job at the historical society for a while. Later, in early
1934, she was hired for a supervisory position, which she kept until *Old Jules*
was about to be published. See Stauffer, *Mari Sandoz*, 84–87, 91, 111.

16. Addison E. Sheldon, *Land Systems and Land Policies in Nebraska* (Lincoln:
Nebraska State Historical Society, 1936).

17. One historian writes, "Sandoz had exceptional hands-on training in
archival research at the historical society; she could have more properly
claimed Sheldon than Hicks as her mentor." Downey, "'She Does Not
Write Like a Historian,'" 10.

18. Roy Marvin Robbins, review of Annie Pike Greenwood, *We Sagebrush
Folks*, and Mari Sandoz, *Old Jules*, in *Mississippi Valley Historical Review*
23, no. 2 (September 1936): 284.

19. Robert L. Dorman, *Revolt of the Provinces: The Regionalist Movement in
America, 1920–1945* (Chapel Hill: University of North Carolina Press, 1993).

20. Sandoz, "Stay Home, Young Writer," 9. Later, she wrote, "I decided early
that most writers do their best work in materials with which they have
emotional identity. Therefore I restricted myself to the trans-Missouri
country. . . . Through the discovery of this one region, this one drop of
water, I hoped to discover something of the nature of the ocean." Quoted
in Bruce H. Nicoll, "Mari Sandoz: Nebraska Loner," *American West* 2,
no. 2 (Spring 1965): 35. Lowry Wimberly, editor of the *Prairie Schooner*
and a mentor of Sandoz, had published an insightful essay on regionalism
in 1932, suggesting, somewhat prematurely, that its days were numbered.
Lowry Charles Wimberly, "The New Regionalism," *Prairie Schooner* 6,
no. 3 (Summer 1932): 214–221. The Lincoln Sunday newspaper reprinted
both Wimberly's and Sandoz's essays on regionalism under the headline
"Wimberly Thinks Regionalism Passe; Mari Sandoz Defends Such a
Theme," *Lincoln Sunday Journal and Star*, May 23, 1937. For an assessment
of Wimberly's treatment of regionalism, see Kathleen A. Boardman,
"Lowry Charles Wimberly and the Retreat of Regionalism," *Great Plains
Quarterly* 11, no. 3 (Summer 1991): 143–156.

21. "Miss Sandoz Quits Lincoln, Sees Culture Dying There," *Sunday Omaha
World-Herald*, April 7, 1940. See also Elizabeth Hughes, "Move to Denver
Will Free Mari Sandoz of Crank Calls," *Sunday Omaha World-Herald*,

June 30, 1940. Sandoz's biographer wrote, "In 1940 she moved to Denver, ostensibly because of research facilities necessary for *Crazy Horse*, her next book, but also to escape the continual unpleasant incidents she faced from irate Lincolnites." Helen Winter Stauffer, *Mari Sandoz* (Boise: Boise State University Western Writer Series Number 63, 1984), 13.

22. Sandoz stayed in Denver from 1940 to early 1943. For her years in Denver, see Stauffer, *Mari Sandoz*, chapter 7; Caroline Bancroft, "Two Women Writers," *Colorado Heritage* 2, no. 1 (1982): 103–111.

23. Mari Sandoz to *Lincoln Journal and Star* (Sunday), May 25, 1960, Mari Sandoz Papers, Archives & Special Collections, University of Nebraska–Lincoln Libraries, Lincoln, Nebraska.

24. Howard Silber, "Mari Is Weak but Still She Writes," *Sunday Omaha World-Herald*, May 23, 1965. Sandoz's "I Hate New York" book may have been a way of talking about an autobiography that, among other topics, would have treated her criticisms of eastern publishers and their editors. For a reference to "my I HATE NEW YORK book," see Mari Sandoz to Bruce Nicoll, July 7, 1963, *Letters of Mari Sandoz*, 412.

25. Norma Carpenter to Mari Sandoz, March 7, 1959, Mari Sandoz Papers, Archives & Special Collections, University of Nebraska–Lincoln Libraries, Lincoln, Nebraska. Carpenter was the promotion director for Miller & Paine.

26. Sandoz, "I Remember Lincoln—As Our Greenwich Village," *Lincoln Evening Journal*, May 8, 1959. Sandoz's biographer observed that this piece "was written long after she had achieved renown. There were other experiences: resentment at what she saw as snubs by important people, illness caused by malnutrition, despair at lack of publishing success, and her extremely negative view of Lincoln itself. That view is inscribed in her 1939 *Capital City*, no matter how she denied it." *Letters of Mari Sandoz*, xvi. A month before the Miller & Paine essay appeared, Sandoz was interviewed by a reporter for the *Daily Nebraskan*, the University of Nebraska student paper: "Describing the University as she knew it, she spoke of the 1920's and 30's as a 'good time for creative people.'" Continuing, she said, "Young people gathered in the local coffee-shops. Art students, literature students, an occasional lawyer or judge and professors discussed life, philosophy, current events." Marilyn Coffey, "University Begins to 'Hum' Says Nebraska Author," *Daily Nebraskan*, April 8, 1959.

27. Rudolph Umland, "Lowry Wimberly and Others: Recollections of a Beerdrinker," *Prairie Schooner* 51, no. 1 (Spring 1977): 17–50. For the Nebraska Works Progress Administration Writers' Project, see David A. Taylor, "Nailing a Freight on the Fly: The Federal Writers' Project in Nebraska," *Prairie Schooner* 78, no. 1 (Spring 2004): 107–119; Stephen Cloyd, "The Nebraska Federal Writers' Project: Remembering Writers of the 1930s," https://lincolnlibraries.org/heritage-room-of-nebraska-authors/the-nebraska-federal-writers-project-remembering-writers-of-the-1930s.

28. Mari Sandoz to Richard Thruelsen, January 16, 1939, Mari Sandoz Papers, Archives & Special Collections, University of Nebraska–Lincoln Libraries, Lincoln, Nebraska.

29. Stauffer, *Mari Sandoz*, 172, 203.

30. Stauffer, *Mari Sandoz*, 181, 200.

31. *Old Jules, Slogum House*, and *Capital City* are among the Sandoz works published under the Bison Book imprint.

32. Stauffer, *Mari Sandoz*, 213.

33. Stauffer, *Mari Sandoz*, 241.

34. Mari Sandoz to J. L. Norris, August 24, 1958, *Letters of Mari Sandoz*, 320.

35. Mari Sandoz, "Outpost in New York," *Prairie Schooner* 37, no. 2 (Summer 1963): 95–106.

36. Stanley T. Williams, "A Nebraska Outpost," *Yale Review* 25, no. 2 (December 1935): 391–393.

37. "Home life, as such, scarcely exists for me. Although I consider the sandhills of Nebraska my home . . . I usually have an apartment somewhere as a base of operations, at Lincoln, say, or Denver, or, the last years, in New York." Mari Sandoz to Ralph Knight, February 4, 1958, *Letters of Mari Sandoz*, 303.

38. For a complete list of Sandoz's publications, including books, stories, and collections edited by others, see *Letters of Mari Sandoz*, 463–467.

CHAPTER 13

How the Midwest Encountered
Mass Consumer Culture

Kenneth H. Wheeler

This chapter explores the impact of a growing mass consumer culture on the Midwest, especially in the 1920s and 1930s. More specifically, it focuses on the relationship between the nation's shift during the 1920s from a producer to a consumer culture and the dramatic fall in reputation the Midwest experienced as a region during the same period. The first two decades of the twentieth century were a heyday for the Midwest. Midwesterners led the nation on many fronts, as the region was a wellspring of invention, creativity, and progressive reforms. After World War I, however, the energies of the Progressive Era dissipated, elites outside the region began to strenuously criticize the Midwest, and a mass consumer culture, having grown in influence for at least decades, perhaps centuries, finally eclipsed the producer culture with which the Midwest was closely identified.

Because consumer culture was a mass culture, all American regional cultures, as Robert Dorman has shown, diminished from the 1920s onward; this chapter suggests that the Midwestern affinity with a producer culture made the region's fall in reputation and image more dramatic, though the actual experiences of Midwesterners during the rise in consumer culture were mixed.[1] Some Midwesterners adored the changes a consumer culture brought to their lives. Others either resisted or bemoaned the cultural changes happening around them and wondered what a growing consumer culture meant for the region and the nation. Still others incorporated elements of the new consumer culture into their existing value systems and communities in self-conscious and even highly creative ways that belied critics' fears.

In the nineteenth century, the Midwest sustained long ties to producer culture. Students attending colleges of the region in the antebellum period expressed interest in "usefulness," work that had a moral dimension to it, reflecting their desire to be true to God's purpose for their life and to be helpful to other people and society. When the term *Middle West* originated in the 1880s to describe Kansas and Nebraska, the people living there were often described as "self-reliant and independent, kind, open, and thrifty. They were pragmatic, and industrious, and they took pride in their work; yet they were also idealistic, moral, and humble." James Shortridge found that from 1902 to 1912, the geographical area considered to be the Midwest expanded dramatically, and by 1920, this growth extended as far as Buffalo and Pittsburgh to the east, the Dakotas to the north, and even Texas to the south and west.[2]

During the first two decades of the twentieth century, Americans associated the idea of pastoralism—the "yeoman-farmer ideal"—with the Midwest, a land rich in natural abundance, its soil worked by this virtuous, humble, independent, egalitarian, self-reliant yeomanry, who in their politics would be "thinking of the public good" and "throwing off the power of vested-interest groups."[3] The pastoral ideal involved a producer culture in which work was valued more highly than leisure, a culture in which status would be gained through the demonstration of industry. Pastoralism did not inherently include a hostile view of cities, which had a legitimate function as the market for farmers' products, especially as long as the cities lived up to pastoral ideals. As the region's cities grew, they came to be known for their vast productive capabilities. In 1914, Carl Sandburg captured this flavor in the opening of his poem "Chicago":

Hog Butcher for the World
Tool Maker, Stacker of Wheat,
Player with Railroads, and the Nation's Freight Handler;
Stormy, husky, brawling,
City of the Big Shoulders

Midwestern cities were different from the finance center of New York or the enticing streets of jazzy, seedy New Orleans. Midwestern cities packed pork and produced goods. The region's cities were in the architectural and cultural vanguard of urban America, and Americans thought of the Midwest "as the most American part of America."[4]

This period of rapid expansion in the Midwest happened during the Progressive Era, which historian Robert Crunden described as "a climate of creativity within which writers, artists, politicians, and thinkers functioned." The "progressive personality," argued Crunden, experienced "its birth in the Middle West," where many young people were reared in devout Protestant homes, devoting themselves "to the figure and example of Lincoln." "To progressives," Crunden contended, "Lincoln was not only a legendary hero who haunted their dreams and talked to their ancestors, but he was a living ideal against which they constantly measured themselves, their friends, and their leaders." Usually after attending one of the denominational colleges dotting the Midwest, these progressives went into one of the newer professions emerging at that time, especially, "journalism, settlement work, higher education, law, or politics." In their new professions, these young progressives found themselves most welcome in the Midwest, where they worked in a "relatively unstructured intellectual and professional climate that encouraged new insights." This Midwestern progressive movement had, of course, national (and international) reach and implications.[5]

World War I, however, changed the national mood, and the Progressive Era ended. During the 1920s, a mass consumer culture dominated over the older producer culture associated with middle-class industry, character, and sacrifice. As consumer culture came to the fore, according to Warren I. Susman, "key words began to show themselves: *plenty, play, leisure . . . public relations, publicity, celebrity.* Everywhere there was a new emphasis on buying, spending, and consuming." At the same time, people increasingly thought of the Midwest as a parochial region fueled by fear and isolationism. Susman found that in the 1920s, East Coast urban intellectuals revolted against "what was considered to be the Midwestern domination of American life and values." Shortridge thought the Midwest represented a pastoral ideal that the nation began to reject as a desirable future during this era. A key turning point was the public's response to Sinclair Lewis's 1920 novel, *Main Street.*[6]

Critics presented *Main Street* as an attack on the provincial and stultifying nature of the small town, which became the general public's understanding of the book as well. But Lewis also praised the natural beauty of small towns, the farmers who lived near them, and the character of Will Kennicott, who was a dutiful and humane small-town man. In a letter written shortly after *Main Street*'s publication, Lewis, who was surprised by the reception of his book, wrote, "If I didn't love Main Street would I write of it so hotly? could I write of it so ragingly?" Authors, however, do not control how people react to what they write, and the response to *Main Street*, parts of which excoriated Midwesterners as provincial, low-brow, and close-minded, showed how the image of the Midwest had changed in the American mind. Midwestern authors of the era who were less critical of the region, such as Booth Tarkington, found their reputations diminishing. Whatever the reality of the Midwest, the image of the region with its producer culture no longer inspired and led a nation dominated by consumer culture.[7]

In the Midwest, responses to the mass consumer culture varied, and important parts of consumer culture began there. For example, Montgomery Ward, in 1872, began his mail-order business from a tiny loft over a Chicago livery stable. Soon Richard Warren Sears of Minnesota partnered with Alvah Curtis Roebuck of Indiana to create another catalog giant: Sears, Roebuck and Co. Free rural delivery made their thousands of consumer items widely available to millions of Americans, creating consumption communities that bound together people who had never met each other but who used the same product. The result was democratic but not regional.[8]

Some producer-minded Midwesterners had trouble coming to terms with consumer culture values. Henry Ford, as is well known, loved his Model T—he believed it was the perfect car. Remarkably inexpensive, yet high in quality, the Model T came from relentless efforts to perfect a mass production system that brought each car to employees on a moving assembly line engineered so workers did not have to stoop to perform their labor. Year after year, beginning in 1915, Model T Fords rolled off the production lines, and by 1927 they comprised more than half of the cars in the world. Sales increased in the 1920s, but Ford's market share fell as General Motors introduced models in "candy dish colors." Not only did General Motors cars change in style and appearance each year, the company introduced installment purchasing through the General Motors Acceptance Corporation (GMAC), which allowed consumers to buy cars on an installment plan at a time when banks did not yet offer loans for cars. Ford dealers saw the problem and urged changes, but Henry Ford remained unyielding and told dealers the problem was poor salesmanship. In 1926, a top Ford executive, Ernest Kanzler, wrote Ford a memo "insisting" Ford produce a new car, but within months, Kanzler was fired. The Ford Motor Company went on "with no budget for research, no accommodation for development of designs and designers." Historian Douglas Brinkley related that when anxious workers secretly created a prototype for a new car, Henry Ford happened upon the unauthorized vehicle and "circled it like an angry cat." Enraged, he seized "a giant pick ax" and "just started ripping into it." [9]

Even Henry Ford and a large pickax, though, could not stop the cultural changes. In 1926, Ford yielded by offering the Model T in not just basic black but also maroon and green. The next year he made the momentous decision to cease production of the "cheap, ugly, durable, efficient, simple, and black Model T" and replace it with the Model A. The damage to the company, though, was done. General Motors surged ahead, and the Ford Motor Company would never again have market dominance. Henry Ford took too long to realize that people didn't want to drive the perfect car if everyone else was also driving the same car. In the new consumer culture, people wanted to feel special—they wanted style and for others to notice their newly purchased car as the latest model. GMAC financing offered the allure of obtaining something immediately and paying it off over time; it allowed consumers to believe that the future would be rosy, that saving for a rainy day was unnecessary, and that delayed gratification was old fashioned. [10]

Another person who witnessed the shift to prominence of consumer culture was sociologist Robert S. Lynd. Born in New Albany, Indiana, Lynd returned to the Hoosier state in 1925 with a team of researchers that descended on Muncie, and he produced in 1929, with his wife, Helen Merrell Lynd, the volume *Middletown: A Study in Modern American Culture*. Among other aspects of life, the Lynds focused on the work Muncie, or Middletown, residents performed. The question posed in the title of their chapter "Why Do They Work So Hard?" had a dismaying answer, from the

Lynds' perspective. Robert came from a Calvinist household that believed in the dignity of work and in finding life's meaning in diligent labor. But in Middletown, as Daniel Boorstin once put it, "The fellowship of skill was displaced by the democracy of cash." In one example, one of the Lynds' researchers asked an executive if an employee working "a complicated machine takes pride in his work" and has "a feeling of proprietorship." The answer was a swift no. The executive mentioned a man "who's ground diameters on gears here for fifteen years and done nothing else. It's a fairly highly skilled job and takes more than six months to learn. But it's so endlessly monotonous! That man is dead, just dead! And there's a lot of others like him." The Lynds did not find many workers in Muncie who felt satisfaction in doing their work, "but both business men and working men seem to be running for dear life in this business of making the money they earn keep pace" with their wants.[11]

For Robert Lynd, the reality of life in Muncie was disconcerting. Where was the feeling of moral purpose in pursuing one's vocation or the feeling that pride in skilled craftmanship was highly valued? Rather, people seemed to be working without any sense of meaning beyond earning a paycheck. The Lynds concluded that people in Middletown had only the faintest idea of why they worked—they were missing the meaning and purpose in work that came from a producer culture. A decade later, when Robert Lynd returned to Muncie in 1935, he concluded that the "master formula" of the town was "Work = Money; Money Buys Leisure; Nonwork = Loss of Opportunity to Make Money, and Therefore Loss of Opportunity to Buy Leisure." A consumer-cultural outlook reigned supreme.[12]

In the 1920s, the Lynds discovered that Middletowners had distinct ideas about what they wanted to do with their money. Some bought radios, others went to the movies, but the product they most desired for leisure was an automobile. One great irony is that producer-minded Henry Ford was instrumental to the spread of a key consumer-cultural item. In Muncie, one mother told the researchers, "We'd rather do without clothes than give up the car." Another woman "emphatically" insisted, "I'll go without food before I'll see us give up the car." Numerous families in the city lived in houses lacking bathtubs yet owned an automobile. The zeal for car ownership was widespread. The Lynds found that the automobile had "revolutionized" Middletown's leisure, was "making leisure-time enjoyment a regularly expected part of every day and week rather than an occasional event," and had "multiplied many-fold" the "readily available leisure-time options." The Lynds also found, however, that the consumer culture could also generate dissatisfaction. The amount of importance people attributed to automobile model years—which the Lynds saw as a result of "commercially manipulated pressure"—amplified the possibility that these people would feel "greatly discouraged." One editor in Middletown attended a car show in 1929 and remarked, "I was driving a car of much better quality than I can afford and only a year old; but, somehow, as I left the auto showroom the vehicle of which I had been proud seemed pitiable."[13]

Robert Lynd worried that in a consumer culture people were falling into the clutches of advertisers who were not looking out for the best interests of consumers. In 1933, Lynd published a chapter on "The People as Consumers" in *Recent Social Trends: Report of the President's Research Committee on Social Trends*. The proliferation of consumer goods available for purchase, Lynd concluded, had actually created "a mounting distaste on the part of both men and women for the labor of buying things, a desire to simplify and to expedite the process as much as possible." While advertisers pitched their efforts as "consumer education," Lynd thought it was "an open question whether factors making for consumer confusion in our rapidly changing culture are not actually outstripping the forces making for more effective consumption. Society is content to allow the buying of a living to remain, like health in the Middle Ages, largely an area of private chaos." He recommended that the government, through agencies and schools, "educate the individual consumer in the practice of the fine art of spending money." Lynd, clearly, personally felt "distaste" for how the world had changed and saw the results of advertising in America's "rapidly changing culture" as creating "private chaos," not consumer education.[14]

Lynd would have shaken his head in exasperation, though, had he seen how his studies were used by advertisers and "business strategists." As historian Sarah E. Igo has shown, the business community readily accepted the idea that Muncie was a representative and typical American city, and businesses proved hungry for the insights the Lynds' scholarship could provide. In Igo's words, *Middletown* was a "godsend to marketers," and in 1934, *Business Week* admitted that *Middletown* was "helpful in charting the course of prospective buyers' expenditures, habits and desires." In 1937, upon the publication of a follow-up volume, *Middletown in Transition*, *Tide* magazine explained that "admen and marketers will read it as a matter of course." Many of these product pitchers actually went to Muncie to do their own research, sure that Muncie was a microcosm of America. Thus, the Lynds, while critical of the consumer culture, unwittingly helped unleash its influences on Muncie and the rest of America through their work.[15]

However, Robert Lynd might have been less alarmed if he had studied how people were actually using the consumer goods they purchased. In Ronald R. Kline's study of how country people used new technologies in the first half of the twentieth century, he found, using a host of examples from the Midwest, that consumers continually used products in ways manufacturers and advertisers never intended. Farmers frequently purchased automobiles and used them for stationary power, lifting the rear tires off the ground and harnessing the belt power of the rear axle to run corn shellers, saws, pumps, and washing machines. Groups of people used their telephone party lines to broadcast gramophone music and even to sing and play instruments to their telephonic audience. In 1937, the head of the New Deal's Rural Electrification Administration, John Carmody, encouraged a consumer-cultural outlook when he said his administration wanted to bring farming families "out of a past of unnecessary denial into a present of reasonable convenience." Yet while Midwestern farm women bought and used some modern household appliances, they were selective about which ones they purchased and how they used them. "Farm people," wrote Kline, "were not passive consumers. . . . Instead, they resisted, modified, and selectively used" consumer goods and "followed their own paths to modernity."[16]

For John Bartlow Martin, the changes in the Midwest were substantial and damaging. Martin was a Hoosier journalist and Midwestern chronicler who, in his 1947 book, *Indiana: An Interpretation*, explained that the late 1800s and early 1900s had been "a golden age," the time of Eugene Debs, the best man he thought Indiana had ever produced, and a time of fine literature, invention, and "constant renewal." But Martin believed that by World War I, Indiana had experienced "a hardening of the arteries" and had never recovered. Martin was not pining for an agrarian past. He celebrated a labor organizer amidst an industrializing region, but he recognized that the Midwest really had produced great Americans, and he thought the pipeline of Midwestern greatness had run dry in a nation that had abandoned the producer culture. Martin complained that "so many farms were 'telephone farms'" and that Brown County, south of Indianapolis, "was little more than a widely advertised commodity, with bearded men in the villages neatly arranged as props for the tourists." To Martin, consumer goods had reshaped farms in negative ways, and towns that previously depended on agrarian commerce had become unproductive and useless tourist destinations.[17]

A related perspective emerged the same year, 1947, when Hoosier Ross Lockridge Jr. published the novel *Raintree County*, which became a best-seller and a Book-of-the-Month Club selection and made its way into the hands of many readers. Lockridge tells the story of John Wickliff Shawnessy, a character who grows up in the mid-nineteenth-century fictional and pastoral eponymous county in Indiana. Young Johnny Shawnessy's father is a doctor and Methodist minister who opposes slavery and tobacco. Johnny fights for the preservation of the Republic in the Civil War but returns to a very different homeplace, with Lincoln assassinated, his father enfeebled, and his childhood sweetheart deceased from the rigors of childbirth after marrying his nemesis. Thinking of the changes, Johnny Shawnessy "would remind himself that nothing remains the same, not even the most ancient scar on the earth of Raintree County." Rather than bemoan his losses, succumb to nostalgia, or give in to the victors of the new era (Cash Carney the capitalist and Garwood Jones the unprincipled politician), Shawnessy quietly moves on with his life. He marries, begins a new family, and teaches children at the local school. Though often saddened by the loss of the pastoral world in which he grew to adulthood, he does not give up trying to live a life worthy of his parents' ideals. And he is rewarded in small but important ways. When Shawnessy runs for a seat in the US House of Representatives against Garwood Jones, Shawnessy is "soundly defeated in the total vote," but "by some miracle" he tallies one more vote than Jones in Raintree County itself.[18]

The most important element in the novel is the Raintree, a life-giving force that symbolizes the world of Shawnessy's youth. Perhaps Lockridge likewise recognized that the Midwestern world in which he had grown up had changed dramatically. Lockridge was the son of a quintessential progressive father, Ross Sr., who, among other things, had written a biography of Abraham Lincoln and taken his namesake son to the southern Indiana grave of Nancy Hanks Lincoln, where he had his son stand and recite from memory the Gettysburg Address. Ross Jr. was not destroying car prototypes or bemoaning a lack of pride in the work done by machinists; he was not trying to turn back the clock. But he wanted assurance that a glimmer of the pastoral world he had once known would continue to exist. In *Raintree County*, the Raintree itself is hidden in the center of a great swamp. Johnny Shawnessy has seen the tree only once, and even then, he could not be sure he had seen it because he was drunk and distracted at the time. As a grown man, Shawnessy wonders if that tree still stands. Is the symbol yet alive? His answer comes when his daughter, Eva, gets lost in the swamp. When she is found, she has leaves and flowers of the Raintree on her person. In Eva's words, "Papa picked up the dress and shook it and little yellow flowers fell out of the pockets. . . . He stood with a strange look on his face sifting the tiny flowers from one hand to the other." Hope was not lost in Raintree County. "Strong yearning possessed him to build again—and better than before—the valorous dream," writes Lockridge. "Did you think that I had lost the way? Did you think that I was drowned in darkness and the swamp? But I was here always, bearing a stem of the summer grass." Shawnessy has found proof that the Midwest of his youth is not dead. Lockridge also wanted to find evidence that the Midwest of his youth, that producer-cultural, pastoral, progressive, vibrant, creative Midwest, was still there in 1947. He wanted to believe that John Bartlow Martin was wrong and that the region had not died from a hardening of the arteries. Ross Jr.'s son, Larry Lockridge, wrote a biography of his father, which maintains that Ross Jr. was uncomfortable with the consumerism and materialism, the "spiritual illness," he sensed in the 1930s and 1940s. It makes sense that Ross Lockridge Jr. yearned "to build again—and better than before—the valorous dream."[19]

Surely other Midwesterners living in the early twentieth century regretted what they had lost. But consumer culture was not imposed on Midwesterners from the outside. To a large extent, people like Montgomery Ward and Henry Ford, the Middletown machinists grinding gears, and the farm wives selectively introducing electrified appliances into their homes were part and parcel of consumer culture. And as Robert and Helen Lynd discovered, many Midwesterners adored what consumer culture brought—greater emphasis on leisure and more options in how to spend their off-work hours. Few Midwestern farmers eschewed telephones. In fact, most common laborers of Middletown were unconcerned with how people thought their spiritual lives had been damaged by the purchase of a car or a trip to the movies. That the regional distinctiveness of the Midwest was weakened in the process seems to be a given, as mass consumer culture affected every part of the nation. And yet the producer-cultural, pastoral Midwest, though derided from outside the region, did not completely disappear. John Wickliff Shawnessy did not give up, and certainly many real-life Midwesterners remained hopeful for a future that could incorporate the best parts of the world they had once known.

NOTES

1. Robert L. Dorman, *Revolt of the Provinces: The Regionalist Movement in America, 1920–1945* (Chapel Hill: University of North Carolina Press, 2003).

2. Kenneth H. Wheeler, "How Colleges Shaped a Public Culture of Usefulness," in *The Center of a Great Empire: The Ohio Country in the Early American Republic*, ed. Andrew R. L. Cayton and Stuart D. Hobbs (Athens: Ohio University Press, 2005), 105–121; Kenneth H. Wheeler, *Cultivating Regionalism: Higher Education and the Making of the American Midwest* (DeKalb: Northern Illinois University Press, 2011); and James R. Shortridge, *The Middle West: Its Meaning in American Culture* (Lawrence: University Press of Kansas, 1898), 17, 22–25.

3. Shortridge, *The Middle West*, 27–30.

4. Carl Sandburg, *Chicago Poems* (New York: Henry Holt, 1916), 3–4. The poem was first published in 1914 in *Poetry* magazine; Jon C. Teaford, *Cities of the Heartland: The Rise and Fall of the Industrial Midwest* (Bloomington: Indiana University Press, 1993); Shortridge, *The Middle West*, 33–37 (quotation, 36).

5. Robert M. Crunden, *Ministers of Reform: The Progressives' Achievement in American Civilization, 1889–1920* (Urbana: University of Illinois Press, 1984), ix, 14–15, 9, 276, 4, 276, 64. See also, on the importance of Lincoln, Ray Ginger, *Altgeld's America: The Lincoln Ideal Versus Changing Realities* (New York: Funk & Wagnalls, 1958).

6. Warren I. Susman, *Culture as History: The Transformation of American Society in the Twentieth Century* (New York: Pantheon Books, 1984), xxiv, 36; Shortridge, *The Middle West*, 39–42.

7. Sinclair Lewis, *Main Street* (New York: Harcourt, Brace, & World, 1920); Lewis quoted in Dorman, *Revolt of the Provinces*, 18; Jeremy Beer, "Midlander: Booth Tarkington's Defense of the Midwest," in *The Midwestern Moment: The Forgotten World of Early Twentieth-Century Midwestern Regionalism, 1880–1940*, ed. Jon K. Lauck (Hastings, NE: Hastings College Press, 2017), 35–53; Shortridge, *The Middle West*, 42–45; and Jon K. Lauck, *From Warm Center to Ragged Edge: The Erosion of Midwestern Literary and Historical Regionalism, 1920–1965* (Iowa City: University of Iowa Press, 2017), esp. 11–35.

8. Daniel J. Boorstin, *The Americans: The Democratic Experience* (New York: Vintage, 1973), 89–164, esp. 118–129. The origins of consumer culture are quite difficult to pin down. Some historians find them as early as the late 1500s. See Daniel Horowitz, *The Morality of Spending: Attitudes toward the Consumer Society in America, 1875–1940* (Baltimore: Johns Hopkins University Press, 1985), esp. xxiv–xxix. David M. Potter, in *People of Plenty: Economic Abundance and the American Character* (Chicago: University of Chicago Press, 1958), argued that all of American history rested upon an assumption of abundance, represented especially by the land that Americans conquered, settled, and developed.

9. Susman, *Culture as History*, 136–137; Douglas Brinkley, *Wheels for the World: Henry Ford, His Company, and a Century of Progress, 1903–2003* (New York: Viking, 2003), 349, 340, 342–345; interview with Douglas Brinkley on *Morning Edition*, National Public Radio, www.npr.org/templates/story/story.php?storyId=1280498.

10. Brinkley, *Wheels for the World*, 346; Susman, *Culture as History*, 136–141 (140, quotation).

11. Richard Wightman Fox, "Epitaph for Middletown: Robert S. Lynd and the Analysis of Consumer Culture," in *The Culture of Consumption: Critical Essays in American History, 1880–1980*, ed. Richard Wightman Fox and T. J. Jackson Lears (New York: Pantheon Books, 1983), 101–141; Robert S. Lynd and Helen Merrell Lynd, *Middletown: A Study in Modern American Culture* (New York: Harcourt, Brace, 1929), 75, 87, 89 (quotations); Boorstin, *The Americans*, 89.

12. Robert S. Lynd and Helen Merrell Lynd, *Middletown in Transition: A Study in Cultural Conflicts* (New York: Harcourt, Brace & World, 1937), 294.

13. Lynd and Lynd, *Middletown*, 251–271 (quotations on 255, 256, and 260); Lynd and Lynd, *Middletown in Transition*, 267–268, fn35.

14. Robert S. Lynd (with the assistance of Alice C. Hanson), "The People as Consumers," in *Recent Social Trends: Report of the President's Research Committee on Social Trends*, 2 vols. (New York: McGraw-Hill, 1933), 857–911 (quotations on 910–911).

15. Sarah E. Igo, *The Averaged American: Surveys, Citizens, and the Making of a Mass Public* (Cambridge, MA: Harvard University Press, 2007), 85–89.

16. Ronald R. Kline, *Consumers in the Country: Technology and Social Change in Rural America* (Baltimore: Johns Hopkins University Press, 2000), 67, 43, 3, 9, 276.

17. John Bartlow Martin, *Indiana: An Interpretation* (New York: A. A. Knopf, 1947; Bloomington: Indiana University Press, 1992), xvi, 113, 121–122, 276. On Martin and his book, see Ray E. Boomhower, *John Bartlow Martin: A Voice for the Underdog* (Bloomington: Indiana University Press, 2015), esp. 87–93.

18. Larry Lockridge, *Shade of the Raintree: The Life and Death of Ross Lockridge, Jr., Author of Raintree County* (New York: Viking, 1994), 4; Ross Lockridge Jr., *Raintree County* (Boston: Houghton Mifflin, 1947), 995, 787.

19. Lockridge, *Raintree County*, 1015, 1058–1059; Lockridge, *Shade of the Raintree*, 43, 76, 151–153, 183–190, 295–297.

"No Place for Artistes"

James Jones's Quest for Authenticity in the Postwar Midwest

Aaron George

I

Following World War II, many Americans became concerned that modernity may have damaged the character of the American soul.[1] Once American men tamed the frontiers; now they donned gray flannel suits. Alongside cultural critiques of the "organization men" who were the "dominant members of society" and the hysterical reactions to "other-directed" men, some Americans pushed back against modernity by idealizing a simpler, lost American past.[2] Some believed a rural Midwest still dominated by corner stores and agricultural production might offer something lost and forgotten in the midst of American modernity.

James Jones, a product of small-town Illinois, offered the simplicity of western America as an antidote to the stifling bureaucratization of American life. The celebrated writer of *From Here to Eternity* and *The Thin Red Line*, Jones has long been considered an important World War II writer. Yet despite his notoriety as a novelist, Jones's contributions to postwar discussions of masculinity and modernity have been overlooked.[3] James Jones, like many Americans, worried that postwar America forced men into lives that betrayed their inner selves. Alienated after his discharge from the army, Jones spent the 1950s trying to translate the practice of self-reflection he learned during the war into a way to combat the fake and position-obsessed society that surrounded him. Both in his novels and in the experimental Handy Writers' Colony he helped to create on the outskirts of Marshall, Illinois, Jones tried to teach men how to withdraw from American culture and to create meaning through societal rebellion.

Jones loved rural America. He spent his postwar years on a commune of his own making in Illinois, close to the town of Marshall. When asked about this choice, Jones's response highlighted the simplicity of the decision: "A lot of people have asked me why, after getting to be 'famous' and making a lot of money with a novel, I would choose to live in Marshall, Illinois. Writers are supposed to go to New York or Mexico City or Hollywood to live after they write a book. My reason is simple. I like living in Marshall better." The rest of his answer included a list of stereotypes of small-town America: Jones admired a bartender who trusted a handwritten check and the "peculiar country humor" spoken by Midwestern men with "nasal drawl[s]." "This kind of a community is the spine," Jones explained, "from which we hang the ribcase and the pelvis of our 'economies' and our politics, our 'policies,' and from which dangle the appendages of our industries."[4]

Jones's anxieties about modernity, and the antidote that the simplicity of Midwestern America represented, were deeply intertwined with his notions of manhood. He wasn't alone; as historians have demonstrated, the end of World War II was punctuated by a collective fear that American men would soon become victims of bureaucracy and suburbia.[5] This incipient modernity, with the interdependence and loss of individualism it seemed to imply, threatened the role of the American male after the war: How could a man claim his autonomy while simultaneously groveling to a boss at work and tiptoeing around a domineering wife at home? James Jones, by advocating separatism as the solution to the feminization of American life, has to be considered as part of this broader cultural crisis. Through Jones, we can see the way some intellectuals tried to advocate for alternatives after World War II, ones that would allow for manhood in a society they felt imperiled individualism and autonomy.

II

From an early age, James Jones was driven by a need to prove himself as a man. Growing up on the westerns and war movies of the 1920s and 1930s had exposed him to a type of turn-of-the-century manhood that was predicated on stoicism, control, and independence. He joined the military in 1938, believing it to be the most likely place to demonstrate his bravery; however, it led to a crisis of faith for Jones. Instead of finding a war like the ones he had seen in films, he found something brutal, vicious, and uncontrolled. As the war taught Jones to distrust popular depictions of heroism, it also helped him redefine the concept of manhood around the rejection of those "heroic" traits and the acknowledgment of them as falsehoods.[6]

Jones entered the war to become a man, but he was stationed in Hawaii as a typist, far away from where he (ironically) thought war might start.[7] Bored with and embarrassed by his safe position, he wrote home to complain to his brother, Jeff, while also heavily exaggerating his sexual exploits. He later admitted to exaggerating these stories in order to present himself as a typical soldier, an especially important performance given his frustration with working as an unmanly typist.[8] Jones also told his brother about his hopes and fears for the impending war: "I'll be goddamned if I'm going to sit behind a typewriter or gas up the planes while other guys fly them and do the fiting [sic]," he wrote in May 1940, just before taking the unusual step of transferring into the infantry. "If I don't get out there," Jones told his brother, "I'll never find out whether I'd have turned yellow or not."[9]

Jones was eating breakfast when the bombing of Pearl Harbor began; he later remembered seeing a plane fly so low to the ground that he could make out the grin of the pilot.[10] Despite the tragedy, Jones was excited; he spent the time between Pearl Harbor and his deployment writing short fragments in which he explored what being a soldier, as well as the concept of manhood, meant. In a two-page fragment titled "December 7th, 1941," Jones described how the bombing transformed the men around him, causing them to stop their womanizing and drinking to become ideal soldiers. Similarly, in an outline titled "The Making of a Man," he drew a comparison between the act of a young man readying himself for war and the forging of steel.[11]

But Jones's expectations were quickly shattered once he actually saw combat. He had harbored worries from the moment he and his fellow soldiers were deployed: as they made their way to Guadalcanal, he noticed other men showing constant insubordination and abandoning their posts. But combat was worse. In a chilling entry in his diary, Jones recorded how the men had "snapped; they went half crazy, kill crazy. They didn't give a damn for anything. They bayoneted sick & wounded Japs. . . . They spit in the faces of dying Japs. Ferrullo shot one sitting head in hands on trail & took his watch. King hunted for them to kill and rob." [12] The men were contemptuous of authority and emotionally out of control—the opposite of the stoic, brave men he had imagined fighting in war. Over the next few months, Jones mused on what he had seen. In his experience, soldiers were neither courageous nor restrained, and actual combat was perverse, disorderly, and fundamentally disinhibiting.

Jones didn't experience much combat. He was transferred to a hospital for a basketball injury—still wanting to appear manly, he lied in letters back home and told his brother he had been grazed by a bullet in combat—and developed trauma, which eventually resulted in his being discharged with a neuropsychiatric condition (a term used at the time that often referred to the condition we now call posttraumatic stress disorder). Not badly injured, Jones wandered the hospital and studied the other men, using the time to meditate on what his experiences had taught him. In one diary entry, he recalled witnessing a seriously injured man being cleaned of his own feces. Entranced by the honesty of the scene, Jones described it in detail, noting, "Every time they moved him, he would moan or say something in a [illegible] voice that reminded me of a child. He was not heroic." [13]

The scene led Jones to further muse on the nature of manliness:

I've seen quite a few wounded men & I've never seen them act as [illegible] –scribed them in his books [illegible] Pearl Harbor. They were not silent. They don't care only whether or not they appear brave. The main reason anyone acts brave anytime is to impress other people & because they have an image in their minds (built up by the tredr [illegible] –tions of the movies, adventure novels, & public opinion) of a brave man suffering immense pain stoicly [sic]

& silently. After being in action, a man does not care what people think of him: he knows those who have been thru what he has will feel as he does, & the opinion of those who haven't is distorted and consequently false. If groaning or crying can make him feel better, he does it. If a man is in a really tight spot, the tremendous fear he feels drives back the curtain so to speak & lets him see the distortions & falseness of the untrue set of values he has been taught. He is never the same again.[14]

Jones was taken aback by both the degree to which his wartime experience differed from what American society had prepared him to expect and the way a real soldier had challenged his previous notions of heroism. Jones started to believe that soldiers were able to access an authentic version of manhood that eluded people who only learned about manhood from "movies [and] adventure novels." Having had the epiphany that war was brutal, scary, and unheroic, Jones saw the possibility for American society to move past its fake, inauthentic expectations of what men should be.

III

Jones had entered the war wondering if he could face the trial before him. He left it with his answer: he ran from the military, convinced he would die if he was sent back overseas, and he went AWOL twice before he was eventually discharged as a neuropsychiatric.[15] But rather than come to terms with this as a manly failure, Jones changed the terms of the debate. The injured man in the hospital seemed to be a model of true manliness: he rejected all the ways society expected him to act and instead let his feelings guide his actions. Jones grew to believe bravery wasn't manly, but foolish: to act brave was to let society dictate your behavior. He thought it took more strength of character to reject this ideal and live uninfluenced by societal approval. Through a rejection of traditional manly virtue, Jones believed, men could live authentically; through authenticity, they could embrace an independence and a sense of individuality that had been denied them and thus reclaim a manhood eroded by postwar America.

Ultimately, Jones determined that a writer could be the ideal man: a hardworking, reclusive individual who could distance himself entirely from society and use his prose to expose the truths of society that others might miss. Many people might believe, for instance, that war was courageous and glamourous; but Jones's writer, offering a perspective from his privileged vantage point, could reveal their mistakes.

Jones's critique came in the midst of a massive upheaval in American society. As millions of veterans returned home, the American population was simultaneously redistributed across the nation. Families moved to the suburbs due to a housing crisis, and the emerging white-collar economy funneled men into corporations and bureaucracies that would have seemed alien to most Americans before the war. These economic and social changes, which many Americans saw as contributing to the feminization of American men, created a societal backlash. David Riesman's *Lonely Crowd*, which argued that modern society produced "other-directed" men, was widely understood by the general public to be evidence that American men were losing the ambition and drive that had defined their frontiersman forebears. The traits Riesman used to define other-direction—cooperation, passivity, selflessness, the ability to get along with others—were traits postwar society identified with femininity, especially motherhood. Many cultural products of the era warned against this encroaching feminization. Pulp literature and movies, for instance, often depicted the fight against communism as a fight between heroic individualism and bureaucratic emasculation.[16]

James Jones found himself trying to reintegrate into a society abuzz with these anxieties. He began to believe society—the same society that had emasculated other-directed men—was to blame for spreading false standards of bravery and wartime heroism in order to trick men into fighting; those who stayed home also seemed to believe these falsehoods.[17] In Jones's mind, his ideal "manly writer" was opposed to society, which was itself opposed to "truth." Echoing nineteenth-century notions of masculinity in which civilization was emasculating, Jones assumed that authenticity could only be found in opposition to society. Writers, on the edges of propriety, would be fully able to critique the values of the world around them.[18]

Jones, like many Americans, often equated modernity with women and feminization. Two of his earliest short stories, for example—"Secondhand Man" and "None Sing So Wildly"—feature male protagonists who have to choose between isolating themselves from civilization, and thus preserving their creativity and vigor, or succumbing to societal demands to get jobs and start families.[19] In both cases, Jones uses a female character to voice the demands of society and implies that by submitting to those demands, his hero would also submit to female domination. Not only does Jones portray women as the mouthpieces of society in his fiction, he also uses misogynist overtones to imply that women are responsible for creating the society that is so damaging to men. In a letter to his friend Peggy Carson in 1947, Jones laid out his understanding of the relationship between writers, women, and society:

> If a man really wants to write, he finds that all of life and Society conspires against him. Even his own body fights him, because the desire in him for a woman is forever pushing him toward marriage, and any writer who marries before he becomes financially self-sufficient in his writing is through. He has to go to work to support a wife and the offspring, and his writing becomes either a childish dream, or else is relegated to the position of an avocation, a hobby. Then too, to find the Truth, the real Truth, unvarnished by the social mores, or the Righteous Ethics, he has to go against everything he has been taught from childhood on, and against everything he is being taught now and urged to do. . . . When a man decides to be a writer, he at once becomes a man against the world, standing out against it, alone, completely.[20]

For Jones, authenticity—the ability to both question the values of society and to live free of societal pressures—was achievable only by men; women, he said, the "arch conservatives of life . . . instinctively hate all radicalism" and thus, unlike men, could never oppose society. Jones believed women to be intrinsically weaker than men and limited by the biological necessities of reproduction and the drive to protect their offspring. Because they needed society, which could offer them protection and a mate, Jones argued women could rarely, if ever, see beyond false notions perpetuated by the society they created. He said a woman has "to fight the hand of Nature much more than a man, and that is why all of them in the end, . . . backslide from truth into conservatism."[21]

Man's search for authenticity, and woman's frustration of that search, is the dominant theme of Jones's early novels. His first novel, the unpublished—and at times incoherent—*They Shall Inherit the Laughter*, for instance, was based upon Jones's own homecoming after the war; it detailed the ways women could use society to rob veterans of the truths they discovered in wartime. His next novel, the career-making *From Here to Eternity*, focused on the army during peacetime and the ways bureaucracy—and the sycophantic men who enforced its rules—forced men of principle to decide between their own values and the values imposed on them by others. But Jones's third novel, the colossal, over 1,100-page failure *Some Came Running*, his self-proclaimed magnum opus and his definitive discussion of postwar America, is especially representative of his philosophy. Set in a fictionalized version of Marshall, the small Illinois town that Jones returned to after the war, the novel follows two brothers, Frank and Dave Hirsh, who represent two opposing male reactions to life in postwar America. Both, it turns out, end in ruin.

Frank, a businessman, welcomes the changes postwar America has brought—obsessed with reputation, he develops a hollow persona and says anything to make others think well of him. But when his wife leaves him after he cheats on her, Frank becomes nothing more than a babbling child, barely able to clean or make lunch. His wife's departure proves Frank's dependency on her; his attempts to preserve his manhood while still remaining enmeshed in society were always, it seems, doomed to fail. By contrast, Dave rejects society and befriends the town's misfits—mainly working-class males who hang around in bars and refuse to work in the town's new shopping mall. Dave buys a house where he and his male friends can live together, away from the demands of society, and where they can practice knife-throwing and other physical pursuits. While women clean for them and sometimes provide sex, the house is a male space, specifically constructed to avoid female influence. Eventually, however, Dave succumbs to the charms of a woman and marries her, believing she will support him domestically and financially while he works on his writing. Yet, his wife—like all women—craves societal approval and forces Dave to take a job at the steel factory, drink in moderation, and become "respectable." Dave loses his creative spark and, at novel's end, suffers a literal death (he is shot and killed) that mirrors his spiritual one.

Critics panned *Some Came Running*. In part, they found Dave's idealized masculinity indulgent and irresponsible rather than inspiring. Instead of challenging the conventions of modern America, one reviewer argued, Dave was just a "self-pitying sore head."[22] Jones, of course, felt that the critics had missed the larger point: he saw Dave's struggle to assert himself in a society that leaves little room for male independence and prerogative as the struggle faced by all men in modern America. Indeed, Jones always maintained that the book was his masterpiece.

Some Came Running took Jones five years to write, time he spent simultaneously living out an experiment in resisting the society his novel decried. From 1948 until 1957, Jones, along with his lover Lowney Handy, worked with an ever-changing cast of aspiring writers, teaching them that if they truly wanted to follow in Jones's footsteps, they'd have to forsake modern America entirely. If society degraded authenticity, then Jones was determined to try to create a community that did not.

IV

Alongside Jones's literary endeavors, he embarked on this material experiment in creating an authentic space in modern America. For almost a decade, he assisted in the development of new writers at the Handy Writers' Colony. Established on a stretch of rural farmland twenty miles from Marshall, the colony welcomed "colonists" who spent each summer typing away at their novels, trying to emulate the brilliance of *From Here to Eternity*. Of course, it took more than typing to become a writer. Jones believed that writing was inextricably linked to the ability to live authentically. The Handy Writers' Colony aimed to teach more than prose; it purported to teach manliness as well.

It wasn't a coincidence that Jones chose for his rebellion a spot of farmland twenty miles outside Marshall. The Midwest, to Jones, was a simple place, less affected by the transformations of American society than urban and suburban parts of the country; as *Some Came Running* demonstrated, it was possible for Jones to imagine the West as a place not completely feminized by the cosmopolitanism of postwar America. Jones spent the decade looking for and admiring the qualities of the West that resonated with his critique of modernity: for instance, when not at the colony, Jones traveled the region in his trailer, believing he was discovering traces of an America more in tune with the ideals he had learned in wartime. By the mid-1950s, he had even begun to wear clothes that made him resemble a cowboy.[23] Jones idealized the West because he saw it as a place where self-reliance, directness, and sincerity—traits that naturally lent themselves to the separatism necessary for authenticity—could be accessed.

Conceptually, the Midwest was a sanctuary to Jones: the rural nature of the region separated it from the suburban and urban centers that Jones associated with feminized modern society. Among these Americans who were less touched by modernity, Jones felt that he could craft an alternative to postwar conformity. Though few men had the luxury, as Jones did, to live as a writer on rural farmland or to travel the West in a trailer, his message still resonated with his readers and the colonists, demonstrating that discontent with male roles in postwar America was more widespread than has been previously considered.

Ironically, it was a woman who helped Jones conduct this experiment. Soon after running away from the army, Jones had fallen under the influence of Lowney Handy, a woman twenty years his senior who was a countercultural icon in his hometown of Robinson, Illinois. Handy helped rehabilitate the traumatized Jones, and the two became nearly inseparable. She came to fulfill an all-encompassing role in Jones's life, becoming at once his therapist, mother figure, muse, editor, and lover. Together, they built the colony. Handy was the quartermaster who could turn men into writers, and Jones was the example of the writer that such an experiment could produce.[24]

Life at the writers' colony was designed to inculcate in men the ideals that Jones believed were necessary for authenticity. First, the men were separated from women. Though Handy ran the colony, and though there were a few female colonists during its years of operation, the Handy Writers' Colony was almost exclusively a male enterprise. Men who lived at the colony were encouraged to abandon girlfriends, focus on their writing, and participate in the male-only environment that they created. Colonist John Bowers, for instance, remembered being admonished by Jones and Handy for having a "mind [so] full of cunt" that he might never finish his novel.[25] However, Jones did believe sex was inseparable from the male experience. As a result, about once a month, the colonists were given money to go to a nearby town and sleep with prostitutes. This opportunity for unattached sex was meant to protect the men from the influence of societal expectations when they left the colony.[26]

Separated from women and the society they represented, the men lived a spartan existence in the colony. Waking up before dawn, they spent mornings in small rooms on the land called barracks, where they copied the works of "manly" writers, hoping to absorb both their writing styles and their character traits through osmosis.[27] Once the colonists had finished copying, they worked on their own novels for a few hours, while Handy patrolled outside their doors barking orders at them. "Queer" foreign authors were banned, lest they encourage the men toward "sissy" writing.[28] Once they finished writing, around noon, they congregated in the open-air "Ramada" where they were encouraged to talk about anything except their writing. While Handy and Jones didn't want the colonists to influence each other's styles, the colony's founders did believe that writers had to learn to break taboos, and so the colonists traded crude curses and loudly discussed bodily functions. In the afternoons, Jones led the rest of the men in knife-throwing, diving, motorcycling, or some type of organized sport, activities meant to bind them together through masculine endeavors.[29]

In Handy's words, the colony was "no place for artistes." Beards and long feminine hair were banned, and both Handy and Jones stressed the harsh physical trials the colonists had to endure in order to become writers.[30] Jones, in particular, promoted the idea that writing was labor; when journalists came to see his colony, he would first show them his prowess as a boxer, bragging about his ability to take a punch in the chest, or show off his skills at Ping-Pong ("It ain't no sissy sport," he explained).[31] One journalist described Jones as "an agony writer. . . . [He] sweats and re-writes, seeking the edge. He used to try to write long hours at a stretch, but found even his tough constitution couldn't take it."[32] Another article published around the same time featured a photo of Jones lifting a massive two-foot manuscript of his new novel, equating the muscles needed to lift it with those needed to write it.

The colony blended Jones's vision of the uninhibited, rebellious writer with a vision of manhood that counterpoised the feminized modern society that had greeted him on his return home from war. Many of the men who joined the colony shared the feeling that they were involved in a project offering more fulfillment than what postwar America could offer. John Bowers, one such colonist, wrote in his memoir that upon arrival, he felt the colony "meant Freedom, Possibilities, Writing the book," while home meant "Marriage, Babies, Responsibilities."[33] David Ray, another colonist, wrote that the colony engaged him after he had found his college courses on writing boring and unappealing. For the time of the colony's existence, from around 1948 until 1957, over seventy different colonists stayed with Jones and Handy; Handy had to continually turn away many more. Something about Jones's vision attracted men—to many, a world without women, without office jobs, and without rules for how to behave seemed preferable to the alternative.[34]

The colony, however, was never very stable; Handy's outbursts and eccentric ideas about women alienated some of the colonists, including both Bowers and Ray. And while she bragged about her success in producing writers, only three colonists besides Jones were ever published.[35] These novels, while not the enduring classics that Jones produced, shared a similar ethos: all featured male protagonists fighting to expose societal mores in a constricting world. The most successful, *Never So Few* by Tom Chamales, fictionalizes the author's experiences of wartime in Burma. It focuses on a Lawrence-of-Arabia type of protagonist, Major Con Reynolds, who comes to respect the primitive Kachin people he assists in World War II for their nobility and their authentic relationship with their world. Replacing Jones's sexism with his own racial essentialism, Chamales sends a message that is essentially the same: alternative societies can provide a truer experience of life than modern America because they are less civilized and thus less apt to create false idols.[36]

The Handy Writers' Colony eventually collapsed in 1957, when James Jones found himself sucked into the society he had spent a decade decrying. Having fallen in love with a minor actress named Gloria Masolino, Jones broke off all contact with the colony after an incident in which the jealous Handy tried to stab Masolino with a bowie knife.[37] Jones and Masolino moved to Paris, where they set up a traditional household, hired a maid, and raised two children. He later excused this behavior by claiming that he was researching a book set in Paris; he also complained that McCarthyism made rehabilitating an inauthentic postwar America impossible.[38] But most seriously, Jones had begun to doubt whether his writers could ever write anything worthwhile. It is possible that Jones had become skeptical about the idea that true authenticity could be taught. More likely, his alienation from Handy and his marriage to Masolino could have made his contempt for modernity suddenly seem childish and unrealistic.

Jones never commented on the paradox of his marrying after decrying the idea for so long. However, his move to Paris implicitly acknowledged the fundamental fragility of his ideal. Even James Jones, a strident opponent of marriage and responsibility, in the end couldn't resist conforming to societal expectations, having children, and moving away from small-town America to live in a bustling metropolis. Like his character, Dave Hirsh, Jones succumbed to the lures of stability and security. Just as Jones's manifesto against domesticity, *Some Came Running*, was released in 1957 to panning reviews, Jones also abandoned his vision. He dropped the colony for domesticity and left rural Illinois for one of the greatest cities of them all. He no longer ran; instead, he raised a family.

NOTES

1. Michael D. Gambone, *The Greatest Generation Comes Home: The Veteran in American Society* (College Station: Texas A&M University Press, 2005); Mark D. Van Ells, *To Hear Only Thunder Again: America's World War II Veterans Come Home* (Oxford: Lexington Books, 2001); Lizabeth Cohen, *A Consumers' Republic: The Politics of Mass Consumption in Postwar America* (New York: Vintage Books, 2003), esp. 112–165, and 166–192; Elaine Tyler May, *Homeward Bound: American Families in the Cold War Era* (New York: Basic Books, 1988), 64–88.

2. William H. Whyte, *The Organization Man* (Philadelphia: University of Pennsylvania Press, 2002), 3–4. For the response to David Riesman's concept of other-direction, see James Gilbert, *Men in the Middle: Searching for Masculinity in the 1950s* (Chicago: University of Chicago Press, 2005), 34–80.

3. William Darby, *Necessary American Fictions: Popular Literature of the 1950s* (Bowling Green, OH: Bowling Green State University Popular Press, 1987), 345–363, is the lone exception.

4. James Jones, "Marshall, Illinois," *Ford Times* 49, no. 3 (March 1957): 53–57.

5. K. A. Cuordileone, *Manhood and American Political Culture in the Cold War* (New York: Routledge, 2005); Gilbert, *Men in the Middle*, esp.

34–80; Barbara Ehrenreich, *The Hearts of Men: American Dreams and the Flight from Commitment* (New York: Anchor Press, 1983).

6. Frank MacShane, *Into Eternity: The Life of James Jones, American Writer* (Boston: Houghton Mifflin, 1985), 14–20.

7. James Jones to Suzanne Rollins, July 8, 1957, James Jones Collection, Beinecke Library, Yale University, series II, box 37, folder 551 (hereafter cited as JJ Collection).

8. James Jones to Jeff Jones, n.d., series II, box 35, folder 512, JJ Collection.

9. James Jones to Jeff Jones, May 22, 1940, series II, box 35, folder 514, JJ Collection.

10. James Jones, *WWII: A Chronicle of Soldiering* (New York: Ballantine Books), 7–8.

11. James Jones, "December 7th, 1941," series I, box 31, folder 410, JJ Collection; James Jones, "The Making of a Man," series I, box 31, folder 371, JJ Collection.

12. James Jones, diary entry, February 1943, series I, box 26, folder 318, JJ Collection.

13. James Jones, diary entry, April 13, 1943, series I, box 26, folder 318, JJ Collection.

14. Jones, diary entry, April 13, 1943.

15. MacShane, *Into Eternity*, 73–77.

16. Whyte, *The Organization Man*; Aaron George, "Gray Flannel Suit or Red Strait Jacket? Anticommunism and the Organization Man in Postwar Fiction and Film," *Journal of Popular Culture* 49, no. 6 (December 18, 2016): 1320–1340.

17. Nelson W. Aldrich Jr, "The Art of Fiction XXIII: James Jones," *The Paris Review*, (Autumn–Winter 1958–1959): 50–51.

18. For discussions of nineteenth-century understandings of civilization and manhood, see Wilfred M. McClay, *The Masterless: Self and Society in Modern America* (Chapel Hill: University of North Carolina Press, 1994) and Gail Bederman, *Manliness and Civilization: A Cultural History of Gender and Race in the United States, 1880–1917* (Chicago: University of Chicago Press, 1995).

19. James Jones, "Second-hand Man," *The Way It Is and Everything Else* (proof copy), box 33, folder 464, 63–88, JJ Collection; James Jones, "None Sing So

Wildly," *The Way It Is and Everything Else* (proof copy), box 33, folder 464, 89–134, JJ Collection.

20. James Jones to Margaret Carson, November 9, 1947, series II, box 34, folder 484, JJ Collection.

21. Jones to Margaret Carson.

22. Theodore M. O'Leary, "A Very Long and Very Bad Novel: His Second Book Indicates That James Jones Hasn't Learned the Rudiments of the Writer's Craft," *Kansas City Star*, January 18, 1958, 6; J. H. D., "Gambit: From Eternity to Here," [ca. 1958], box 72, folder 5, HWC Collection; or "Life Is a Four-Letter Word," *Time Magazine*, January 13, 1958, 96.

23. James Jones, "Living in a Trailer," *Holiday Magazine*, July 1953, 74–120; MacShane, *Into Eternity*, 117; George Hendrick, Helen Howe, and Don Sackrider, *James Jones and the Handy Writers' Colony* (Carbondale: Southern Illinois University Press, 2001), inserts.

24. For a good description of her role as a mentor, see A. B. C. Whipple, "James Jones and His Angel," *Life* (May 7, 1951). For an in-depth look at their relationship, see Frank MacShane, *Into Eternity*, esp. 73–78. Also see the extensive correspondence between Lowney Handy, Harry Handy, and James Jones at the Handy Writers' Colony Collection, University of Illinois, Springfield.

25. John Bowers, *The Colony* (New York: Dutton, 1971; New York: Greenpoint Press, 2014), 100. For a description of the colony, see Hendrick, Howe, and Sackrider, *Handy Writers' Colony*.

26. David Ray, "Mrs. Handy's Curious Colony," *Chicago* 3, no. 7 (September 1956): 22–27. Bowers, in *The Colony*, describes one of these adventures on pages 42 through 46 and elsewhere in his memoir.

27. See Hendrick, Howe, and Sackrider, *Handy Writers' Colony*, 50–51; MacShane, *Into Eternity*, 118; Bowers, *The Colony*, 28–30; Ray, "Mrs. Handy's Curious Colony," 24–27.

28. Ray, "Mrs. Handy's Curious Colony," 22–27, 24–25.

29. Ray, "Mrs. Handy's Curious Colony," 23–24, Bowers, *The Colony*, 168–174, 186–188.

30. Whipple, "James Jones and His Angel," 152.

31. "The Good Life and Jim Jones," *Life*, February 11, 1957, 83–86.

32. John Keasler, "Life of a Best-Selling Author," *St. Louis Post-Dispatch*, box 64, folder 13, Handy Writers' Colony Collection.

33. Bower, *The Colony*, 77.

34. Hendrick, Howe, and Sackrider, *Handy Writers' Colony*, 56.

35. William Leonard, "Lowney Handy's Colony Turning Out Novels," *Boston Sunday Herald*, August 4, 1957.

36. Tom T. Chamales, *Never So Few* (New York: Scribner, 1957).

37. MacShane, *Into Eternity*, 155–157.

38. Aldrich Jr., "The Art of Fiction," 37–41.

CHAPTER 15

Newton Minow, John Bartlow Martin, and the "Vast Wasteland" Speech

Ray E. Boomhower

Novice political speechwriter John Bartlow Martin found himself in a quandary after joining Democrat Adlai Stevenson's 1952 presidential campaign staff in the Illinois governor's race against his Republican opponent, Dwight D. Eisenhower. A former reporter and a nationally known freelance writer who had made a comfortable living in suburban Chicago crafting stories for such "big slick" magazines of the day as the *Saturday Evening Post*, Martin had abandoned his trade for a time to offer his writing talents to Stevenson's campaign, which was headquartered in the state capital, Springfield. Martin had gravitated from aiding Stevenson's media relations with press secretary William Flanagan to becoming a member of a group of remarkable speechwriters dubbed the "Elks Club Group" (so named because the Stevenson campaign had rented space for them in the local Elks Club building). "All my life, I had been a reporter, on the outside looking in," Martin recalled. "Now suddenly I was on the inside looking out." Unfortunately, Martin, who had come to Springfield in late August, discovered in early October the "unhappy fact" that he had not been paid his promised salary of two hundred dollars per week plus expenses (he was accustomed to making approximately five hundred dollars a week as a freelancer).[1]

For assistance with his payroll problem, Martin turned to Stevenson's assistant counsel, Newton N. Minow, a lawyer and former law clerk to Chief Justice Fred M. Vinson of the US Supreme Court. Minow had quickly become one of Stevenson's most trusted advisors and had served as the governor's surrogate on state matters ("Everybody else was gone," Minow noted) while Stevenson campaigned for the presidency. "I had felt insecure in my general position, which was somewhat anomalous," Martin admitted. "There really hadn't been a job for me at the Elks; I had, in effect, just moved in and made one." In addition to his responsibilities with state government, Minow had worked with Stevenson's speechwriting staff, for example, arranging housing for them at the Elks building and securing them secretarial assistance. Receiving Martin's plea for help, Minow managed to cut through any red tape and, upon his return from a campaign trip with Stevenson, Martin discovered a full payment for his time waiting for him. He continued to be paid on schedule for the rest of his time with the candidate. "If you wanted something done, Minow was the one," said Martin. For his part, Minow observed that Martin appeared to be a "natural at writing anything," was particularly good at writing political speeches, and, thanks to his days as an "extraordinary" reporter, possessed skills as a "great human observer." [2]

Nearly nine years after Stevenson's failed 1952 presidential run, Martin and Minow, who had remained friends after the campaign, found themselves called to serve by the new young president, John F. Kennedy— Minow as the chairman of the Federal Communications Commission (FCC) and Martin, eventually, as the US ambassador to the Dominican Republic. Before accepting his posting in the Caribbean, Martin had turned down two other diplomatic jobs, in Switzerland and Morocco, but had made early contributions to the administration, producing speeches for Attorney General Robert F. Kennedy, Ambassador to Denmark William M. Blair Jr., and Minow. Of the three speeches, Martin recalled, the one he aided Minow in drafting "had the most impact"—quite an understatement, considering that Minow's May 9, 1961, talk before the annual convention of the National Association of Broadcasters (NAB) in Washington, DC, stunned his audience of two thousand industry representatives and imprinted on the American psyche a phrase, "vast wasteland," still used today when critiquing television programming. The phrase, using imagery inspired by T. S. Eliot's 1922 poem "The Waste Land," has also been commemorated in numerous newspaper and magazine articles, editorials, cartoons, books, and documentaries. Minow himself had to endure being lampooned by Hollywood producer Sherwood Schwartz, who named the doomed ship (SS *Minnow*) from the television series *Gilligan's Island* after him. Minow's daughters have joked to him that on his tombstone will be engraved the words: "On to a Vaster Wasteland." Minow, who has said he expects the phrase will be included in the first sentence of his obituary when he dies, probably could not have realized the lasting effect of his speech, especially considering the reaction he received from one audience member. He recalled that he was talking with LeRoy Collins, NAB president and a former governor of Florida, after finishing his remarks when a member of the audience approached the two men and said to Minow, "I didn't particularly like your speech." The man left, only to return a few minutes later to say to Minow, "The more I thought about it, your speech was really awful." The man retreated, only to return for a final time to comment: "Mr. Minow, that was the worst speech I ever heard in my whole life!" Collins attempted to console Minow, gently putting his arm around the FCC chairman's shoulder and telling him, "Don't let him upset you, Newt. That man has no mind of his own. He just repeats everything he hears."[3]

Although both were Midwesterners—Martin was born in Ohio and raised in Indianapolis, Indiana, and Minow spent his youth in Milwaukee, Wisconsin—as well as survivors of the Great Depression, the two had starkly different views of their childhoods. In his memoirs, Martin reflected that most people who write such books seemed to have enjoyed happy, carefree childhoods. "I hated mine," he recalled. "Many seem to regard the years of their youth as the easiest years of their lives. Mine were the hardest." Minow, who received an excellent education in Milwaukee's public schools, remembered "a very ideal childhood and a happy life." Both were college graduates (Martin attended DePauw University in Greencastle, Indiana, and Minow, ten years younger than his friend, graduated from Northwestern University in Evanston, Illinois, after service with the US Army in World War II). From an early age, Martin, who "read all the time," had wanted, in spite of his father's disapproval, to be a writer, following in the footsteps of his favorite authors Ernest Hemingway, Thomas Wolfe, and John Dos Passos. Martin did so, beginning his long career earning a living from putting words down on paper as a reporter for the *Indianapolis Times*. Martin abandoned the daily grind of newspaper work for the sometimes-uncertain life of a freelance writer for true-crime magazines, eventually advancing to having his work appear in such respected national magazines as *Esquire*, *Harper's*, and the *Post*. Minow selected the law as his career, obtaining his law degree from Northwestern with the assistance of the GI Bill (graduating first in his class and serving as editor of the *Law Review*), joining a Chicago law firm (Mayer, Meyer, Austrian and Platt), clerking with Vinson, and joining Stevenson's gubernatorial staff. "Two of my father's brothers, two of my uncles, were lawyers, but I don't know that that had a big impact on me," Minow recalled. "I think it was because the law and government were essential to each other, and I was fascinated by that."[4]

Martin and Minow took quite separate paths to be able to forge their unique partnership on the NAB speech. In Kennedy's successful 1960 campaign against his Republican opponent, Richard Nixon, Martin devised a niche for himself as what he termed an editorial advance man, attempting to bring together two vital aspects of any campaign—scheduling and speechwriting. "I'd go into a state in advance of the candidate to interview people, trying to find out what the local issues were," he recalled. "I would talk to the local Democratic leaders, businessmen, taxi drivers, waitresses, bartenders, anybody I could find." Once he had ferreted out enough information, he produced a report and joined the campaign party as it traveled through the area he had just visited. The candidate took the briefing sheets Martin produced and used them to speak extemporaneously and expertly about the issues facing a community, and he never had to arrive at a speech without "knowing what to expect and what was expected of him," said Martin. Such editorial advance work, noted Martin's friend and fellow speechwriter Arthur M. Schlesinger Jr., "sharpened the impact of speeches and also influenced political strategy."[5]

When first asked, Minow had turned down an offer for a job in the Kennedy administration, but he did agree to help the president's brother-in-law, Sargent Shriver, with recruiting people to fill the many open positions in the new government. Minow made it known that the only job he might be interested in was FCC chairman because of his interest in television, which he called "the most important invention since the atom bomb." To his "great surprise," he became Kennedy's first appointment to a federal regulatory body. The job might well have been appointed to Minow due to the influence of the president's brother, Robert F. Kennedy, who had gotten to know Minow well while traveling with the Stevenson presidential campaign in 1956 in anticipation of John Kennedy's run for the White House four years later. On a couple of occasions, Robert Kennedy and Minow were roommates, sharing a hotel room while on the road. "He and I were the same age; we had children the same age," Minow said. "And we were very inclined to talk about the effect of television on children and the lack of good programming for children." Once, walking back to their hotel in Springfield after a visit to the Abraham Lincoln home, Kennedy had told Minow that when he was growing up, he believed there were three great influences on a child—home, school, and church. "Now, in my home with my kids," Kennedy told Minow, "I see there's a fourth. It's the television set. My kids are fascinated. They're watching television too much." As lawyer for the Encyclopedia Britannica Film Company, which made educational films, Minow occasionally was able to mail a film to Kennedy. "He showed it to his kids on Saturday morning and sent it back," Minow recalled. "These were films shown in school. Bob remembered that." [6]

By accepting the FCC position and its $20,500 yearly salary, Minow made a significant financial sacrifice, doing so because he supported the new administration. "You've got to look at the period of American history that it was," he later said. "It was the Kennedy era. It was the young people who had served in World War II . . . who were now taking on the public responsibility, who had a sense of idealism and who cared about the country, who felt that public service was an honorable thing to do." Established by Congress in 1934, the FCC had the power to issue broadcast licenses in "the public interest, convenience, or necessity," but for many years it had been lax in its oversight and sometimes corrupt in its practices. In the 1950s during the Eisenhower administration, the FCC had come under fire as being too closely tied to the industry it was charged with overseeing in an era that saw radio disk jockeys bribed with cash to play certain songs and television quiz shows, most notably the program *Twenty-One*, accused of unfair and rigged shows. John Charles Doerfer, who had become FCC chairman in 1957, had come under fire from congressional investigators for accepting complimentary air travel from George B. Storer, president of Storer Broadcasting, which owned seven radio stations and five television stations. Doerfer later admitted that he had also stayed for nearly a week on a Storer yacht, *Lazy Girl*, and had traveled on it to Key West, Florida, for a golfing trip. Although Doerfer defended his actions and said his conscience was "absolutely clean," in March 1960, he submitted his resignation to Eisenhower, who had sought such an action and indicated that Doerfer's decision to resign was "a wise one." [7]

In March 1961, Minow, who believed that broadcasters had not been meeting their public-interest obligations as outlined in their government licenses to use the airwaves, prepared to make his inaugural speech as the head of the FCC to industry executives at the thirty-ninth annual convention of the NAB, the industry's trade association, set for May 9 in Washington, DC. "The morality had sunk in both places [radio and television]," Minow remembered. "I knew we had to straighten it out. And I also knew that television was changing the lives, particularly of children, without much attention being paid to what it was doing." At the time of his speech, he later recalled, there were only two and a half networks, some cities had only one television station, and there existed no cable television or telecommunication satellites. Broadcasters were expecting the worst, as Minow had said at his confirmation hearings before the US Senate in early February that the FCC should have a role in "encouraging better programs," and he expressed a determination "to do something about it." If a television network decided to put a "lousy Western" on the air, it was none of the government's business, the thirty-five-year-old Minow told the senators, but if a network "put on nothing else for three years, then it is." Among the issues he wanted to address during his time in office, he aimed to encourage competition by increasing the allocation of channels through the ultrahigh-frequency (UHF) band by mandating that television sets have UHF tuners (most televisions at the time did not, blocking viewers from watching channels between 18 and 83); to obtain from Congress enhanced authority to regulate the industry; to encourage educational and pay television; and, especially important to him, to develop intercontinental television through communication satellites. Asked by President Kennedy why he advocated so strongly on behalf of communication satellites, Minow said he told him satellites were more important than "sending a man into space, because they launched ideas, and ideas last longer than people." Minow possessed two essential attributes that made him eminently qualified for the job—he had no interest in being reappointed, and he would seek no job in the television industry after leaving government employment.[8]

According to Minow, his friend Martin, who knew just how important the NAB speech would be, volunteered to produce a draft for him. "I wouldn't have imposed on him," Minow said years later. Before Minow took over the FCC, Martin recalled, the two men "discussed the office, and I promised to help him with his speeches if I could." He wrote Minow in March 1961 that he expected to have some ideas to pass along to him in a few weeks and suggested that Minow refrain from leaking any information about what he intended to say to reporters, including Jack Gould, a noted television critic for the *New York Times*. "I suggest you store everything up until May then drop the bomb," Martin wrote. Minow responded by thanking Martin for his assistance and said his staff at the FCC had "all become John Bartlow Martin fans, and the great debate here is whether you look like Ernie Pyle or Abraham Lincoln."[9]

Before volunteering his speechwriting skills to Minow in the chairman's effort to give the television industry a much-needed jolt, Martin had, for several months, been researching and writing a series for the *Post* on the state of American commercial television—a business that had grown by leaps and bounds since the end of World War II. In 1946, there were television sets in eight thousand American homes, but by the time John Kennedy took office, that number had skyrocketed to forty-seven million homes. Nearly nine out of ten households had one or more television sets, and the average American spent six hours a day watching programs. Advertisers had noted television's penetration into family life, spending more than $1.5 billion on commercials in 1959. Minow observed that the public seemed to spend more time with television "than it does on anything else except working and sleeping." He also decried the broadcast industry's thirst for increasingly greater profits. "These fellows, the television broadcasters, think this is an oil well," Minow noted. "Unless they're making 30 percent a year they consider it a failure. Some stations gross nine million [dollars] and make five million profit before taxes. What other business is like that?"[10]

To gain perspective on television's quality and its effect on American society, Martin decided to spend almost an entire day, twenty hours, watching programs. He woke up at 5:30 a.m. at his Highland Park home, ate a hearty breakfast, tuned his family's set to Chicago's WNBQ Channel 5, sat down, and kept his eyes glued to the screen until the NBC affiliate ended its broadcast day at 1:52 a.m. "The channel and the day were chosen at random," Martin noted. After watching Dave Garroway on the *Today* program, Martin felt besieged by a seemingly endless stream of game shows, programs that had disappeared from the airwaves for a time after the quiz show scandals. By the end of the morning, Martin had also witnessed approximately seventy commercials advertising such products as soap, detergent, lipstick, orange juice, salad dressing, baby food, hair cream, hair spray, vitamins, soup, headache remedies, bleach, frozen food, appliances, and patent medicines. "The commercials, loud and frequent and long, seemed stupefying," he said. In the afternoon, after having watched television for nine straight hours, Martin observed that, except for news broadcasts and two brief interviews on the *Today* program, "nobody on Channel 5 had discussed a single idea." He persevered, enduring such banal hit programs as *Sing Along with Mitch* and *The Jack Paar Show*, as well as the violence of a show called *Official Detective*, which featured several fistfights, three shootings, four killings, and a suicide. "After Paar," Martin laconically noted, "it was a pleasure." All in all, he wrote in a draft of the article, what he had seen had been "a vast wasteland of junk." Obviously, Martin added, no one would normally have watched television as he had done, just as few people would sit down and in one day read an entire issue, cover to cover, of a magazine such as the *Post*. "Nonetheless," he said, "this is what was sent over the airwaves by one television station, owned by a leading network in a big city. The station is licensed by the Government to use the people's air; this is how it used it that day." [11]

On April 8, Martin sent Minow a rough draft of his proposed NAB speech, which he admitted might be "too tough" on the industry. He also shared the draft with Schlesinger, asking him, if he found the time, to "mark it up and return it to me or to Newt direct." In preparing his remarks, Martin had consulted with Albert P. Wiseman, a former Stevenson campaign aide and public relations director for Foote, Cone, and Belding, a Chicago advertising agency. In his letter to Minow, Martin said the broadcasters expected the new FCC chairman to "tell them to clean house or you'll do it for them. I would do it—but at the same time not do it." Instead, Martin advised Minow to take a conciliatory tone, because if he "hit them on the nose," it might have a negative effect on the new NAB president, Collins, who had been a supporter of reform in the industry. Martin advised elevating the controversy between the industry and its critics by calling the broadcasters' attention not only to their "mundane failings—too much violence—but to the larger context of intercontinental TV. At present the broadcasters' main concern is that there is too much mayhem and sadism on TV. They also bear a great guilt burden because of the quiz-payola scandals. . . . All this seems beneath you. I would like to see you enlarge enormously the whole context of the TV controversy." Wiseman, who had offered Minow some suggested "gags" to use in his speech, had reviewed Martin's draft and told Minow that it represented "a great high-level statesmanship speech that will gain widespread approval. It's a speech that they will least expect—thinking that you will attack them on violence, westerns, situation comedies, etc. Thus, they will be quite surprised when they hear these ringing words of world-wide challenges." Minow appreciated Martin's work, writing him on April 17: "I cannot, cannot, cannot thank you enough. I'm deeply moved by your giving me so much of your thought and time, and the country will benefit from it—and so will I!"[12]

In addition to Martin's contribution for his NAB speech, Minow also received assistance from Tedson Meyers, an FCC aide; Stanley Frankel, his brother-in-law and a former newspaper reporter and magazine publisher; and others. Of all the drafts he received, however, "the best one by far" came from Martin, said Minow, who noted he was a much better editor than he was a writer. Minow's editing skill came in handy and ensured him everlasting fame when he cut two crucial words from one of Martin's drafts. The original draft, which owed much to Martin's experiences watching Channel 5, included the following: "I invite you to sit down in front of your television set when your station goes on the air and stay there . . . and keep your eyes glued to that set until the station goes off. I can assure you that you will observe a vast wasteland of junk." According to Martin, Minow "had the wit" to cut "of junk." Much of what Martin wrote remained in the forty-minute speech Minow gave before the approximately two thousand broadcasters assembled for lunch at the Sheraton Park Hotel. At the start of his remarks, Minow tried to let his audience know that he respected their profession, noting that they toiled in "a most honorable profession," and he admired their courage. "I can think of easier ways to make a living," he said. "But I cannot think of more satisfying ways." Still, Minow let the broadcasters know that they were using the public airwaves "as trustees for 180 million Americans," and, as public trustees, they were obligated to "deliver a decent return to the public—not only your stockholders. So, as a representative of the public, your health and your products are among my chief concerns." The portion that received the bulk of the media's attention, however, came later. After praising some programs from the past season, including *The Fred Astaire Show*, *The Bing Crosby Special*, *CBS Reports*, and *The Twilight Zone*, Minow reminded broadcasters of the following:

> When television is good, nothing—not the theater, not the magazines or newspapers—nothing is better.
>
> But when television is bad, nothing is worse. I invite each of you to sit down in front of your television set when your station goes on the air and stay there, for a day, without a book, without a magazine, without a newspaper, without a profit and loss sheet or a rating book to distract you. Keep your eyes glued to that set until the station signs off. I can assure you that what you will observe is a vast wasteland.
>
> You will see a procession of game shows, formula comedies about totally unbelievable families, blood and thunder, mayhem, violence, sadism, murder, western bad men, western good men, private eyes, gangsters, more violence, and cartoons. And endlessly commercials—many screaming, cajoling, and offending. And most of all, boredom. True, you will see a few things you will enjoy. But they will be very, very few. And if you think I exaggerate, I only ask you to try it.[13]

Ironically, Minow's speech, which left many broadcasting executives looking as if they were "refugees from an atomic blast," reported one magazine, received attention for all the wrong reasons and was "badly misinterpreted," noted Minow. "Today that speech is remembered for two words—but not the two I intended to be remembered," Minow later said. "The words we tried to advance were 'public interest.' To me, the public interest meant, and still means, that we should constantly ask: What can television do for our country? For the common good? For the American people?" He said he wanted the broadcasters to know that there was a new team in town who really cared about the public interest and that if television failed in that area, they would find themselves in difficulty with the government. At the same time, he added, the FCC stood ready to back television executives if they decided to tackle controversial issues.[14]

The speech, noted Martin, made Minow a symbol of the "newness and boldness of the Kennedy administration." The overwhelming media attention, however, did cause Martin some trouble with his *Post* series on television, as he had to alter his original passage of television as a "vast wasteland" as not his own summary of what he had seen, instead quoting Minow as the source of the phrase. For his concluding article for his *Post* series, Martin profiled Minow, his NAB speech, and its aftermath, including one television executive issuing a "call to arms" against the FCC chairman. Nowhere in the article, however, does Martin reveal the key role he played in the "vast wasteland" address. In his memoirs, Martin acknowledged that in this instance he had approached a conflict of interest, but he concluded: "It didn't bother me." (The *Post* might have been willing to overlook any improprieties by Martin because of the pressure the magazine industry was feeling from the television industry when it came to advertising revenue.) Martin also took great pains to note that his origination of the "vast wasteland" phrase took nothing away from Minow. "This thing happens all the time," he said, noting that Louis Howe came up with "the only thing we have to fear is fear itself" for President Franklin D. Roosevelt's first inaugural address. "It is the business of holders of high public office to broker ideas to the public; Newt Minow had the wit to recognize a good phrase and the courage to throw it in the teeth of the broadcasters and thus show the public the need for reform," said Martin. Minow noted that later he and Martin often saw one another in Washington, DC, and he believed Martin was "very pleased" with the NAB speech. After all, Martin in his career had written "for political people, for the Kennedys, for the Stevensons, [but] the FCC speech is the one that got the most attention."[15]

Although broadcasters believed that Minow, through his speech, had alienated "the whole goddam industry," public reaction was overwhelmingly positive. Analyzing the first 2,542 letters it received regarding

Minow's remarks, the commission reported that 2,049 (80.6 percent) were in agreement with its chairman's sentiments, while only fifty-five letters opposed what Minow had to say. Newspaper columnists, including Gould, praised Minow. When he returned home after his speech, Minow received two telephone calls. The first came from President Kennedy's father, Joseph, from whom the FCC chairman expected "sharp criticism." Instead, the senior Kennedy told Minow that he had just finished talking to the president and had told his son that Minow's speech "was the best one since his [JFK's] inaugural address on January 20th. Keep it up; if anyone gives you any trouble, call me!" The second call came from Edward R. Murrow, the former newsman and commentator, who had joined the Kennedy administration as director of the US Information Agency. "You gave the same speech I gave two years ago," Murrow told Minow. "Good for you—you'll get a lot of heat and criticism, but don't lose your courage!" Those messages, said Minow, gave him "the backbone" he needed to focus the FCC's mission on requiring that broadcasters serve the public, as well as their private, interest, and to increase choices for American viewers. "In the long run," he noted, "we believed that competition was preferable to governmental regulation, especially where a medium of expression was involved."[16]

Minow, who received the Presidential Medal of Freedom from President Barack Obama in 2016, has often been asked for his opinions regarding television over the years since his 1961 speech. One of the most troubling changes he witnessed was the rise in both the "quantity and quality" of violence he has seen on programs. During the time of his NAB speech, he had worried that his children would not benefit much from television, but thirty years later, he worried that his grandchildren would actually be harmed by viewing television, citing a statistic that by the time a child reached the age of eighteen, he had seen twenty-five thousand murders on television. "In 1961 they didn't make PG-13 movies, much less NC-17," he observed. "Now a 6-year-old can watch them on cable." Over the years, he has called for enhanced financing for noncommercial television, and he has said he believes news—television's most important public service—has not lived up to its potential. "Too much deals with covering controversy, crimes, fires, and not enough with the country's great issues," he said. Also, while Minow believed expanding choices when it came to programming would serve a public good, he also believed there is a downside: "People used to have the same set of facts, and partly the result of opening up choices and cable TV, there are so many voices now a lot of the division in this country is about not having that common set of facts anymore. As in most of life, there is good and bad." The vast wasteland has grown vaster still, with programming in the public interest a distant ideal.[17]

NOTES

1. John Bartlow Martin, *It Seems Like Only Yesterday: Memoirs of Writing, Presidential Politics, and the Diplomatic Life* (New York: William Morrow, 1986), 147–148; and John Bartlow Martin, memorandum to Newton Minow, October 9, 1952, John Bartlow Martin Papers, Manuscripts Division, Library of Congress, Washington, DC (hereafter cited as Martin Papers).

2. John Bartlow Martin, 1952 Presidential Campaign Journal, Martin Papers; Newton Minow interview with Mark DePue, May 31, 2017, p. 8, Abraham Lincoln Presidential Library, Springfield, IL; and Newton Minow, telephone interview with the author, June 27, 2013.

3. Martin, *It Seems Like Only Yesterday*, 202–203; and Newton N. Minow, *How Vast the Wasteland Now?* (New York: Gannett Foundation Media Center, 1991), 6.

4. Martin, *It Seems Like Only Yesterday*, 17; and Minow interview with DePue, 4–5.

5. "Memo on Memoirs," December 5, 1980, Martin Papers; and Arthur M. Schlesinger Jr., "John Bartlow Martin, 1915–1987," in *The Century Yearbook, 1987* (New York: Century Association, 1987), 265.

6. Minow interview with author; Mary Ann Watson, *The Expanding Vista: American Television in the Kennedy Years* (New York: Oxford University Press, 1990), 20; Minow interview with DePue, 10.

7. Watson, *The Expanding Vista*, 20; Bruce Lambert, "John Charles Doerfer, 87, Is Dead, Headed F.C.C. in Era of Scandals," *New York Times*, June 8, 1992; Jay Walz, "F.C.C. Chairman Defends Record at House Inquiry," *New York Times*, February 4, 1958; and William M. Blair, "Doerfer Resigns as F.C.C. Chairman at President's Bid," *New York Times*, March 11, 1960. After his resignation, Doerfer started a law practice in Washington, DC, and later did legal work for Storer Broadcasting and served as a vice president with the company. See Lambert, "John Charles Doerfer, 87, Is Dead," and Watson, *The Expanding Vista*, 19.

8. Minow interview with DePue, 15; John Bartlow Martin, "Television USA: The Big Squeeze," *Saturday Evening Post*, November 11, 1961, 62–63; James Warren, "Never Mind the 'Vast Wasteland.' Minow Has More to Say," *New York Times*, May 7, 2011; Christopher Borrelli, "The Long, Long Reach of Newton Minow, Former FCC Chairman," *Chicago Tribune*, January 22, 2017; Newton N. Minow, "Commentary: A Medal after Ignoring Presidential Orders," *Chicago Tribune*, December 7, 2016; and Watson, *The Expanding Vista*, 19.

9. Minow interview with author; Martin, *It Seems Like Only Yesterday*, 202–203; and John Bartlow Martin to Newt Minow, March 20, 1961, and Newton Minow to John Bartlow Martin, March 22, 1961, Martin Papers. The correspondence between Martin and Minow is also contained in the Newton N. Minow Papers, Wisconsin Historical Society, Division of Library, Archives, and Museum Collections, Madison, Wisconsin (hereafter cited as Minow Papers).

10. John Bartlow Martin, "Television USA: Wasteland or Wonderland? A Famous Writer's Close-up Report on the Controversial State of TV," *Saturday Evening Post*, October 21, 1961, 20–21; and Martin, "Television USA: The Big Squeeze," 62.

11. Martin, "Television USA: Wasteland or Wonderland?," 20–21; and James L. Baughman, "Minow's Viewers: Understanding the Response to the 'Vast Wasteland' Address," *Federal Communications Law Journal* 55, no. 3 (2003): 452.

12. John Bartlow Martin to Newt Minow, April 8, 1961; John Bartlow Martin to Arthur M. Schlesinger Jr., April 8, 1961; and Newton Minow to John Bartlow Martin, April 17, 1961, Martin Papers. See also Albert P. Wiseman to Newt Minow, April 12, 1961, Minow Papers. Some of the "gags" Wiseman offered Minow included "I've heard TV programs are marvelous for shut-ins: By showing them what's going on in this frantic world, they're happy that they aren't out in it" and "I notice by the ratings that the top shows are three westerns. This shows the industry is in the right rut." For his part, Minow wrote Wiseman, joking, "Thanks for your nice letter and your suggestions, some of which are helpful and some of which are lousy!" See Newton Minow to Albert P. Wiseman, April 19, 1961, Minow Papers.

13. Watson, *The Expanding Vista*, 22; Minow interview with author; Martin, *It Seems Like Only Yesterday*, 203; and Minow, *How Vast the Wasteland Now?*, 21–22, 24.

14. Newton Minow, "Television," *Vital Speeches of the Day* 57, no. 18 (July 1, 1991): 556; Newton Minow interview, Archive of American Television, www.emmytvlegends.org/interviews/people/newton-n-minow#/; and Minow, *How Vast the Wasteland Now?*, 4.

15. Martin, "Television USA: The Big Squeeze," 65; Watson, *The Expanding Vista*, 27; and Martin, *It Seems Like Only Yesterday*, 203.

16. "Minow's Viewers," 450, 452; and Minow, *How Vast the Wasteland Now?* 8–9.

17. Warren, "Never Mind the 'Vast Wasteland'"; and Borrelli, "The Long, Long Reach of Newton Minow."

CHAPTER 16

CLEVELAND'S ANISFIELD-WOLF BOOK AWARDS AND MIDWESTERN RACIAL LIBERALISM

Andrew Seal

"There is a race problem in Cleveland, but it is not acute," the African American novelist Charles Chesnutt wrote in late 1930. He was writing for a mostly white audience in the *Clevelander*, the periodical for the city's Chamber of Commerce,[1] but Chesnutt—who was born in Cleveland in 1858 and had, after growing up in the South, lived there since 1883—was admonishing rather than reassuring his readers.

> From the Negroes' side [the race problem] is mainly concerned with a fair living, a decent place to live, making his way in the world on equal terms with others, and living at peace with his neighbors. With these things, or any of them, denied to any material extent, that the problem might become acute is evidenced by the race riots which a few years ago convulsed Chicago, Detroit, and St. Louis.

Chesnutt suggested that one factor in the city's relative placidity was the philanthropy of "the better class of white people," who, even in the first full year of the Depression, were generous toward causes benefiting the city's African American population.[2] Their money, however, was a relatively sterile gift, Chesnutt argued: "They could render [African Americans] a better service by cultivating fraternal or, if that be too much, at least friendly relations with them, not so much by way of condescension, as from man to man, thereby making their advancement easier along all lines."[3]

Charles W. Chesnutt is an apt representative of Cleveland's intellectual history: Midwesterners—even those proud of and interested in the region's culture—often overlook both the writer and the city. But Chesnutt and Cleveland go well together for reasons beyond their existence on the margins of Midwestern history. Chesnutt's second book of short fiction was subtitled *Stories of the Color Line*, and although most of his stories were about the South, his explorations of the complicated and never-settled location of the color line were in many ways rooted in the anxious uncertainties of life in Cleveland, a city that wavered between exuberant progressivism and sullen reaction for much of the twentieth century. Cleveland's most famous novelist today—Celeste Ng—is still writing about the color line in the city, about the force of unspoken racial conventions arbitrarily and enigmatically applied.[4] As W. E. B. Du Bois said of the world, the problem of Cleveland's twentieth century *was* (and is) the problem of the color line, and that is true especially of its intellectual history.[5]

Chesnutt was also typical of Cleveland's intellectuals throughout history in his answer to that problem. As you can see from the preceding quotes, Chesnutt responded to what he (and most genteelly educated people of his day) called "the race question" partly with optimism but also with a cool earnestness intended to snap people to collective attention rather than incite them to collective action. The point for Chesnutt was to "face facts"—those "better sorts" of Clevelanders needed to be brought to a consensus about what the problem was, and after this agreement was achieved, each man or woman could take appropriate individual action.[6] In Chesnutt's eyes, mass mobilizations for redress or reform, such as pickets or rallies, achieved only ephemeral understandings of the race problem—a consensus of feet and voices rather than minds and hearts.

Chesnutt's approach to the race question was a variety of racial liberalism, and it was largely well-to-do Cleveland's tack on race as well. Of course, just as Chesnutt was a national writer, so was racial liberalism a nationwide intellectual project, but both Chesnutt and the form of racial liberalism he articulated were shaped and angled in ways that are clearly marked by their origin in the Midwest.

This chapter explores that particularly Midwestern variety of racial liberalism, and it does so through a literary prize based in Cleveland that Chesnutt almost certainly would have won had he lived long enough. The Anisfield-Wolf Book Award was instituted in 1934 to honor a "sound and significant book published either in the United States or abroad in the previous twelve months on the subject of racial relations in the contemporary world."[7] Bestowed for fiction, nonfiction, and poetry, these prizes are still awarded annually, and the roster of recipients is formidable, from Zora Neale Hurston in 1943 to Louise Erdrich in 2009. But while the scope of the prize is global and its recipients have hailed from all over the world, it was endowed by a Cleveland philanthropist and has been administered by the Cleveland Foundation since 1963. This Midwestern origin has subtly shaped not just the kind of books that have been awarded but the overall message the prize has propagated. We can better understand what Midwestern racial liberalism was (and perhaps is) by understanding what makes the Anisfield-Wolf Book Award Midwestern.

Racial liberalism was a body of thought and practice that flourished in the United States across the middle of the twentieth century, roughly between the end of World War I and the end of what has been called the "heroic period" of the civil rights movement (1954–1965).[8] According to the legal theorist Lani Guinier, it "emphasized the corrosive effect of individual prejudice and the importance of interracial contact in promoting tolerance."[9] Racial liberals intended to leverage social scientific knowledge and psychological insights to combat prejudice at its root as a supposedly natural aversion to difference. Racial liberals hoped to circumvent this truth of human nature by increasing the total number of positive interactions "across the color line" and by minimizing the number of negative or alienating contacts, demonstrating how greater familiarity with and knowledge about racial or ethnic others could, over time, dissolve preconceptions of difference. To use the title of a famous midcentury work about anti-Semitism, racial liberalism argued all people were "brothers under the skin."[10]

Starting from this interpersonal level, racial liberals believed they could manage racial and ethnic tensions between whole groups. Ideally, racial liberals wanted to achieve a durable settlement across a number of different concerns—what jobs were open to whom, what homes could be bought by whom, who could send their children to which school, which clubs and other social organizations accepted whom as members. They have been criticized by later scholars and activists for pursuing this settlement in a way that did not so much seek justice as it wished for peace.

Early examples of racial liberals were those early Gilded Age and Progressive Era benefactors from what Chesnutt called the "better class of white people" who funded groups such as the Cleveland Council of Sociology, a sort of debating society founded in 1893 for which Chesnutt himself served as president in 1911. These organizations were made up of "leading ministers, judges, lawyers, educators, and social workers of Cleveland who studied and discussed the city's civic and social problems and tried earnestly to find solutions for them." [11] They were most common and most active in big cities during the Progressive Era, and, particularly in Cleveland, they rode high on the optimism of reformers such as Newton Baker, the city's mayor from 1912 through 1916. [12]

After World War I, both philanthropy and reform were increasingly professionalized and increasingly consolidated in large foundations and research clearinghouses. Institutions such as the Russell Sage Foundation, the Carnegie Corporation, the Rockefeller Foundation, the Laura Spelman Rockefeller Memorial, the Rosenwald Fund, and (later) the Ford Foundation underwrote the work of groundbreaking research by the Social Science Research Council, the Brookings Institution, the National Bureau of Economic Research, and other centers. While these large, highly professional institutions covered a wide array of social scientific topics, the race question was nonetheless a frequent focus of the studies they funded or carried out. [13]

The scholarship that has examined the history of racial liberalism has typically focused on these elite and mostly New York– or Washington-based organizations, and it has emphasized particularly their Cold War– era interventions into "race relations," rarely examining the interwar period in any depth. Often, scholars have directly tied the flourishing of racial liberalism to the pressures of anticommunist foreign policy on domestic race relations. In competition with the Soviet Union for allies among the emerging Third World nations, US elites recognized that the nation's horrendous record on racial equality was a serious diplomatic vulnerability, one that the USSR frequently exploited. Many Americans already committed to redressing these inequalities took full advantage of this situation, but others more reluctantly began to support the cause of civil rights: together, they made a coalition born of idealism and necessity. This was the heyday of racial liberalism.[14]

The Anisfield-Wolf Book Awards fit awkwardly within this narrative, however. The prize was established well before the Cold War, and so it obviously cannot be attributed to the Cold War–era desire to improve the public image of the United States as a nation at least *trying* to improve its "race problem." The prizes began, in fact, in the depths of what has often been characterized as a period of deep isolationism for the United States—especially for the Midwest—when Americans were supposed to be wholly uninterested in the problems of people (ostensibly) unlike themselves. While recent scholarship from the "transnational turn" has convincingly contested this overgeneralization,[15] the prize clearly imagined Americans as citizens not just of their nation but of the globe, who ought to be informed about and who might be affected by race relations not just in the industrial cities of the northern United States or in the cotton fields of the South but also in South Africa or in eastern Europe.

The awards did, however, mean to attack the provincialism of a particular group: publishers. As the novelist Lillian Smith—who joined the panel of judges in 1956—put it, "At the time Mrs. Wolf set up this fund there was an urgent need to arouse publishers' interest in publishing books on race relations and books about Negroes for there had been almost a taboo against doing so. The Anisfield-Wolf Award dramatized the need for more books and better books about people of all races and their relations with each other."[16]

The Anisfield-Wolf Book Awards were rooted in Cleveland, not New York, Washington, DC, or even Chicago, which had its own major research foundations and had an ample reserve of both raw and experienced social science researchers based at the University of Chicago. Sociologists and political scientists from what was becoming known as the Chicago school were extremely well connected to (and in some cases helped to administer) the giant nationwide institutions, directing much of the funding for new projects back to Chicago. The Windy City therefore famously became the nation's premier "laboratory" for social scientists during the first half of the twentieth century, especially on questions of race and ethnicity.[17] Cleveland simply could not boast of that kind of intellectual pull.

That is not to say, however, that the awards were wholly unconnected to the intellectual powerbrokers of New York and Chicago. The first three judges for the prize were Henry Pratt Fairchild, a nationally prominent sociologist at New York University; Henry Seidel Canby, a Yale professor of English and the editor of the *Saturday Review of Literature*; and Donald Young, the executive director of the Social Science Research Council and a sociologist of race relations. Early on, these judges emphasized cutting-edge social science in their choices both for the recipients of the award and for a grant-in-aid program that ran unsuccessfully for a few years.[18] The first five selections were straightforward sociology monographs, and the judges were especially impressed by the Chicago school approach: in four of the first eleven years, a product of the University of Chicago took home the award.

The composition of the panel of judges had much to do with this emphasis on serious social science—Canby, as a man of letters, was outnumbered by the sociologists Fairchild and Young. That is not to say there was conflict. Instead, the vagueness of the terms of the prize made it possible for the judges to interpret according to their preferences and predispositions. It also meant that the parameters of the award could be reinterpreted, as was the case after 1941, when Louis Adamic's *From Many Lands* was selected. The judges acknowledged that this choice marked a departure from the previous five selections, announcing in the *Saturday Review of Literature* that they intended henceforth to broaden their scope. "We wish this very useful award for scholarly works in the field of racial relations might be twinned with another offered for creative literary work, such as novels, or plays which deal with or are inspired by the same theme," they wrote, noting that Adamic's work adroitly straddled literature and sociology. "Mr. Adamic's book, which is a series of case histories, very well told, of what might be called the drama of racial contacts in America, lies close to the area of fiction and dramatic composition," and this aesthetically conscious method was, they believed, just as important as more rigorous social science. Calling *From Many Lands* "a human, warmly written account of the racial contacts and blendings of America's more recent immigrants," the judges recognized that the book might—because of its engaging style and emotional depth—thereby give a wider range of readers the same kind of clear-sighted encounter with the facts of race relations and the difficulties facing racial minorities that social scientific monographs provided to specialists.[19]

Edith Wolf, the founder of the awards, also had a hand in pushing the judges to orient their choices for the prize toward a broader audience. Although she was exceptionally hands-off in the committee's affairs, she had also stipulated at the outset that the prize was to be handled through the offices of the *Saturday Review of Literature*—arguably the nation's premier middlebrow tastemaker.[20] This connection was made in part because of her friendship with Amy Loveman, a member of the *Saturday Review*'s editorial board, but it also indicated that Wolf cared about the ability of the awards to guide the reading choices of the "common reader." She also cared about encouraging writers—often people of color—to see their stories about and research on the race problem as deserving of a wide audience, even if they were struggling to obtain one. Wolf's correspondence with some of the prize-winning authors shows that the difficulty of getting more publicity for the award was often a subject of mutual regret and frustration. Zora Neale Hurston wrote to Wolf, "Good will towards men is not popular enough. I would like the world to think about it more. . . . I think the Award and the soul behind it has not been sufficiently publicized."[21]

On the other hand, the judges did not give up on their goal of honoring pathbreaking scholarship. Nor did they have to—the *Saturday Review* covered books of all kinds, including rigorous social science texts and sometimes even books not yet published in English, so the judges' selection of more specialized titles was not necessarily out of step with the mission of the book awards implied by its connection with the *Review*. Rather than shift entirely one way or another, the judges split the prize. In most years thereafter, they granted two awards, one to a more academic work and one to a more creative work. Both had to achieve the same objective: they were not merely to depict the race problem, but to "clarify" it. The books were also supposed to advance each other's cause. As one history of the awards put it, "In writing to Mrs. Wolf, Mr. Canby expressed the opinion that such a balance would be admirable, in that the so-called scholarly award would lend importance and dignity to the creative literary book, which being in all probability more popular would in turn help to carry the more serious work."[22]

But with this new development, it seems that Canby had asserted more influence over the prize committee's selections. In addition to his editorship of the *Saturday Review*, Canby was the editor-in-chief of the Book-of-the-Month Club (BOMC), and he had already in that guise distinguished Louis Adamic as one of the preeminent interpreters of the experiences of the "newer immigrant" in the United States. The BOMC's selection of *Native's Return* in 1934 was a career-launching event for Adamic, who would go on to direct the antifascist and antiracist organization Common Council for American Unity, which forcefully advocated the importance of cultural pluralism, especially during World War II.

That embrace of cultural pluralism was a departure from the attitudes of many sociologists regarding racial and ethnic heterogeneity during the interwar period—including the attitude of Henry Pratt Fairchild, one of the Anisfield-Wolf judges. Fairchild was a vehement hawk on immigration restriction, and even after the Johnson-Reed Act of 1924 accomplished that goal, he continued sounding the alarm about the dangers of an unassimilable immigrant mass in the body politic, publishing *The Melting-Pot Mistake* in 1926. Where Fairchild seems to have found common ground with Canby and with Donald Young was in the scholarship on African Americans, where his expressed views were more in line with the racial liberalism of the other two judges. Young's work was generally focused on African Americans (alongside his own work, he assisted with Gunnar Myrdal's *An American Dilemma*), but he also wrote *American Minority Peoples*, a massive sociological text that argued "that the problems and principles of race relations are remarkably similar, regardless of what groups are involved; and that only by an integrated study of all minority peoples in the United States can a real understanding and sociological analysis of the involved social phenomena be achieved." [23]

As Canby and Wolf pulled the awards toward the middlebrow, the overall message expressed by the prize-winning books shifted increasingly toward this broad construal of the dimensions of the race problem as something more like "the problem of racial or ethnic minorities everywhere." The awards opened up not just in terms of the audience they intended to address but also in terms of coverage; although books on African Americans continued to win the award frequently, the judges began to think globally. A book on Haiti was chosen in 1942; the world of eastern European Jews was highlighted in 1944; the awards drew attention to Latinos in Texas in 1947, American Indians in 1948, and Hawaii and South Africa in 1949. Any readers who followed the Anisfield-Wolf Book Awards through the 1940s would have been encouraged to stretch their awareness of the global dimensions of the color line and the multiple groups it touched.[24]

These trends only became more entrenched as the panel of judges began to turn over due to the retirement or deaths of the original three. After a few reshuffles, a second lineup emerged consisting of an anthropologist, Ashley Montagu, who acted as the chief judge; two novelists, Pearl Buck and Lillian Smith; and a historian, Oscar Handlin. Considerably less tied to the social sciences, these judges chose books that were at the center of popular debates about the emerging civil rights movement. The books they selected also shed light on aspects of US and world history that many people were keen to forget or to ignore, including apartheid in South Africa, the Leo Frank case, and the internment of Japanese and Japanese Americans during World War II. One of the first choices this new slate of judges made as a group was to award Gilberto Freyre's *The Masters and the Slaves: A Study in the Development of Brazilian Civilization*, which was a fairly bold choice relative to most of the books that had been previously chosen.[25] In 1966, they honored both Claude Brown's *Manchild in the Promised Land* and *The Autobiography of Malcolm X*.

Although none of these judges were Midwesterners, their reshaping of the awards' implicit purpose—to reach a wider audience, to balance social science and literary "warmth," to think not just along one plane but in many directions—followed a recognizably Midwestern pattern of thought. One of the greatest works of sociology was, after all, Robert and Helen Lynd's two-volume *Middletown* project (*Middletown: A Study in Contemporary American Culture* [1929] and *Middletown in Transition: A Study in Cultural Conflicts* [1937]), which—although it notoriously evades the issue of race—checks the boxes on all three of those qualities just named. A bestseller that was as widely praised for its social scientific innovativeness as for its evocative intimacy, *Middletown* was breathtakingly multidimensional in its analysis of the city of Muncie, Indiana. Likewise, so much of Midwestern fiction has been lauded for its sociological richness, from Theodore Dreiser and Sherwood Anderson to Jane Smiley and Bonnie Jo Campbell. That blending of the scientist's eye and the novelist's heart is a trademark of Midwestern culture.

In addition, unlike other regions of the United States, the Midwest has never been oriented geographically or intellectually in one direction exclusively: unlike the Northeast, the Midwest's points of reference are not always transatlantic, nor has either a North–South or East–West division of the country always been dominant. Midwesterners are used to looking around themselves in 360 degrees, perhaps in order to get a sense of where they are in the world. One could, for example, point to the extraordinary success of Midwestern journalists—especially around the mid-twentieth century—in interpreting events from all four corners of the earth, from Lowell Thomas's genial expeditions to the sober clarity of Walter Cronkite, the daring of Vincent Sheean to the comprehensiveness of John Gunther.[26] The Anisfield-Wolf Book Awards' global reorientation starting in the 1940s seems to be an excellent reflection of that genuinely global perspective.

The final way in which this revision of the awards' terms seems to jibe with Midwestern ideas about race and with a distinctively Midwestern racial liberalism is in its consistent emphasis on the identification of a person's private life as the source of that person's similarity to or commonality with other people. Across the color line or across an ethnic divide, Midwesterners seem to believe, it is especially our needs and our wants, our dreams and our quirks, that are truly held in common. This idea stands in contrast to a more traditional egalitarianism premised on the idea that formal rights and protections demarcate the location of a common ground among differing peoples. Where others might emphasize equality before the law as the only valid meaning for human commonality, Midwesterners—including Midwestern intellectuals—have often added and at times even prioritized what might be called a similarity of the heart. It is not necessarily in public life—in courts or at the polling booths—that democratic equality is confirmed, this idea might argue, but in the nearly universal responses people have to common private experiences: to births and deaths, to marriages, rites of passage, games, pain, romance, suspense, pity, and compassion.[27] What was needed to unknot the tangle of racism among whites was simply testimony to this basic, person-to-person commonality.

Lillian Smith articulated the philosophy behind the awards in a 1960 letter, writing, "We cannot separate race relations from the totality of human relations. Set one real person (free of prejudice, who has intelligence and character and talent) in any community and by his very presence he will begin to change that community. We Americans, perhaps of all the Western world, have forgot the value and sheer power of *presence*. We have almost forgot that the frail individual has great power when he himself has depth and integrity and concern for others." [28]

Perhaps no book that won the Anisfield-Wolf Book Award emblematizes this idea better than the 1946 winner *One Nation*, produced by *Look* magazine (based in Des Moines) and edited by the novelist Wallace Stegner (who, though primarily identified with the American West, also had considerable Midwestern ties). *One Nation* was a photographic essay somewhat in the vein of *Let Us Now Praise Famous Men*, but it also reached forward to the famous photographic exhibition *The Family of Man*, by Edward Steichen. Like the latter, its purpose was not so much to document an existing social ill as to reveal the tremendous significance of fundamental human similarities.

In fact, it did both. A foreword written by Harlan Logan, the editor of *Look*, explained the reason for the book: the "growing wave of intolerance and prejudice" that had swelled during World War II. Logan stated,

> Our purpose is to focus attention upon one of the gravest social problems facing our country in this critical time: to present an objective treatment of individual minorities in picture-text which may be communicable to those of our fellow citizens who stand to profit most from its revelations. The tone of the book is neither reactionary nor radical; the editorial point of view is forthright, fact-finding, liberal. [29]

In five parts—"Pacific Races," "Mexicans," "Oldest Americans," "Negroes," and "Culture and Creed"—the book's photographs covered an immense range of experiences and emotions. Exclusion, segregation, and discrimination were everywhere present, but so was joy and affection and camaraderie among these excluded individuals. On one page might be a stark trio of pictures portraying the bleakness and menace of the "relocation centers" of Japanese and Japanese Americans; on the facing page, a family sharing a pot of tea. The captions on two successive photographs, broken by an ellipsis, read, "Though beggary is still a guest in many an Indian house, and poverty a visitor with whom the tribes are all too familiar, and though the pitiful slums of 'agency Indians' still clutter the reservations . . . hope has moved in, and self-reliance and self-respect." [30]

Nearly all of the photographs—like so many of the Farm Security Administration photographs of the Depression—were candid and intimate, catching people in their everyday business of life. One photograph depicted an African American man eating, and then a subsequent shot showed the insignia of segregation: a "Whites Only" sign. A woman read a newspaper on one page; a scrap of print on the next page showed a racist cartoon. The juxtaposition tacitly made the argument that it is only the latter images—the public assertions of prejudice—that are truly alien or strange: they are not part of the common life of eating and reading and living.

This refusal to believe that any human is really an incomprehensible "other" is a kind of vote for the moral potency of human similarity, and it is not hard to see how that faith in human unity can become a formula for action. This is the recipe for racial liberalism: the belief that maximal progress can be made toward abolishing prejudice by reminding people from a majority background of how much they have in common with people in the minority.

To its proponents, racial liberalism has often seemed like common sense: you can best appeal to people by finding common ground with them. Prejudice is either just a species of ignorance or a kind of myopia in which differences can be seen with perfect clarity and similarities appear as indistinguishable blurs. But racial liberalism's critics point out that invocations of "natural" human traits or habits often smuggle in norms that are unconsciously particularistic. [31] Consider, for instance, how in photo-essays like *One Nation*, in any of the montages featured in *Look* magazine, or in *The Family of Man*, heterosexual marriage is presented as a "universal" experience that can bridge and even transcend particular cultures. Even if legally valid same-sex marriage did not yet exist in the mid-twentieth century, the concept of a "Boston marriage" had been around for over half a century, and hundreds of thousands of Americans lived as lifelong "spinsters" or "bachelors." Different-sex marriage was no more a default aspect of being human than driving a Ford or wearing a mustache.

Even more fundamental to the critique of racial liberalism is the observation that it places a great deal of the burden of overcoming prejudice on the victims of prejudice. Racial liberals presume that each human shares some common ground with every other human, but someone still has to do the work of finding that common ground and making it visible to others. Additionally, in this system victims of prejudice must *want* to find that common ground; they must find the process of identifying and emphasizing similarities while diminishing or marginalizing differences valuable.

Obviously, not all Midwesterners are racial liberals, and not all racial liberals are Midwesterners. But there is perhaps nothing more characteristically Midwestern than the belief that everyone wants to belong to the majority, to be on the team, to be included. Many of the most eloquent Midwestern writers have testified to their communities' incapacity to understand that some people prefer to be different, to stand out, to not join in. It is an attitude that goes beyond conformism—a term many eastern-based critics have mistakenly used in describing a Midwestern ideology—because conformists, while disagreeing with eccentrics, can still understand them; they just want to hammer them back into line. The stereotypical Midwesterner, however, simply cannot process the idea that someone might yearn to be unusual.

The original idea of the Anisfield-Wolf Book Awards and the principles guiding the judges' decisions over many decades seem to be imbued with this same incredulity that anyone would truly not want to be part of the majority, would want to retain and continue to emphasize the features that make them different. While not full-blown melting pot assimilationism, this was a conviction that, ultimately, similarity would prevail. Racial liberalism—even when espoused by people from a minority background like Charles Chesnutt or Edith Wolf (who was Jewish)—sees membership in the majority as the ultimate goal. For racial liberals, the majority isn't a calcified segment of the populace set on maintaining its position and its borders, but an infinitely expandable blob eager to absorb new people like an amoeba. In this line of thinking, the majority and the common ground will become the same thing; when everyone finds what they have in common, that will be the basis of a universal majority.

In the Anisfield-Wolf Book Awards' defense, it should be said that this incredulity in the face of deliberate eccentricity can turn a forceful rejection of any ideology that elevates racial difference into an absolute principle of enmity and subordination. How does one person hate another because of the color of their skin? Why would anyone make difference into such an obsession? These questions are audible as the subtext of Midwestern racial liberalism, and at a time when the news confronts us with ample evidence that many Americans remain obsessed with expelling or dominating racial "others," such incredulity seems noble and humane.

NOTES

1. I have drawn basic information about the *Clevelander* and many other Cleveland-related items from the invaluable *Encyclopedia of Cleveland History*, which is hosted online by Case Western Reserve University and edited by John J. Grabowski. *Encyclopedia of Cleveland History*, https://case .edu/ech/.

2. Chesnutt was describing a racial status quo as seen from above, and he was speaking comparatively rather than absolutely—compared to Detroit or St. Louis, Chicago or Cincinnati, Cleveland was considerably more progressive with regard to race. The placidity he speaks of, however, was about to be upended by the formation of the Future Outlook League (FOL), a hybrid of community organizing and labor union that began in 1935 and was most active in its first decade. Made up mostly of relatively recently arrived, unemployed African American migrants from the South, the FOL's first activities were part of a nationwide "Don't Buy Where You Can't Work" campaign among African Americans protesting hiring discrimination in retail shops. The FOL's creatively confrontational tactics and highly participatory, vigorously working-class culture are well chronicled in Kimberley L. Phillips, *AlabamaNorth: African-American Migrants, Community, and Working-Class Activism in Cleveland, 1915–45* (Urbana: University of Illinois Press, 1999). A much earlier history—Charles H. Loeb, *The Future Is Yours: The History of the Future Outlook League, 1935–1946* (Cleveland: Future Outlook League, 1947)—is also highly useful.

3. Charles W. Chesnutt, *Essays and Speeches*, ed. Joseph R. McElrath Jr., Robert C. Leitz III, and Jesse S. Crisler (Stanford, CA: Stanford University Press, 1999), 542.

4. Ng's two novels so far are *Everything I Never Told You* (New York: Penguin, 2014) and *Little Fires Everywhere* (New York: Penguin, 2017).

5. Other useful works about the history of African Americans in Cleveland during this period include Kenneth L. Kusmer, *A Ghetto Takes Shape: Black Cleveland, 1870–1930* (Urbana: University of Illinois Press, 1978); David A. Gerber, *Black Ohio and the Color Line: 1860–1915* (Urbana: University of Illinois Press, 1976); William Wayne Giffin, *African Americans and the Color Line in Ohio, 1915–1930* (Columbus: Ohio State University Press, 2005); and Virginia R. Boynton, "Jane Edna Hunter and Black Institution Building in Ohio," in *Builders of Ohio: A Biographical History*, ed. Warren R. Van Tine, Michael Dale Pierce, and Michael Cain Pierce (Columbus: Ohio State University, 2003): 228–240.

6. Two works that do not address these issues directly but do provide some valuable intellectual historical background of a comparative nature are Holly Case, *The Age of Questions* (Princeton, NJ: Princeton University Press, 2018); and David Shi, *Facing Facts: Realism in American Thought and Culture, 1850–1920* (New York: Oxford University Press, 1996).

7. "John Anisfield Award," *Saturday Review of Literature*, July 21, 1934, 11.

8. Peniel Joseph, "Waiting Till the Midnight Hour: Reconceptualizing the Heroic Period of the Civil Rights Movement, 1954–1965," *Souls* 2, no. 2 (Spring 2000): 6–17.

9. Lani Guinier, "From Racial Liberalism to Racial Literacy: *Brown v. Board of Education* and the Interest-Divergence Dilemma," *Journal of American History* 91, no. 1 (June 2004): 95. See also Walter A. Jackson, *Gunnar Myrdal and America's Conscience: Social Engineering and Racial Liberalism, 1938–1987* (Chapel Hill: University of North Carolina Press, 1990) and Eric Schickler, *Racial Realignment: The Transformation of American Liberalism, 1932–1965* (Princeton, NJ: Princeton University Press, 2016).

10. Carey McWilliams, *Brothers Under the Skin* (Boston: Little, Brown, 1944).

11. Helen M. Chesnutt, *Charles Waddell Chesnutt: Pioneer of the Color Line* (Chapel Hill: University of North Carolina Press, 1952), 245.

12. For more on Cleveland's reform tradition, see David D. Van Tassel and John J. Grabowski, eds., *Cleveland: A Tradition of Reform* (Kent State University Press, 1986); Hoyt Landon Warner, *Progressivism in Ohio, 1897–1917* (Columbus: Ohio State University, 1964); Shelton Stromquist, "The Crucible of Class: Cleveland Politics and the Origins of Municipal Reform in the Progressive Era," *Journal of Urban History* 23, no.2 (1997): 192–220; Alexandra W. Lough, "Tom L. Johnson and

Cleveland Traction Wars, 1901–1909," *American Journal of Economics and Sociology* 75, no. 1 (2016): 149–192; Thomas F. Campbell and Edward M. Miggins, eds., *The Birth of Modern Cleveland, 1865–1930* (Cleveland, OH: Western Reserve Historical Society, 1988); Kenneth Finegold, *Experts and Politicians: Reform Challenges to Machine Politics in New York, Cleveland, and Chicago* (Princeton, NJ: Princeton University Press, 1995); and two firsthand accounts—Frederic C. Howe, *The Confessions of a Reformer* (New York: Scribner, 1925); and Tom L. Johnson, *My Story* (New York: B. W. Huebsch, 1911).

13. John D. Rockefeller was originally a Clevelander, but the Rockefeller Foundation was incorporated in New York. Rockefeller did, however, exert his influence philanthropically in Cleveland through the auspices of one of his lawyers, Frederick H. Goff. Goff established the Cleveland Foundation, which still exists, and now administers the Anisfield-Wolf Book Awards. For more on the broader context of philanthropy and social science, see Alice O'Connor, *Social Science for What?: Philanthropy and the Social Question in a World Turned Rightside Up* (New York: Russell Sage Foundation, 2007).

14. For background on this dynamic, see Mary L. Dudziak, *Cold War Civil Rights: Race and the Image of American Democracy* (Princeton, NJ: Princeton University Press, 2011); Martha Biondi, *To Stand and Fight: The Struggle for Civil Rights in Postwar New York City* (Cambridge: Harvard University Press, 2003); Karen Ferguson, *Top Down: The Ford Foundation, Black Power, and the Reinvention of Racial Liberalism* (Philadelphia: University of Pennsylvania Press, 2013); and Inderjeet Parmar, *Foundations of the American Century: The Ford, Carnegie, and Rockefeller Foundations in the Rise of American Power* (New York: Columbia University Press, 2012). A notable exception to this general postwar emphasis is Karen R. Miller, *Managing Inequality: Northern Racial Liberalism in Interwar Detroit* (New York: New York University Press, 2016).

15. A sampling of excellent studies focusing on the interwar period and informed by the transnational turn might include Nancy F. Cott, "Revisiting the Transatlantic 1920s: Vincent Sheean vs. Malcolm Cowley," *American Historical Review* 118, no. 1 (February 2013): 46–75; Joseph Fronczak, "The Fascist Game: Transnational Political Transmission and the Genesis of the US Modern Right," *Journal of American History*

105, no. 3 (December 2018): 563–588; and especially Brooke L. Blower, "From Isolationism to Neutrality: A New Framework for Understanding American Political Culture, 1919–1941," *Diplomatic History* 38, no. 2 (April 2014): 345–376.

16. Lillian Smith to Ashley Montagu, April 5, 1960, MS 2129, Hargrett Rare Book and Manuscript Library, University of Georgia Libraries (hereafter cited as Hargrett—UGL).

17. The literature on the Chicago School is enormous. See, especially, Stow Persons, *Ethnic Studies at Chicago, 1905–45* (Urbana: University of Illinois Press, 1987); Henry Yu, *Thinking Orientals: Migration, Contact, and Exoticism in Modern America* (New York: Oxford University Press, 2001); Mary Jo Deegan, *Jane Addams and the Men of the Chicago School, 1892–1918* (New Brunswick, NJ: Transaction Books, 1988); and Andrew Abbott, *Department & Discipline: Chicago Sociology at One Hundred* (Chicago: University of Chicago Press, 1999).

18. Among the recipients of this grant, however, was future Nobel Peace Prize winner Ralph Bunche, who also won the Anisfield-Wolf Award in 1939.

19. "Anisfield Award," *Saturday Review of Literature* (February 2, 1941): 8.

20. Both of the classic studies of middlebrow culture feature Canby heavily: Joan Shelley Rubin, *The Making of Middlebrow Culture* (Chapel Hill: University of North Carolina Press, 1992); and Janice Radway, *A Feeling for Books: The Book-of-the-Month Club, Literary Taste, and Middle-Class Desire* (Chapel Hill: University of North Carolina Press, 1997). Also pertinent to this chapter as background regarding middlebrow interest in non-US cultures are Christina Klein, *Cold War Orientalism: Asia in the Middlebrow Imagination, 1945–1961* (Berkeley: University of California Press, 2009); and Hua Hsu, *A Floating Chinaman: Fantasy and Failure across the Pacific* (Cambridge: Harvard University Press, 2016).

21. V. Leslie Thomson, "The Anisfield-Wolf Awards," (PhD diss., Florida State University, 1959), 2, 1–10. The awards' ability to encourage potential authors to write about race was a continuing mission for the judges. See Lillian Smith to Ashley Montagu, March 10, 1959, MS 2129, Hargrett—UGL.

22. Thomson, "The Anisfield-Wolf Awards," 10.

23. Donald Young, *American Minority Peoples: A Study in Racial and Cultural Conflicts in the United States* (New York: Harper, 1932), xiii.

24. A full list of winners can be found at "Winners by Year," Anisfield-Wolf Book Awards, www.anisfield-wolf.org/winners/winners-by-year.

25. It was also an unusual choice in that the judges—led by Lillian Smith, who lobbied enthusiastically for it—selected it in 1957 even though it was originally published in Portuguese in 1933 and first translated into English in 1946. Lillian Smith to Dr. Ashley Montagu, February 20, 1957, MS 2129, Hargrett—UGL.

26. The pathbreaking history of the Missouri School of Journalism—especially its importance in reporting in East Asia over the first half of the century—is another case in point. See Steve Weinberg, *A Journalism of Humanity: A Candid History of the World's First Journalism School* (Columbia: University of Missouri Press, 2008). Two good general histories of foreign correspondents are Morrell Heald, *Transatlantic Vistas: American Journalists in Europe, 1900–1940* (Kent, OH: Kent State University Press, 1988); and John Hamilton Maxwell, *Journalism's Roving Eye: A History of American Foreign Reporting* (Baton Rouge: Louisiana State University Press, 2009).

27. The best example of this idea is the 1955 photography exhibition (and later book) *The Family of Man* by Edward Steichen, who lived for many years in Milwaukee and was the brother-in-law of Carl Sandburg. Sandburg contributed the introduction to the book version, *The Family of Man* (New York: Museum of Modern Art, 1955). One might also look to the novels of some of the Midwest's most significant writers and artists for other examples, for instance, Willa Cather and Grant Wood.

28. Smith to Ashley Montagu, April 5, 1960, MS 2129, Hargrett—UGL. In fact, this mini-manifesto was written as a protest: Smith was writing Montagu because she was discouraged by what she saw as the mediocrity of many of the books they were awarding. Rather than honoring new books yearly, she argued that the Anisfield Wolf money should be used to fund original research. Yet in her larger vision of the awards' purpose, she was upholding a more fundamental allegiance to the primacy of the personal and the value of private action in tackling racism—a position characteristic of Midwestern racial liberals.

29. Wallace Stegner, *One Nation* (Boston: Houghton Mifflin, 1945), v.

30. Stegner, *One Nation*, 54–55, 166–167.

31. Among many analyses of the limits of racial liberalism, see especially Robin Marie Averbeck, *Liberalism is Not Enough: Race and Poverty in*

Postwar Political Thought (Chapel Hill: University of North Carolina Press, 2018); and Leah N. Gordon, *From Power to Prejudice: The Rise of Racial Individualism in Midcentury America* (Chicago: University of Chicago Press, 2015). For a philosophical treatment of the subject, see Charles W. Mills, *Black Rights/White Wrongs: The Critique of Racial Liberalism* (New York: Oxford University Press, 2017).

CHAPTER 17

How the Midwestern GOP Encountered Modernity

Robert Taft, Mobility, and Individualism

William Russell Coil

In the mid-twentieth century, US Senator Robert Alphonso Taft fit no one's picture of modernity. Think modernity and think instantly of early-twentieth-century bohemian intellectuals. Centered in Greenwich Village, bohemians were painters and poets and novelists and activists. They sought liberation from political, social, and economic traditions, conventional yet restrictive customs that limited individual creativity and possibility. Think of public intellectual Walter Lippmann, who described Greenwich as a place where people were "so impatient of old and crusty things," meaning the failed ideas, values, and leaders of the past. Or think of Hutchins Hapgood, a journalist and anarchist, who said modern bohemians, wherever they might gather, were "bored by some small place in the Middle West" and sought the freedom "to lead their own lives." And think especially of Emma Goldman, a Russian Jewish immigrant to the United States. In the years before World War I, Goldman toured America championing labor militancy, free love, free speech, birth control, and anarchism. She was modernity's "New Woman," challenging gender roles, sexual mores, and male authority. She and other bohemian intellectuals were, in the words of Gertrude Stein, exploring how to live "life without father."[1]

But Robert Taft? He was "father." For several generations, Taft men, Republicans all, made rules that everyone else followed. From the 1870s to the early 2000s, one male Taft or another served in politically prominent national and international positions, making Robert a part of America's most durable political dynasty. They were Midwesterners, but the landscapes of Yale and Washington, DC, were as familiar to the Tafts as the rivers and hills that define Cincinnati, Ohio, the place they called home. Alphonso Taft, the founder of the dynasty and Robert's grandfather, was neither "flashy, profound," nor "even reflective." Nor was Robert. He always dressed the part of "father," favoring the intellectual and material fashions of a small-town Midwestern banker; stalwart and stolid in pursuit of respectability; ever ready to pronounce on the importance of character, thrift, and perseverance; usually sporting delicate rimless glasses and three-piece business suits with vests, like his mind, buttoned up.[2]

Robert Taft campaigned mainly as an opposer. Elected to the US Senate from Ohio in 1938, he served until his death in 1953. In between, he ran three failed campaigns for the Republican presidential nomination, each time running as the "Midwestern Resistance to the Eastern Establishment." He often opposed American military intervention in global affairs, even as totalitarians around the world threatened democracy. He opposed a social safety net because he believed it weakened an individual's moral fiber. He opposed experimental government programs, evaluating policies on the basis of how well they aligned with sound principles of constitutional law and free enterprise. The "only object" of government, he argued, was to help citizens develop their character, industry, and self-reliance. President Franklin Delano Roosevelt and New Dealers, and increasingly the Wall Street wing of the Republican Party, had cravenly reduced the "intellectual and moral purpose" of government to the crass mission of providing better "plumbing."[3]

Was Taft for anything? His platform seemed boiled down to a simple dichotomy: the old-fashioned over the modern. That Taft lost his party's presidential nomination three times seemed to suggest that the nation had rejected him and his region, that important elements of modernization—machine-age technology; anonymous and expansive bureaucratic authority; global communications, migrations, and markets; and centralized economic power—had exposed his cherished and "eternal" American values of hard work, thriftiness, and self-reliance as hoary incantations to a dead past, that the Midwest, once vital and distinct, had drifted into homogenized "fly-over country." In other words, Taft failed because he seemed to be a spokesperson for the traditional world, a voice for the rooted provincial in a mobile cosmopolitan world. In a classic account of US modernization in the late nineteenth and early twentieth centuries, historian Robert Wiebe analyzed the friction between the traditional and modern worlds and seemed to summarize Taft: people like him "tried desperately to understand the larger world in terms of their small, familiar environment . . . to impose the known upon the unknown, to master an impersonal world through the customs of a personal society."[4]

And yet Taft and his Midwest, like the bohemian intellectuals in Greenwich Village, were both producers and products of modernity. Taft reminds us that modernity is not a tidy, unidirectional, and monolithic process but a messy, contingent, reciprocating loop. Taft and his followers created their regional identity in conversation with the transnational forces of modernity, selectively embracing, rejecting, negotiating, and adapting their way to building the Midwest. Taft Republicans invented a most American region even as they helped build a deterritorialized America.

British philosopher Herbert Spencer influenced Taft's modernity. Spencer selectively borrowed and popularized the scientific ideas of Charles Darwin. As historian George Cotkin wrote, modernity and the "Darwinian revolution in science" were intertwined. Like modernism, Darwinism "posited change, process, and struggle as essentials" and provided a justification for "ceaseless change and challenge to authority." After the Civil War, Spencer's American adherents argued that struggles among conflicting interests ended not in a brutal, competitive free-for-all but a harmonious, evolutionarily strengthened community.[5]

Young Taft learned crucial lessons from Spencer's ideas on evolution. "Character," his father wrote, was "formed by the practice of self-restraint and self-sacrifice, by overcoming obstacles." Historian James Patterson concluded that, as a child, Taft was made to understand "the necessity of strenuous effort, of overcoming competition. The world was harsh, and only the fittest could survive in it." Here was the philosophical core of Taft's political agenda, the foundation of his critique of the New Deal: government assistance only hindered the process by which people progressed. Struggle. Suffering. Perseverance. Survival. These natural selection mechanisms made individuals, and thus society, better.[6]

It was a cruel philosophy during the Great Depression when millions of people were out of work, hungry, and homeless through no fault of their own. Taft, however, saw progress. Spencer, historian Jackson Lears wrote, "provided a social scientific sanction for the popular tendency to link material and moral progress." He and his followers "could dismiss the suffering and death of individuals as unimportant, the necessary friction on the high road of progress." Taft wanted individuals to "rise above the average standard of living and enjoy a little more luxury or a little more power." Government had only to assure that "reasonable success" would receive the "recognition it deserve[d] from [a person's] friends and neighbors." For Taft, individual struggle was an optimistic process. Current suffering from exploitation and inequality was, in his view, merely a prelude to a better place.[7]

Taft seemed out of place in the modern world because he struggled with mass communications. He was a three-time failure for the Republican presidential nomination, after all, and Patterson summarized well the essential Taft persona: "his apparent coldness, the forced harshness of his speaking voice, the stiffness of his public posture." And then there was the fashion. Taft committed to the look of a small-town Midwestern banker—of "father"—so fully that he undermined his political tacticians when they dictated that Taft change his image. In 1939, his staff contrived a "candidate goes hunting in Texas" event. The goal was simple: to impart a hint of rural masculinity to an Ivy League lawyer who preferred the nature of the golf course, especially the DC area's elite, all-male Burning Tree Club. Taft, however, complicated the event. After the hunt, he changed from his hunting clothes into one of his beloved vested business suits and then—and only then—posed for a photograph, holding a dead bird that someone else had just shot.[8]

At first look, the resulting confused image exposed an incompetent public relations staff and a candidate uncomfortable with the idea not just that he must earn the consent of the governed but also must persuade them through the distasteful artifice of mass communication. Why was this prosperous and paunchy man holding a dead bird? Who actually killed the bird? Why were there were no other props in the photo? Just Taft and the dead bird? Why was there no gun in sight? The photo clearly revealed that Taft was out of his element. The message might as well have been, "My campaign is as dead as this bird."

As a clue to Taft's modernity, however, the image tells a different story. The important element of the image is not the action within the photo but the action before the photo was taken. Taft changed his clothes—not because he suffered from repressed emotions and unconsciously needed to "button up" his appearance for the public, nor because he was inept, mistakenly believing that a lone man dressed in a business suit and holding a dead bird made sense. He changed his clothes on purpose. The image tells us that Taft did not want us to believe he was a hunter. He inserted a different image than the campaign staff had tried to project, and Taft's choice was closer to the truth than "I'm a manly hunter."

In this photo, Taft pointedly rejected violence as a symbol of male authority. To Taft, this symbol was outmoded because it recalled the mythical American frontier, a world in which brave pioneers and soldiers tamed an uncivilized place, a world where masculine authority was derived from an ability to kill, a once necessary but now regressive world where "father" was a fighter. That had been Theodore Roosevelt's game, and Taft, by reason of temperament and experience, could never win that game, let alone play it. He was a privileged urbanite. He had no personal connection to the notion that hunting could be a local ritual of generational male bonding. Roosevelt, moreover, was suspect. In the 1912 presidential election, Roosevelt ran as a third-party candidate, split the Republican vote, and denied Taft's father, William Howard, a second term as president. Robert Taft therefore rejected Roosevelt's version of authority. Roosevelt's skill in hunting and killing communicated virility, craft, and individuality in a world in which ever more people worked in an urban, hierarchical setting completing repetitive tasks. Mastery of violence, according to Roosevelt, revealed righteous leaders of a nation entangled with and threatened by the modern world. Roosevelt's strenuous life was, according to historian Jackson Lears, "antimodern," suggesting that Roosevelt was ill at ease with overcivilized modern life and searching for an "intense experience" as an antidote to it.[9]

Taft constructed his small-town, Midwestern banker identity as a contrast, choosing a version of "father" to communicate respectable stability and local, personal authority in an interconnected modern world that had little of either. He communicated "manager," not predator. That conscious choice to change clothes resulted in failed political art but nevertheless reflected Taft's worldview. From 1889, the year Taft was born, through 1953, the year he died, the world had experienced two major economic depressions (1893 and 1929), the rise of America as a military and financial world power, two catastrophic global wars (World Wars I and II), and the emergence of the Cold War, which threatened existential destruction. In Taft's lifetime, the world became increasingly connected and complex through technology—technology that facilitated the movement of people across borders, spread information farther and faster than ever before, consolidated economic power, and made it easy to obliterate civilization. Taft chose to be the paternal face of modernization. Americans no longer needed a gunslinger. They needed a steady hand, an orderly decision-maker, someone from a special place with tried-and-true values in an unsettled world.

The Midwest, Taft had good reason to believe, was that special place. In 1939, the same year Taft went hunting in Texas, Hollywood film studio Metro-Goldwyn-Mayer released *The Wizard of Oz*. Its popularity at the box office at the time and its enduring power since suggest that its message made sense to Americans. The Midwest was reliable. It was home, the place to which you could return when the thrill of modernity's ceaseless change turned into mere chaos, when the liberating bounty of personal and material choices turned into the enervating anxiety of uncertainty. The film documented both the fear of and the thrill produced by modernity. The abundant and magical technology in Oz, its prosperity on gaudy display, its vibrant colors swirling in constant motion—all of it was exciting. Disorienting, too. In fact, so disorienting that Dorothy, in the end, chose to return home to the refuge provided by her family and her community. Home was Kansas and, by extension, the Midwest. It was dependable, if bland. It was made productive through honest toil rather than wizardry. It placed trust in local authority (Dorothy's family, the male farm workers). It feared and, ultimately, rightly doubted an all-powerful and seemingly unknowable elite (the Wizard) who planned and controlled the community (the Emerald City). In the responsible Midwest, community authority guided individuals through the disorientation of modernity.[10]

Mobility is a defining element of modernity and can be a source of disorientation. Migration undermines the comfort of borders, both physical and intellectual, and disrupts the production and reproduction of a place. Locality, as anthropologist Arjun Appadurai wrote, is a "fragile and difficult achievement," one "shot through with contradictions, destabilized by human motion." In the nineteenth century, however, migration was so common that "homesickness" emerged as a modern condition. In keeping with the rise of Darwinism, a good modern citizen, one who could compete in a market economy, needed to overcome this disease, to struggle and, through self-control, defeat the psychological impulse to return home. A successful, autonomous, adaptable person was a survivor of this disease.[11]

Taft's steadfast defense of rugged individualism was an adaptation to rootlessness, his region's guide through the disorientation of modern mobility. Through the "ethic of self-control"—character, perseverance, hard work, thrift—individuals could struggle, remake themselves, and rise above the station into which they were born. This ethic of self-control was, according to Jackson Lears, "a moral gyroscope," a way of ensuring that communities in flux, churned by the upheaval of mobile "self-seeking individuals," avoided fragmentation and chaos because of the breakdown in traditional authority. Mobile individuals, in fact, undermined "communal pride." As a result, the ethic of self-control translated into social control, into stability despite the constant pressure of change.[12]

Taft himself was rootless. Born in Cincinnati, Taft spent his youth where elites learned their craft (New England prep school, Yale undergrad, and Harvard Law), where they exercised imperial authority (the Philippines, where his father was appointed governor after the Spanish-American War), and where they expanded American influence (Washington, DC, where his father, as Theodore Roosevelt's secretary of war, oversaw the building of the Panama Canal and served as provisional governor of Cuba, and then, in 1908, was elected to the US presidency). Before he was fourteen, Robert had traveled to Japan, Hong Kong, and Europe. How many American children met the Pope, as he did in 1902? The Pope asked Robert "what he wished to be." Taft said, "Chief Justice" of the United States Supreme Court—a job that was William Howard Taft's personal ambition. His son's admiration must have made him happy. He must have been proud, though, when Horace Taft, William Howard's brother and the headmaster at the Taft School, wrote to William Howard just after Robert, nearly fourteen years old, had arrived at the prep school. Despite spending over a month traveling alone from the Philippines to Connecticut, despite arriving two weeks late to enroll at a new school, despite now living thousands of miles from his parents, Robert betrayed "no signs of homesickness." [13]

Mobility also shaped the development of the Midwest. Consider Cincinnati, Ohio, the Tafts' home. By the 1850s, communications, transportation, and mass production technology made Cincinnati a crucial node in a modernizing global network, rewarding an individual's ability to adapt to the new, to struggle against chaos, to demonstrate character, perseverance, and self-reliance. First steamboats, then canals, and finally railroads and telegraphs facilitated the mobility of people, goods, and ideas. Assembly-line techniques found early acceptance in Cincinnati's slaughterhouses. Farmers in the fertile Miami Valley, just north of the city, grew the corn that fed the pigs that city workers processed into pork that fed, among others, slaves on southern cotton plantations and textile mill workers in Lowell, Massachusetts, and Lancashire, England. Cincinnati lard oil, too, was used as an industrial lubricant and cleaner in the mills of the Atlantic world. As early as the 1830s, visitors to Cincinnati described the specialized and regimented labor along the "disassembly line." They used a metaphor for work that was distinctly modern: killing and dismembering a pig went off like "clockwork." [14]

The technological forces of modernity had stitched Cincinnati into an impersonal, synchronized, sometimes liberating, often contentious, increasingly cruel world. Cincinnati's booming prosperity created demand for more labor, luring tens of thousands of migrants and immigrants, testing their strength to fend off homesickness. By 1847, nearly half the city was foreign-born. Modernity exacted high costs, however, throwing together mobile, diverse people who all sought something better, perhaps, but did not all expect to abandon their languages, faiths, and traditions in the process. Persistent race riots and flashes of xenophobia convulsed the city. [15]

Alphonso Taft, Robert's grandfather, tested his mettle in chaotic Cincinnati. A migrant from Vermont, Taft arrived in Cincinnati in 1839. He became a lawyer for the railroads. As a local judge, he wrote an "opinion against compulsory Bible reading in schools." In the 1870s and 1880s, he was the secretary of war and attorney general in the Grant administration. In the 1880s, he served abroad as the ambassador first to Austria-Hungary and then to Russia. Here was the Taft family relationship with modernity in one life: a lawyer for the railroads, the symbol of modernity; a judge striking at traditional religious authority; and a national elite representing emerging American power in the world.[16]

And Cincinnati, though urban and industrial, was indicative of the trends that shaped the rise of the Midwest. Immigrants, for example, settled not just in cities but in rural areas too. According to historian Jon Gjerde, before the Civil War, foreign-born people dominated the movement into Midwestern rural areas: "Until at least 1880, the proportion of residents of foreign birth in the middle western states roughly paralleled the proportion of the foreign-born in the urbanizing East." Moreover, Gjerde continued, in 1880 "over two-thirds of all foreign-born farmers" resided "in the Old Northwest and the states of Iowa, Minnesota, and Nebraska and the territory of Dakota to the west." As it emerged in the nineteenth century, the Midwest was no more rooted than the Tafts. Disruptive mobility, an essential element of modernity, was fundamental to the establishment of the Midwest.[17]

Gjerde demonstrated that these farmers selected the bits of modernism that suited them and resisted what they found inconvenient. Their mobility, while a brave rejection of the failed past, often occurred in the context of family and community migration. They were, in other words, modern in their desire to find new opportunities away from home but traditional in that they moved within support groups of kith and kin. Their desire to start anew, moreover, to escape their version of Lippmann's "old and crusty things," was prominent. A German immigrant justified his radical move by saying that in Germany, "the old institutions seemed rotten and sick unto death," while a Norwegian enjoyed "the satisfaction of being liberated from the effect of all yoke and despotism." Just as prominent, however, was their wish to mitigate their modernity. Immigrants saw in the Midwest a fluid and free place to maintain ethnic traditions, to be, for example, more Norwegian than they had been in Norway. Modernity had therefore not destroyed small, rural communities in the Midwest; modernity had given people an opportunity to reproduce or invent community traditions to manage change. Like Robert Taft, these travelers created a "complementary identity" capacious enough to contain several seeming opposites: Midwestern and transnational; local and distant; traditional and modern.[18]

Ceaseless cultural and demographic change, however, only reinforced the importance of the ethic of self-control. If Midwesterners continued to be mobile, then community authority no longer held individual behavior in check. Immigrant grandparents and parents prioritized their individual desires over the commonweal when they left Europe. Once in the Midwest, they struggled to enforce their community power. In similar fashion, their children and grandchildren moved on, this time from rural Midwestern communities, in search of something new and better, to live, as Hapgood said, "a life of their own." Or as Gertrude Stein said, "without father." Leaders of rural Midwestern ethnic enclaves concluded that mobility, one of the "acids of modernity," eroded the power and stability of family and community. One priest even recommended that parents who left the community "throw their children into the river that their bodies and not their souls should be lost in the outside world." It seemed more humane, though, just to teach a child the ethic of self-control.[19]

For Midwesterners, the ethic of self-control did the difficult work of producing and reproducing a sense of place, a locality, in a world that was becoming "deterritorialized, diasporic, and transnational." As Appadurai wrote, "Much that has been considered local knowledge is actually knowledge of how to produce and reproduce locality under conditions of anxiety and entropy, social wear and flux, ecological uncertainty and cosmic volatility." Some societies, moreover, inscribe locality onto the body. "Ceremonies of naming and tonsure," for example, "scarification and segregation, circumcision and deprivation" mark a person as local, defined against an "Other." Midwesterners, though, inscribed the mind, adopting the ethic of self-control as an essential marker of being Midwestern, as an essential set of values in the uncertain and volatile context in which the Midwest developed. As a set of inscribed values, the Midwest was less a specific place on the map and rather more like a compass, helping to navigate modernity regardless of one's location. Robert Taft might have been rootless, but he bore the intellectual mark of the Midwest wherever he went.[20]

The problem with Taftian modernity and the moral gyroscope is that risk, too, was internalized and individualized. Modernity increased risk and exposed more of the world's population to intense economic exploitation. An individual was newly vulnerable to economic decisions made by distant corporate executives; to industrial accidents in dangerous mechanized workplaces; and, because of the interconnected nature of the economy, to global economic competition, change, and collapse. Rugged individualism, moreover, failed to account for restrictions on individual behavior based on race, gender, or class. In the first half of the nineteenth century, communities held individuals accountable for economic insecurity, their poverty or injury blamed on the shortcomings of their character. Failure was an individual problem. In the second half the nineteenth century, however, reform movements around the world challenged these assumptions. Poverty, industrial accidents, and unemployment slowly became a condition of modernity that required state intervention to assist people harmed by modern life. This movement came comparatively late to the United States, finding a coherent national expression only in the 1930s with the Great Depression and New Deal.[21]

As historian David Kennedy argued, whatever else the New Deal accomplished or failed to accomplish, however patchwork and improvised its programs, it "left in place a set of institutional arrangements that constituted a more coherent pattern than is dreamt of in many philosophies. That pattern can be summarized in a single word: security." Whether establishing pensions for the elderly, guaranteeing the right of workers to join a union and collectively bargain, or insuring savings accounts, the New Deal sought to socialize the risks of modern life. People could be injured on the job, could be poor through no fault of their own, could suffer because capitalists had too much power over individual workers. New Dealers believed that modern life had changed too much and too fast, rendering past ideas unworkable and lending urgency to the pragmatic experimental effort to resolve the human crisis.[22]

Taft criticized the New Deal because it replaced rugged individualism and the ethic of self-control with material security. New Dealers, Taft said, judged their programs "on the question of whether they give men more money, more bathtubs, more automobiles, and less time to work." Taft believed that opportunity was, in fact, the source of freedom. Material security merely made free citizens into slaves. The Declaration of Independence, Taft pointed out, offered only the pursuit of happiness, not its guarantee. Security, he further argued, had never been important to the American tradition: "This nation would never have been founded if our forefathers had not considered freedom ahead of security, ahead of wealth, ahead of peace itself." The "burden of security" hindered the diligent worker. Opportunity worked best for the disciplined individual who understood that "the ways of freedom do not always give instantaneous results." The problem with Taft's celebration of rugged individualism was not that it marked him as inadequately modern but that rugged individualism was an aspect of an all too brutal modernity.[23]

Taft was not a cranky regionalist raging against the standardizing, integrating nationalism of the New Deal and bemoaning the disappearance of village values. His defense of rugged individualism, however miserly and uncaring it could be, was consistent with the rise of the Midwest as a specific geography, a symbolic spatial invention of a people reacting and contributing to—indeed, participating in—modernity. The Midwestern identity was tied to the disciplined, thrifty, persevering sovereign self, bound to no other person or place or tradition or idea except through voluntary association. These values—middle class and bourgeois—may seem like your grandparents' tired nostrums. Historically, however, they were transformative. "The rise of middle class values and the institutions of capitalism," Andrew Cayton and Peter Onuf argued, "were synonymous with the rise of the Midwest." And while framing their history of the Midwest primarily as a story of national integration, a rebirth of the nation in the "image" of the Midwest, Cayton and Onuf called attention to the transnational context of the Midwest's founding. "The institutions of capitalism"—communications and transportation technology, global movements of capital and labor, the rise of bureaucratic power—knit the cities and farms of the Midwest to the wider world. Taft's Midwestern Republicanism and its deep affinity for rugged individualism developed as an expression of Americanness just as global modernity began to undermine the notion of America's geographical isolation.[24]

Robert Wiebe said late-nineteenth-century America "was a society without a core," a nation without "national centers of authority and information," which could have ordered the ceaseless and chaotic changes of modernity. Midwesterners offered themselves to be that authority. And why not? In the nineteenth and early twentieth centuries, Midwesterners were essential to modernity. In Chicago, architect Louis Sullivan leveraged new technology to develop skyscrapers, the icon of the modern built environment. Chicagoans also pioneered the "democratization of owner-occupied housing," aiding in "the transition of working-class families to the modern age and modern conveniences." In Detroit and in Dayton, Henry Ford and the Wright Brothers, respectively, revolutionized transportation, granting individuals even more leverage over space and time than the nineteenth century's steamships and railroads. The automotive and aviation industries were not just global symbols of American technological genius. They were symbols, as well, of global modernity. By the late 1920s, Ford had become a worldwide term synonymous with modernity: Fordism, describing the transition from craft production to assembly lines. The resulting mass production worked to deskill industrial work, speed up its pace, lower its costs, and democratize access to goods. These innovations, in turn, enhanced geographic and social mobility. Midwesterners made it easier for Americans to break from the past and start anew. No wonder, then, that from 1860 through 1920, Americans elected a Midwesterner to the presidency eleven times in fifteen elections—all of them Republicans. Taft defended a Midwest that had been central to the spread of modernity.[25]

NOTES

1. Christine Stansell, *American Moderns: Bohemian New York and the Creation of a New Century* (Princeton, NJ: Princeton University Press, 2000), 44, 120–144, 7.

2. James T. Patterson, *Mr. Republican: A Biography of Robert A. Taft* (Boston: Houghton Mifflin, 1972), 11.

3. Robert A. Taft, *Congressional Record*, 80th Congress, 1st Session, A793–A794; Caroline Thomas Harnsberger, *A Man of Courage: Robert A. Taft* (Chicago: Wilcox and Follett, 1952), 132–137.

4. Robert Wiebe, *The Search for Order, 1877–1920* (New York: Hill and Wang, 1967), 12.

5. George Cotkin, *Reluctant Modernism: American Thought and Culture, 1880–1900* (New York: Twayne, 1992), xii; T. J. Jackson Lears, *No Place of Grace: Antimodernism and the Transformation of American Culture, 1880–1920* (New York: Pantheon Books), 21.

6. Patterson, *Mr. Republican*, 14; Andrew R. L. Cayton, *Ohio: The History of a People* (Columbus: Ohio State University Press, 2002), 323–326.

7. Lears, *No Place of Grace*, 7–8, 20–23 (quotes, 21); Robert A. Taft, *A Republican Program: Speeches and Broadcasts* (Cleveland, OH: David S. Ingalls, 1939), 29–31, 43, 45–47 (quotes, 29–30 and 43).

8. Patterson, *Mr. Republican*, 20, 332, 496.

9. Richard Slotkin, *Gunfighter Nation: The Myth of the Frontier in Twentieth-Century America* (New York: Athenaeum, 1992), 51–57; Lears, *No Place of Grace*, xii, 96, 108, 159, 222.

10. Warren Susman, *Culture as History: The Transformation of American Society in the Twentieth Century* (New York: Pantheon Books, 1984), 28, 268; James R. Shortridge, *The Middle West: Its Meaning in American Culture* (Lawrence: University Press of Kansas, 1989), 1–2.

11. Arjun Appadurai, *Modernity at Large: Cultural Dimensions of Globalization* (Minneapolis: University of Minnesota Press, 1996), 33–34, 181, 191–192, 198; Susan J. Matt, *Homesickness: An American History* (New York: Oxford University, 2011), 5–6, 122–123, 167–168; and Matt, "You Can't Go Home Again: Homesickness and Nostalgia in US History," *Journal of American History* 94, no. 2 (September 2007): 469–497.

12. Lears, *No Place of Grace*, 12–13, 66.

13. Patterson, *Mr. Republican*, 23–26, 30.

14. Daniel Walker Howe, *What Hath God Wrought: The Transformation of America, 1815–1848* (New York: Oxford University Press, 2007); Sven Beckert, *Empire of Cotton: A Global History* (New York: Vintage Books, 2015); Steven J. Ross, *Workers on the Edge: Work, Leisure, and Politics in Industrializing Cincinnati, 1788–1890* (New York: Columbia University Press, 1985); Steve C. Gordon, "From Slaughterhouse to Soap-Boiler: Cincinnati's Meat Packing Industry, Changing Technologies, and the Rise of Mass Production, 1825–1870," *IA: Journal of the Society for Industrial Archeology* 16, no. 1 (1990): 55–67 ("clockwork," 56); Richard G. Arms, "From Disassembly to Assembly. Cincinnati: The Birthplace of Mass Production," *Bulletin of the Historical and Philosophical Society of Ohio* 17

(July 1959): 195–203; Ian Tyrrell, "Robert Wiebe's *The Search for Order*: Fifty Years On," *Journal of Gilded Age and Progressive America* 17 (2018): 397–411; Daniel T. Rodgers, "Tradition, Modernity, and the American Industrial Worker: Reflections and Critique," *Journal of Interdisciplinary History* 7, no. 4 (Spring 1977): 655–681.

15. Andrew Cayton, *Ohio*, 21, 26–27, 118–119, 124–126, 148–150.

16. Patterson, *Mr. Republican*, 10; Richard White, *Railroaded: The Transcontinentals and the Making of Modern America* (New York: W. W. Norton, 2012); Tony Judt, "The Glory of the Rails." *New York Review of Books*, December 23, 2010, www.nybooks.com/articles/2010/12/23/glory-rails.

17. Jon Gjerde. *The Minds of the West: Ethnocultural Evolution in the Rural Middle West, 1830–1917* (Chapel Hill: University of North Carolina Press, 1997), 4–5; Appadurai, *Modernity at Large*, 188, 191–192.

18. Jon Gjerde, "The Perils of 'Freedom' in the American Immigrant Church," in *Crossings: Norwegian-American Lutheranism as a Transatlantic Tradition*, ed. Todd W. Nichol (Northfield, MN: Norwegian American Historical Association, 2003), 8, 5–8; Gjerde, *Minds of the West*, 60, 63–64, 72, 101, 130, 284; Tyrrell, "Robert Wiebe's *The Search for Order*," 399.

19. Gjerde, *Minds of the West*, 68, 317, 238.

20. Appadurai, *Modernity at Large*, 179, 188, 181.

21. Thomas Bender, *A Nation Among Nations: America's Place in World History* (New York: Hill and Wang, 2006), 275–280; Jacob Hacker, *The Great Risk Shift: The New Economic Insecurity and the Decline of the American Dream* (New York: Oxford University Press, 2006), 25–26; Wiebe, *Search for Order*, 4.

22. David M. Kennedy, *Freedom from Fear: The American People in Depression and War, 1929–1945* (New York: Oxford University Press, 1999), 363–380; Bender, *Nation Among Nations*, 278; Eric Rauchway, *The Great Depression and the New Deal: A Very Short Introduction* (New York: Oxford University Press, 2008), 87–102.

23. Taft, *A Republican Program*, 44–47; Robert A. Taft, "No Substitute for Freedom," *Colliers* 119, no. 5 (February 1, 1947): 13, 58; Matthew Karp, "The New World Order," *Boston Review*, October 3, 2016, http://bostonreview.net/books-ideas/matthew-karp-new-world-order.

24. Andrew R. L. Cayton and Peter S. Onuf, *The Midwest and the Nation: Rethinking the History of an American Region* (Bloomington: Indiana

University Press, 1990), 118, 123; Eric Foner, "Ohio and the World: The Civil War Era," in *Ohio and the World, 1753–2053: Essays Toward a New History of Ohio*, ed. Geoffrey Parker, Richard Sisson, and William Russell Coil (Columbus: Ohio State University Press, 2005), 73–92.

25. Wiebe, *Search for Order*, 12; Jon C. Teaford, *Cities of the Heartland: The Rise and Fall of the Industrial Midwest* (Bloomington: Indiana University Press, 1993), 73–77; Robert M. Crunden, *Ministers of Reform: The Progressives' Achievement in American Civilization, 1889–1920* (New York, Basic Books, 1984) 139–140; Robert J. Gordon, *The Rise and Fall of American Growth: The US Standard of Living Since the Civil War* (Princeton, NJ: Princeton University Press, 2016), 108; Ian Tyrrell, *Transnational Nation: United States History in Global Perspective Since 1789* (London: Palgrave McMillan, 2007), 151, 162–163.

CHAPTER 18

The Fusionist Mind of Stephen Tonsor

Gleaves Whitney

I

The people who remember Stephen Tonsor nowadays tend not to be academics but movement conservatives.[1] What they recall is "the insult," and they can tell you exactly where and when the University of Michigan historian served it up: in downtown Chicago, in a ballroom at the Drake Hotel, in 1986, at a Philadelphia Society meeting.[2] Delivering prepared remarks to a mostly friendly audience of conservatives, Tonsor played the scold. It was time to put neoconservatives in their place. Embellishing a figure of speech uttered by an obscure US senator,[3] the barrel-chested Tonsor let fly: "It is splendid when the town whore gets religion and joins the church. Now and then she makes a good choir director, but when she begins to tell the minister what he ought to say in his Sunday sermons, matters have been carried too far."[4]

What was behind Tonsor's provocation? It was rooted, I believe, not just in his convictions but also in his insecurities. The dramatic rise of neoconservatives inside the movement and inside the Reagan administration had real consequences. Jobs were at stake. Status was at stake. The battle over ideas was at stake.[5] By the mid-1980s, it was apparent that the neocons were capturing the big money in the foundations as well as the plum assignments in the Reagan administration—at the expense of some very fine traditionalists. So Tonsor fell back on his instincts: he attacked.

A combat veteran, Tonsor had won three Bronze Stars in World War II. Now, in the battle over the fate of his tribe—a congeries of fusionists and traditionalists[6]—he argued that the conservative movement was not to be confused with the Republican Party or Washington think tanks. The true roots of conservatism were not political, but cultural, extending back to ancient Jerusalem, Athens, and Rome, pagan and Christian.[7] True conservatives, believing civilization was a fragile achievement, owed an incalculable debt to the stewardship of generations of Roman- and Anglo-Catholics. These conservatives also gleaned lessons from the "dynamic stability" of early modern Britain and the "stable dynamism" of the American founding.

Against the backdrop of crises caused by the Great Depression, World War II, and the 1960s cultural revolution, a new generation of conservative fusionists and traditionalists coalesced mostly in the Midwest around the work of Richard Weaver, Russell Kirk, Frank Meyer, Eric Voegelin, Thomas Molnar, and Peter Stanlis. Although he himself did not want to be labeled, Tonsor allied himself with these fusionists and traditionalists. They valued Catholicism's role in the creation and development of Western civilization. They were wary of the impact of nominalism on modern philosophy, of the French Revolution on modern politics, and of the Industrial Revolution on modern society. They believed the problem with the neocons was that they had turned their backs on tradition. Mostly secular New York Jews, the neocons tended to be Nietzscheans in outlook, nihilists in the pursuit of power, and modernists who had forgotten God.

Some Catholic traditionalists and fusionists responded gleefully to Tonsor's putdown of the neocons; others, not so much. Before he delivered his remarks, Tonsor's wife, Caroline, and best friend Henry Regnery pleaded with him to soften the message. They worried it had the taint of anti-Semitism even though Tonsor was not anti-Semitic. They recalled his first love affair with a Jewish refugee from Nazi Germany named Rose Epstein; he always had feelings for her and remained in touch with her until death did them part.[8] But the attendees in the room would not have known about this love affair. Nor did they know how much the Old Testament permeated his thought. They would fail to see, Caroline and Henry argued, that Tonsor was attacking the neocons not for being Jewish but for not being Jewish enough—because he believed the neocons had turned their backs on God.[9]

Tonsor was unmoved by Caroline's and Henry's pleading—and the rest, as they say, is history. Tonsor's public reputation took a hit from which it never fully recovered. Yet it was a price he seemed willing to pay. He expressed no regrets when I asked him one year later about the speech. In fact, he proudly gave me a copy of his type-written manuscript. The carefully calculated insult was textbook Tonsor. His fierce prejudices, probing intellect, and prickly personality combined to define a distinct intellectual style: always fortissimo, never pianissimo.

In addition to the notorious Drake Hotel speech, movement conservatives recall Tonsor's pique between 1981 and 1992, during the Reagan and Bush administrations. Rather than rejoice that a conservative had finally made it to the White House, Tonsor expressed dismay at how easily traditionalists were seduced by power. A depressed Tonsor intoned, "When conservative scholars swap their tweed jackets for blue suits and go to Washington, you know the end of the movement is near."[10]

He was particularly perturbed by William J. Bennett's contest with M. E. Bradford for the prize of running Reagan's National Endowment for the Humanities. The eventual selection of Bennett, who had the backing of the neocons, and the rejection of Bradford, who had the backing of the southern and Midwestern paleocons, triggered Tonsor's outrage. It confirmed in his mind that the neocon will-to-power wins out over less well-funded and less well-connected traditionalists every time.[11]

II

As telling as the fights over status are, there is so much more to recall about Stephen John Tonsor III than an insult here or a premonition there. Bookish conservatives know that one of his most enduring achievements is found in the scores of elegant, erudite essays that he produced for journals including *Modern Age*, *Intercollegiate Review*, *National Review*, and *First Things*.[12]

Tonsor's sparkling essays compare favorably with those composed by the giants of the genre—Lionel Trilling, George Orwell, Matthew Arnold. They certainly stand in stark contrast to the dull monographs he produced.

Each essay is like a winding mountain trail that rewards its reader with a succession of grand views. The monographs proceed as though one were riveting together parts on an assembly line in a factory that generates units of knowledge with industrial efficiency.

In the essays, Tonsor's brilliance shines. Many of them grew organically out of lectures to his students at Michigan. During a typical academic year, Tonsor would deliver up to 150 talks—in his Western civilization survey, in his History of History class, and in two advanced courses in modern European intellectual history. In addition, he led graduate seminars on special topics such as the idea of decadence. Over a career of forty years at Michigan, a biblically suggestive span, Tonsor's fierce intellect attracted serious students to his classes. He cultivated a cadre of loyal young scholars who treasured him as a teacher and mentor. They fondly remembered him long after leaving Michigan and credited him with changing their lives for the better. They also knew that their professor could be demanding, confrontational, and feisty. Full disclosure: Tonsor served as my graduate advisor for five years. I experienced firsthand his generosity as a mentor and his brilliance as an intellectual historian and cultural critic. More, he was my godfather when I was received into the Catholic Church. On occasion, however, I experienced another side of his personality that would cause me no end of grief, more about which below.

What are some of the important things that students learned from Tonsor? Since his passing in 2014, I have asked that question to a score of Michigan alumni who studied under him either as undergraduate or graduate students. Their answers are revealing. Except for the perceived injustice of it, they could not care less that Tonsor is relatively unknown in academic circles today or that he is not the most cited academic they ever had as a professor. What they do care about is the personal connection with him. They felt that studying with him was a privilege and an adventure. Under his tutelage, they caught something—the nobility of the life of the mind, the romance of discovery, the fight for truth. They learned that to dedicate one's life to humane learning is not a job, but a calling. That to fulfill that calling is not for the faint of heart, but for those with focus and discipline. That the liberal arts are not easy, but hard—really hard—often requiring years of dogged study. That the imagination is not just helpful to inquiry, but essential to pouring old wine into new wineskins. That in what we today call a STEM world, divergent thinking is even more important than convergent thinking if modern civilization is to preserve the dignity of the human person. That in a society with many pressing needs, to pursue truth, goodness, and beauty for their own sake is not a diversion, but a privilege. That religion and myth are keys to historical meaning. That history is not a science, but a humane discipline that embraces all the messiness of life and the many conflicting ways it might be interpreted. That to understand a cultural problem often requires not just training in history, but also inquiry into religion, art, music, literature, architecture, philosophy, and philology. That to express a thought well is not just ornamental, but essential in a pluralistic society with a short attention span.[13]

I would be remiss not to mention a tradition that a number of Tonsor's students remember and cherish. Our professor was well known for approaching a student after the late-morning intellectual history class. He would invite the student to accompany him on his twenty-minute walk home to have a glass of sherry and enjoy a hot lunch prepared by his wife, Caroline. It mattered not what the student's political views were—one of the founders of Students for a Democratic Society, Tom Hayden, enjoyed the tradition. Stephen and Caroline Tonsor had been married since 1949, and the modest house they kept in the cozy neighborhood of Burns Park was a welcome respite for young people shoehorned into student housing or a studio apartment. Indeed, for Tonsor's students, these midday jaunts were one of the highlights of a Michigan education. They invited illuminating conversation on the walk to and from 1505 Morton Avenue. Once in the house, Tonsor might invite the student to look at the flower arrangement from his garden or pore over his latest exhibit catalogues. In the background, the university's NPR station played classical music. Once Caroline announced that lunch was served, everyone would sit down and Tonsor would offer a blessing under a Bavarian crucifix. With Caroline present, the conversation often took a more relaxed turn, and people would speak of their families, hometowns, holiday traditions, and weekend outings. It was truly lovely—an oasis of civility. To this day, the Michigan alumni who were fortunate to be welcomed into the Tonsors' home speak warmly of these unforgettable occasions.[14]

III

Tonsor's brilliance was evident both in conversation and writing. If he was intimidating, it was because his mind managed to hold, in dynamic tension, the thought of an exceedingly diverse stable of authors—from the philosophy of Aristotle to the poetry of Goethe to the history of Lord Acton.

When I was preparing to move to Ann Arbor and study under Tonsor's direction, I discovered the method and metaphysic he had developed by the mid-1960s. He called it "the organic reconciliation of opposites." [15] It was shorthand for the polarities he used to approach inquiry, order understanding, and develop rhetorical strategies. The concept seemed to run like a golden thread through many of the essays he produced.

If the concept of the organic reconciliation of opposites needed an introduction that most of his readers could understand, Tonsor would point to the work of Frank Meyer, the founder of a closely related method and metaphysic known as *fusionism*. Tonsor regarded Meyer as a mentor.[16] They spent countless hours on the phone in the 1960s—always, alas, at dinnertime, to the consternation of Caroline. Meyer endeavored to find common ground among diverse schools of conservative thought. He could do so because, in Tonsor's words, he "is a great debater [who has] first debated with himself every idea which he publicly defends or opposes. He is such a worthy combatant because every issue which he confronts publicly has first been fought out as a civil war with himself." Meyer saw that these interior battles were reflected in the movement's external battles, especially those between Libertarians and Catholic traditionalists. Freedom stripped of order led to anarchy and licentiousness. Order stripped of freedom led to clerical fascism. Meyer thus tried to bring harmony to conservatism "by insisting that freedom and order, innovation and tradition, are not irreconcilable antitheses." Rather, he believed people needed to maintain the symbiotic relationship of the two in order to live in a humane polity. More, such polarities could be yoked in an act of fusion that would build a movement.[17]

If the organic reconciliation of opposites needed grounding in reality, Tonsor would point to Walt Whitman: "Do I contradict myself? Very well then, I contradict myself, I am large, I contain multitudes." Just as Tonsor acknowledged his debt to Frank Meyer, he also acknowledged his debt to "the Romantic appreciation of the dialectic of opposites and polarities." When he studied poetry at the University of Illinois as an undergraduate, he steeped himself in the sensibilities of Whitman and the Romantics because it was they who "expressed eloquently and frequently the profound observation that the essence of life is polarity, opposition, contradiction; and that these—when integrated, harmonized, synthesized, their warring forces harnessed by the sovereign personality, institution, or society—enrich and energize the larger context of which they are a part."[18]

If the organic reconciliation of opposites needed to be unpacked in philosophical terms, Tonsor would point to the polarities that demark our lives—sacred and secular, transcendence and immanence, faith and reason, Jerusalem and Athens, Christian and pagan, church and state, eternity and time, infinity and space, absolute and relative, permanent things and historicism, philosophical truth and historical contingency, classic and modern, Enlightenment and Romantic, liberty and equality, justice and mercy. Already in his 1958 review essay about the British Catholic historian Christopher Dawson, Tonsor was staking out the polarities to be harmonized.[19]

If the organic reconciliation of opposites was in search of case studies, Tonsor would point to the great thinkers who set out to mediate the polarities. In the Age of Heroes, it was Homer mediating between the humanizing traditions of home and the existential tests from abroad. In classical Greece, it was Plato mediating between Parmenides's absolute and Heraclitus's relative. In medieval Europe, it was Thomas Aquinas mediating between the reason of Athens and the faith of Jerusalem. In the eighteenth century, it was Madison mediating between the Lockean liberal and Ciceronian republican traditions. In the nineteenth century, it was Goethe mediating between the Enlightenment and Romanticism. In the twentieth century, it was Dawson mediating between two forms of modern extravagance, that of the spiritual Baroque and that of the material Bourgeois. No matter how capable the workers in the vineyard are, the work of mediation is never finished. As Tonsor noted, "These principles are ever held in precarious balance by individuals and by societies; the resolution of their forces is never final; their synthesis is never complete."[20] Note that it would be a gross misunderstanding to conflate Tonsor's idea of the organic reconciliation of opposites with anything resembling Hegel's dialectic. Even to suggest such a thing would draw Tonsor's swift ire, as I discovered during one of his office hours!

If the organic reconciliation of opposites needed to be translated into a philosophy of civilization, Tonsor would observe that modern man lives with tensions, paradoxes, and contradictions—polarities that arise from our civilization's conflicting sources of intellectual and moral authority. In our shorthand way, we call those conflicting sources Christendom, Enlightenment, and Romanticism. These three civilizational sources have a complex and overlapping relationship to one another, something like that of a parent to strong-willed children. They are continually clashing, continually generating conflicting ideas and discourse in our public affairs. As a result, the conservative must be discerning, for he believes in freedom as well as in order. He believes in the individual as well as the community. He believes in the equality of all as well as in hierarchy, natural aristocracy, and excellence. He believes in private enterprise, competition, and market mechanisms as well as in those human, moral, and cultural values that cannot be quantified by the competition of interests in the marketplace.[21]

If the organic reconciliation of opposites were applied to higher education, Tonsor would point to the challenge of the denominational Christian college preserving its mission in a secularizing society. His passionately delivered speech at Augsburg University in 1969 explored the tension between civilizational unity and educational diversity. Recall, he was a Roman Catholic delivering the keynote at a Norwegian Lutheran college that was celebrating its one-hundredth anniversary:

> Those who consciously or unconsciously seek to purchase unity at the price of individuality and diversity contradict one of the most pervasive tendencies in our experience. We are able to be one effectively because we have been many individually. Our differences and our distinctions in this ecumenical world are not sources of weakness and anarchy but are the very basis out of which a rich and harmonious unity can develop.
>
> This process of diversification within a larger unity has been one of the distinguishing characteristics of our whole civilization.

No other civilization has possessed the essential unity and
the fascinating multiplicity characteristic of western society.
Christianity has divided and subdivided, each branch emphasizing
in some distinctive way an important aspect of a common belief.
Our political institutions have been structured in such a way that
pluralism has been given concrete expression in our society. And
our public lives are characterized by debate and constant, even
acrimonious, discussion of alternative solutions to our problems.
Our experience with diversity of belief and practice has led us to
recognize that alternative lifestyles, alternative political solutions,
alternative social institutions, and most especially, alternative
educational programs are a major source of strength, stability, and
richness in our society.[22]

Indeed, Tonsor declared, an education that empowers students to negotiate the dialectic between unity and diversity helps shape "the civilized,
educated, and rational man."[23]

If the organic reconciliation of opposites needed a method, Tonsor
would point to one of the most civilized, educated, and rational men
he had studied, Lord Acton. This great Catholic historian counseled
students to know their opponents' thinking better than the opponents
did. Keep an open mind. Test beliefs against reality. Cross-examine the
evidence. One's opponent just might know something you don't and teach
you something of value.[24] To illustrate, Tonsor would point to Acton's
willingness to revisit the evidence and soften his initial hostility to the
French Revolution.[25] A related piece of advice from Acton to students
was to be both-and, not either-or, thinkers. In the nineteenth century,
the number of accessible archives in Europe and the United States
multiplied. It was the golden age of history. For the first time, scholars
could travel to distant archives with relative ease and explore different
perspectives of the same events in a systematic way. So Tonsor counseled
apprentice historians to make the pilgrimage to the archives, explore
them imaginatively, mine them thoughtfully, and expand the horizon
of credible interpretations. It is hard work, but there is no shortcut to
understanding the past as it actually happened, *wie es eigentlich gewesen*.
Tonsor warned: "Only silly men write quickies."[26]

If the organic reconciliation of opposites needed a moral imperative in our day, Tonsor would insist that truth matters—and it often hurts. He would look again to his hero, Lord Acton, who urged students to have the courage to follow the evidence wherever it leads, no matter who might be offended, no matter what the cost. To illustrate, Tonsor would look to Lord Acton's mentor, Ignaz von Döllinger, about whom Tonsor had written his dissertation. Döllinger was a Catholic priest and scholar. Discovering material in the archives that was unpopular with the majority of the hierarchy in Rome, he paid dearly for rejecting the dogma of papal infallibility at the First Vatican Council: the penalty for his independence of mind was excommunication. Döllinger valued his integrity as a historian more than his standing as a priest.[27]

As this golden thread running through Tonsor's early work has attempted to show, the Michigan historian belonged to a great tradition in the West, that of the Christian humanist who accepted the Herculean if not Sisyphean task of trying to reconcile polarities. Given that human beings' aspirations are framed by limitations, there will always be a dynamic tension between God and man, faith and reason, the absolute and relative, the universal and the particular, unity and diversity, Jerusalem and Athens, authority and liberty. The work is never finished. Yet to strive for reconciliation is ennobling: "My behavior," Tonsor confessed, "would be less honorable and my world more impoverished were I to abandon any one of these contradictory ideals."[28]

IV

Stephen Tonsor lived from 1923 until 2014, a tumultuous period of depression, global war, and cold war that abundantly illustrates what happens when world-historical opposites go unreconciled. Perhaps his career as an intellectual historian and cultural critic were inspired, in part, by the widespread human misery he witnessed. Due to limited space, I can give only a few biographical highlights, but they are richly suggestive of the link between his life and times.

Interviews with the people who knew him intimately, as well as research in several archives, paint a discordant picture of Tonsor's interior life, where he waged his own fierce struggle to reconcile opposites. Like all of us, he was a mare's nest of contradictions. At his best, he was the happy warrior who could go to campus and spar for hours with the New Left as they threw SDS slogans in his face. Then he'd come home to the joy of laboring in his two gardens or of hiking with Caroline and their four children in the forested glacial moraines around Ann Arbor. He loved the traditions surrounding holidays with family and made much of them, especially around Christmas and the Epiphany, which the Tonsors celebrated each year with a spirited party.[29]

Yet Tonsor was also tormented by a dark side that filled him with resentments and pessimism. One should never forget that he experienced much hardship as a boy. The oldest of seven children, he grew up in and around Jerseyville, Illinois, in the Great Depression, in a poor working-class family. One of his brothers, Bernard Tonsor, explained that the family had to move so many times "because Mom and Dad could not pay the grocer." There were other times when, to get to school on snowy winter mornings, young Stephen either had to walk barefoot or suffer the humiliation of wearing his mother's shoes so as not to get frostbite.[30] For the rest of his life, Tonsor struggled to reconcile his attachments to Jerseyville with his blessed escape from its confinements.

Tonsor grew up in a family that loved the routines and rituals of the Catholic Church. He enthusiastically shared in the faith of his fathers; it kept him close to his German heritage and to his God. But at an early age, he became aware of how a beautiful thing can become polluted. A pedophile priest assigned to the parish made Tonsor angry forever after. "That son-of-a-bitch should have rotted in prison," he would say.[31]

Most conservative Catholics who knew Tonsor probably assumed that he embraced the doctrines of their church. Most of them he did, yet his letters also reveal quite an independent parishioner. His independence is of a piece with his admiration for Tocqueville, Döllinger, and Acton, all of whom had a problematic relationship with Rome. While Tonsor was conservative in his aesthetics, and while he bristled at leftwing homilies from the pulpit, he was quite liberal in the reforms he advocated. It began with his anger at the bishops: from the start, they should have adopted a policy of zero-tolerance for pedophiles and for the church leaders who abetted them. He also maintained that he could find nothing theologically wrong with allowing priests to marry and admitting women into the clergy.[32]

Tonsor's letters to Henry Regnery and my interviews with his widow Caroline reveal that he suffered from severe bouts of depression most of his life. A letter to Joseph Amato and an interview with his sister Mary Jean describe his first crushing disappointment in life. When he was a high schooler preparing for the priesthood, he was rejected by the seminary at the Pontifical College Josephinum in Worthington, Ohio, after the campus interview. Tonsor was quite open about the reason for the rejection: he struggled with his sexuality.[33]

The year 1940 found Tonsor beginning his freshman year at a school associated with the Presbyterian Church, Blackburn College, in Carlinville, Illinois. There he struggled with the war that had broken out in Europe. He thought seriously about declaring himself a conscientious objector because he did not want to fight Germans, but then he reconciled himself to being drafted after the attack on Pearl Harbor. He would become part of the Army Signal Corps, rise to the rank of staff sergeant, and earn three Bronze Stars in General MacArthur's campaign to retake the Philippines.[34]

Also in his freshman year at Blackburn, Tonsor fell in love for the first time. As noted previously, her name was Rose, and she was a Jewish refugee from Nazi Germany. Alas, her father, Fritz Epstein, did not want his daughter to marry a Catholic. But Tonsor and Rose formed a lifelong attachment. Even after he married Caroline (1949), whom he dearly loved, he always found a way to visit Rose in her adopted hometown of Boston. In fact, it was on one of these visits that he first heard Christopher Dawson lecture;[35] the great British historian briefly held a chair at the Harvard Divinity School (1958–1962).

One should never forget where Tonsor came from. He was eighteen when he was ripped from his home in the Corn Belt to fight in a distant war. He was twenty-two when he came back to the Midwest, a combat veteran hardened but determined to resume his studies. Some of the people close to him have wondered whether his experience of combat in the Pacific and his exposure to a pedophile priest in his parish caused posttraumatic stress or even a traumatic brain injury. This is speculation—I have found nothing in the archives to confirm such a diagnosis—and the circumstantial evidence is inconclusive.[36] But awareness of the hardships Stephen Tonsor suffered surely softens any harsh judgments one is tempted to make about the man.

V

Before ever meeting him, I read Tonsor's early essays, written in the 1950s and 1960s, and they drew me into his mind. After arriving in Ann Arbor, I was slow to discover that he was changing his mind. In letters to Henry Regnery in the 1980s, he often complained of being depressed and tired.[37] Life was increasingly difficult for him. He was in the seventh decade of his earthly pilgrimage and his views were hardening. Maybe his youthful quest to seek the organic reconciliation of opposites had lost its luster. Maybe he had soured on the contemporary scene in the conservative movement, the Republican Party, and the Catholic Church. Maybe the Drake Hotel speech signaled that his muscular intellect was beginning to ossify. By and by, his conversation would veer in a predictable direction— more authority and less freedom, more paleo and less neo, more fission and less fusion. Tonsor was drifting away from the organic reconciliation of opposites that he had found so compelling as a young man, and I got the memo late. I was assuming one thing; he was saying another. Our diverging perspectives became the source of disagreements. He did not like being challenged. He seemed jealous that I was driving up to Mecosta and becoming closer to Russell Kirk. It didn't help when one day I swapped my tweed jacket for a blue suit and went to the capital city to work with Michigan's new governor, John Engler. Tonsor would never invite me over for lunch again.

Thankfully, that's not the end of the story. More than two decades later, the Tonsors' oldest daughter, Ann, invited me to his memorial Mass. The date was June 26, 2014. The place was St. Mary's Catholic Church on the road west out of Jerseyville. I was the only one outside the family in attendance. It meant the world to me to re-establish a connection with Caroline, Ann, and the rest of the family after so many years.

Stephen Tonsor was a difficult personality, no doubt about it. We had differences that our similarities could not overcome. But he formed my mind and spirit for the better, and I will always honor him as a mentor. I still call him my godfather and *Doktorvater*. Not a day goes by when I do not think of him. Welcome to my challenge—reconciling opposites.

NOTES

1. This chapter originally appeared as "The Fusionist Mind of Stephen Tonsor" in *Modern Age* 61, no. 1 (Winter 2019): 41–50, and it is reprinted here with permission from *Modern Age*. Many learned readers kindly offered their critiques of this chapter when it was in draft form. My heartfelt thanks to Dr. Bradley Birzer, Mr. Winston Elliott, Mrs. Annette Kirk, Dr. George Nash, Dr. Jeffrey Nelson, Dr. Gregory Schneider, Dr. Antony Thrall Sullivan, and Ms. Ann Tonsor Zeddies for the time they put into making my work better.

2. See the April 1986 Philadelphia Society program at https://phillysoc.org/wp-content/uploads/2015/06/Conservatism-Identity-its-Limits-4.18-20.86.pdf.

3. The source of this figure of speech is apparently Indiana Senator James Watson, who refused to endorse the 1940 Republican candidate for president, Wendell Willkie, because Willkie was a former Democrat. Watson said, "I may welcome a repentant sinner into my church, but I wouldn't want him to lead the church choir." See www.senate.gov/artandhistory/history/common/generic/People_Leaders_Watson.htm.

4. For the text of the talk, see Stephen J. Tonsor, "Why I Too Am Not a Neoconservative," in *Conservatism in America since 1930: A Reader*, ed. Gregory L. Schneider (New York: New York University Press, 2003), 373–378. For insights from the panel's chairman, I interviewed John Ryan by phone. For another panelist's impressions of Tonsor's talk, see Paul Gottfried, "Remembering a Crucial Battle in the 'Conservative Wars,'" *The Imaginative Conservative* (December 26, 2016), https://theimaginativeconservative.org/2016/12/remembering-the-conservative-wars-paul-gottfried.html. See also Gottfried's interpretation of neoconservatism in *The Conservative Movement*, rev. ed. (New York: Twayne, 1993). For contemporary reporting on Tonsor's speech and the dustup it caused, see Jeffrey Hart, "Gang Warfare in Chicago," *National Review* 38, no. 10 (June 6, 1986), 32–33; and John B. Judis, "The Conservative Wars," *New Republic*, August 11–18, 1986, 15–16. For the toxic charge of antisemitism in Tonsor's attack on the neoconservatives, see David Frum, "The Conservative Bully Boy," *American Spectator* 24, no. 7 (July 1991), 12.

5. Authors of various studies have offered context to Tonsor's 1986 speech to the Philadelphia Society. See, for example, J. David Hoeveler Jr.,

"Conservative Intellectuals and the Reagan Ascendency," *History Teacher* 23, no. 3 (May 1990): 305–318; and Benjamin Ginsberg, *The Fatal Embrace: Jews and the State* (Chicago: University of Chicago Press, 1993), 233.

6. For more on fusionism, see George H. Nash, *The Conservative Intellectual Movement in America since 1945*, 2nd ed. (Wilmington, DE: ISI Books, 2006), 173–187.

7. Cf. Russell Kirk, *The Roots of American Order*, foreword by Forrest McDonald (Wilmington, DE: ISI Books, 2002). Tonsor in several of his essays and talks, including "Why I Too Am Not a Neoconservative," acknowledges a great intellectual debt to Kirk that went back to 1953 or 1954.

8. Caroline Tonsor occasional interviews with author, Chelsea, MI, July 2014–August 2018; and Stephen J. Tonsor, "Why I Am a Conservative," *Modern Age* 49, no. 3 (Summer 2007).

9. Tonsor's papers, in the Hoover Institution Archives, contain a fascinating, if angry, letter exchange between Tonsor and Werner Dannhauser. The exchange rolled out between April and June 1986 in response to Tonsor's Philadelphia Society speech. In the exchange, Tonsor indicted the neoconservative Dannhauser, a scholar of Nietzsche, for not being faithful to Yahweh and thus not being Jewish enough.

10. Tonsor used this line or some slight variation of it repeatedly when I worked with him in the 1980s. See also the formulation in his essay, "The Haunted House of the Human Spirit," *Modern Age* 29, no. 4 (Fall 1985): 292.

11. See, for example, John L. Kelley, *Bringing the Market Back In: The Political Revitalization of Market Liberalism* (London: Macmillan, 1997), 188–189.

12. A number of Tonsor's best essays are collected in *Equality, Decadence, and Modernity: The Collected Essays of Stephen J. Tonsor*, ed. Gregory L. Schneider (Wilmington, DE: ISI Books, 2005). Tonsor's earlier essays are collected in *Tradition and Reform in Education* (La Salle, IL: Open Court, 1974).

13. For some of Tonsor's most powerful prose on the value of humane letters, see Tonsor, "Haunted House," 292.

14. Caroline Tonsor interviews with author. For more descriptions of these special times with the Tonsors, see Gleaves Whitney, History Gadfly blog, starting with "Tonsor #8—1505 Morton Ave.," September 19, 2016, http://gleaveswhitney.blogspot.com/2016/09/tonsor-4-part-4-1505-morton-ave.html.

15. Stephen J. Tonsor, "The Conservative Search for Identity," in *What Is Conservatism?*, updated ed., ed. Frank S. Meyer, (Wilmington, DE: ISI Books, 2015), para. 2.

16. Tonsor, "Why I Am a Conservative."

17. Stephen J. Tonsor, "The Drift to Starboard," *Modern Age* 13, no. 3 (Summer 1969): 330. It was not just Tonsor who was trying to figure out a way to understand common ground. Meyer's "Fusion" and Tonsor's "organic reconciliation of opposites" are different ways of describing the same paradigm. Many postwar conservatives wanted to express the paradigm using their own terms. Russell Kirk, in *The Conservative Mind*, rev. ed. (Washington, DC: Regnery Publishing, 1985), 185 ff, speaks oxymoronically about "liberal conservatives" such as Tocqueville. What Tonsor called the "organic reconciliation of opposites" was his putting his scent on Meyer's and Kirk's earlier expressions of the paradigm.

18. Tonsor, "Conservative Search for Identity," first paragraphs.

19. Stephen Tonsor, "History and the God of the Second Chance," *Modern Age* (Spring 1958): 199–201.

20. Tonsor, "Conservative Search for Identity," para. 3.

21. Stephen J. Tonsor, "Why I Am a Republican and a Conservative," in *Equality*, 235.

22. To hear Tonsor's speech, "The Church-Related College," delivered at Augsburg University on October 15, 1969, go to www.youtube.com /watch?v=N-PQ7DlHVUk.

23. Tonsor, "Church-Related College."

24. Stephen J. Tonsor, remarks to the National Association of Manufacturers, Orlando, FL, April 1969. Draft manuscript copy in the Stephen J. Tonsor papers, Blackburn College Archives, Carlinville, IL.

25. Stephen J. Tonsor, foreword, in John Emerich Edward Dalberg-Acton *Lectures on the French Revolution* (Indianapolis: Liberty Fund, 2000), Kindle ed., loc. 47.

26. Said by Tonsor to author, office hours, 1988.

27. Stephen J. Tonsor, "Ignaz von Döllinger: A Study in Catholic Historicism," (PhD dissertation, University of Illinois, 1955), chapter 1; Stephen J. Tonsor, "Ignaz von Döllinger: Lord Acton's Mentor," *Anglican Theological Review* 41, no. 2 (1959): 211–215; Stephen J. Tonsor, "Lord Acton on Döllinger's Historical Theology," *Journal of the History of Ideas* 20, no. 3 (1959): 329–352.

28. Tonsor, "Why I Am a Republican and a Conservative," 235.

29. Ann Tonsor Zeddies occasional interviews with author, Grand Rapids, MI, 2014–2018.

30. Bernard Tonsor interviews with author, Jerseyville, IL, July 1, 2014, and June 27, 2015.

31. Bernard Tonsor interviews with author.

32. Stephen J. Tonsor to Joseph A. Amato, 2001, in the Amato Papers, University of Minnesota Archives.

33. Caroline Tonsor interviews with author; Joseph A. Amato interviews with author, Grand Rapids, MI, April 30–May 1, 2015; Mary Jean Jarvis interviews with author, Jacksonville, IL, June–July 2015; Tonsor to Amato, Amato Papers, University of Minnesota Archives.

34. Bernard Tonsor interviews with author.

35. Tonsor, "Why I Am a Conservative"; Caroline Tonsor interviews with author.

36. Ann Tonsor Zeddies interviews with author.

37. I am in possession of hundreds of pages of Stephen Tonsor's letters to Henry Regnery from the 1970s to the mid-1990s, thanks to the generosity of Henry's son, Alfred Regnery.

CHAPTER 19

The Rise and Demise of Rural and Regional Studies at Southwest Minnesota State University, 1977–2010

David Pichaske and Emily Williamson

Southwest Minnesota State University (SMSU) was established as South-west Minnesota State College in 1966, part of a surge of new institutions built to serve baby boomers. Some early years saw total enrollments of more than 3,000 students, but by 1977, enrollment had dropped to 1,522.[1] At that time, in an effort to rejuvenate the institution, new president Jon Wefald—former state commissioner of agriculture—proposed a program in rural and regional studies, based on "urban studies" programs popular elsewhere, "to make [SMSU] into a school that people in south-western Minnesota would want to send their children to."[2] Minnesota Governor Rudy Perpich supported the program, noting, "There is pride in rural Minnesota, where a program of rural studies at Southwest will make it an even stronger regional university."[3]

The college described Wefald's Rural and Regional Studies Program (commonly referred to as simply rural studies) as one that would provide "students with opportunities to study, understand, and appreciate our rural heritage and to seek ways to improve contemporary rural life." The program defined "rural" places as those with "direct economic dependence on the resources of the land; an immediate relation between society and the natural environment; a low population density; and smaller and more closely knit human communities."[4] Though the program's focus was not limited to the region, the definition could easily have been describing southwestern Minnesota. This was not a program in agriculture or creative writing like those mentioned by President Wefald in a memo to faculty on January 15, 1980, reviewing faculty experiences in such programs as the Prairie Writing Program at Moorhead State and Great River Writing at Winona State.[5] In a memo from April 17, 1981, program director Alec Bond described the Rural and Regional Studies Program as "unique, so far as I have been able to discover, in that it is a liberal arts and interdisciplinary approach to rural values, themes, ideas. The faculty has resisted, I gather from discussions with them, attempts to 'agrify' the program or turn it toward a more rural sociology program, of which there are many throughout the United States. . . . No one in the administration or faculty has pointed me toward a similar program antedating ours."[6] On the other hand, the program's next director, Joseph Amato, in a 1982 interview with the student newspaper, noted a "convergence between what we call the new history and rural studies. New history deals with the less than official people who didn't turn up on the pages of the old books. It's the underside of history."[7]

Wefald's rural agenda did not erase an increasingly global consciousness at the university that had produced, for example, campus seminars on nuclear power and the 1979 Iran hostage crisis, an International Students Organization, and dorms named House of Buckingham, Camaraderie, Kamasutra, and Aquarius; but at least some people at the college prided themselves on being part of "A College in the Cornfield" or "The College on the Prairie." A father writing in the 1979 student newspaper stated that his son "off in the boonies" claimed to enjoy life in "Camp Rural Studies."[8]

The program prospered in the late twentieth century, survived into the early twenty-first century, faded around 2005, and disappeared entirely in 2011, the victim of several converging events, including a national shift of emphasis in academia from local to global and diverse;[9] a Minnesota Transfer Curriculum imposed on all state institutions, which promoted the global and the diverse but found no room for the rural and the regional; population shifts from the countryside to cities; and internal politics. The history of rural and regional studies at SMSU mirrors the shifting focus of intellectual activity across America in the late twentieth century. That

intellectual history impacted students taking classes to meet general education graduation requirements; those admittedly few students who chose
to minor in rural studies (the program never developed a major); faculty
in the classes they taught, the research they pursued, and the conferences
they attended; the still-extant Society for the Study of Local and Regional
History; and several published books and pamphlets.

In April 1980, the State University Board approved a twenty-eight-hour,
seven-class minor for the program, but until 1999, all faculty, including
the program director, were officially housed in other departments, and
the rural studies minor simply required that students take courses in those
departments plus a study or seminar taught by the program director. The
program's real population base came from a university requirement that all
SMSU students take classes in rural studies. All students took Introduction
to Rural Studies taught by instructors in the social science department,
then selected eight additional hours (two courses) from other disciplines,
including physical education, biology, history, and English. These rural
studies requirements were separate from the university's general studies
requirements, but many courses fulfilled both general and rural studies
requirements. Inevitably, then, the 200-level Literature course, invented in
1978 as a parallel to Literature & Humanities and designed for students who
wished to count the course toward both general and rural studies, replaced
the 100-level Literature class in course offerings. In other departments,
rural studies courses that "double counted" quickly expanded as faculty
saw a golden opportunity to increase department enrollments and thereby
secure their positions—courses such as The History of Minnesota (history)
and American Folklore (taught by folklorist Alec Bond in the English
department, who was researching vestiges of Belgian folklore in the
nearby town of Ghent, Minnesota, at the time).[10]

By 1982, a rural studies committee was meeting monthly, and with
the help of historian Thaddeus Radzilowski, a Regional History Center—
funded in part by the National Endowment for the Humanities (NEH)
and the Minnesota Resources Commission—had been set up on the fifth
floor of the library. A high-profile, three-room Center for Rural and Regional Studies opened in 1987, absorbing a Southwest Minnesota Regional
Research Center dating back to 1972. This was a joint venture between
the Minnesota Historical Society and members of the college's history

department. Starting in 1990, the center housed the Society for the Study of Local and Regional History, which published books and, as pamphlets, the senior research projects of rural studies minors. The center also hosted conferences and, for a time, offered grants to faculty proposing projects in rural studies and projects for aiding elementary and secondary teachers developing local and regional curricula.

As the Rural and Regional Studies Program prospered, it added personnel, including a dean in 1999. Its budget rose irregularly, although direct costs to the university are impossible to track, as the program received numerous grants from sources credited in the 2000–2002 college catalog, including the Otto Bremer Foundation, the Gunlogson Regional Research Fund, the Minnesota Humanities Commission, the US Department of Agriculture, and even the NEH.[11] After Amato retired as dean of the program in 2003, budgets dropped measurably (by $1,100 in 2007) and then disappeared as the program was incorporated into the geography department in 2011.

In its glory days, the program set a standard of excellence that attracted considerable attention and support. As early as May 4, 1981, the First Bank System announced a grant to the university "to bring to the campus and to the region outstanding performers and lecturers that would focus on a central theme highlighting aspects of America's rural heritage," which ended up including Gregg Campbell on Food Control and Modern Agriculture, Larry Remele on The Changing Image of the American Farmer, and 1972 graduate Annette Atkins on Refuge from the Asylum (the poor in nineteenth-century Martin County).[12] From the late 1980s to the early 2000s, the program held conferences on many rural and regional themes, including one in 1995 focused on the floods of 1993, a topic spun out of a book edited by Joe Amato and Janet Timmerman, *At the Headwaters*; one on New Immigrants of Southwest Minnesota in 1996; one on Business and Banking in the Countryside in 1998; one on Rethinking Home: A Case for Writing Local History in 2001, based on the book written by Amato; and The Rivers of History: the Minnesota and Mississippi Rivers in 2005.[13]

In addition, teaching and research being done within the program attracted financial support beginning in the program's early days. In 1980, the Bush Foundation gave the college $27,000.[14] A $12,500 1983 grant supported teleconferencing courses in rural-regional literature. In the 1984–1985 school year, the McKnight Foundation gave $44,000 to develop a cooperative network to bring rural studies to junior colleges in the Minnesota towns of Worthington, Canby, Jackson, Granite Falls, Morris, Willmar, and Pipestone. In 1985, on an NEH grant, members of the literature and history departments toured the region giving presentations (usually to small audiences) on rural history and literature as part of a two-year summer institute called Heritage of the Prairie. Another grant from 1985 underwrote correspondence classes in rural literature. Funds from the Bremer Foundation underwrote grants of $500 to $1,000 to faculty visiting sites and centers and attending conferences. In 1986, a Bush Foundation grant brought writers—including Paul Gruchow—to campus to conduct seminars for SMSU faculty, and a State Arts grant brought high school teachers to the university to focus on teaching rural and regional material in their curricula, including Illinois rural poet Dave Etter and Wisconsin rural writer Norbert Blei. For the 1989–1990 school year, the Rural Studies Center received a $224,108 grant from the NEH for the Heritage of the Prairie Institute. Ted Radzilowski, who designed the program and administered the grant, said it was the only rural studies grant ever funded by the NEH and that it was "prompted by the increasing demands from teachers in rural areas for classroom materials that reflect the experience of their students. Most texts and curriculum materials available for rural schools are prepared with an urban or suburban audience in mind, and they seriously neglect rural history, culture and literature." [15]

The English department contributed to the program's success by promoting rural authors and rural writing events. In 1977, the college hosted several writers with rural and regional connections, including William Kloefkorn, Joe and Nancy Paddock, and Robert Bly. Cornstock Readings (a parody of Woodstock) were held three or four times a year at the Silver Dollar Bar in Ghent. In 1986, Phil Dacey created a week-long Minnesota Writers' Festival, bringing to the campus nationally recognized celebrities and such rising stars as Linda Hasselstrom, Dave Etter, Leo Dangel, and Bill Holm. [16] During the festival, brown-bag lunches and picnics (not to mention informal late-evening sessions at the Silver Dollar Bar and a special session of Cornstock) connected the writers and their audiences in an uncommonly intimate setting. Mari Ann Grossman of the *St. Paul Pioneer Press-Dispatch* wrote, "It seems unlikely that such a stellar group of men and women of letters will ever be gathered in one place in the state again."[17] "I have never seen a group of people so happy to see one another," wrote Ted Kooser.[18] Another festival was held in 1989 (bringing in Senator Eugene McCarthy), with others following in 1992 and 1995.[19] In September 2000, a two-day mini-festival called Marshall Minifest was held.[20] Early festivals were cobbled together with grants from the Bush and Bremer Foundations, patrons such as Tom Sand, and just plain ingenuity, but by 1998 the fifth incarnation of the week-long Minnesota Writers' Festival was so well known that the Minnesota State Arts Board handed the school $45,000 to host the fifth incarnation of the festival.[21]

Grant money also funded the program's publications. In 1999, the Center for Rural and Regional Studies received a three-year $85,000 grant from the Otto Bremer Foundation to support five doctoral or postdoctoral students who would research the area "and publish articles or books based on their findings."[22] Also, as late as 2001, the Bremer Foundation was underwriting a two-part project to hire journalist Nancy Torner "to write weekly columns about southwest Minnesota," which would be offered "free of charge to regional newspapers" and to create a webpage where others could post their region-related stories.[23] Over the three decades of the Rural and Regional Studies Program's existence, the Society for the Study of Local and Regional History's series of printed books exceeded thirty titles.

Grant funding also underwrote other presses connected to the region. SMSU's librarian Don Olson operated a letterpress called Ox Head Press at the university starting in the 1970s.[24] And in 1981, David Pichaske brought with him from Illinois two small presses, Spoon River Poetry Press and Ellis Press, which had been publishing rural authors for years. Additional grant funds fathered two additional presses: Crossings Press and Plains Press, which published Bill Holm's book on Minnesota, *The Music of Failure*; Gerritt Groen's *Bringing the Humanities to the Countryside*; David Nass's book on the farm holiday movement in Minnesota, *Holiday*; and David Allen Evans's book *Remembering the Soos*.[25] Crossings Press published in 2000 *Southwest Minnesota: The Land and the People*, a coffee table book of photos and selections from many significant writers who had written about the region (including Henry David Thoreau and Allen Ginsberg), and in 2007 *Southwest Minnesota: A Place of Many Places*. Crossings Press also published Joe Amato and John Meyer's *The Decline of Rural Minnesota* in 1994.[26]

The arc of the Rural and Regional Studies Program at SMSU can be tracked by Joseph Amato's transformation from history professor to program director (in 1996) to dean of rural and regional studies (in 1999). He described his grand scheme for a Center for Applied Rural and Regional Studies as "a grant-soliciting, book-producing and conference-developing unit" that would support "ongoing seminars, workshops, leadership development, publications and forums."[27] During this time, members of the administration proposed an International Center for Rural Literary Arts with its own building, a Regional Hall of Fame, annual rural writers festivals, outreach programs for grades K–12, summer workshops, a retreat facility, and a press doing publications, anthologies, and perhaps a journal. Amato realized his plan for a Center for Applied Rural and Regional Studies; the Center for Rural Literary Arts and the Regional Hall of Fame never got built.

Enrollments at SMSU grew right along with the Rural and Regional Studies Program. Thanks to President Wefald's rural program and his other efforts, enrollments increased from 1,522 in 1977 to 2,024 in 1980.[28] The expanding programming and growing student population continued through the presidencies of Robert Carothers (1983–1986) and Douglas Treadway (1987–1991). The college reached what was announced as an all-time enrollment high in 1999,[29] then increased another 13.2 percent in 2002.[30]

But this period of growth did not last. A non-rural/regional movement was gathering strength, even on the SMSU campus.[31] The summer Teachers Institute of 1990, sponsored by the National Rural Education Association, was organized around the theme of Rural Studies in a Global Society,[32] but ultimately rural studies did not fit the new national agenda focusing on globalization and diversity. In 1993, for example, the school received a grant from the State University System to fund not rural and regional projects, but global studies projects (this was possibly a result of the Minnesota State University System opening a campus in Akita, Japan, in 1990), aggressively promoted study-abroad programs, and began offering one or two global studies cluster trips every semester. The 1994–1996 university catalog reflected this shift in its subtitle: "A World of Difference." Some faculty who had been most involved in rural studies led global studies cluster trips to Poland and Italy and began writing about places far from Southwest Minnesota, such as David Pichaske's *Poland in Transition* (1994) and, years later, Joseph Amato's *My Three Sicilies* (2016). Gradually, interest in the diverse and the global expanded, while interest in the rural and the regional shrank.

In addition, in the late 1980s and early 1990s, the rural studies part of the school's general studies requirement came under attack. In 1978, the initial requirement had been twelve credit hours (the school year was divided into three ten-week terms, and classes were four credit hours). By 1985, the rural studies requirement was trimmed to eight of the sixty-eight general studies hours. With the change from three ten-week terms to two fifteen-week semesters in the 1996–1997 school year, the requirement changed to two three-hour classes. In 2002, the requirement dropped to one three-hour class. Finally, in 2005, it disappeared.

Another development contributed to the demise of rural studies: the Minnesota Transfer Curriculum (MTC) imposed on all state institutions in 1998 by the State University System (headquartered in St. Paul). In addition to meeting SMSU's liberal arts core requirements (forty-four semester hours), students needed to meet MTC requirements (fifteen hours could count for both requirements) as well as the rural studies requirement. The ten MTC areas of required study included earlier SMSU requirements plus critical thinking, human diversity, global perspective, civic and ethical responsibility, and people and the environment. Although inventive minds might have found a way for Rural Literature, for instance, to count as a course focusing on critical thinking skills or people and the environment, the unconscious urban bias of the MTC agenda did not leave much room for rural studies courses: studying rural places, even one's home, was not one of the MTC requirements.[33] The new focus on the global and the diverse provided an opportunity for new courses taught by new faculty, regardless of their connections to or affection for their location in southwestern Minnesota. As the Rural and Regional Studies Program had sired a string of courses in the 1980s designed to meet its requirements, the MTC requirements produced a rash of classes in the early 2000s designed to teach critical thinking, civic responsibility, and diversity, including but not limited to Politics of the Global Economy,

Diversity Management, the Literature of Human Diversity, Gender Issues, and Computers and Society.

For a time, the rural studies program survived. As recently as fall of 2004, the university offered five sections of Rural and Regional Literature, two sections of Rural Geography, and two sections of Rural World. But Dean Joseph Amato retired in 2003, and the new program head, his son Anthony Amato, focused rural studies, especially the minor, increasingly on geography. The changing agendas and changing administrations inevitably took their toll, and in 2005 the Rural and Regional Studies Center closed (the rooms became the Southwest Marketing Advisory Center/Southwest Business Development Center), and the center moved to a single room on the first floor of the building before disappearing entirely. Nonfaculty personnel working for the center were fired or reassigned. In an op-ed piece in the Marshall *Independent*, former information officer for the Center for Rural and Regional Studies Janet Timmerman wrote, "I was called in, about an hour after my direct supervisor was notified, and told my job was ended and I would be laid off as of July 1, 2005. . . . Two months later . . . another co-worker, Jan Louwagie, was removed from the Center." [34] On October 2, 2005, in another op-ed published in the Marshall *Independent*, six faculty members [35] responded to what they referred to as

> several misleading letters in the *Independent* during the last several months that would seem to support the Rural and Regional Studies Center (RRSC) at any cost to Southwest Minnesota State University (SMSU). These letters, including ones from Joe Amato and Geoff Cunfer [former dean of rural studies and director of the RRSC, respectively] may make it seem as if rural and regional studies at SMSU stand or fall with the fate of the RRSC. This is not true. . . . Rural and regional studies are an important part of the SMSU mission and of our general studies.

In 2010, the rural studies requirement disappeared entirely (study abroad was "encouraged" through the Global Studies and Common Market programs), and thus the courses designed to meet rural studies requirements disappeared and the program ended.

The focus of attention—nationally, in Minnesota, and at SMSU—had shifted, and both interest in and funding for rural studies waned. When the Sweetland Administration in 1997 proposed cutting the low-enrollment Indigenous Studies program, the faculty responded not with the charge that the school disesteemed the region but that SMSU "doesn't value diversity." "I find it strange that diversity isn't one of our 'basic values,'" wrote history professor Jeff Kolnickel.[36] Today, a focus on diversity prevails even without Indigenous studies, but since the diversity rubric does not recognize the ethnic heritages of the local southwest Minnesota populace—Norwegian, German, Polish, Icelandic, Belgian, Irish, and English—as diverse, the intellectual focus of southwest Minnesota has become not what the local population is, but what it is not. The Marshall festivals celebrating rural writers have ended. Marshall Festival 5, directed by a master of fine arts student with few rural connections, turned out to be a turning point for the festival, as it mixed well-known rural writers with new-agenda panel discussions on Postmodern Minnesota and Writers of Color and Ethnicity in Minnesota. Held in 2010, the festival was described by the director as "shorter" than previous festivals, and it featured less-prominent writers than those who had attended past festivals. Sadly, twelve people showed up for the closing day luncheon, where three hundred prepaid meals had been prepared. Today, the Rural and Regional Studies Program is gone, the Society for the Study of Local and Regional History publications series has ceased (though the society itself survives), and virtually all rural studies classes have either been cancelled or not offered due to anticipated low enrollments.

Enrollments at SMSU began to taper with the school's shift in focus from rural and regional to global and diverse.[37] A system-wide study in 2011 showed SMSU enrollments down 4.1 percent with a projected 5.5 percent drop for 2012.[38] An external study titled Higher Education Needs of Southwest Minnesota (done in 2011 by MGT of America, Inc., in Tallahassee, Florida) notes that "the recent curriculum mix has not consistently generated the enrollment levels needed to maintain targeted revenue goals and efficiencies";[39] enrollments have dropped steadily; the Akita campus closed some time ago; and global studies travel abroad destinations were reduced to Selma, Alabama, and New York City. However the global/diverse agenda prevails. Post hoc is not always propter hoc, but evidence suggests that SMSU's best years were concurrent with its prominent Rural and Regional Studies Program. The recent decline in enrollments—like the drop in the late 1970s—has been attributed to "national trends" beyond the university's control. The university might be wise, however, in deciding not to follow those national trends, which have not produced student interest and enrollments comparable to those produced by the Rural and Regional Studies Program. Resurrecting the program could, in the words of President Wefald, make SMSU into a school that people in southwestern Minnesota would want to attend.[40]

NOTES

1. Marshall *Independent*, January 13, 1977, 1.
2. SMSU student newspaper, the *Reader*, August 30, 1979, 7a. President Wefald himself was a guest instructor in a two-credit course, The Rural School, in spring 1978 (*Reader*, February 17, 1978).
3. *Reader*, November 6, 1978, 1.
4. *General Studies 1978–1979* booklet, SMSU McFarland Library, Striegel Archives. The program description in the 1983–1985 catalog reads, "The Rural Studies Program at SSU offers students an opportunity to study and appreciate their rural heritage and contemporary rural life; to gain insight into present and future rural problems and prospects for rural people; and to appreciate, cultivate, and revitalize rural values for the sake of future generations" (27).
5. Striegel Archives, "SUFA 9/1/1980–8/31/1981, March 11, 1981."
6. Striegel Archives, "Faculty Assembly 1980–81." The school at that time did offer a program in agribusiness management and now offers a degree in agribusiness management.
7. The SMSU *Statement*, May 14, 1982, 6.
8. *Reader*, September 14, 1979, 2. On November 9, 1979, the *Reader* reported, "The unique SSU rural history program gained national recognition last weekend when four SSU history professors presented a summary of the program to a gathering of the Social Sciences History Association at Cambridge, Mass," invited there by SMSU history graduate Annette Atkins (3). Throughout America there was at this time an interest in things rural, a response to the abstractions of urban postmodernism, reflected in songs such as "Country Roads" and "Goin' Up Country," which brought

to prominence writers such as Garrison Keillor, Robert Bly, Annie Dillard, Wendell Berry, and Edward Abbey. That national interest would continue through the 1980s and even the 1990s.

9. In this regard, academic thought has changed 180 degrees in the last four decades. The rationale for programs such as Afro-American studies and women's studies was always, "We have a substantial black population/ female population, and these students deserve to study their own culture. *Nosce te ipsum.*" Today we tell students they need to study "diverse" cultures to know what they are not.

10. The list of courses that could double-count to meet the twelve-hour rural requirement included Agribusiness Management 210, 475; Biology 180, 185, 190, 195; Earth Science 120; Education 230; Literature 200, 280, 336, 350, 360 (including Western American Literature and Writers of the Land); Music 170; nine classes in the physical education department (including Beginning Canoeing and Folk and Square Dancing); Economics 330; History 101, 295; Political Science 324; and Sociology 135, 435.

11. $3,075 for 1981–82; $6,700 for 1985–86; $7,300 for 1989–90; $8,050 in 1996; $9,430 for 2000; $9,930 for 2002; $7,800 for 2004 (Striegel Archives, "Budgets"). In a February 1, 2001, letter to the school newspaper, the *Impact*, history professor Jeff Kolnickel claimed the program's operating and research budget was costing the university $42,000, but he did not say how much of that was underwritten by grants.

12. Striegel Archives, Faculty Assembly file, May 4, 1981.

13. Dan Flores on "Bioregionalism," Molly Rozum on "Grasslands Grown," Jerry Perkins on "Regional Journalism: How Newspapers Make a Region," Gijs Schilthuis on "A Decade of New Agricultural Cooperatives in Minnesota: A Viable Solution," Bill Hoffman on "Electronic Connections: How Web Pages Can Make a Region," Susan Marie Green on "West Central Minnesota and New Chicano History," and Cedric Chatterley on "Spencer: A Town's Recovery from the 1998 Tornado," SMSU Digital Archives, November 1, 2000.

14. This and subsequent grant figures come from boxes 10, 22, and 37, Striegel Archives. These are not the only grants to the RRS program reported.

15. The program ran June 8 to July 14, 1989; the thirty teachers received a $1,500 stipend and $600 for expenses. The *Impact*, February 22, 1989, 14.

16. These included Wendell Berry, William Kloefkorn, Ted Kooser, Donald Hall, Jon Hassler, and Meridel LeSueur, and a host of Minnesota luminaries such as Carol and Robert Bly, Thomas McGrath, Fred Manfred, Roberta Hill Whiteman, and Jim Heynen.

17. Cited in the program for *Marshall Festival '05*, 5.

18. Ted Kooser, "Good Spirits Under the Comet's Tail: The Marshall Festival," *Coda*, November/December 1986, 27.

19. Speakers included Robert Bly, Carol Bly, Linda Hasselstrom, Bill Stafford, Bill Holm, Howard Mohr, Dave Etter, Norbert Blei, Paul Gruchow, Twyla Hansen, Robert Hedin, Jim Heynen, William Kloefkorn, Fred Manfred, Dan O'Brien, Kim Stafford, Mark Vinz, and scholars such as Ed Griffin, Agnieszka Salska, and Deb Wylder.

20. Even in non-festival years, the department hosted writers with rural and regional connections: William Kloefkorn in 1981, Robert Bly and Carolyn Forsche in 1983, Meridel LeSueur in 1984, Joan Colby in 1987, Linda Hasselstrom and Jim Heynen in 1988.

21. "SSU English Department Plans Marshall Festival V," *Focus*, Winter 1998, 3.

22. "Center for Rural and Regional Studies Receives $85,000 Otto Bremer Foundation Grant," September 14, 1999, MSU Digital Archives.

23. "Journalism Project Kicks Off at Southwest State," March 6, 2001, SMSU Digital Archives.

24. Olson used cold type and a letter press to publish broadsides, cards, and miniatures. His booklist included many notable authors, such as Robert Bly, Bill Holm, Ursula Le Guin, Joy Harjo, Phil Dacey, and Meridel LeSueur. In 2003, Norbert Blei's Cross+Roads Press published a book on Olson titled *A Butterfly Sleeps on the Temple Bell*.

25. Publication of *Holiday* coincided with a farmer's demonstration in St. Paul supporting legislation offering debt relief from the 1980 farm crisis. In advance of the demonstration (Southwest State President Robert Carothers was on the bus from Marshall to St. Paul, as were David Nass, Joe Amato, and David Pichaske), two hundred copies of the book had been sent to the capitol building to be placed in the mailboxes of all legislators as "a gift from the new press at Southwest State." The book was cited in speeches at the demonstration . . . and shortly after the demonstration, the legislation passed.

26. Plans for an anthology of *Tales from the Yellow Medicine River* (based on Illinois *Tales from Two Rivers*—new history in which old ones tell their stories) never produced a book.

27. *Impact*, March 25, 1999, 1.

28. *Reader*, April 1, 1980.

29. *Impact*, October 7, 1999.

30. *Impact*, October 10, 2002.

31. A 1983–1985 addition to the description of a program that placed "special emphasis on both the upper Great Plains and Southwest Minnesota" (catalog, 28) may have been written to defend the program against or perhaps accommodate the rising agenda of diversity and globalism, those trends that ultimately did the program in: "Rural life is not singular or homogenous," wrote program moguls Joseph Amato, David Nass, and Ted Radzilowski; "Diversity of typography, climate, class, culture, ethnicity, mode of production and stage of technology are distinguishing features of rural areas" (27). In a retrospective essay, Amato writes, "local historians can enrich their narratives of a singular and unique place by joining them to larger regional, national, and even global histories." Joseph Amato, "Local History a Way to Place and Home," in *Why Place Matters*, ed. Wilfred McClay and Ted McAllister (New York, Encounter Books, 2014), 217.

32. *Focus*, Spring 1990, 2.

33. Paradoxes apparent to even the most casual observer reveal the barely hidden agenda of the new requirements: studying women's literature and the psychology of women met the MTC's critical-thinking requirement, but studying American or British literature did not. Classes in gender issues, women's literature, and Native American literature met the diversity requirement, but rural society in pre-industrial times did not. The class in gender issues also met the global perspective requirement. The history class in early America met the civic and ethical responsibility requirement, but rural literature did not.

34. "SMSU's Handling of Center," Marshall *Independent*, September 1, 2005, 4A.

35. The authors were Stewart Day, Eric Markusen, Chris French, Chris Mato Nunpa, Steve Kramer, and Jack Hickerson. Joseph Amato and President Douglas Sweetland had invoked the wrath of Nunpa when the administration proposed cutting his American Indian & Dakota Studies

THE SOWER AND THE SEER

Program in 2001. "How can you propose expanding Rural & Regional Studies while cutting American Indian & Dakota Studies?" demanded a letter in the student newspaper (*Impact*, March 8, 2001). The real problem was that American Indians could attend University of Minnesota–Morris tuition-free (the campus had once been the Native American School), so virtually no American Indians attended Southwest.

36. *Impact*, October 2, 1997, 2.
37. Statistics are clouded by the rise of a College Now program that allowed high school students sitting in their high school classrooms and being taught by their high school teachers to count as college students, thereby adding those high school students to the university enrollment. Consequently, numbers increased as the halls emptied.
38. David Pichaske, "Papers," 2011.
39. Pichaske "Papers."
40. One blueprint for recovery might be Zachary Michael Jack's essay "History's Way Homeward: A Regionalist Approach to the Renovation of a Discipline," *Midwest Quarterly* 60, no. 1 (Fall 2018): 72–86.

CHAPTER 20

MIDWESTERN LITERATURE AND THE LITERARY CANON

Where, When, and How?

Sara Kosiba

Midwestern literature has been intertwined with American literature for as long as the region has been part of the development of
the United States; however, it has had a continually fraught presence in
the literary academy. Despite the efforts of prominent critics, publishers,
writers, and scholars to increase the recognition of Midwestern literature
as a distinct subject area, Midwestern literary study has found opposition
in many of the same powerful forces that work as gatekeepers to the literary canon for so many writers as well. To date, there is no comprehensive
book on the history of Midwestern literature that carries the examination
to the present day, although several contemporary scholars have done
strong work in broadening our understanding of particular genres or areas
within Midwestern literature (the Chicago Renaissance, the literary left,
individual author studies, the Revolt from the Village, etc.). There is also
a significant paucity of scholarship on the teaching of Midwestern literature, which is likely due to the almost nonexistent place Midwestern
literature, as a subject in its own right, has in educational curricula. This
chapter is far too short to take on the entire history of Midwestern literature in academia, but I explore some of the basics of what we do know
and how that information might shape our intentions in recognizing and

developing Midwestern literary study moving forward. If we truly want to "map the Midwestern mind," we need a more distinctive overview of the place Midwestern literature has held in American literary history and culture, particularly in how the subject has been represented in postsecondary education and how the region's literary contributions are still relevant in the present day and deserve a greater place in the academy.[1]

Delving into the politics of Midwestern literature and the literary canon involves situating some of that discussion within the evolving history of American literature and literary canon formation. English, as a formal discipline, gained status in postsecondary study in the late nineteenth century,[2] and American literature, as a subspecialty of broader literary scholarship, gained formal recognition several decades later. Elizabeth Renker notes that "published histories of the field typically cite the late 1920s as the turning point toward professionalization: the foundation of the American Literature Group of the Modern Language Association in 1921 was followed by the inauguration of professional journals (*The New England Quarterly* in 1928 and *American Literature* in 1929)." Renker also notes that published research and dissertations increased during that time.[3] As American literature gained ground in academic settings, questions of which authors to include in the canon were continually debated. Who were the American literary greats? The various answers to this question are often weighted with social and political baggage. Paul Lauter explains that traditionally,

> our choice of these texts is rooted in assumptions derived from the particular characteristics of our class, race, sex, reshaped to be sure by the powerful influence exerted—particularly those of us from "minority" or otherwise "marginal" origins—by the professors of the dominant culture. From this limited set of texts, this canon, we project standards of aesthetic excellence as well as the intellectual constructs we call literary history. And once we have developed such constructs, we view other works in their terms, whether the works originate from that initial "text milieux" or from outside it.[4]

The politics of the literary canon, and particularly the American literary canon, have been well documented in scholarship. The debates regarding greater representation of women and ethnic perspectives have been particularly important, and despite great gains in those areas, the discussion is far from over. I am not alone in arguing that regional bias also plays a significant role in canon formation.[5] Eric J. Sundquist has argued, in contrasting writers who receive the more widely valued "realist" as opposed to "regionalist" moniker, that "economic or political power can itself be seen to be definitive of a realist aesthetic, in that those in power (say, white urban males) have more often been judged 'realists,' while those removed from seats of power (say, Midwesterners, blacks, immigrants, or women) have been categorized as regionalists."[6] Many Midwestern writers and scholars spent their lives fighting either an internalized sense of regional inferiority encouraged by mainstream attitudes or explicit external hostility or bias to their regional location or identity.

As American literature as a whole was arguing for its place in literary studies,[7] it is not surprising that Midwestern literature did not have much of an early formal presence on college or university campuses, especially with a literary locus of power generally located on the East Coast of the United States in publishing hubs like New York or on long-established college campuses like Harvard and Yale. However, informal study of Midwestern literature was taking place throughout the country in such venues as women's clubs. Members of the Century Book Club met in Charlotte, North Carolina, in April 1908 to hear three papers on regional American literature: "Southern Literary Life and Letters," "Middle West Literature and Writers," and "Pacific Coast Literary Life and Letters."[8] A collection of similarly regionally oriented papers was presented at the women's club in Des Moines, Iowa, in February 1916.[9] The Shakespeare Department of the Billings, Montana, Women's Club had a program on "The Middle West in Fiction" in December 1921. The presentations focused on the work of Hamlin Garland, Theodore Dreiser, Zona Gale, and Sinclair Lewis, and there was a roundtable discussion of Lewis's *Main Street*.[10]

Two early twentieth-century literature professors were instrumental in founding Midwestern literature as a subject worthy of attention in college classrooms. John T. Frederick (1893–1975) was a formidable figure in the foundation of Midwestern literary studies. Frederick studied American literature while attending the University of Iowa and prior to graduation founded a little magazine called *The Midland* focused on regional writing. He built a career teaching at universities throughout the Midwest, including the University of Iowa, Northwestern, and Notre Dame. In an address at Kansas State Agriculture College in December 1924, Frederick focused on his preferred subject of "Literature in the Middle West" and

> opened his lecture with a discussion of regional literatures and with a defense of them. He pointed out the beginnings of middle western literature in the writings of Hamlin Garland, and classified middle western writers into two groups, according to the subject matter with which they deal. He placed such writers as Willa Cather and John Neihardt in the group which deals with the historical background of building the middle west, and classified Carl Sandburg, Edgar Lee Masters, and Sinclair Lewis with those who write of modern middle western life.[11]

While studies of Midwestern literature today can extend back to diaries of explorers who first traveled the region or to early histories preceding national or state distinctions, Frederick's comments give contemporary readers a sense of how Midwestern literature may have been defined in the early twentieth century to students and the public.[12]

In addition to teaching and presenting in public venues, Frederick's position as editor of *The Midland* would also be influential in shaping public perceptions of Midwestern literature. That early little magazine would last an impressive eighteen years, spanning 1915 to 1933. The first issue declared that the journal was "a modest attempt to encourage the making of literature in the Middle West," although the magazine's regional perspective would become broader over the years.[13] Milton M. Reigleman notes that, within the magazine, the "comments about literature from other regions reflected [the editors'] desire to make those other regions better known to Midwesterners."[14] Many familiar literary names from the early twentieth century appeared in its pages, among them Sanora Babb, Cleanth Brooks, Paul Corey, Paul Engle, James T. Farrell, William March, John G. Neihardt, Ruth Suckow, and Mark Van Doren.[15] Frederick J. Hoffman, Charles Allen, and Carolyn F. Ulrich, in their mid-twentieth-century analysis *The Little Magazines*, noted,

Because of its contribution to the development of regionalism, *The Midland* must be ranked alongside *The Dial*, *The Little Review*, and *Poetry*. It was a magazine that discovered and helped many young authors. It published a great volume of excellent fiction. Of the 337 *Midland* stories that came to Edward O'Brien's notice [editor of the annual *Best American Short Stories* collection], 324 were judged of high merit, 105 of them being of such distinction that he gave them his highest rating. Few magazines can boast such a high percentage of excellent stories.[16]

Frederick was a strong advocate for literature from the Midwest through his work on *The Midland*, his own literary production, and his work anthologizing Midwestern writers.[17] The body of work that he participated in and produced provides one of the strongest foundations for early twentieth-century Midwestern literary study.

The second prominent name in early Midwestern literary studies was John T. Flanagan (1906–1996). In his essay "A Specialist Before My Time," Flanagan reflected on his studies in American literature as a graduate student at the University of Minnesota and his eventual interest in Midwestern literature. He noted that in addition to his teaching at the University of Minnesota and the University of Illinois, he "taught courses in middle western literature at both Indiana University and Southern Methodist University." His scholarly credentials also included "two Fulbright lectureships in France and Belgium," where he spoke about Midwestern writers, and Flanagan noted that he "directed doctoral dissertations on figures such as Sinclair Lewis, O. E. Rølvaag, Vachel Lindsay, Edgar Lee Masters, Ruth Suckow, Sherwood Anderson, Ernest Hemingway, and Mark Twain."[18]

While Flanagan, like Frederick, also edited an anthology of Midwestern writing among other scholarly books,[19] his greatest contributions to the intellectual history of Midwestern literature are the many scholarly articles he wrote exploring various aspects of Midwestern literary history. Flanagan said that one of his early influences in studying Midwestern writing was Ralph Leslie Rusk's two-volume collection *The Literature of the Middle Western Frontier* (1925) and that he once hoped to pick up where Rusk's history left off.[20] While he never accomplished a project of that scope, Flanagan's overviews of "The Middle West Farm Novel" and "The

Middle Western Historical Novel" are valuable for even contemporary scholars, as they provide comprehensive surveys of pre-1940 Midwestern literature in those categories.[21] In the 1950s, he authored a few articles contributing to a sense of Midwestern literary history. In "A Soil for the Seeds of Literature" and "A Half-Century of Middlewestern Fiction," Flanagan brought Midwestern literary history into the twentieth century by building off of the historical work of scholars he admired, like Rusk and Dorothy Dondore, and incorporating contemporary authors and perspectives.[22]

Despite the efforts of these two men and many others,[23] Midwestern literature never achieved firm standing in academia. Barbs and parodies suggesting Midwestern cultural blandness contributed to some of the region's marginalization. In 1925, Harold Ross, cofounder and editor-in-chief of *The New Yorker*, would distinguish the audience for his magazine by stating that it was "not edited for the old lady in Dubuque."[24] In 1929, *Vanity Fair* would parody the best short story of the year awards and note "The Gloomy Mid-West Story." Its protagonist, Minnie Timkins, spent her time staring "out the window across the desolate prairie, drab and flat and hopeless" and eventually she "broke her own arm at the elbow, just to hear it snap," with the implication that it would break the monotony of her life.[25] These stereotypes of the Midwest continue today in the idea that the region remains a place to "fly over" and not stop. Scholars over the years have also tended toward privileging regional literature from places like the South over that of the Midwest. In 1939, Tremaine McDowell asserted that "The Middle West, endowed with no glamorous tradition comparable to that of the South, has capitulated more frequently to the metropolis."[26] Southern literature, focused significantly on exploring pre– and post–Civil War conceptions of southern culture, gained a larger and more distinctive audience in the twentieth century. Much of that attention was encouraged by individuals like the Southern or Nashville Agrarians, a group of writers and scholars, including John Crowe Ransom, Donald Davidson, and Allen Tate, who used their platforms at major universities to argue for the significance of southern literature and culture.[27] Their influence in defining regional literature extends well into the late twentieth and early twenty-first centuries. For example, while Ronald Weber noted at the end of *The Midwestern Ascendancy in American Writing* (1992) that there is some promise in the future of Midwestern writing, he contributed to the continued marginalization of the region's literature by stating that the early-twentieth-century ascendancy he describes did not "run particularly deep" and that the region lacks "novelists of towering stature" (using William Faulkner as one example) and lacks a "gathering of critical thinkers the match of the Nashville Agrarians or ambitious cultural journalists the equal of W. J. Cash."[28]

The difficulty in pinning down a clear definition of Midwestern literature often lies in the perpetual ignorance of so many to the region's history and culture. In the twenty-first century, there are still too many questions about what counts as Midwestern literature or whether there is anything particularly distinctive or cohesive in literature emanating from the Midwest. For example, David Pichaske, in his article "Where Now 'Midwestern Literature'?" (2006), argues for a Midwest style of writing, one incorporating "realism bordering on naturalism, with elements of humanism and social critique. Plain, colloquial speech, with elements of self-conscious doubt. Guarded experimentation. Limited theory," but he questions whether contemporary writers are still using that Midwest style or if they have been corrupted by a modern sense of placelessness.[29] In 2014, Anna Clark explored the question "What Is the Midwestern Literary Tradition?" in the *Chicago Tribune*, compiling reflections from nine individuals, including professors, authors, publishers, and people knowledgeable about books. The contributors all highlight the difficulty in pinning down an exact definition of a place with so many characteristics.[30] The region is rural, urban, universal, distinct, and diverse. It is, essentially, amorphous and hard to elucidate, according to these voices.

Scholarship about the Midwest continues to share similar challenges. The irony is that the difficulty cited by many in defining the Midwest is still present in other regional literatures, such as southern literature, but it tends to be less confounding there than it is in Midwestern literary scholarship. Southern literature has had a much more cohesive sense of disciplinary identity than Midwestern literature despite combating the same pressures of oversimplification and the negotiation of a similar diversity of perspectives. Barbara Ladd noted the challenge of southern literature's complex perspectives while also recognizing the increased academic legitimacy of the subject within university environments in the 1950s and continuing today.[31] If a more prominent presence for southern literature helped to better codify its presence in academia, what might happen if Midwestern literature were also granted some of that more prominently visible territory?

The Society for the Study of Midwestern Literature (SSML), founded in 1971 by David D. Anderson, Russel B. Nye, C. Merton Babcock, Bernard Duffey, William Thomas, Robert B. Hubach, and William B. McCann, has worked to build more academic legitimacy for Midwestern writing. The founding principle of SSML was to "encourage and assist the study of [Midwestern] literature in whatever direction the insight, imagination, and curiosity of the members may lead," and that mission is still a core component of the organization's philosophy today.[32] SSML publishes two scholarly journals, *MidAmerica* and *Midwestern Miscellany*, dedicated to the exploration of Midwestern literary texts and topics, and the society was instrumental in sponsoring volumes one and two of the reference work *Dictionary of Midwestern Literature* (2001; 2016). The society holds an annual conference and sponsors paper sessions at other major national conferences, such as at the Modern Language Association (MLA) conference. SSML also presents the MidAmerica Award to recognize outstanding contributions to Midwestern literary study and the Mark Twain Award to recognize distinguished contributions to Midwestern literature. It is fitting that the first MidAmerica Award was presented to John T. Flanagan in 1977.[33]

In terms of placement within universities, however, Midwestern literature has never had the formal presence southern literature often enjoys. In a brief survey of the twelve largest state universities in the Midwest, one university per Midwestern state, Midwestern literature does not appear in any of the current course offerings or in any of the course catalogs. Only four universities within the twelve offer general courses on regional American literature, and one university (Michigan State) offers a course in state writers. While Midwestern literature could still have a presence within these universities as a special topics course or under another designation, it has no formal legitimacy as part of a literary curriculum. In contrast, of the sixteen largest state universities in the South, highlighting one major state university per southern state (using the US Census definition for the South), nine of the sixteen universities either currently offer a course in southern literature or have one listed in their course catalog (around 56 percent). Five of those universities offer a course in some kind of regional literature, and seven of the sixteen offer a course in state literature. While this is just a small sampling, the South clearly eclipses the Midwest in terms of literary legitimacy at the collegiate level.[34]

A more thorough survey, however, suggests that Midwestern literature does have a presence in some Midwestern college and university settings. In April 2018, I conducted an email survey of English department chairs and curricular heads at 158 postsecondary institutions, among them public, private, and two-year institutions, throughout the Midwest. I asked whether Midwestern literature had a place in the curricular offerings.[35] The return rate on my survey was not large (15 percent), but it did provide a sense of the few places in the Midwest where Midwestern literature or the literature of Midwestern states may have a presence. Six of twenty-four responses noted that the institutions were either currently offering Midwestern literature on a periodic basis (often as a special topic course) or had taught it as a subject in the past.[36] One school, Upper Iowa University, noted that Midwestern literature has been taught as part of the course curricula since 1983. Three schools claimed to be either currently teaching a state literature or having taught a course in state literature in the past.[37] While the University of Nebraska does not offer a course specifically in Midwestern literature, its course offerings Willa Cather and Her World and Plains Literature highlight Nebraska and its surrounding territory, even if not invoking the state name. Hastings College, also in Nebraska, has similar course offerings, with a course in Great Plains Literature and one in Regional Modernisms. Four colleges or universities currently offer or have offered courses in literature from the western United States, and five have offered or currently offer courses in literature of the American South.[38] While not comprehensive, the sampling does show that Midwestern literature has a presence in some academic corners of the Midwest, although it clearly lacks the same widespread presence within its own region as southern literature has within the South.

Shortly after receiving the MidAmerica Award in 1977, John T. Flanagan wrote, "It is pleasant to know that regional literature no longer needs an apology and that specialists in the writing from and about the Middle West now occupy a respectable place in academia."[39] While scholars are still pursuing inquiry into Midwestern writers and literary topics, there is still a gap in collective knowledge and awareness of what Midwestern literature is and what it can teach us. One source of that knowledge gap is clearly the diminished place Midwestern literature has within the literary academy. Midwestern writers make appearances in contemporary literary classrooms as part of a larger focus on overall American writers; however, they are rarely featured as Midwestern writers.[40] SSML is also working hard to keep Midwestern literature alive in scholarly circles, but it is clear that more needs to be done. In recent decades, for example, the MLA has hosted a discussion forum on the southern United States (the only regional forum the organization sponsors) and has focused on developments in southern studies in its flagship journal, *PMLA*. While MLA recognizes SSML as an allied organization, SSML has provided no similar focus or opportunity for Midwestern studies.[41]

In many ways, it is not surprising that writers, scholars, critics, and even the general public cannot find firm footing in defining a literary Midwest, as we have done so little to formalize it as a field of study within the academy or to provide ample opportunity for the discussions necessary to build a better understanding of what that subject should entail. It is impractical and unrealistic to expect all institutions to embrace Midwestern literary study, particularly when American higher education is facing so many financial and strategic concerns, but it is also surprising that so few colleges or universities in the Midwest have focused on exploring local historical and cultural contributions as part of providing a comprehensive education. While there are exceptions, such as the University of Nebraska's Center for Great Plains Study and courses in Great Plains literature, and promising new initiatives focused on the Midwest or Midwestern states,[42] there is still substantial room to grow. It would be nice to see similar focus applied to formalizing a comprehensive Center for Midwestern Studies[43] or providing a similar academic platform by which Midwestern literature, history, politics, and culture could be explored.

This overview of Midwestern literature's place within the literary canon is far from comprehensive, particularly due to the limitations of what can be covered in a single chapter, but my hope is that it draws attention to some of the necessary discussions we need to have as we explore the significance of the Midwestern mind and the place of Midwestern culture. While Midwestern writers have often been recognized as part of an overall American literary identity, we need to dedicate more time to understanding their contributions to a regional literary discourse, one that helps us to better understand the rich intricacies of place amidst the broad diversity that is American literature and culture.

NOTES

1. It is worth noting that my argument is resonant with Jon K. Lauck's recent overviews of the place of Midwestern history in the academy, which he explores in *The Lost Region: Toward a Revival of Midwestern History* (Iowa City: University of Iowa Press, 2013) and *From Warm Center to Ragged Edge: The Erosion of Midwestern Literary and Historical Regionalism, 1920–1965* (Iowa City: University of Iowa Press, 2017).

2. For example, the Modern Language Association, one of the long-standing academic organizations supporting the study of language and literature, was founded in 1883. "About the MLA," Modern Language Association, www.mla.org/About-Us/About-the-MLA.

3. Elizabeth Renker, *The Origins of American Literature Studies* (Cambridge: Cambridge University Press, 2007).

4. Paul Lauter, "History and the Canon," *Social Text* 12 (1985): 95.

5. Scholars have explored the intersections of gender and race with region and the effect that has on marginalization, such as in Marjorie Pryse and Judith Fetterley, *Writing Out of Place: Regionalism, Women, and American Literary Culture* (Urbana: University of Illinois Press, 2003).

6. Eric J. Sundquist, "Realism and Regionalism," in *Columbia Literary History of the United States*, ed. Emory Elliott (New York: Columbia University Press, 1988), 503.

7. Jay B. Hubbell, in his foreword to the first issue of *American Literature*, noted some of this debate, commenting that "until recent years our scholars were slow to study the national letters or their relation to European literatures and to American life and thought." *American Literature* 1, no. 1 (1929): 2.

8. "In the Realm of North Carolina Society: Monroe," *Charlotte [NC] Daily Observer*, April 26, 1908.

9. "Club Calendar for the Week," *Des Moines [IA] Register and Leader*, February 13, 1916.

10. "Yuletide Work of Club to Be Meeting Topic," *Billings [MT] Gazette*, December 4, 1921.

11. "Midwest Great Theme," *Kansas Industrialist* (Manhattan, KS), December 10, 1924, 1.

12. Edward Watts, *An American Colony: Regionalism and the Roots of Midwestern Culture* (Athens: Ohio University Press, 2002), provides a strong overview of Midwestern culture during its territorial phase prior to being parceled into states.

13. "The First Person Plural," *The Midland* 1, no. 1 (1915): 1.

14. Milton M. Reigelman, *The Midland: A Venture in Literary Regionalism*, (Iowa City: University of Iowa Press, 1975): 72.

15. Reigelman, *The Midland*, 72.

16. Frederick J. Hoffmann, Charles Allen, and Carolyn F. Ulrich, *The Little Magazines: A History and Bibliography* (Princeton, NJ: Princeton University Press, 1946).

17. Frederick's fictional contributions include the novels *Druida* (New York: A.A. Knopf, 1923) and *Green Bush* (New York: A. A. Knopf, 1925). Early anthologies edited by Frederick include *Stories from the Midland* (New York: A.A. Knopf, 1924), which included early work by Ruth Suckow, and *Out of the Midwest: A Collection of Present-Day Writing* (New York: McGraw-Hill, 1944) containing urban- and rural-focused works from throughout the region.

18. John T. Flanagan, "A Specialist Before My Time," *Minnesota History* 46, no. 1 (Spring 1978): 23.

19. John T. Flanagan, ed., *America Is West: An Anthology of Middle Western Life and Literature* (Minneapolis: University of Minnesota Press, 1945).

20. Ralph Leslie Rusk, *The Literature of the Middle Western Frontier*, 2 vol. (New York: Columbia University Press, 1925; New York: Frederick Ungar Publishing, 1962); Flanagan, "A Specialist," 21.

21. John T. Flanagan, "The Middle Western Farm Novel," *Minnesota History* 23, no. 2 (1942): 113–123; John T. Flanagan, "The Middle Western Historical Novel," *Journal of the Illinois State Historical Society* 37, no. 1 (1944): 7–47.

22. John T. Flanagan, "A Soil for the Seeds of Literature," *The Heritage of the Middle West*, ed. John J. Murray (Norman: University of Oklahoma Press, 1958); John T. Flanagan, "A Half-Century of Middle-Western Fiction," *Critique* 2, no. 3 (1959): 16–34; Dorothy Anne Dondore, *The Prairie and the Making of Middle America: Four Centuries of Description* (Cedar Rapids, IA: Torch Press, 1926).

23. I feel remiss in not including a section on Walter Havighurst (1901–1994) here, as he is another important figure in shaping early Midwestern literary perspectives, but there is not enough room in the scope of this chapter. Havighurst's substantial contributions include editing *Land of the Long Horizons* (New York: Coward-McCann, 1960), which collects historical and literary perspectives on the Midwest from its early exploration period to the mid-twentieth century.

24. Harold Ross, "Of All Things," *The New Yorker*, February 21, 1925, 2.

25. John Riddell, "J. Riddell Memorial Award Short Best Stories," *Vanity Fair*, April 1929, 95.

26. Tremaine McDowell, "Regionalism in American Literature," *Minnesota History* 20, no. 2 (1939): 114.

27. One of the key texts in defining the southern agrarian critical platform is *I'll Take My Stand: The South and the Agrarian Tradition* (New York: Harper, 1930).

28. Ronald Weber, *The Midwestern Ascendancy in American Writing* (Bloomington: Indiana University Press, 1992), 3–4.

29. David Pichaske, "Where Now 'Midwestern Literature'?," *Midwest Quarterly* 48, no. 1 (2006): 111.

30. Anna Clark, "What Is the Midwestern Literary Tradition?," *Chicago Tribune*, September 19, 2014, www.chicagotribune.com/lifestyles/books /ct-prj-rust-belt-midwestern-literature-20140919-story.html.

31. Barbara Ladd, "Literary Studies: The Southern United States, 2005," *PMLA* 120, no. 5 (2005): 1628–1639.

32. "Society for the Study of Midwestern Literature, The," *Dictionary of Midwestern Literature*, vol. 2, ed. Philip A. Greasley (Bloomington: Indiana University Press, 2016): 786.

33. "1970s MidAmerica Award," Society for the Study of Midwestern Literature, www.ssml.org/resources/awards/the-midamerica-award/70s _midamerica_award_recipients.

34. US census definitions were used to define the two regional areas. According to the US census, the Midwest consists of Ohio, Indiana, Michigan, Wisconsin, Illinois, Iowa, Nebraska, North Dakota, South Dakota, Missouri, and Kansas. The South consists of Delaware, Maryland, West Virginia, Virginia, Kentucky, Tennessee, North Carolina, South Carolina, Georgia, Florida, Mississippi, Alabama, Arkansas, Louisiana,

Oklahoma, and Texas. To gain a relative sense of size, universities were selected by searching *US News and World Report* data for greatest enrollment based on state (which I recognize is not perfectly definitive, as a university's self-reported data can be imperfect, but this was intended as a small initial sampling and not a full scientific study). This data was collected on November 23, 2018, using course catalogs and offerings listed on the university's own websites. In the Midwest, the four universities offering regional literature courses included Ohio State University (American Regional Cultures in Transition), Michigan State University (Methodologies of Literary History: Region, School, or Movement), South Dakota State University (Literature of the American West), and the University of Nebraska (Literature of Place, Willa Cather and Her World, Humanities on the Plains, and Plains Literature). Michigan State University offers a course in Michigan Literature. In the South, West Virginia University, Virginia Tech University, University of Tennessee, North Carolina State University, University of South Carolina, University of Central Florida, University of Mississippi, University of Arkansas, and Texas A&M University all have southern literature courses, although the titles can vary slightly. Five southern universities offer courses in some kind of regional American literature: West Virginia University (Literature of Place, Appalachian Fiction, and Topics in Appalachian Studies), Virginia Tech (Appalachian Literature), University of Kentucky (Literature Across Borders), Kennesaw State University (Regional Literature), and Texas A&M University (Life and Literature of the Southwest). Seven southern universities offer courses in their respective state literatures: University of Maryland–College Park, University of Kentucky, University of South Carolina, University of Central Florida, Louisiana State University–Baton Rouge, University of Oklahoma, and Texas A&M University.

35. My list was compiled of the top five public colleges or universities, top five private colleges or universities, or top five two-year colleges based on size (using *US News and World Report* enrollment data). Some states had fewer than five schools in those categories, and in those situations, I sent emails to all the schools I could find even if there were fewer than five. I could not find email addresses or clearly listed curricular coordinators for thirteen schools, most of them community colleges or other two-year schools. The 158 number reflects actual emails sent and not the omitted schools.

36. I define a "special topic" course as one that generally has a broad general distinction that can be tailored by the faculty member or department to fit a broad range of potential subjects. These are generally different from core or canonical course titles (survey courses, Shakespeare, African American literature, etc.) that often have particular distinction in a course catalog. The six colleges or universities that self-identified as currently teaching Midwestern literature or as having taught it in the past are the University of Michigan, the University of Wisconsin Colleges (since my survey, these colleges have been restructured and no longer share one common curriculum), Upper Iowa University, Maryville University, Dakota State University, and Western Michigan University.

37. University of Michigan, the University of Wisconsin Colleges, and Maryville University.

38. Colleges or universities that self-identified as currently teaching western American literature or having taught it in the past include the University of Michigan, the University of Dubuque, Maryville University, and Western Michigan University. Colleges or universities that self-identified as currently teaching southern American literature or having taught it in the past include the University of Michigan, Saint Louis University, Creighton University, Benedictine University, and Western Michigan University.

39. Flanagan, "A Specialist," 23.

40. For example, in the widely used *Norton Anthology of American Literature* (9th edition), a book used in many undergraduate literary survey courses, several canonical Midwestern writers make an appearance, from Edgar Lee Masters and Sherwood Anderson to Theodore Roethke and Gwendolyn Brooks.

41. Most recently, a *PMLA* section on "The Changing Profession" was titled "Adjust Your Maps: Manifestos From, For, or About United States Southern Studies" and contained eleven short pieces reflecting on various aspects of southern literature and culture *PMLA* 131, no. 1 (2016).

42. The Andrew W. Mellon foundation has provided funding for the Newberry Library's "What Is the Midwest?" initiative and also to Indiana University to explore Indiana studies. See "Newberry to Advance Public Humanities with $1 Million Mellon Grant," June 2015, www.newberry.org/newberry-advance-public-humanities-1-million-mellon-grant; and "IU Bloomington Receives $1 Million Grant to Support Research in Arts and Humanities,"

June 18, 2018, https://news.iu.edu/stories/2018/06/iub/releases/18-million-dollar-grant-to-support-research-in-arts-and-humanities.html.

43. A Center for Midwestern Studies does currently exist at the University of Missouri–Kansas City, but the focus of its programing is primarily limited to history and culture in the Kansas City area.

CHAPTER 21

THE STARS HAD BECOME *MY* STARS

Leslie C. Peltier, Starlight Nights, *and Amateur Astronomy*

Robert L. Dorman

I

"Astronomy has always occupied a surprisingly high place in the cultural life of Ohio," a statewide survey noted in 1946. The Cincinnati Observatory, dedicated in 1843, was one of the two oldest in the country. A major manufacturer of astronomical equipment, Warner & Swasey, had been operating in Cleveland since 1881. The world's third-largest telescope was installed at Perkins Observatory near the Ohio town of Delaware in 1931. And Ohio was home to Leslie C. Peltier, the famous comet hunter who would go on to write a book beloved by generations of amateur and professional astronomers, *Starlight Nights: The Adventures of a Star-Gazer*.[1]

To characterize Peltier as a literary meteor risks mixing a metaphor. "Comet" best captures the arc of his writing career—a periodic comet, one that is known and long in coming, yet the final magnitude of which remains a surprise. Peltier published *Starlight Nights*, his first book, in his sixty-fifth year. He had already achieved substantial renown thanks to his astronomical discoveries. He had been writing short pieces for thirty years and lecturing around Ohio even longer. Though he had come to see himself as "fundamentally a writer," no one suspected that he had this book in him. Walter Scott Houston, the long-time columnist for *Sky & Telescope* magazine, declared that *Starlight Nights* had "the widest impact of any astronomy book" since the turn of the century.[2] It also won the Ohioana Book Award, because "the adventures of a stargazer" took place around Delphos, Ohio.

Comets made Leslie Peltier famous enough to believe that his life might constitute literary material. His fame—how his discoveries were presented to the public—suggested certain themes. A rural Midwestern birthplace helped; so too his status as a high school dropout. His self-made career, emerging out of modesty and obscurity, aligned neatly with regional and national myths, just as his birthday (January 2, 1900) ran in sync with the twentieth century. At age sixteen he bought a telescope. During World War I, he quit school to work on the family farm. He was fortunate in his parents, who personified the Ohio idyll—a farmer and a homemaker, two hands-off nurturers in a "family of readers" who gave Peltier room to roam, collect, and tinker.[3] He lived with his parents on their farm, where the observatory was, until he married at age thirty-three.

Peltier once denied that the title *Starlight Nights* had been "suggested by anyone or anything," yet he received detailed advice on every aspect of the book from his friend the nature writer Edwin Way Teale, who got him partway there: "The Starry Night (Or Under the Stars, or The Stars of the Night)." In any case, the phrase has some intriguing literary resonances. It appears in *The Prelude, or Growth of a Poet's Mind* by William Wordsworth, a preeminent regionalist with a passion for astronomy, who wrote of that "sublimer joy" felt when he would "walk alone . . . in starlight nights / Beneath the quiet Heavens." The affinity to Peltier's book runs deeper than this turn of phrase, in fact. *The Prelude*—also a memoir—depicts a young mind becoming integrated with a place, how "the earth / And common face of Nature spake to me / Rememberable things." Most strikingly, Wordsworth (like Peltier) extends the "common face of Nature," his local landscape, to include astronomical objects in the sky, as when he describes how the moon "hung / Midway between the hills, as if she knew / No other region; but belong'd to thee, / Yea, appertain'd by a peculiar right / To thee and thy grey huts, my darling Vale!"[4]

Another preeminent regionalist, Willa Cather, has the narrator of her novel *My Ántonia*, Jim Burden, look out on a rather different set of huts and recall when "on starlight nights I used to pace up and down those long, cold streets, scowling at the little, sleeping houses" where "the life that went on in them seemed to me made up of evasions and negations."[5] While Burden comes to cherish Black Hawk, Nebraska, from afar, Peltier—thanks to his comets—was able to find peace right at home, fulfilling his ambition in the wider world while remaining nestled in the local. If Jim Burden had stayed in Black Hawk, married Tony, skipped Harvard, opened a law office for a major railroad—and at retirement age, published *My Ántonia*—his life would have proceeded like Peltier's.

At one point in *Starlight Nights*, Peltier performs a thought experiment that suggests he may have felt a sense of alienation. He confesses that his favorite boyhood books dealt with shipwrecked survivors, castaways, exiles—*Robinson Crusoe, Swiss Family Robinson, Rolf in the Woods*. How can it be so? He was born, raised, and spent his whole career in and near the town of Delphos. As late as age thirteen he had never been more than fifty miles from home. Yet, although he belonged to Delphos, he did so entirely on his own terms. This is part of the rhetorical power of *Starlight Nights*: Peltier was someone who, in the twentieth century, had found a way to live deliberately. To every appearance, he was conventional; he married, had children, worked for local businesses. He and his family were fully a part of the community. "We were variously involved in church affairs [Methodist-Episcopal], in Eastern Star, in garden clubs, and in a devious maze of Cub Scout work," he wrote. He might also have mentioned the Grange, school band, and the library board. But Peltier was not conventional—not at all. His mind was elsewhere. In the thought experiment, which can be interpreted not as a fantasy but as Peltier's psychological reality, he is completely alone on an island. His only concern is how to re-create his astronomical observing program "*without a telescope*," using just pencil and paper and his own eyes. It can be done, he determines; he will be fine. Often, Peltier notes, castaways don't want to come back, or regret it if they do.[6]

The origin story of Leslie Peltier's storybook life was detailed in "The Strawberry Spyglass" chapter of *Starlight Nights*: how sixteen-year-old Leslie picked nine hundred quarts of strawberries on the family farm (at two cents per quart) to buy his first telescope. His initial interest in astronomy had come late, he admits, and appropriately, it was fostered by a book given to him by his mother. Leslie's new telescope—a collapsible affair with a two-inch aperture—was literally the product of his father's passion, growing strawberries. In this very immediate and concrete way, the home soil became the means by which Peltier transcended the local and familial, entering into the cosmopolitan and the universal, living in rural Ohio but in a different dimension.

The book from his mother provided an address for the American Association of Variable Star Observers (AAVSO), an amateur group based at Harvard College Observatory (HCO), which in that era was "the greatest storehouse of astronomical data in the world." The AAVSO compiled amateur observations of variable stars, that is, stars varying in brightness for reasons then unknown. The data could be processed into tables or graphs and made available to professional scientists. The organization was small; variable-star observing was a painstaking business, involving specialized charts and meticulous magnitude estimates of stars often visible only in telescopes. The larger one's telescope, the better one was able to observe stars throughout their fluctuations, and Peltier's scope was undersized. When AAVSO organizers saw what an assiduous observer he was (monthly reports were required), they arranged for the loan of a four-inch instrument from HCO, later upgraded (in 1921) to a six-inch refractor from Princeton. The prestige of these affiliations to Ivy League institutions bestowed legitimacy on Peltier's unorthodox scientific career. With help from his omnicompetent father, he built a classic domed observatory out in the middle of a pasture, "where he does research work for Harvard University," a Lima newspaper reported.[7]

The Princeton telescope was a widefield design, optimized for "comet seeking." Peltier, with his prodigious memory, ultimately dispensed with the AAVSO's star charts, and his ability to memorize large segments of the sky (as enhanced by a telescope) served him well in his comet program, which was his own idea. The undertaking suggests a measure of ambition. Comet-hunting offered the possibility of "becoming astronomically world-famous overnight," as a Canadian astronomy journal later remarked, pointing to Peltier as an exemplar. Comets also fit the pattern of what most attracted Peltier's attention as an observer: along with novae and some types of variable stars, comets embodied a changeful, dynamic, unpredictable nature. "Perhaps it is their suddenness," Peltier wrote about novae, "and their element of surprise that have made them so fascinating to me." His decades of routine—the monthly reports to AAVSO continued, uninterrupted, for more than fifty years—were a lifelong vigil for novelty. Thousands of hours of persistent searching might elapse between each comet discovery, resulting in a dozen altogether scattered across three decades between 1925 and 1954. For twelve years he kept watch on one nova, RS Ophiuchi, before it finally erupted.[8]

Ohio as yet did little directly to aid Peltier in this vigil—that support would come later in his career—but the importance of home as an indirect facilitator should not be overlooked. Peltier did not forget this in his work. "Make the reader feel acquainted with your environment and take him into your world," Teale advised. In fact, *Starlight Nights* at times seems an almost phenomenological account of the life-world that enabled Peltier's scientific enterprise.[9] The striving for novelty required regularity, routine, and flexibility, all of which were to be had on a family farm nested within a relatively stable local economy that mixed agriculture and industry. Delphos was known for its honey production, yet it also featured a truck manufacturer (Gramm Motors) as well as the Delphos Bending Company, a maker of children's furniture and toys where Peltier worked for decades as a draftsman and designer. These opportunities for employment allowed him to remain in the area long term. His life-world gifted him with the luxury to become a creature of habit—something essential to the science that he practiced.

Around the time Peltier discovered his first comet in 1925, he had taken a job as a clerk at the truck factory. This detail might seem to belie the bucolic setting of *Starlight Nights*, as does the fact that an interurban railway connecting Delphos to Lima ran within a half mile of the Peltier farm. Paradoxically, these urban-industrial elements of Peltier's life serve only to heighten the sense of his work as a Midwestern idyll. In Ohio, birthplace of Thomas Edison and home to those legendary unschooled tinkerers the Wright brothers, traditional values had found an equipoise with modernity, it seemed; change and innovation could be transmuted from the simple virtues. Peltier's unlikely story was filled out by these cultural referents: the native genius, the whiz kid. Many Americans of the day (including Peltier) had read the same boy books, most especially the adventures of that man-boy inventor-hero, Tom Swift. Initial reports of Peltier's 1925 comet emphasized how "youthful" the nearly twenty-six-year-old was.

He had spotted the comet at his "home-made observatory on the family farm," they remarked. "Peltier's knowledge of the heavens is self gained," another account marveled. "He never studied astronomy in any school or college." A June 1926 article in *Popular Mechanics*, his first major national coverage, began by describing Peltier as "a young farmer boy." [10]

Writing of his momentous first discovery in *Starlight Nights*, Peltier took his cues from this good-copy version of himself. Young Les is home alone. His parents have gone out for the evening, taking the family car. In the crisp autumnal air, a Friday the thirteenth, he walks out to the observatory to begin his session. Like Wordsworth's moon, the star Arcturus hovers over the "strawberry patch whose fruitful runnered rows had once produced a spyglass"; Jupiter and Venus quiver above the river to his west. With the Princeton scope, Peltier sweeps the sky systematically. He spots the new comet and determines its magnitude, position, and motion. According to procedure, he must wire Harvard for confirmation, but the Western Union office is closed. He will have to send a telegram from the railroad depot in Delphos. Without a car, Peltier hauls out his trusty old bicycle and speeds off into the night, dramatizing his boyishness. The illustration accompanying the chapter (drawn by Peltier himself, of course) shows him bundled up, pedaling, scarf flying, neighbor dogs barking. [11]

Future Peltier coverage reinforced the boy-book tropes that would find their way into *Starlight Nights*, underwriting its long-lasting appeal. As late as 1939, an interviewer from *Country Home Magazine* would comment that Peltier was "not greatly changed from the simple farm boy." A 1940 feature in *Popular Science* offered a cutaway illustration of his new invention, the "merry-go-round observatory," which allowed Peltier to scan the skies at the turn of a steering wheel. An early biography of Peltier, published in 1942, was presented in the form of a comic strip. In the space of just nine panels, it was twice mentioned that he worked at a toy factory. [12]

II

By the conclusion of Peltier's "Friday, the Thirteenth" chapter, the reader is more than halfway through *Starlight Nights*. The chronology thereafter jumps to 1933, his marriage, and the end of his extended boyhood. The divide is marked off by the next four chapters (out of twenty-eight), which recount the newlyweds' months-long honeymoon trip to the Southwest. Perhaps Peltier did experience the trip that way, as a watershed, just the two of them living out of a car, wholly unsettled, the desert environment so different—even some of the stars were new to him. Providing continuity with his old life, he had his wife, Dottie, who was a neighborhood woman he'd grown up with, and his telescope. Honeymoon or no, he did not miss any reports to the AAVSO.

In a page or two covering the 1930s, Peltier then rounds out the bildungsroman that has been taking shape in the first half of *Starlight Nights*: he starts his job of forty-plus years at Delphos Bending; he and Dottie live in his grandfather's former farmhouse; after their first son's birth, they move to Delphos proper. The boy becomes a father; he moves from agriculture to industry, country to city; and he assumes a public, authoritative role. As Peltier's comet discoveries mounted, his national fame surged. He was presented with the AAVSO's first-ever merit award in 1934; he was written about in *Time* magazine; he was interviewed on the radio by Eleanor Roosevelt. The coverage peaked in 1936, when Comet Peltier (1936a) reached global naked-eye visibility. At that time, reports cast him in the mold of a Depression-era everyman, a paragon of democracy. As one syndicated columnist wrote, Peltier was the "farmer genius" who offered "an amazing example of what persistence and application will accomplish [when] specialized education" was lacking.[13]

All this publicity, though it underscored his amateur status, necessarily elevated Peltier in terms of respectability and stature, coaxing him into speaking engagements and literary endeavors. Peltier at this point seems to have grown into the idea of himself as a science popularizer— and more significantly, he was being accepted as such. Since 1923, he had been hosting community and school groups at the observatory. By 1929, he was taking the show on the road, delivering public lectures on "cosmic evolution." Famously shy face-to-face, Peltier found his voice in these performative situations. After a 1936 presentation to the Cleveland Astronomical Society, he was deemed a "ready and fluent lecturer" with a "charming" personality.[14]

Thus, Peltier took advantage of his 1930s moment to begin a sporadic writing career. He published several short articles in *Nature Magazine*, among other venues, developing the genial, informal style that would become familiar to readers of *Starlight Nights*. His subjects were on hand around the farm—fairy shrimps from a pond, tree crickets—the kinds of things that he had been collecting all his life. Similar Thoreauvian close-ups of local flora and fauna (one illustration in *Starlight Nights* shows Peltier on his hands and knees, studying an insect) would help ground his cosmic-themed book in the concreteness of an intimately known eco-system, not to mention in the comfortable tropes of nature writing. "The night sky is part of all nature," Teale agreed.[15] And like Arcturus hovering over the berry patch, such depictions extended the concept of a holistic nature—as well as the depiction of Peltier's life-world—beyond the bounds of Earth: a homebody's cosmos.

The other primary theme of Peltier's 1930s writings, not surprisingly, concerned the status of the amateur in the field of astronomy. This topic had been something of a staple of astronomical society journals until the amateur-professional divide grew so wide that it was no longer relevant. That day was at hand by 1940, if not already past. Astronomy was becoming Big Science, and astrophysics was its cutting edge. In 1929, Edwin Hubble had announced the expansion of the universe, a discovery that he made with the one-hundred-inch telescope that George Ellery Hale built at Mount Wilson Observatory; such observations were far beyond detection with amateur-sized instruments. Hale began construction of the two-hundred-inch telescope for Mount Palomar in 1936, completing it in 1948, the first of a wave of large telescopes to be built in the postwar western United States. The growth of research focused on radio and other segments of the electromagnetic spectrum was also taking astronomy in directions where the amateur could not follow. The fate of the AAVSO in this new world revealed the widening gulf between amateurs and professionals in a very stark way. The organization was evicted from its quarters at HCO in 1953, as the university's astronomy department began to reinvent itself into what would become known as the Harvard-Smithsonian Center for Astrophysics.[16]

Tom Swift got his "giant telescope" in a 1939 adventure, but Peltier, perhaps in the whirl of his growing fame, failed to grasp these trends fully, overstating the amateur's prospects. In a 1936 article, for example, he declared that variable stars, comets, occultations, meteors, novae, the moon—all provided chances for research that the amateur could do "as well [as] or better than can the professional astronomer." In a 1939 *Science News Letter* article, Peltier, described as "America's Foremost Amateur Astronomer," elaborated: "None of these astronomical by-paths requires any special mathematical training"; all that they needed was "diligence and persistence." Indeed, taking the longer view, he asserted, "Probably no other science has received so much advancement . . . through the work of the amateur as has the science of astronomy. . . . A large share of the important discoveries in the past were made by men who . . . earned their living at some entirely unrelated task."[17] But that past belonged to the era before nuclear physics, relativity, electronics, and the modern research university.

HCO director Harlow Shapley, who once carefully dubbed Peltier the "world's greatest non-professional astronomer," provided a reality check in a 1936 article on amateurs (featuring Peltier) that appeared in *Reader's Digest*. "These amateurs will not discover the secret of the universe," Shapley stated, "but they are giving us a solid body of recorded data on which we can study the secret." Shapley's colleague Cecilia Payne-Gaposchkin, Peltier's almost exact contemporary—the two were born and died within about five months of each other—makes for a telling comparison. Despite the hurdles confronting women in the sciences, Payne-Gaposchkin earned all the requisite degrees, including a doctorate in astronomy from Radcliffe College. During the same year that Peltier discovered his first comet, Payne-Gaposchkin proved (in her epochal dissertation) that stars are composed mainly of hydrogen and helium, using stellar spectra and equations drawn from the field of physical chemistry. She herself thought that the AAVSO's data was of "enormous value"—and in 1938, she used it to literally write the book on variable stars.[18]

By the time he wrote *Starlight Nights*, Peltier had gained a greater sense of proportion regarding the amateur's role, chastened by technological change and his own limits as a visual observer. Postwar advances in photoelectric photometry, for example, held the promise of "rendering automatic the actions otherwise performed by the observer" in measuring variable stars, a 1952 report foretold. In that same year, Peltier had shifted his own program away from the AAVSO's voluminous list of long-period variables to focus on a smaller number of more specialized categories. After 1954, he also stopped finding comets. Whether or not these developments account for the strongly nostalgic tone of *Starlight Nights*, they may well have led Peltier to reconsider the value of amateur astronomy, shifting the emphasis from objective (scientific discovery) to subjective (self-realization). As he wrote in *Starlight Nights*, the professionals "with their big wide-angle cameras" had tallied fifty-two new comets to the amateurs' twelve between 1948 and 1960. On the same page, while ostensibly defending the amateur's contribution, he made a more striking admission—that under an observing routine, "one becomes a veritable automaton." All those decades of monthly reports stretched out behind him. He recommended comet-seeking as a "leisurely, pleasant" pursuit, very calming and relaxing.[19]

Age may account for some of this attitude. Peltier substantially finished writing a draft of *Starlight Nights* by early 1964, but it is not known exactly when or why he began it. He suffered a heart attack around 1960 (he managed his variable observations with binoculars from his hospital bed)—perhaps this event was a spur as well as a root cause of nostalgia. Peltier had been seeing details of his biography handled by other writers since at least 1926. Most recently, Teale had told Peltier's story yet again in a chapter of *Autumn Across America* (1956), a first-person account of a visit to Peltier's home in Delphos (Teale was one of a string of distinguished pilgrims hoping to meet the farmer genius) that may well have given Peltier inspiration. Certainly by the period of Teale's editorial involvement with *Starlight Nights*, Peltier was being directly coached to "whenever possible . . . link an act to some memory of the past."[20]

Peltier's alienation was never so much from a place as from a time (and a time of life), the very definition of nostalgia. By 1960, as professional astronomy ascended to unreachable heights (Peltier also railed against the hubris of the US space program), he had reason enough to feel warmly toward Delphos and Ohio. A decade earlier, the Peltier family had moved to Brookhaven, a modest Delphos estate featuring a historic home on twelve acres—large enough to provide "country life in town," in Peltier's words. Here he came to appreciate that a landscape "also has a depth dimension"—historical, ecological, and geological. *The Place on Jennings Creek*, his lesser and grumpier 1977 sequel to *Starlight Nights*, chronicled Peltier's efforts to restore both gardens and wilderness to Brookhaven's grounds and woods in a more crowded and polluted world. The centerpiece of the estate arrived in 1959, a token of Ohio's esteem. Miami University offered him a disused twelve-inch Clark refractor and its observatory, all of which had to be disassembled and reconstructed at Brookhaven. If here Peltier enjoyed "country life in town," then the observatory installation, detailed late in *Starlight Nights*, had the air of a barn-raising. Local contractors, along with the owner of Delphos Bending, voluntarily oversaw every detail of the project, which required multiple trucks and large construction cranes. The telescope tube alone—a classic brand considered the "Stradivari" of refractors—was sixteen feet long and extremely heavy, far too much for one person to handle, even for a devoted do-it-yourselfer like Peltier.[21]

The glow of camaraderie occasioned by the installation of the Clark had its effect on the tone of *Starlight Nights*, as did the advent of Peltier's first long-term collaborator, Carolyn Hurless. After 1958, and for much of the next two decades, she and her husband (Peltier's "nearest neighbor AAVSOers," from Lima) would be his regular weekly visitors. Hurless and Peltier took advantage of the Clark's larger aperture to pursue special projects for the AAVSO. The refractor's greater light-gathering power compensated for the fact that Peltier no longer had "youthful eyes," an admission that he did not make until the *Jennings Creek* sequel. Hurless's participation was significant enough that Peltier's merry-go-round was renovated to seat two rather than the one lone wolf at the steering wheel.[22]

The two observatories situated amid the homemade landscaping of Brookhaven were the spatial expression of science as the nexus of a holistic and integrated life, binding together the natural, communal, historical, and personal. In the central passage of *Starlight Nights*, the materialist and reductive burgeon out into the emotive and aesthetic as Peltier seeks to communicate this experience of wholeness, to *popularize* it. His observatories might have looked like "quite ordinary wood and metal, concrete and stucco," Peltier writes, but to him they were "vital and alive . . . compounded of the visual delights, the unexpected thrills, the lasting friendships, the expressions of good will and the multitude of kindred blessings that have come to me, all mixed with starlight, from the skies of three score years."[23]

It was this life that Peltier was offering to anyone taking up the pursuit of astronomy. If amateurs were not going to discover the secrets of the universe, neither were they mere data collectors. At the beginning of

Starlight Nights, Peltier locates himself, standing in his backyard, relative to three prominent stars in the sky. This sense of connectedness to universal nature was available to a "rural rustic" from Delphos, Ohio, just as it was to anyone on the face of planet Earth. When he had first memorized the constellations as a teen, the revelation had come to him. After spending a year learning the stars, he wrote, "Each one recalled for me a place, a time, a season. Each one was now a personality. The stars, in short, had now become *my* stars." [24]

The broad and enduring appeal of *Starlight Nights* was rooted not just in the conventions of boy-books and nature writing, but also in passages like this one, bridging the earlier scientific wing of the amateur astronomy movement and its rapidly expanding "recreational" wing of the 1960s and 1970s, drawing new adherents who looked through mass-produced telescopes for beauty and sublimity rather than data. Peltier's book showed that the two impulses were not mutually exclusive. While privately he might grouse to Teale about the erosion of amateur standards after the influx of space-age enthusiasts, his book's focus on the personal experience of observing struck a more generous tone. *Starlight Nights* thus avoided becoming merely an elegy for the "serious" amateur, undermined by dabblers and ignored by professionals. As Teale emphasized to Peltier, "The real heart of the story—the thing that others can get pleasure out of imagining themselves doing even if they never do it—is your discoveries with modest equipment made in your own cornfield and backyard." [25]

In 1968, the AAVSO convened its annual meeting in Lima in honor of Peltier's fifty consecutive years of observations, complete with a pilgrimage to Brookhaven. Over the previous year, the group had begun the "computerized data processing" of its decades of records. Peltier continued sending in his monthly reports, but he preferred to think of stars "still uncaptured by chemical emulsions and still unsentenced by the instant verdicts of computers," each and every observation record bearing the author's signature, the "human touch" of individual experience and perception. He published a guide to the stars for beginners in 1972. On the day that he died in 1980, he was tending a garden next to his observatories. [26]

NOTES

1. J. Allen Hynek, *Stars Over Ohio: Commemorating the Fiftieth Anniversary of the Emerson McMillin Observatory* (Columbus: Ohio State University, 1946), 1, 14, 20; Leslie C. Peltier, *Starlight Nights: The Adventures of a Star-Gazer* (New York: Harper and Row, 1965; Cambridge, MA: Sky Publishing, 1999).

2. Leslie C. Peltier, *Leslie Peltier's Guide to the Stars* (Cambridge: Cambridge University Press, 1986), xii, xi.

3. Peltier, *Starlight Nights*, 32.

4. Peltier, *Starlight Nights*, x; Edwin Way Teale [EWT] to Leslie C. Peltier [LCP], February 2, 1964, Edwin Way Teale Papers, Archives and Special Collections, University of Connecticut Library (hereafter cited as EWTP/ASC-UCL); William Wordsworth, *Poetry & Prose* (Cambridge, MA: Harvard University Press, 1955), 308, 298, 305.

5. Willa Cather, *Early Novels and Stories* (New York: Library of America, 1987), 850–851.

6. Leslie C. Peltier, *The Place on Jennings Creek* (Chicago: Adams Press, 1977), 28; Peltier, *Starlight Nights*, 201, 73–78.

7. Cecilia Payne-Gaposchkin, *An Autobiography and Other Recollections* (Cambridge: Cambridge University Press, 1984), 207; "Delphos Astronomer Speaks to Kiwanians," *Lima (OH) News*, July 30, 1929.

8. Peltier, *Starlight Nights*, 126, 192, xiii; H. B. Brydon, "Telescope Making for Beginners," *Journal of the Royal Astronomical Society of Canada* 29, no. 4 (April 1935): 142; Leon Campbell, "Variable Stars," *Popular Astronomy* 41, no. 8 (October 1933): 441.

9. EWT to LCP, August 23, 1963, EWTP/ASC-UCL.

10. Tom D. Crouch, *First Flight: The Wright Brothers and the Invention of the Airplane* (Washington, DC: National Park Service, 2002), 18–20, 140; "Medal Promised for Delphos Astronomer," *Lima (OH) News*, December 17, 1925; Associated Press, "Peltier Discovers New Comet," *Hamilton (OH) Evening Journal*, December 31, 1925; "Peltier Comet Has Faded from Sight," *Lima (OH) News*, February 7, 1926; "Hunting Comets," *Popular Mechanics* 45, no. 6 (June 1926), 919.

11. Peltier, *Starlight Nights*, 132–133, 136.

12. Clarence Woodbury, "Heaven's Night Watchman," *Country Home Magazine* 63, no. 5 (May 1939): 32; "Merry-Go-Round Observatory," *Popular Science*

136, no. 2 (February 1940): 108–109; Leslie C. Peltier and B. W. Schlatter, "Here's My Story: The Career of Leslie C. Peltier," *Popular Science* 140, no. 3 (March 1942): 112–113.

13. Peltier, *Starlight Nights*, 172–173; Thomas R. Williams and Michael Saladyga, *Advancing Variable Star Astronomy: The Centennial History of the American Association of Variable Star Observers* (Cambridge: Cambridge University Press, 2011), 100–101; "Amateur & Amateurs," *Time* 27, no. 22 (June 1, 1936): 58; "Mrs. Franklin D. Roosevelt to Interview Leslie Peltier," *Lima (OH) News*, August 23, 1939; Talbot Lake, Profiles for Today, *Elyria (OH) Chronicle Telegram*, May 29, 1936.

14. "Science Class Calls," *Lima (OH) News*, April 10, 1923; "Delphos Astronomer Speaks to Kiwanians"; Don H. Johnston, "Notes from Amateurs," *Popular Astronomy* 44, no. 10 (December 1936): 574.

15. L. C. Peltier, "Fairy Shrimps," *Nature Magazine* 23, no. 3 (March 1934): 120; L. C. Peltier, "An Insect Serenader," *Nature Magazine* 22, no. 4 (October 1933): 165; Peltier, *Starlight Nights*, 180; EWT to LCP, February 2, 1964, EWTP/ASC-UCL.

16. Williams and Saladyga, *Advancing Variable Star Astronomy*, 153–170.

17. Victor Appleton, *Tom Swift and His Giant Telescope* (Racine, WI: Whitman Publishing, 1939); L. C. Peltier, "Comet-Hunting for the Amateur Astronomer," *Nature Magazine* 28, no. 6 (December 1936): 342–343; Leslie C. Peltier, "Amateur Astronomers Can Make Vital Contributions," *Science News Letter* 36, no. 9 (August 26, 1939): 135.

18. Carolyn Hurless, "Our Friend, Leslie Peltier: A Personal Reminiscence," *Journal of the American Association of Variable Star Observers* 9, no. 1 (October 1980): 33; Webb Waldon, "Consider the Heavens," *Reader's Digest* 29, no. 172 (August 1936): 51; Richard Williams, "January 1, 1925: Cecilia Payne-Gaposchkin and the Day the Universe Changed," *APS News* 24, no. 1 (January 2015), www.aps.org/publications/apsnews/201501 /physicshistory.cfm; Payne-Gaposchkin, *Autobiography*, 152; Cecilia Payne-Gaposchkin and Sergei Gaposchkin, *Variable Stars* (Cambridge, MA: Harvard College Observatory, 1938), 108.

19. Theodore Walraven, "A New Photoelectric Variable Star Photometer," *Monthly Notes of the Astronomical Society of South Africa* 11, no. 4 (April 30, 1952): 36; Williams and Saladyga, *Advancing Variable Star Astronomy*, 142; Peltier, *Starlight Nights*, 230.

20. Carolyn Hurless, "Leslie Peltier Remembered," *Sky & Telescope* 60, no. 2 (August 1980): 104; Edwin Way Teale, *Autumn in America* (New York: Dodd, Mead, 1956), 43–51; EWT to LCP, August 23, 1963, EWTP/ASC-UCL.

21. Peltier, *Starlight Nights*, 200, 203, 210–215, 218–220; Peltier, *Place on Jennings Creek*, 83.

22. Peltier, *Starlight Nights*, 219; Williams and Saladyga, *Advancing Variable Star Astronomy*, 227; Peltier, *Place on Jennings Creek*, 167; Hurless, "Our Friend," 32.

23. Peltier, *Starlight Nights*, 2.

24. Peltier, *Starlight Nights*, 1–2, 40; Peltier, *Place on Jennings Creek*, 79.

25. Thomas R. Williams, "Getting Organized: A History of Amateur Astronomy in the United States" (PhD diss., Rice University, 2000), 1–3, 328–331, 367–368; LCP to EWT, January 31, 1965, and EWT to LCP, September 25, 1964, EWTP/ASC-UCL.

26. "Delphos Astronomer Notes 50 Years of Star Observing," *Delphos (OH) Daily Herald*, June 3, 1968; Elizabeth O. Waagen, "Archiving of Variable Star Data—The AAVSO Experience," in *The Study of Variable Stars Using Small Telescopes*, ed. John R. Percy (Cambridge: Cambridge University Press, 1986), 190; Peltier, *Place on Jennings Creek*, 166; Leslie C. Peltier, *Guideposts to the Stars: Exploring the Skies Throughout the Year* (New York: Macmillan Publishing Co., 1972); Hurless, "Our Friend," 34.

CHAPTER 22

George McGovern

An Intellectual in Politics

John E. Miller

A s an intellectual in politics, George McGovern of South Dakota rose to the pinnacle of the profession during the 1960s and 1970s.[1] Most politicians are not likely to be considered intellectuals, but that is the word that best describes McGovern, who learned to read before he entered school, continued to be a voracious reader for the rest of his life, excelled in the classroom, aspired to become a history teacher or college professor, and briefly was one before entering politics.[2] He frequently told people that he always thought of himself more as a teacher than anything else. "It's simple," he told a *Wall Street Journal* reporter in 1983, "I'm basically a teacher, and politics is just a great big classroom."[3]

It should also be said that McGovern was a *Midwestern* intellectual in politics. Having been born and gone through grade school, high school, and college in the Midwest, he remained in the region to attend graduate school at Northwestern University on the north side of Chicago. He was a finalist for a job as a history professor at the University of Iowa, and had it been offered to him, perhaps he would have stayed in the region for the rest of his career. Since it was not, he switched paths, went into politics, built up the South Dakota Democratic Party, and made a career for himself in politics, representing his home state in Congress for twenty-two years. After retiring from politics, he returned to live in his hometown.

Unsurprisingly, McGovern's signature political issue while building up the Democratic base and during his early years in Congress was agriculture, since farming was central to the economy of his state and that of the entire region. Many—but by no means all—of the intellectuals who influenced him were Midwesterners, including professor Ray Allen Billington, frontier historian and biographer of Frederick Jackson Turner; the La Follettes of Wisconsin; former Secretary of Agriculture and Vice President Henry A. Wallace of Iowa; and McGovern's congressional colleagues such as Hubert Humphrey, Gaylord Nelson, and John Culver. Many of McGovern's personal qualities were, in fact, stereotypes often associated with the region, such as friendliness, modesty, religiosity, candidness, industry, and integrity.

In the House of Representatives and the US Senate between 1957 and 1981, McGovern associated with and established close personal friendships with a number of other former college professors, including Mike Mansfield of Montana, Democratic majority leader in the Senate; J. William Fulbright of Arkansas, chairman of the Senate Foreign Relations Committee; Eugene McCarthy of Minnesota, who dramatically contended for the presidency in 1968; and Daniel Patrick Moynihan, who served as Richard Nixon's domestic policy advisor before becoming a senator from New York. There were other professorial types, too, in McGovern's cohort in Congress—Gale McGee, John Brademas, Paul Douglas, and Mark Hatfield among them. McGovern's long-time political nemesis from South Dakota and Senate colleague between 1963 and 1973 was the Republican Karl Mundt, who, like McGovern, had been a college professor and a debate coach before entering the political merry-go-round.

McGovern's political ascent got a big boost from the friendship that developed between him and John F. Kennedy during the election of 1960. The two connected immediately when then Congressman McGovern, who was running against Mundt for the latter's Senate seat, flew from Sioux Falls to Mitchell with the Democratic presidential nominee, who gave a speech there in the Corn Palace on his tour through Midwestern farm states. On their short flight, Kennedy absorbed McGovern's quick briefing on local agriculture, incorporating the information into his own remarks for the waiting crowd. The Massachusetts senator had acquired a reputation as something of an intellectual himself, having authored (with help from speechwriter Ted Sorensen) a Pulitzer Prize–winning book,

Profiles in Courage, and for reputedly being able to read twelve hundred words a minute. As president, Kennedy surrounded himself with brainy advisors and aides. Many of the men (they were mostly men) with whom he filled his administration were impressive enough intellectually that they achieved a reputation for being "the best and the brightest." Their gauzy credentials did not prevent them, however, from soon stumbling into the morass of Vietnam. Among them were Secretary of Defense Robert McNamara, Secretary of State Dean Rusk, National Security Adviser McGeorge Bundy, Ambassador John Kenneth Galbraith, and Council of Economic Advisers Chairman Walter W. Heller. After narrowly losing his bid to unseat Mundt in 1960, McGovern vied for a place in Kennedy's cabinet as Secretary of Agriculture. Reserving that position for former Minnesota governor Orville Freeman, the incoming president carved out a special niche for McGovern as director of the Food for Peace program, a position Kennedy elevated to cabinet status for his new friend, whom he had singled out as a comer in the Democratic Party and one who could help him in South Dakota. McGovern used the position as a platform from which to run two years later for South Dakota's other Senate seat—this time he was successful, but just by a whisker (597 votes). Ten years later, he would be running for the presidency himself.

The 1960s and 1970s were a time of turmoil and achievement—one marked by antiwar demonstrations, civil rights marches, women's liberation, other reform movements of all types, urban riots, and men landing on the moon. It was a time when drugs, rock and roll, and hippie be-ins shook traditional culture and one in which education at all levels went through a period of extraordinary growth and tension. As books poured off the presses, magazines and newspapers flourished, and intellectual movements of all kinds proliferated, ideas, debates, manifestoes, and high-flown rhetoric were the order of the day. The intellectual give-and-take, from the classroom to the street and from television studios to book discussion groups, was stimulating, exhilarating, and in some cases violent. McGovern felt right at home in the middle of all of it.

I spoke with him three times between 2003 and 2012. Each time, he greeted me holding a book in his hand, one of them being a new history of the Democratic Party that he had been up reading until two or three in the morning, which explained why he had shown up at his door barefoot five minutes after I rang the doorbell at 8 a.m. When I asked him in 2012 whether he could envision himself as having been a college history professor his entire life, he quickly and without any hesitation answered yes. The academy is what he had aimed at joining soon after he returned from Europe, where he had been a B-24 bomber pilot during World War II. He got a brief taste of teaching as a history professor at his college alma mater in Mitchell, South Dakota—Dakota Wesleyan University—where he quickly emerged as one of the most popular professors on campus. The student yearbook, the *Tumbleweed*, which was dedicated to him in 1952, observed that during McGovern's short time on campus, he had "found a place in the hearts of students, both in and out of the classroom. He is one of those capable few who can associate intimately with the students and share their problems, yet command their respect in the deepest sense of the word." Students found McGovern to be stimulating, encouraging, intelligent, well-organized, inspirational, and hard-working, with high expectations for their own industry. Dorothy Schwieder, who went on to a long career as a historian at Iowa State University, recalled that she and others thought his reading list for classes "seemed long."[4] Among two finalists for a job at the University of Iowa in 1952, McGovern lost out to a "guy from Harvard," something he still seemed perturbed by sixty years later.

Although he soon departed academia to enter politics, McGovern never stopped thinking of himself as a teacher, something he mentioned often in interviews with reporters. During the years he served in Congress, plus the time he spent as the Food for Peace director and in the years that followed, McGovern remained an "intellectual in politics." This endeared him to many people, casting him as a man of deep intelligence, wide learning, and dedication to reason in the service of making life better for ordinary people. For others, this was part of what alienated him from them—his ideological bent, his reputed impracticality, his "ivory-tower" dreaminess, and his alleged radicalism. McGovern, despite his modest and unpretentious approachableness and his measured, thoughtful speaking style, was a polarizing figure. People tended to admire him or dislike—even hate—him. His ability to succeed for as long as he did as a liberal Democrat in one of the most conservative Republican states in the Union testifies to his intelligence, capacity for empathy, charm, persuasiveness, appealing ideas, organizational skill, political savvy, and plain dumb luck.

For McGovern, being an intellectual in politics meant several things. For one, he arrived in Washington, DC, with well-formed ideas about how society and the economy worked, about problems that needed to be addressed, and about possible solutions for dealing with them. He brought with him a well-thought-out political ideology—progressivism or liberalism, a banner he was always proud to claim—which suggested a broad range of policy options that might be considered when proposing legislation. He did not feel obliged to follow blindly—or, perhaps, advisedly—fellow congressmen, party leaders, political consultants, or outside experts when staking out his own political positions on things, when running reelection campaigns, and when interacting with the public. He would listen to others, but he would "be his own man"—pushing out front on issues and not remaining content to be a follower or "one of the pack." Although McGovern did not, for the most part, become a recognized floor leader in the House or the Senate, he did emerge as a shaper of opinion, including on such national issues as the Vietnam War (especially), agricultural policy, food, and poverty. These often involved him in controversy and attracted attention, things he did not shy away from.

McGovern's intellectual progress traced back to his childhood in small-town South Dakota, and he remained a "small-town boy" and a child of the prairie to the end. As he emerged from the pack to become the frontrunner for the Democratic nomination in the spring of 1972, *Time* magazine ran a cover story about him under the headline "Here Comes the Prairie Populist." He was born on July 19, 1922, in Avon, a town of around six hundred people, but after a brief hiatus in Calgary, Canada, so they could be near his aging grandmother, the family settled down in the larger town of Mitchell, with a population approaching eleven thousand, when he was six years old. His father, Joseph McGovern, was a Wesleyan Methodist minister, strict, straight-laced, and a stern disciplinarian, while also being a loving but emotionally undemonstrative man. Having been for a time a second baseman in the St. Louis Cardinals organization and aspiring to a place in the major leagues, Joseph later repudiated the loose living and rough atmosphere surrounding him in the minors during his short baseball career. He discouraged his two sons from engaging in organized sports, and although young George joined other boys in the usual playground games, he never got involved in competitive interscholastic sports. From the beginning, his would be more a life of the mind.

George's mother, tall and stately and two decades younger than her husband (he had remarried after his first wife died), offered the boy the generous warmth and nurturing that was less forthcoming from his father. She provided a steady rock of love and stability in a family that grew to include four children—two girls and two boys. George was second in line. Every day was punctuated by morning reading of Scriptures and prayers at mealtimes. The weeks were marked by Sunday services, both morning and evening, and by Wednesday prayer sessions. Several times a year, revivalists arrived in town to lead a week of Christian outreach and renewal. George later described the household atmosphere as devout and conservative, but not oppressive or overbearing. As his sister Olive put it, the children knew they were "not quite the same as other children. We were expected to be a standard for the community. Everything that other Christians did, we had to do double." [5] Growing up, George managed to express his individuality and a bit of rebelliousness in several ways, including sneaking off to the local movie theater, an activity forbidden by his father. Journalist Robert Sam Anson observed, "For George, going to the movies was more than just entertainment; it seemed sometimes like an act of personal liberation." [6]

Setting George apart from other boys and girls was a seriousness of purpose and a studiousness that made him seem someone special. His attraction to reading, more than anything else, shaped his identity early on. Having learned the rudiments of it before entering school, he developed a habit as a grade school student of checking out books every week from the local Carnegie library, which became a sort of home away from home. A noticeable bashful streak heightened his early bookishness. At a young age, he displayed, according to biographer Thomas J. Knock, "a maturity beyond his years." [7]

On Sunday afternoons, George would sit beside his father listening to the radio as Social Gospel minister Harry Emerson Fosdick delivered his weekly sermons from his Riverside Church in New York City. Reverend McGovern counseled his son that while the celebrated minister was well-versed in Scriptures and a dedicated churchman, his liberal brand of Christianity needed to be carefully scrutinized and accepted only with major reservations, because on many counts the message contradicted the elder McGovern's conservative theological tenets.[8] How long it took the boy to veer away from his father's more traditional, conservative interpretation of the Bible and assimilate liberal deviations from it is uncertain, but by the time he was in college, George McGovern had pretty much made the transition.[9]

Despite his native intelligence and early ability to read, McGovern's extreme shyness and refusal to talk in first grade led his teacher to consider holding him back a grade, promoting him only "on condition." A more understanding second grade teacher kept him after school to read aloud to her, and his third-grade teacher, Grace Cooley, took him under her wing and helped build up his confidence, setting him on a path to scholastic excellence that continued all through grade school, high school, college, and graduate school. He really came into his own as a high school sophomore under the tutelage of English teacher Rose Hopfner, who encouraged him to talk to the school's history instructor and debate coach, Bob Pearson. That, McGovern later observed, was the most important piece of advice he ever received.[10] Although Pearson's political views leaned conservative, his youthful enthusiasm and personal charisma quickly impressed McGovern, leading him to want to follow in Pearson's footsteps as a history teacher. More consequentially, Pearson soon engaged his precocious charge in debate competition, and McGovern's competitive, winning style garnered many trophies and speaking awards during the rest of his high school career and on into college.

Besides building self-confidence and speaking acumen, debate and participation in other forensics events developed McGovern's research skills, his understanding that every issue has more than one side, his curiosity, his openness to argument and discussion, his persuasive talents, his democratic inclinations, his love for facts and reasoned thinking, and his general respect for the life of the mind. Nothing could have been more intellectually stimulating for this budding scholar than to enthusiastically engage in debate competition. "It really changed my life, no question about it," McGovern later reflected upon the experience. "If I had not gone out for debate, there is not a chance in the world, in my opinion, that I would have ever come to the United States Senate. It was the one thing that I could do well. It really became the only instrument of personal or social power that I had."[11]

Along with debate, McGovern won numerous oratorical contests, usually speaking on the topic of peace. While attending college in his hometown at Dakota Wesleyan University, he won the South Dakota Peace Oratory Contest as a sophomore with a speech titled "My Brother's Keeper." It was chosen by the National Council of Churches as one of the best dozen speeches given in the United States during 1942.[12] By then, the United States was deep into World War II, and a year later McGovern was in flight-training school, soon to be off to Europe to pilot B-24 bombers, mostly over Austria and Germany. Even in the midst of thirty-five bombing missions and several near-escapes with his life, McGovern did not give up his intellectual pursuits. In late 1944 and early 1945, between bombing runs while operating out of the American base in Cerignola, Italy, he worked his way through works of progressive and other historians, such as Vernon L. Parrington and Charles and Mary Beard (their 1,700-page *Rise of American Civilization*). His goal now was, after returning to finish up his undergraduate degree at Dakota Wesleyan, to go on to postgraduate work and become a college professor. "I've discovered that old driving interest to learn rather than make money is still dominant," he wrote his brother-in-law, Bob Pennington. "I'm afraid I'm 'doomed' to the life of a student and a teacher."[13]

Back in the states, however, McGovern took another direction, opting to follow in his father's footsteps and enter into the ministry. The reverberating shock of his wartime experience led him to enroll at Garrett Theological Seminary in Evanston, Illinois, in the fall of 1946, opening up an opportunity for him to make a different kind of impact on society. During his senior year at Dakota Wesleyan, Professor Donald McAnnich, a recent PhD from Boston University, had introduced him to the influential early-twentieth-century theologian Walter Rauschenbusch, whose *Christianity and the Social Crisis* established him as the main explicator of the Social Gospel movement in the United States. Rauschenbusch became one of the intellectual lodestars of McGovern's career. Later, when he was a senator, the *Wall Street Journal* assigned McGovern to review a new Rauschenbusch biography. Prefacing his comments on the book, McGovern wrote, "As a combat bomber pilot in World War II, I emerged from that experience with an enhanced interest in understanding the central values of life and in creating a more humane and peaceful world. The writings and concepts of Walter Rauschenbusch did more than anything else to help me understand the relevance of the Judeo-Christian ethic to my search for meaning and my hopes for peace and justice. He exerted a similar influence over the lives of countless other idealistic young Americans."[14] Books, then and later, would operate as more than a diversion or a minor presence in McGovern's life. They would help establish his identity and guide his thinking and actions.

Part of McGovern's theological training was assignment as pastor of a small Methodist church in the town of Diamond Lake, thirty miles north of Evanston. It took only several months for him to suspect that the detour he had taken had been a mistake; he enjoyed his classes, preaching on Sundays, and interacting with his parishioners—all activities at which he excelled. But the pressures placed on him to build up numbers in the pews and in the collection plates, the priestly rituals he was obliged to perform, and the duty to counsel people on marital problems and other issues gnawed at him. When Bob Pennington, who was enrolled in the history PhD program at Northwestern, encouraged McGovern to listen in on some history classes, he enthusiastically accepted the invitation and quickly decided to switch over into the history PhD track himself.

He emerged as the top student in the program. His three most important professors—Lefton ("Lefty") Stavrianos, who taught eastern European history; Ray Allen Billington, the noted frontier historian; and McGovern's dissertation advisor, Arthur Link, who became Woodrow Wilson's major biographer—all held McGovern in high regard and stayed in touch with him over the years, corresponding with him, sending him money, and organizing other historians and intellectuals to back his reelection and presidential campaigns.[15] McGovern's association with them and with other members of the profession; his constant reading; his frequent writing on historical subjects, including the publication of his dissertation; and the reputation he acquired for fact-based analysis and argumentation all helped burnish his reputation in Washington, DC, as one of America's leading "intellectuals in politics."

As a young scholar, McGovern had gotten into the practice of underlining, marking, and writing in the margins of books and articles that he read. At the time of his death in October 2012, I was able to spend six hours perusing and taking images of several hundred of his books remaining on the shelves of the home in Sioux Falls where he lived during the last several months of his life. I was also able to interview him twice during the last two months before he died. It was obvious from my discussions with him at the time and from his books and his markings in many of them that he had never given up his devotion to reading and to translating the information and knowledge that he obtained in the process into practical political action. My brief perusal of a small remnant of probably thousands of books that he had acquired and read over seven decades revealed him to have been a highly eclectic, though also a focused, reader. His preferences ranged from history and biography to current events, political and social analysis, and cultural matters. But there was also a large smattering of religious books, economic treatises, fiction, and even poetry.

McGovern's inveterate, eclectic reading habits introduced him to a wide trove of ideas of the kind that the ordinary run of practical politicians might have been too busy or too uninterested in to bother with. Most politicians possess a filtering mechanism that, if in working order, leads them to tone down or withhold their private sentiments and beliefs, translating them into what they deem to be more moderate or acceptable language. McGovern, while more outspoken than many of his colleagues, also understood, as does any successful politician, how to tailor his rhetoric to the moment and to the circumstances. He was often pilloried in the press and by political opponents for being an extremist. The term *McGovernism* was coined as a mark of opprobrium—indicative of his alleged radicalism, naiveté, budget-busting spending schemes, softness on communism, and even anti-Americanism. His opposition to the Vietnam War, especially, triggered these charges, but so did his calls for military budget cuts and multilateralism in foreign affairs; his support for women's groups, blacks, American Indians, and other minorities; his association with Hollywood stars and entertainment figures; and his alleged softness on crime. Ironically, it was a snide statement by his initial 1972 running mate, Senator Thomas Eagleton of Missouri, associating McGovern with advocacy of "amnesty, acid, and abortion" that helped doom his bid for the presidency that year.

Many criticisms aimed at McGovern over the years were half-baked or off-kilter, while others had some merit. His valedictory remarks upon leaving the Senate in the wake of the 1980 "Reagan Revolution" indicated his own sense that he had "tried to be faithful to the enduring values of the Judeo-Christian ethic and the American democratic experiment" and that being "steeped in the soil" and in the small towns and cities of South Dakota, he had always stayed close to his constituents. There was no crossroads or community, no matter how small, he said, that he had not visited several times.[16]

It may come as some surprise to readers that he privately harbored even more extreme views on many issues than he was willing to express publicly. My best evidence for this is the interest the senator exhibited in Yale University law professor Charles Reich's widely discussed *The Greening of America*, published in 1970 at the end of the tumultuous 1960s and two years before the presidential campaign of 1972. I was able to acquire McGovern's marked-up copy of the book at the estate sale held after his death. His extensive markings in it are revealing. While it is, admittedly, impossible to ascertain exactly what McGovern was thinking as he underlined and highlighted sentences and paragraphs, the mere fact that he read the book so carefully and marked it so extensively demonstrates his unusual interest in its contents. Frequent comments in the margins, such as "note," "use," "key," and "important," indicate that he might have wanted to use the material in a speech or in something he was writing. McGovern mentally compared Reich's far-reaching critique of American society and his call for "a deep personal commitment to the welfare of the community" to the Biblical injunction to "Love thy neighbor as thyself" by writing those words from Matthew 22:39 in the margin. He wrote "Use" with two underlines by Reich's statement:

> All of Consciousness III's criticisms of society were brought into sharpest focus by the Vietnam War. For the war seemed to sum up the evils of our society: destruction of people, destruction of environment, depersonalized use of technology, war by the rich and powerful against the poor and helpless, justification based on abstract rationality, hypocrisy and lies, and a demand that the individual, regardless of his conscience, values, or self, make himself into a part of the war machine, an impersonal projectile bringing death to other people.[17]

McGovern's wide reading marked his personality and threw a bright light on his approach to public office. As a long-time debater and debate coach; as a PhD recipient in American history and an enthusiastic student of the subject; as a frequent writer on historical and political subjects; as one who obviously appreciated and depended upon the knowledge and expertise of scholars and specialists in many subject areas; as a careful user of language and one who appreciated all kinds of language, including poetry; and as one who sought after and valued the truth, while understanding the pernicious effects of lies, half-truths, unbridled public relations, and political spin, McGovern was a model of a politician who took ideas seriously, who recognized their value and importance in the political process, and whose entire career demonstrated the importance of facts, accuracy, rational discussion and debate, expertise, and science in democratic decision-making and governance.

This is not to say that he never engaged himself in a bit of dissembling, shaded the truth, withheld evidence, exaggerated, or participated in myth-making while on the campaign trail or in front of various audiences. But McGovern, in large measure, consistently displayed his commitment to accurate reporting of and upholding the value of truth.

Nowhere were these qualities of mind revealed more starkly than in the passionate way in which he approached the United States' military posture, issues of war and peace, and especially the Vietnam War. At Northwestern, he was one of twenty-three out of twenty-six history graduate students who supported Henry Wallace's futile Progressive Party presidential bid in 1948. The former vice president's major emphasis that year was on the need to reduce Cold War tensions and work out some sort of accommodation with the Soviet Union. The twenty-six-year-old McGovern and his wife, Eleanor, attended the rump party's nominating convention in Chicago as delegates from Illinois, and he later gave a speech about the Progressive Party at a Kiwanian meeting back in Mitchell in September, by which time it was obvious Wallace would get only a handful of votes. Since the former vice president was not on the ballot in Illinois, where McGovern was registered to vote, and since he could not bring himself to accept voting for Truman that year, he wound up not voting at all. McGovern's familiarity with Cold War history, his informed reading on Vietnam and what was going on in Southeast Asia, and his long-time dedication to peace and peaceful resolution of disputes led him to become one of the early outspoken critics of American military policy in Southeast Asia as it developed after 1963. Some of his harshest, most outspoken rhetoric was stimulated by his impassioned thoughts on the subject and occasioned some of the bitterest reactions against him.

On other issues, too—including budgetary policy, welfare programs, civil rights, women's rights, agricultural policy, and the environment—books and articles in journals and magazines provided McGovern with the information, ideas, and considerations that helped shape his thinking and the policy positions that he took. All this was evident to perceptive observers who were able to stay around him for a time. Most notably, in 1972 the drug-addled, unpredictable, but frequently insightful *Rolling Stone* reporter Hunter S. Thompson found McGovern to be an unusual and admirable sort of presidential candidate—one whose "painfully earnest style," up-close likability and sincerity, basic decency, and integrity and honesty set him apart from the usual run of politicians. Yet Thompson ironically noted that the candidate—who, like a number of others, was talking at the time about the need for "a New Politics"—drew upon his own experience and historical understanding to formulate his campaign strategy. Thompson observed, "For all his integrity, he is still talking to the Politics of the Past. He is still naïve enough to assume that anybody who is honest & intelligent—with a good voting record on 'the issues'—is a natural man for the White House." [18]

For all of McGovern's obvious characteristics that were mentioned by many reporters and pundits—his rural, small-town South Dakota roots; religious upbringing; intellectual bent; liberal tenets; sincerity; and basic decency (Robert Kennedy called him "the most decent man in the Senate")—McGovern retained a distance and impenetrability that often baffled observers. This found expression in the incredulity pundits expressed when he first announced his candidacy, then their piling on the bandwagon of exaggerated praise that was heaped upon him when he broke out from the pack in the spring, only to be followed by a virtual 180-degree turn against him after the bungled convention (punctuated by his 2:30 a.m. acceptance speech) and the Eagleton disaster. No other presidential nominee had ever seen his star rise and fall so quickly.

McGovern was accused of excessive moralism and hypocrisy; incompetence and clever maneuvering; naiveté and poor management. Conservatives accused him of radical plans for the economy and the military; left-wingers accused him of cutting corners. Most damaging of all, few people took seriously enough his accusations of corruption, immorality, and illegality in the Nixon administration. Two *Newsweek* reporters condemned him for his moral absolutism and for his resorting to the harshest rhetoric of any campaign in memory. Stewart Alsop echoed that notion, claiming that no presidential candidate in modern history had "imputed to his rival such foul and evil motives." [19] McGovern's academic credentials and his strident criticism of the Nixon administration failed to convince the majority of the electorate and left many in the press unconvinced and nonplused. Being an intellectual helped him no more than, twenty years earlier, the "egghead" label had assisted Adlai Stevenson—the man McGovern told people had most inspired him to get involved in electoral politics and after whom he named his only son.

There were those, however, who were not put off by intellect and who responded to it positively or enthusiastically. McGovern benefited from having a large coterie of historians in his corner, solicited and organized by his former Northwestern professors. Other intellectual friends, such as historian Arthur M Schlesinger Jr., political scientist James MacGregor Burns, and economist John Kenneth Galbraith, sent personal checks for his campaigns, wrote supportive articles about him, and solicited votes for him. [20] Because of his unsuccessful 1972 campaign, George McGovern goes down in many minds and in some history books as a loser, but just like William Jennings Bryan, another three-time loser (McGovern also lost Senate bids in 1960 and 1980, while winning three times in between), McGovern retains a place in the minds and hearts of many followers. That is partly because of his stance on the issues, especially his opposition to the Vietnam War, but it is mostly because of who he was—a decent, warm-spirited, inspired, visionary, dedicated, patriotic, democratic, and talented man. That he was also flawed, like the rest of us, is a given. Ultimately, he was a teacher and an intellectual in politics. We could use more of them.

NOTES

1. For the facts of McGovern's life and career, I have relied primarily upon Thomas J. Knock, *The Rise of a Prairie Statesman: The Life and Times of*

George McGovern (Princeton, NJ: Princeton University Press, 2016); Robert Sam Anson, *McGovern: A Biography* (New York: Holt, Rinehart and Winston, 1972); and George S. McGovern, *Grassroots: The Autobiography of George McGovern* (New York: Random House, 1977).

2. Michael Barone applied the term in "George McGovern: Veteran Notions," *Washington Post*, January 1, 1984. Asking how McGovern arrived at his views about reducing tensions with the Russians, cutting defense spending, and increasing domestic spending, Barone opined, "Largely by reading books. Shy as a child, he was and is a voracious reader, rising at 5 a.m. and reading for a couple of hours before getting on with the work of the day."

3. McGovern quoted in James M. Perry, "Teacher McGovern Considers Politics Another Classroom," *Wall Street Journal*, October 19, 1983.

4. Don Bohning, "'George' Warmed His Students: History Professor Was a Campus Favorite," *Miami Herald*, reprinted in *Madison Capital Times*, July 20, 1972; Dorothy Schwieder, "Historical Musings: Reflections on George McGovern, Teacher and Mentor," *South Dakota History* 44 (Summer 2014): 163–174.

5. Olive McGovern quoted in Anson, *McGovern*, 20.

6. Anson, *McGovern*, 21.

7. Knock, *The Rise of a Prairie Statesman*, 13.

8. McGovern interview, by the author, Sioux Falls, South Dakota, August 31, 2012.

9. Mark A. Lempke, "Senator George McGovern and the Role of Religion in South Dakota Political Culture," in Jon K. Lauck, John E. Miller, and Donald C. Simmons Jr., eds., *The Plains Political Tradition: Essays on South Dakota Political Culture*, vol. 2 (Pierre: South Dakota Historical Society Press, 2014), 151–155. Over the years, A. James Armstrong, Methodist Bishop for the two Dakotas, would become one of McGovern's closest personal friends and political allies as well as an intellectual mentor.

10. McGovern, *Grassroots*, 12; Anson, *McGovern*, 28.

11. McGovern quoted in Anson, *McGovern*, 31.

12. He would come back after the war and win another peace oratory contest with a speech titled "From Cave to Cave," inspired by the emergence of the atomic age, his own wartime experience, and his newfound appreciation for Social Gospel teachings. Knock, *Rise of a Prairie Statesman*, 83–84.

13. McGovern quoted in Knock, *Rise of a Prairie Statesman*, 72.

14. George McGovern, "A Progressive's Progressive," *Wall Street Journal*, June 14, 1989.

15. See extensive correspondence files and lists of donors in the George McGovern Papers, Seeley G. Mudd Archives, Princeton University.

16. McGovern's speech reprinted in *Brookings (SD) Register*, January 2, 1981.

17. Charles A. Reich, *The Greening of America: How the Youth Revolution Is Trying to Make America Livable* (New York: Random House, 1970), 230. Robert Sam Anson has a long footnote (p. 146) reflecting McGovern's stated enthusiasm for the book and quoting a memo he wrote to his staff about it.

18. Hunter S. Thompson, *Fear and Loathing on the Campaign Trail '72* (New York: Popular Library, 1973), 73.

19. Peter Goldman and Richard Stout, "McGovern's Politics of Righteousness," *Newsweek*, November 6, 1972, 43; Stewart Alsop, "The Devil and George McGovern,'" *Newsweek*, November 6, 1972, 136.

20. Arthur Schlesinger Jr., "The Case for George McGovern: 'It's Hardly a Sin to Support the Best Man,'" *New Republic*, February 26, 1972, 15–17; James MacGregor Burns, "The Democrats on the Eve: McGovern and America's Future," *New Republic*, July 1, 1972, 15–19; John Kenneth Galbraith, "The Case for George McGovern," *Saturday Review*, July 1, 1972, 23–27.

CONTRIBUTORS

Kerry Alcorn is an independent scholar who lives and works in Saskatoon, Saskatchewan, Canada. He completed his PhD in Educational Policy Studies and Evaluation at the University of Kentucky's College of Education, where he specialized in the history of education. His dissertation explored the parallels between educational developments within the progressive period of educational reform in the US, particularly as it manifested itself across the American Midwest and Plains, and his home province of Saskatchewan. Ultimately, this led to the publication of *Border Crossings: US Culture and Education in Saskatchewan, 1905–1937* (McGill-Queen's University Press, 2013). He maintains an interest in continental perspectives in comparative history.

Jenny Barker Devine serves as an associate professor of history at Illinois College, a four-year, residential liberal arts college in Jacksonville, Illinois. Her research focuses on Midwestern women's activism, as indicated by her numerous articles, book chapters, and one monograph: *On Behalf of the Family Farm: Iowa Farm Women's Activism Since 1945* (University of Iowa Press, 2013). After committing several years to developing Illinois College's archives, she has turned to a new project tentatively titled *American Athena: Cultivating Victorian Womanhood on the Midwestern Frontier.*

Ray E. Boomhower is senior editor at the Indiana Historical Society Press, serving as editor of the quarterly popular history magazine *Traces of Indiana and Midwestern History* since 1999. He is the author of numerous biographies of Hoosier notables, including John Bartlow Martin, Ernie Pyle, Lew Wallace, May Wright Sewall, and Benjamin Harrison.

Allan Carlson taught history and politics at Hillsdale College. For twenty-two years, he also served as the series editor for Marriage and Family Studies at Transaction Publishers. He has lectured at academic institutions in more than twenty nations and has appeared as a guest commentator on BBC, CBS,

MSNBC, ABC, CNN, CBC, C-SPAN, PBS, NPR, and many other media outlets. His books include: *The New Agrarian Mind: The Movement Toward Decentralist Thought in Twentieth Century America* (Transaction Press, 2000), *Third Ways: How Bulgarian Greens, Swedish Housewives, and Beer-Swilling Englishmen Created Family Centered Economies . . . And Why They Disappeared* (ISI Books, 2007), and (as editor) *Land and Liberty: The Best of* FREE AMERICA (Wethersfield Institute, 2019).

Justin Clark is a public historian and serves as the digital initiatives director at the Indiana Historical Bureau, a division of the Indiana State Library. He holds a BS in History/Political Science from Indiana University Kokomo and an MA in Public History from Indiana University–Purdue University Indianapolis. His graduate research focused on orator Robert Ingersoll and his contributions to Midwestern freethought. In Clark's spare time, he loves books, music, movies, and traveling. You can contact him at justinclarkpubhist@gmail.com or follow him on LinkedIn at www.linkedin .com/in/justinclarkph.

William Russell Coil is a lecturer in the history department at Ohio State University. He graduated from Ball State University and earned his MA and PhD in History from Ohio State University. With Geoffrey Parker and Richard Sisson, Coil edited *Ohio and the World, 1753–2053: Essays Toward a New History of Ohio* (Ohio State University, 2004). Coil also contributed entries on Midwestern Republicans to *The American Midwest: An Interpretive Encyclopedia* (Indiana University Press, 2006) and to *Builders of Ohio: A Biographical History* (Ohio State University, 2003). He has also explored America's global past in several invited public presentations.

Cherie Dargan is a retired community college teacher, volunteer with the League of Women Voters, writer and blogger, family historian, and webmaster of the websites for Ruth Suckow (www.ruthsuckow.org) and the Cedar Falls Authors Festival (www.cfauthorsfestival.org), among others. She writes columns on technology for the Western Home Communities publication, the *Journal*, and has published columns in *The Waterloo Courier*. Her chapter "The Realistic Regionalism of Iowa's Ruth Suckow" is included in *The Midwestern Moment: The Forgotten World of Early-Twentieth-Century Midwestern*

Regionalism, 1880–1940 (Hastings College Press, 2017). Dargan earned a BA from Buena Vista University and MAs from Iowa State University and the University of Northern Iowa. She is a member of the Cedar Falls Supper Club and continues to write about Iowa author Ruth Suckow.

Robert L. Dorman is a professor of library science at Oklahoma City University. He is the author of *Revolt of the Provinces: The Regionalist Movement in America, 1920–1945* (University of North Carolina Press, 1993). His most recent publications include *Hell of a Vision: Regionalism and the Modern American West* (University of Arizona Press, 2012) and an essay on Nebraska writer Mari Sandoz in the volume *Regionalists on the Left: Radical Voices from the American West* (University of Oklahoma Press, 2013). His latest book, *Alfalfa Bill: A Life in Politics* (University of Oklahoma Press, 2018) received the Oklahoma Book Award for Non-Fiction. Dorman is also a lifelong amateur astronomer.

Aaron George received his PhD in American History and the History of Sexuality from Ohio State University in 2017. His interests include American intellectual history, the history of masculinity, and the history of LGBT communities in the twentieth century. He is currently revising his book manuscript, *When Cowboys Come Home: Re-Imagining Manhood in Post-World War II America*, for publication; this manuscript investigates the way veterans of World War II wrote about manhood after the war, rethinking the importance of male camaraderie, authenticity, and emotional honesty in forging male identities. He is currently an assistant professor of American history at Tarleton State University in Stephenville, Texas.

Joseph Hogan is the director of fact-checking at Retro Report. He received his MA in English and American Literature at New York University, where he was a Charles Whickham Moore fellow. He has written for the *New York Times*, *The Nation*, and the *Middle West Review*, among other publications. He is also a co-editor of *Finding a New Midwestern History* (University of Nebraska Press, 2018).

Brian M. Ingrassia teaches history at West Texas A&M University in Canyon, Texas. He is author of *The Rise of Gridiron University: Higher Education's Uneasy Alliance with Big-Time Football* (University Press of Kansas, 2012) and series editor of the Sport and Popular Culture Series at the University of Tennessee

Press. He has published articles in the *Journal of the Gilded Age and Progressive Era*, *Journal of Illinois History*, and other scholarly journals. A native of central Illinois, Ingrassia earned degrees at Eureka College and the University of Illinois.

Sara Kosiba has dedicated her career to studying authors and literature from the American Midwest. A past president and current board member of the Society for the Study of Midwestern Literature, she has published on a variety of authors including August Derleth, Josephine Herbst, Ernest Hemingway, and Dawn Powell. She is currently working on a biography of Michigan-born writer John Herrmann and has written introductions to reissues of two of Herrmann's novels.

William C. Kostlevy has degrees from Asbury College, Marquette University, Bethany Theological Seminary, and the University of Notre Dame (PhD) where the focus of his work was American Intellectual and Religious History. He is the director of the Brethren Historical Library and Archives in Elgin, Illinois. He is the author of *Holy Jumpers: Evangelicals and Radicals in Progressive Era America* (Oxford University Press, 2010) and editor of the *Historical Dictionary of the Holiness Movement* (Scarecrow Press Inc., 2009). His work has appeared in *Wisconsin Magazine of History*, *Christian History*, *Brethren Life and Thought*, and the *Journal of the Gilded Age and Progressive Era*. He has served as a professor of history and political science at Tabor College and as an archivist and special collections librarian for Asbury Theological Seminary and Fuller Theological Seminary. He is a fellow of the Center for the Study of Anabaptist and Pietist Groups at Elizabethtown College in Pennsylvania.

Jon K. Lauck is the author of several books, including *The Lost Region: Toward a Revival of Midwestern History* (University of Iowa Press, 2013) and *From Warm Center to Ragged Edge: The Erosion of Midwestern Regionalism, 1920–1965* (University of Iowa Press, 2017). Lauck has worked for several years as a full-time professor, a part-time professor, and a lawyer, and he is currently serving as an adjunct professor of history and political science at the University of South Dakota and as the editor-in-chief of the *Middle West Review*.

John Linstrom is series editor of the Liberty Hyde Bailey Library for the Comstock Publishing Associates imprint of Cornell University Press. He coedited

The Liberty Hyde Bailey Gardener's Companion: Essential Writings (Comstock-Cornell University Press, 2019), and he prepared the centennial edition of Bailey's ecospheric manifesto *The Holy Earth: The Birth of a New Land Ethic* (Counterpoint Press, 2015), which features a new foreword by Wendell Berry. Linstrom's poetry has been published in numerous journals, including *North American Review*, *The New Criterion*, *Atlanta Review*, *Vallum*, and *Cold Mountain Review*. He formerly worked as curator and then director of the Liberty Hyde Bailey Museum in South Haven, Michigan, and he currently lives with his wife and their joyful window garden in Queens, New York, where he is a MacCracken Doctoral Fellow in English and American Literature at New York University.

The late **John E. Miller** grew up in six small towns in the Midwest as well as in a suburb of Chicago, graduating from the University of Missouri in 1966. He received his MA and PhD degrees in History from the University of Wisconsin–Madison in 1968 and 1973. He taught mostly twentieth-century American history courses for a year at the University of Tulsa and then for twenty-nine years at South Dakota State University before becoming a full-time writer in 2003. His last published books were *Small-Town Dreams: Stories of Midwestern Boys Who Shaped America* (University Press of Kansas, 2014) and *Democracy's Troubles: Twelve Threats to the American Ideal and How We Can Overcome Them* (McFarland Publishers, 2020).

Paul Murphy is a professor of history at Grand Valley State University. He is the author of *The New Era: American Thought and Culture in the 1920s* (Rowman & Littlefield, 2012) and *The Rebuke of History: The Southern Agrarians and American Conservative Thought* (University of North Carolina Press, 2001). He published, most recently, "The Last Progressive Historian: Warren Susman and American Cultural History" in *Modern Intellectual History* 14, no. 3 (November 2017). He is currently working on a study of humanist thought in the US entitled "The Dividing of the American Mind: The Search for a New Humanism and the Debate over the Role of Intellect in the United States, 1900–1950."

Marcia Noe is a professor of English and the director of Women's Studies at the University of Tennessee at Chattanooga. She edits *MidAmerica* and *Midwestern Miscellany* for the Society for the Study of Midwestern Literature, and she is the author of *Susan Glaspell: Voice from the Heartland* (Western

Illinois University, 1983) and more than twenty other publications on Susan Glaspell, winner of the 1931 Pulitzer Prize for drama.

David Pichaske is a professor of English at Southwest Minnesota State University. He has edited or authored over two dozen published books, including *Southwest Minnesota: The Land and the People* (Crossings Press, 2000), *Rooted: Seven Midwest Writers of Place* (University of Iowa Press, 2006), *Song of the North Country: A Midwest Framework to the Songs of Bob Dylan* (Continuum Press, 2010), a memoir titled *Here I Stand* (Ellis Press, 2015), and a collection of previously published articles titled *Crying in the Wilderness: Essays Public and Private* (Ellis Press, 2017).

William C. Pratt is a professor emeritus of history at the University of Nebraska at Omaha. He served as a distinguished Fulbright lecturer in American history at Moscow State University in 2000 and as a senior Fulbright lecturer at the University of Warsaw in 2007. Recent publications include "Observations from My Life with Farm Movements in the Upper Midwest," *South Dakota History* 44, no. 2 (2014), and "Communists and American Farmers in the 1920s," *American Communist History* 17, no. 2 (2018).

Raised among the coastal redwoods of Humboldt County, California, **Daniel Rinn** has been captivated by the natural world since childhood. As a result, his research and writing generally focus on the history of environment and ideas. His work has appeared in academic journals, as well as the *Washington Post* and various digital mediums. He is completing his dissertation at the University of Rochester on the history of twentieth-century American environmental thought.

Andrew Seal is a lecturer in the Peter T. Paul College of Business and Economics at the University of New Hampshire. He has often written about the Midwest and its history, including for the *Middle West Review*. He grew up in Indiana, and the poetry of James Whitcomb Riley therefore comes to him unbidden every Halloween.

Michael C. Steiner is a professor emeritus of American studies at California State University, Fullerton. He is the author or editor of five books, including

most recently *Regionalists on the Left: Radical Voices from the American Left*
(University of Oklahoma Press, 2013). Since retiring and returning to his
native Midwest in 2016, Steiner has written five journal articles and book
chapters on the region's intellectual and social history. His book, *Horace M.*
Kallen in the Heartland: The Midwestern Roots of American Pluralism, was
published by the University Press of Kansas in May 2020.

Edward Watts is a professor of English and American Indian and
Indigenous Studies at Michigan State University. His previous
contributions to the field of Midwestern cultural history are: *An American*
Colony: Regionalism and the Making of Midwestrn Culture (Ohio University
Press, 2002), *The First West: Writing from the American Frontier, 1776–1860*
(an anthology; Oxford University Press, 2002), and *In This Remote Country:*
Colonial French Culture in the Anglo-American Imagination, 1760–1865
(University of North Carolina Press, 2006). His most recent book on
regionalism is *Mapping Region in Early America* (coeditor; University of
Georgia Press, 2015). Among other courses, he teaches on Michigan's
cultural history and American Indian literature.

Kenneth H. Wheeler, professor of history at Reinhardt University,
graduated from Earlham College and earned his MA and PhD degrees at
Ohio State University. Wheeler is the author of *Cultivating Regionalism:*
Higher Education and the Making of the American Midwest (Northern
Illinois University Press, 2011), and he is a contributor of the entry on
"Intellectualism" to *The American Midwest: An Interpretive Encyclopedia*
(Indiana University Press, 2006) among other chapters and essays on
Midwestern history and culture.

Gleaves Whitney has been the director of the Hauenstein Center for
Presidential Studies at Grand Valley State University since 2003.
With Jon K. Lauck and the Midwestern History Association, Whitney has
hosted the largest gathering of historians of the Midwest each year since
2015. Each of those gatherings at GVSU has resulted in new scholarship and
books about the Midwest—Lauck and Whitney have collaborated to edit and
contribute to several of them. A historian by training with many years in the
classroom and in public service, Whitney was educated at Colorado State

University and the University of Michigan. He has lived in the Midwest for more than three decades and makes his home in Grand Rapids, Michigan.

Emily Williamson is a graduate of Southwest Minnesota State University, and she currently teaches high school in Pipestone, Minnesota. This is her first publication.

INDEX